Practical Business Writing

Practical Business Writing

Arn Tibbetts
University of Illinois

with
Charlene Tibbetts and
Louise Steele

Little, Brown and Company
Boston   Toronto

Library of Congress Cataloging-in-Publication Data

Tibbetts, A. M.
   Practical business writing.

   Includes index.
   1. Business report writing — Study and teaching.
I. Tibbetts, Charlene. II. Steele, Louise. III. Title.
HF5719.T53   1987   808′.066651   86-20904
ISBN 0-316-84500-0

Copyright © 1987 by Arn Tibbetts with Charlene Tibbetts and Louise Steele

All rights reserved. No part of this book may be reproduced in any form or by any electronic or mechanical means including information storage and retrieval systems without permission in writing from the publisher, except by a reviewer who may quote brief passages in a review.

Library of Congress Catalog Card No. 86-20904

ISBN 0-316-84500-0

9 8 7 6 5 4 3 2 1

Don.

Published simultaneously in Canada
by Little, Brown & Company (Canada) Limited

Printed in the United States of America

Credits

Overview

   Pages 11–12, Figures 0.1 and 0.2: LACO Limited Warranty and MECO Limited Warranty from *Writing in the Professions*, by Goswami, Redish, Felker, and Siegel, November 1981, Document Design Center. Reprinted by permission of the Document Design Center.
   Pages 16–17: Mortimer Smith, letter of appeal for contributions to Council for Basic Education. Reprinted by permission of The Council for Basic Education.
   Page 21: Daniel McDonald, Mitchell Shortfall letter, "The World's Worst Business Letter: A Candidate" from the *ABCA Bulletin*, 9-82. Reprinted by permission of Daniel McDonald.

Chapter 2

   Pages 39–40: WILL Priority Transmittal Letter. Reprinted by permission of Dr. Donald P. Mullally.

   Page 45: From Transco Energy Company's *Quarterly Report*. Reprinted by permission of Transco Energy Company.

Chapter 3

   Page 58, Figure 3.5: Diagram of company organization from Felker, et al., *Guidelines for Document Designers*. Reprinted by persmission of Document Design Center.
   Page 60, Figure 3.8: "Changes in Air Pollutants" from Felker, et al, *Guidelines for Document Designers*. Reprinted by permission of Document Design Center.
   Page 60, Figure 3.9: Changes in Air Pollutants from Felker, et al., *Guidelines for Document Designers*. Adapted by permission of Document Design Center.
   Page 61, Figure 3.10: 1970 "Population" from

CONTINUED ON PAGE 507

"Tell the truth, but make the truth fascinating."

— David Ogilvy
Confessions of an Advertising Man

Preface

Our experience in business and in teaching communication led us to believe that a somewhat new approach might be useful to you as an instructor and to your students. How did we arrive at this approach?

First, using a sabbatical, two of us travelled the country, from Minnesota to Texas and from New York to California. We talked to instructors in little colleges and big universities. You told us your problems in teaching business communication and what you would like to see in a helpful text. We put much of what you told us into the book.

Next, we discussed certain problems in communication with business people. We asked them what skills they wanted new graduates to have. Almost always, they mentioned one thing at the top of the list — the *general ability* to write and speak efficiently. They assumed that if students can generally be taught to make a point in a message, to worry about the reactions of the reader or listener, to give all necessary detail, to write literate sentences (an important skill!), they won't have serious problems with specific assignments that come up on the job. Two of us have had our own business for many years, and we have found these remarks to be both true and practical.

Putting together, then, what *you* want in a communication course and what the business world wants graduates to be able to do, we designed this book. It is a new course but, as we said earlier, by no means entirely new. The fine old tradition of business writing and speaking has many useful approaches — too many for any sensible person to believe that they should be abandoned. So we have kept a great deal of the long-tested past, and you will find that past honored in these pages. To this tradition we have added special emphases on:

- The modern, informal tone in business messages.
- The human approach to communication — real people "speaking" to other real people. Written messages have a *voice* that none of us can ignore.
- Writing and speaking as a process, but not to the detriment of the product. Product and process must be interrelated.
- The uniqueness of the typical message, each one deserving its own special planning and execution.

Along with these emphases, we have tried to de-emphasize a little the use of set models, set patterns of response, and check-off lists. Yet, as you well know, these can be helpful to you and your students, so we have included them where many of you said you would like to have them.

Accordingly, the book represents a balance between old and new, a balance which should be practical, handy to teach, and (dare one hope for it?) engaging. Indeed, we worked as hard on the style of the book as on its content. We hope that you and your students will find it pleasant to read. (We have paid particular attention to the complaint from business people that too often messages just aren't *attractive.*)

Finally, we made the book as short as possible, while still including everything in it. Quite frankly, we tried to give you a good product at a lower price, one that would serve your needs well without cleaning out the pocketbooks of your students!

The material you find in this book, then, is the result of three and a half decades of synthesizing materials from business, research, and teaching. We have had one major goal in mind: to encourage students to deal successfully with genuine problems in writing business communications.

This is not a book about failure — but about success and how your students can attain it.

HOW THE BOOK IS ORGANIZED

Our present courses in business writing are, we believe, the best-taught courses in all of college composition. One reason is that you teachers of business writing agree pretty well on what your students should learn. But you don't always agree, and shouldn't have to, on the order of many assignments.

Accordingly, we have organized the book in groups of more or less "free-standing" parts. There are ten of these, each covering a particular problem in business communication. We have arranged the parts in what many instructors have suggested is a reasonable order for teaching. Thus Parts 1, 2, and 3 cover *planning, organizing,* and *writing* the message. However, since these and the other parts are free-standing, you can change the order as you teach. (For example, we often teach Chapter 6 — on words, usage, and *bizbuzz* — in the second week of the term.)

You can also change the order of many later chapters. If for any reason you would like to cover Part 10 (on office machines) earlier in the course, you can do so without violating the logic of the text.

You will also note two other special things — Appendix C, *A Short Handbook of Grammar and Punctuation,* and Appendix D, *Nice to Know* (which covers writer's block, outline forms, sex and the language, legal issues, and dictating skills).

Be encouraged to move around in the book — find a sequence of chapters for teaching that satisfies you best. But we would also encourage you (at the beginning of the course) to have students read and absorb the ten basic suggestions in the Overview. Our testing of material in the whole book suggests (1) that much of what you teach can be taught in different arrangements, but (2) that certain basic suggestions for good communication can be taught early to provide a base for what follows.

THE PROBLEMS AND CASES (FOR WRITING)

A new teacher of business writing said: "You know all that trouble in freshman comp about *finding a topic?* That drove my students crazy — and me too! Now all I have to do is to assign a business writing problem or case, and the trouble disappears."

Like that teacher, we too enjoy the luxury of assigning problems and cases. Each of the major chapters has its own set of problems, and we have grouped another 19 of them in Appendix A (pp. 414–430).

ACKNOWLEDGMENTS

Our editor at Little, Brown, Joe Opiela, deserves thanks for his sound advice at various stages in the development of this book. Virginia Shine, Alex Rubington, and Elena Giulini did a fine job putting the book together. The very helpful reviewers provided many valuable suggestions and criticisms. William J. Buchholz, Bentley College; Raymond Dumont, Southeastern Massachusetts University; Melinda Kramer, Purdue University; Gene Krupa, University of Iowa; Robert Mehaffey, American River College; and Michael Rossi, Merrimack College, all deserve recognition.

We are deeply indebted to many splendid practitioners and scholars in the field of communication. To name only a few: Francis Christensen, E.D. Hirsch, Jr., Mary P. Hiatt, Melba Murray, Robert A. Day, John H. Dirckx, M.D., Sir Ernest Gowers, Wayne Booth, Dwight Bolinger, Robert Gunning, Francis Weeks (long-time executive secretary of the Association for Business Communication — ABC), and Robert Gieselman, Director of Business and Technical Writing at the University of Illinois.

Also, as editor of the *Bulletin* and *Journal* of ABC, Arn Tibbetts has profited greatly from the scholarship and ideas of dozens of men and women who teach around the world.

The publications of the Document Design Center in Washington, D.C., have been invaluable. We also owe a particular debt to two writers whose work always gives us pleasure and instruction: David Ogilvy, whose *Confessions of an Advertising Man* is a beautifully written example of how to think about writer, reader, and situation; and David Mellinkoff, Professor of Law at UCLA, whose *Legal Writing: Sense and Nonsense,* proves once and for all that the law does not have to be impenetrable.

A.T.
C.T.
L.S.

Contents

Introduction		xiii
Overview: Ten Basic Suggestions for Successful Communication		1

PART 1   PLANNING YOUR MESSAGE — 29

1	Hang Your Message on a Hook	31
2	"Listening to the Look": The Power of Visual Effect	37
3	Should You Use Graphics?	54

PART 2   ORGANIZING YOUR MESSAGE — 73

4	Block Out the Big Picture	75
5	How *Not* to Lose Your Reader	89

PART 3   WRITING YOUR MESSAGE — 101

6	Words—and the Problem of Bizbuzz	103
7	Style: Make Your Writing Readable	120

PART 4   TYPICAL MESSAGES — 143

8	Goodwill	145
9	Selling a Product or Service	156
10	Inquiries, Orders, and Replies	170
11	Claims	182
12	Credit	191
13	Collections	201
14	Letters of Evaluation and Recommendation	210

PART 5   NEGATIVE MESSAGES — 221

15	Negative Messages	223

PART 6   REPORT WRITING — 239

16 Reports in General — 241
17 Proposals — 283
18 Progress Reports — 298

PART 7   JOB HUNTING (*SELLING YOURSELF*) — 301

19 Your Job Campaign — 303
20 The Application (Letter and Résumé) — 310

PART 8   ORAL MESSAGES — 323

21 Picking a Form for Your Speech — 325
22 Shaping a Speech for Your Audience — 333
23 Convincing Your Audience — 344
24 Managing the Dramatic Elements of Speaking — 356

PART 9   THE LIBRARY — 371

25 Using the Library — 373

PART 10   OFFICE MACHINES — 391

26 The Least You Should Know About Office Machines — 393

Appendix A   Extra Problems — 414
Appendix B   Message Format and Mechanics — 431
Appendix C   A Short Handbook of Grammar and Punctuation — 459
Appendix D   Nice to Know — 475
   Avoiding Writer's Block — 475
   Outline Forms and How They Are Used — 478
   Sex Terminology — 481
   Legal Issues — 484
   How to Become a Good Dictator — 492

Index — 495

Introduction

To: Students
From: Arn Tibbetts *aT*
Subject: Business Communication and You

Are you ambitious? You are, I suppose, or you wouldn't be taking a course in business writing (and speaking) — and reading this book.

Can business writing (as I will call it to save space) help you fulfill your ambitions? It can — more so, probably, than you imagine. Business people need you if you can write well. All the major surveys of executives and opinion makers say the same thing:

Give us graduates who can handle the language.

When DuPont's retired chairman, Irving S. Shapiro, was asked what special skills employees needed, he answered: "Writing!" He added: "Everything turns on it in a business."

When Fortune magazine interviewed recruiters, the magazine reported that "the most frequent observation was a simple wish that business schools do a better job teaching their students to write and speak effectively."

Will business writing be hard for you to learn?

You should find it fairly easy — compared, for example, to most other writing courses. Why? Three reasons:

1. The ideas you write about usually exist "outside" of you, in your experience or in the cases and problems included in this book. You won't have to dredge so many ideas out of your brain, as you may have done in other writing courses — although you do have to be imaginative.

2. You can write more simply and straightforwardly, without feeling compelled to be fancy or literary. You can be yourself.

3. Most important, perhaps, you have the luxury of designing your messages for various readers. A freshman theme, for instance, ordinarily has only one reader, the instructor. But in business writing, you will design your messages for different readers (and for different kinds of readers) — seldom for your instructor alone. You will not be writing in a vacuum.

Professor Francis Weeks is one of the world's authorities on business writing. He often refers to what he calls "the great curse of business writing" — dullness. Too many people, says Weeks, "write about themselves or they write about subject matter." To help avoid dullness, he says, they should "write about their readers." Well, we want to avoid dullness!

You will discover that planning <u>to influence your readers</u> will make business writing more interesting, and much easier. Readers are (like you) human beings with human desires. They want to be:

- well thought of
- improved in status or situation
- improved financially
- improved in their work or play
- more interested in life generally

If any business message you write can do one or more of these things for your reader, they — and <u>you</u> — will benefit.

Good luck!

Practical Business Writing

TEN BASIC SUGGESTIONS

- Sharpen the *point* of your message (p. 1)
- Define your role as writer of each message and project the right image (p. 2)
- Write from your *reader's* viewpoint (p. 3)
- Decide how you want to *influence* your reader (p. 4)
- *Anticipate* and answer any *questions* your reader may have (p. 5)
- Design your message for both *situation* and *context* (p. 7)
- *Keep it simple!* (p. 9)
- Break your writing into manageable *chunks* (p. 10)
- Use simple, familiar *words* (p. 13)
- Think *action* and write *who does what* (p. 15)

And: BE HUMAN

OVERVIEW

Ten Basic Suggestions for Successful Communication

SUGGESTION ONE: SHARPEN THE POINT OF YOUR MESSAGE

In the business world, there is ordinarily only one reason to write: to send a message from writer to reader. The message is not about the writer, at least not usually. It is about something the writer wishes to communicate, and it must have a point.

This point should not be blurred or vague. Usually, it should not be stated like this:

- Something should happen tomorrow.
- Your idea has something good in it.
- They found a flaw in the setup.
- Let's have a discussion.

Before you start to write, consider your point carefully and sharpen it. Instead of *Let's have a discussion,* sharpen your point into something like *Before we sign the contract, let's discuss Section 3A.* Or, perhaps, *Section 3A of the contract seems loosely worded to me. Can we talk it over?*

It will often help you to write your proposed point on scratch paper. Use a sentence or two. Underline key words; they will help you organize your message and stay on the subject.

Examples:

- Please <u>pay</u> your <u>overdue bill</u>.
- Can you <u>fix</u> my <u>roof</u>? (The wind <u>damaged</u> it.)
- Will you please let my <u>company</u> fix your <u>roof</u>?
- Here is a <u>plan</u> that will <u>reduce pollution</u>.
- Put your <u>money</u> in our <u>bank</u>.
- Plan <u>X</u> is <u>impractical</u> at <u>this time</u>.

Each underlined word helps sharpen the point of the message.

Know your point before you start writing. Keep thinking about it as you write. Don't send the message until you check to see whether you stayed on the point. Avoid irrelevancies.

SUGGESTION TWO: IN EACH MESSAGE, DEFINE YOUR ROLE AS WRITER, AND PROJECT THE RIGHT IMAGE

Who am "I"?

As the writer, look into an imaginary mirror and answer that question. It may seem foolish to ask who you are, but the fact is that every writer wears different hats. At various times the same writer can be a supervisor of office workers, an accountant, a representative of the company, a user of computer hardware, a seeker after a loan, a business executive, a United Fund canvasser, a supervisor of three different groups, an employee responding to a supervisor, and so on. Dr. Jekyll and Mr. Hyde have nothing on you when it comes to the number of people inhabiting a body.

For every different person living inside you, you write somewhat differently. You have a slightly different role to play for each one. Your role as supervisor is different from your role as United Fund canvasser, and when you write messages in those roles you should take that fact into account. Your reader expects you to. If you don't shift gears smoothly from role to role, you will make a reader uneasy. If you don't believe this, try writing a United Fund request to your peers as if you were sending a memo to the Division of Security and Maintenance, reminding its people to lock all inside doors at night.

In different situations you will project different images as a writer. To readers, you can appear (in various messages) as careful, cold, warm, helpful, kind, stingy, grateful, mean, indulgent, craftsmanlike, bold, or timid, and so on, almost without limit.

What do you want your readers to think of you? Look at your message from their viewpoint. Is the resulting image the one you want to project? While you are trying to be firm and hard-headed, are you actually projecting an image that is harsh or selfish? Read your message aloud. How does it sound?

SUGGESTION THREE: WRITE FROM YOUR READERS' VIEWPOINT

Who are your readers, and what do they want?

First, why do we say *readers* rather than *reader*? Because you will be more successful if you understand that many messages (perhaps even most messages) have more than one reader. Your previous school experiences may have led you to believe that a message has only one reader: your instructor. But in business, many messages are designed for a multiple readership. A memo may reach three people or thirty. A letter may have copies that are sent to half a dozen people.

A report directed only to Ms. X in Transportation may be photocopied and eventually reach any number of readers, some of whom (in large companies) you don't even know exist. (They may not know you, either.) For that matter, when you write a letter to John B., how do you know who is going to read it at this time — or later? Your letter will be filed, and five years from now Susan F. and Mike Q. may read it to learn what you thought back in 1986.

In their excellent book on report writing, *Designing Technical Reports*, J.C. Mathes and Dwight Stevenson make these flat statements about readers:

- "It is false to assume that the person addressed is the audience." (Almost anybody can read a report — and will do so, if he or she is interested or involved in some way in the issues raised by the report.)
- "It is false to assume that the report has a finite period in use." (A good report is often useful for months, even years, after it is written.)

These observations apply to many other messages besides reports. So when you plan your message, take every possible reader into account, for now and for years from now.

Ask questions like these: What do your readers know, or not know? How do they feel about the subject of your message? Do they want to hear what you have to say? Maybe they will hate it. What then? Are they prejudiced against your idea to begin with?

In 1983, the editors of the *Wall Street Journal*, a Dow Jones publication, quoted Clarence Barron, the owner of Dow Jones, as follows: "Never write from the standpoint of yourself, but always from the standpoint of the reader. Economize his time."

Reader, reader, reader. Readers.

The more successful you are as a writer, the more you will worry about your readers. Through questions to yourself, you will analyze them as human beings with feelings, thoughts, and knowledge of various kinds:

- What would Ms. Lebedaux, who runs the company's Department of Customer Service, prefer to hear about her department? What is she most proud of? What does she do well? Not so well?

- What do my employees want in a description of retirement benefits? How many statistics, and what kind, will they grasp immediately? What would they most appreciate my telling them? Not appreciate?
- As Dean of the College, you ponder: Certain college seniors must take a required course in a field other than their own. How will they feel about the course? Will they have any positive reactions I can build upon?
- What does the typical gasoline buyer feel about a company credit card? Why do buyers carry a credit card, anyway? If they save a few cents a gallon by paying cash, would they prefer to pay cash?
- Mr. Higgins is going to buy a small fleet of panel trucks from my company. How much does he know about truck use? How much would he understand, for example, about rough service as my company defines the term?
- What are the thoughts and attitudes of the users of oil for home heating about oil, about our service, about our pricing? I'll make a list of what the typical home owner might think.

In trying to answer such questions you learn to *be* your readers, to get inside their skins.

SUGGESTION FOUR: DECIDE HOW YOU WANT TO INFLUENCE YOUR READER

One author of this book tells a story:

> A few months out of college, I was suddenly dropped into a situation no one had prepared me for. I was doing field work on an oil exploration crew employing seismic geophysics. My work was mostly plain hard labor on the end of a shovel. On a minute's notice, my supervisors trucked me off to the field office, brushed off the dust, and spoke as follows:
>
> "We're understaffed and overworked. The new contract calls for seven-day weeks. From now on, you will prepare all the structure maps for Repro and write all the reports. Here's what they are: *Daily progress report;* that's a letter. *Weekly report on the main reflector beds;* ditto. *Final report* for each project; check the standard report form. But DON'T use the form for every report. Reports can't all look alike. If they do, the client won't read 'em carefully enough. Answer any business correspondence; show your drafts to the party chief."
>
> I said: "I've never done all that before."
>
> They said: "You're trained as an engineer, aren't you? You took writing courses in college? Get cracking; we're working seven to seven this week. Here's the data for the daily report; Sam's got the stuff for the weekly. If you have any questions, ask him or the party chief."
>
> They went away, and I sat down feeling limp. In my university, there had

been no courses in either business or technical writing. I'd taken two terms of English composition in the engineering college — got a B and a C in them. I went to the man who ran the geophysics department. What he told me has been of help for thirty-five years. "Well," he said, "try thinking this way. Imagine that every piece you write is an argument that asks a reader to *believe* or *do* something. Or both. Your job is to convince the reader to believe what you want him to, to do what you suggest. Lead him by the hand through your report or letter. When you think he might stumble, stop and find out why, and where you went wrong — because *you* are responsible for keeping him on his feet."

It was an interesting idea: the message as *argument,* and the reader as a traveller through a partly unknown land, a reader who might stumble and fall if I didn't lead him along carefully.

In the business world, almost every message you write, every speech or presentation you give, is an argument, an attempt to convince and influence the reader.

As David Farkas in *The ABCA Bulletin* suggests, you create influence by convincing the reader to:

- learn practical information, or
- learn to perform a task, or
- make a decision, or
- agree with you on an issue, or
- take action on a problem, or
- respond with intellectual or esthetic satisfaction, or
- approve of you, your ideas, or the group you represent.

Each of these classes of influence has its own subclasses, and each can blend into one or more of the others. Each class also has its own relationship to your message and its point.

SUGGESTION FIVE: ANTICIPATE (AND ANSWER) ANY QUESTIONS YOUR READER MAY HAVE

Typically, a reader is full of questions. The smallest thing can start them coming.

After you read "a reader is full of questions," didn't you wonder: What does that mean? Why *questions?*

Readers read for information: to get answers to questions, many of which are raised by you, the writer. Take this sentence from an article in *Business Week,* for example:

> Experts are convinced that it is only a matter of time before these "thinking" computers open up awesome new applications in offices, factories, and homes.

Upon reading this, the reader automatically asks such questions as these:

1. What does the writer mean by *awesome?*
2. What kinds of applications? In what fields?
3. How long will this take to happen?

Question number one leads to the second sentence from the *Business Week* article:

> "AI (artificial intelligence) will change civilization in a profound way," says Nils Nilsson, director of the AI center at SRI International.

Questions the reader asks about this are:

1. What does he mean by *civilization?* By *profound?*
2. How will AI change the world?
3. Can you tell me more about Nilsson and his qualifications for making such a statement?

Question number two leads to the third sentence in *Business Week:*

> It will change the way we work, the way we learn, the way we think about ourselves.

Questions that follow from this are:

1. How will it change the way we learn?
2. How will it change the way we think about ourselves?
3. How will it change the way we work?

Question number three leads to the fourth sentence:

> Nilsson and his fellow computer scientists see the coming commercialization of AI as the most significant advance in computer science since the invention of the computer.

As you can see from these examples (taken from an article by Steven Darian), a message is so tightly tied to the reader's viewpoint that question-raising happens automatically. Indeed, in some types of specialized writing, authorities have argued that the message should be designed around the question. A journalist will, for instance, design a news story around: What? Why? Who? Where? When? How? If these questions aren't answered in most news stories, readers come away feeling cheated.

Every message has its own questions-from-the-reader built into it. Deliberate duplication aside, no two messages are exactly alike. So in order to satisfy your readers and influence them as you wish, anticipate their questions.

Here's a little postscript to that principle. If you can't answer the questions, don't raise them!

SUGGESTION SIX: DESIGN YOUR MESSAGE FORM FOR BOTH SITUATION AND CONTEXT

Everyone knows that people in the business world write things called memos, letters, and reports. But what are these, and what is the difference between them?

It is often customary for companies to use memos for "inside" messages and letters for messages to the outside. But this convention is elastic. Letters inside a company are common. And the memo form, or a variation of it, may be sent outside the company. In addition, a memo can be a report; a report can be a letter; a letter can have a subject line, as a memo does; a memo can be twenty pages long; a report can be one page long. Such variations occur time and again.

The point here is that we should avoid acting like one manager of affairs (an ancient mythological Greek, actually, named Procrustes), who on occasion had people sleep over at his place. He put them on an iron bed. If they were too long for the bed, he cut them off to fit. If they were too short, he stretched them to fit. For thousands of years this vigorous solution to problems has been called the procrustean solution. It does work, but only at some cost to the problem or person involved.

Successful writers are wary of the solution of Procrustes: that is, they don't always insist on chopping and shaping a message into a certain form, such as a memo, letter, or report. (All these forms are discussed later in this book; see the index for page numbers.) Instead, they try to design their messages for both situation and context.

Situation

Every situation is slightly (sometimes greatly) different from every other. A situation on Wednesday is not exactly the same as it was the previous Friday. Inflation today is not exactly what it was a year ago. The TV habits of Americans are not those of Germans; their situations are different.

It is not a good idea to use a "canned" solution to a writing problem. Readers may resent it. They may conclude that you have not thought the matter through. So take a fresh look at the situation; define the problem; think up a fresh solution. Then write a fresh message that fits.

But in what form: letter, memo, or report? In the form that best fits your situation and the prevailing convention. If your company insists on memos for certain situations, there is nothing wrong with that. But if it doesn't insist on set forms, consider designing one of your own.

Students often ask: When I go to work for a company, how will I know which message forms to use and how long they should be?

Some answers: Go to the company files and see what others are using in various situations. Ask around to see whether the forms and techniques are "set in concrete" or can be varied. Ask a number of people, including those you work for. Consider the situation you are being asked to write in. Can you design a message and a form especially for that situation? If you can't, don't worry. But we're betting that in many cases you can. American business runs on ingenuity.

Context

Here are some of the commonest howls heard in an office:

- Why am I reading this?!
- I understand the solution, but what is the problem?
- What am I supposed to do with ten copies of this report?

In each case, the writer wrote a message but forgot to put it into a context, the special circumstances involved.

What is involved in a context? Mainly, those things you read earlier in this overview: the writer, the reader, the point of the message. Here is a simple example of creating context. It's a brief note that starts:

> Dolores, I know you were interested in what the judgment was on the Marsten case, even though we were not directly involved. Did you know that Marsten's son had been running the business since the father had a stroke? Well, the son decided to call us in. . . .

If the writer of the message had started by saying: "Marsten's son decided to call us in," it is likely that Dolores would have been confused about why she was receiving information when she was not involved in the case. With context provided, she knows what the point of the message is, one that is summed up in the familiar abbreviation FYI ("for your information").

A context can be created in a number of ways:

1. Use a specific subject line.

> Subject: Spaces in the Learning Center

Follow up the subject line with an explanation that completes the context:

> Recently, I announced that the registration for the Learning Center was closed and that we would not be taking any more children. But we have had two cancellations, so . . .

2. Give some background.

>   Last year, we decided that the church could not afford to finish paving the back parking lot. Since Hans Tatum's bequest, however, our financial condition has changed somewhat. After consulting our accountants, we have decided to approach you with some alternatives. . . .

3. Be simple and direct.

>   Here is your new System Six Marvel Computer.
>
>   We have improved your health care coverage, starting the first of the year.
>
>   Bob, here's the information you asked for on the Watson file.

SUGGESTION SEVEN: KEEP IT SIMPLE — BUT NOT, OF COURSE, SIMPLE-MINDED

A book you might enjoy reading is *In Search of Excellence: Lessons from America's Best-run Companies*, by Thomas J. Peters and Robert H. Waterman, Jr. After years of studying successful companies, Peters and Waterman wrote this book about their findings. Some of them are fascinating. One finding relevant to our discussion is that excellent companies simplify. The authors say:

>   Most acronyms stink. Not KISS: *Keep it Simple, Stupid!* One of the key attributes of the excellent company is that they have realized the importance of keeping things simple despite overwhelming genuine pressures to complicate things.

How do excellent companies simplify? Peters and Waterman's evidence indicates that they force simplicity on nearly every aspect of their business, particularly on paper work. The average length of a new-product plan at their company, 3M, is only five pages, not the 200 pages that the authors found typical in many large companies. And 3M's success with new products is legendary.

By contrast, unsuccessful companies tend to drown in paper. The authors investigated a company that gave them a sense of "hopeless bureaucracy." Not one task force in the company had finished its job in the past three years. One reason was too much paper work. They investigated another unsuccessful client and discovered that the typical length of its task-force reports was more than 100 pages.

When Rene McPherson became head of Dana Corporation, he threw out twenty-two and a half inches of policy manuals and substituted a one-page statement of philosophy. On most projects, Texas Instruments pares down its list of objectives; a statement of more than two objectives, says TI, "is no objective."

Procter and Gamble insists on its legendary one-page memo. A brand new manager at P & G submitted a memo a page and a quarter long and it was kicked back as too long. The past president of P & G, Richard Deupree, used to return a long memo with this order: "Boil it down to something I can grasp." Deupree said to an interviewer, "Part of my job is to train people to break down an involved question into a series of simple matters. Then we can all act intelligently."

Why all this insistence in successful companies on keeping it simple? There are two answers, both supported by considerable research.

The first answer has to do with the human brain. Research suggests that most of us cannot grasp, much less assimilate, much data at one time. We can't deal with it, analyze it, or (most important) act on it. Successful people and companies believe in talking and writing, but not as a substitute for action. You must get things done and move on. For the second answer, see below.

SUGGESTION EIGHT: BREAK YOUR WORK, AND YOUR WRITING, INTO MANAGEABLE CHUNKS

A second answer as to why companies like to simplify is related to what we call *chunking*. If you had to carry a ten-foot log (to be used for firewood) from one place to another, you would not try to lift it all at once and carry it to a saw. Too much trouble. It would be easier to carry a portable saw to the log, saw it into chunks you can handle, and then carry the chunks to your place of storage. *Chunking* is breaking big things into smaller pieces so that you can handle the pieces. A successful company chunks in every part of its system.

One executive, for example, starts her day by dividing her task for that day into the important and the unimportant. She then grades them according to importance from least important to most important. Her chunking done, she gets down to work, handling the tasks in whichever order she thinks is sensible.

When she communicates, she chunks the material: a letter chunk to this person, a memo chunk to that committee, a report chunk to a district manager. Each of these messages usually covers one problem or task; she cuts "areas of difficulty" into manageable chunks so that they can be dealt with easily.

Her messages are also chunked.

- Her memo to X has five paragraph chunks.
- Her report to Y has three parts, or chunks.

Ten Basic Suggestions

- Her letter to the vice-president has twenty-two sentences (statement chunks), and those twenty-two sentences have thirty-one phrase and clause chunks marked by punctuation.

Chunking is basic to successful communication. You start by simplifying your material so that chunking is possible. Then you break the parts of the message into mental "bite sizes" so that your reader can swallow them one at a time.

Chapters 6 and 7 in this book will discuss Suggestions seven and eight in more detail. For the moment, note the differences between the messages in Figures O.1 and O.2. The complicated message presents the reader with one large, black blob of words. Nothing stands out. The sentences are too long. Readers feel as though, in order to comprehend the total message, they have to swallow it mentally all at once — an almost impossible task. Authorities on

---

LACO Black and White Television

LIMITED WARRANTY

LACO warrants this new set to be free from defective materials and workmanship, and agrees to remedy such defect or to furnish new parts for any unit which discloses such defect under normal installation, use and service, for a total period of one year after date of sale to original purchaser. LACO will supply parts and service at no charge for the first 90 days of this warranty and charge a service charge of $9.00 for the balance of this warranty with no charge for parts, provided that your set has not been dropped or abused or damaged during alterations or repairs by any person other than an authorized LACO Service Center, and provided that your set is delivered by its owner to us, or to an authorized LACO Service Center, all transportation charges prepaid. Antenna, power cords and any other accessories used in connection with this product as well as broken cabinets or parts damaged by misuse are not covered by this warranty. This warranty is in lieu of all other expressed warranties and no representative or person is authorized to assume for us any other liability in connection with the sale of our product. Your set sent in for repair must be dispatched in original packing together with an original sales receipt to validate the date of purchase. After the first 90 days, the service charge of $9.00 must accompany your set. Any set sent in for repair without sales slip or dispatched for repair after warranty has expired may be subject to a charge for labor plus cost of parts and transportation charges. This warranty gives you specific legal rights and you may also have other rights which vary from state to state.

Figure O.1. "Unchunked" and Complicated

MECO Black and White Television
LIMITED WARRANTY

Who is Covered?

This warranty covers the original buyer of this MECO TV set.

What Is Covered?

This warranty covers your new MECO TV set for any defects in materials or workmanship.

What is NOT Covered?

This warranty does not cover . . .
- the antenna
- the power cord
- any accessories used with the TV
- a broken cabinet
- parts damaged by misuse.

This warranty will not apply if the TV set was dropped, abused, or damaged when altered or repaired by anyone except an authorized MECO service center.

What MECO Will Do and For How Long

For the first 90 days, MECO will supply parts and labor free to repair or replace any defects in materials or workmanship.

After 90 days and up to 1 year, MECO will supply the part free but you will pay a $9.00 service charge. The $9.00 service charge must be paid when you bring or send in the TV.

After the warranty period (one year), you will pay for labor and parts.

At all times, you are responsible for bringing or sending your MECO TV in for repairs.

What You Must Do

The set must have been installed and used normally during the warranty period.

If you bring or send the TV in to an authorized MECO service center, it must be in its original packing case.

You must present an original sales receipt, showing the original date of purchase.

How To Get Warranty Service

Look in the Yellow Pages of your telephone book for the authorized MECO service center nearest you.

Ten Basic Suggestions 13

> This warranty gives you specific legal rights, and you may also have other rights which vary from state to state.
>
> The warranty that this product will work normally is limited to one year. No one has the right to change or add to this warranty.

Figure O.2. "Chunked'" and Simplified

readability point out that such messages are often not read at all; readers are so intimidated by them that they give up after looking at them for a few seconds.

By contrast, the chunked and simplified message, which gives similar information, is not nearly so intimidating. The big boldface headings allow readers to see and comprehend each chunk of information at a glance. The list under "What Is NOT Covered" is chunked into five short phrases that are easy to understand. And the sentences themselves are shorter, chunked into little pieces that are easy to read. Example:

chunk	*chunk*	*chunk*
After the warranty period	(one year)	you will pay for labor and parts.

Compare that sentence with this one from the complicated message:

> LACO will supply parts and service at no charge for the first 90 days of this warranty and charge a service charge of $9.00 for the balance of this warranty with no charge for parts, provided that your set has not been dropped or abused or damaged during alterations or repairs by any person other than an authorized LACO Service Center, and provided that your set is delivered by its owner to us, or to an authorized LACO Service Center, all transportation charges prepaid.

SUGGESTION NINE: USE SIMPLE, FAMILIAR WORDS

HEURISTICS AS A CONCOMITANT TO LEARNING COMMUNICATIONS SKILLS

What does that heading say? Possibly no more than: "This writer doesn't know what he's talking about, so he's going to fake it for a while."

About the type of words in that fake heading, G. K. Chesterton remarked, "You can go on talking like that for hours with hardly a movement of gray matter inside your skull." As it happens, Chesterton was commenting on this sentence:

> The social utility of the indeterminate sentence is recognized by all criminologists as part of our sociological evolution towards a more humane and scientific view of punishment.

Chesterton said that if you translate this sentence into, " 'I wish Jones to go to jail and Brown to say when Jones shall come out,' you will discover with a thrill of horror that you are obliged to think."

Some words are vague or unclear by nature: *function, in terms of, eventuate, media, expeditious.* Such words are swampy quicksand for the writer. One false step with your left foot into *function* or *in terms of* and you have lost your mental balance. Before you know it, your right foot blunders into *media*, causing you to fall headlong into *expeditious*. Unless you are rescued in seconds, you are going to drown in nonsense.

Many a writer lies in a damp grave, his resting place marked only by jargon like the fake heading: *Heuristics as a concomitant to learning communications skills*. Would you believe that this was a title of a speech given at a convention of communications professors? Would you believe that the speech was poorly attended?

Keep it simple applies not only to actions but to words as well. We think in words. If our words are fuzzy or jargon-ridden, our thoughts are likely to be fuzzy, even unintelligible. And then we will have failed; our message did not get through.

At this point in a class discussion, someone usually raises a hand: "Aren't some jargon terms necessary — for example, to professionals, who need them to communicate with each other?"

A second question follows: "Isn't some jargon necessary for legal purposes? I mean, in business, you've got to be legal!"

These are good questions, and they deserve more detailed answers than we have space for here. (See Chapter 6 for more discussion on the problem of words in business.)

For the time being, though, we can collapse the two questions into one and answer it by considering the necessity of jargon in making a message "legal." It is surprising to learn that much legal jargon is unneeded, even by lawyers. Consider the opinion of David Mellinkoff, professor of law at the University of California at Los Angeles and an expert on writing and the law. In his book, *Legal Writing: Sense and Nonsense*, Mellinkoff says: "Most law can be expressed in ordinary English." He argues that much legal jargon is neither exact nor precise, not even to lawyers. His premise, which is supported by his bookful of examples, is: "If it's good writing by the standards of ordinary English, it is more likely to be good legal writing."

Perhaps the major lesson here is that the standards of good writing do not change from job to job. It does not matter whether you work in accounting, advertising, sales, or engineering. To paraphrase Mellinkoff: If it's good writing by the standards of ordinary English, it is more likely to be good accounting, advertising, sales, or engineering writing.

SUGGESTION TEN: THINK ACTION. THEN WRITE *WHO DOES WHAT*

Here are two sentences that fail as messages:

1. There are three characteristics of consumer behavior involved in product purchase.

2. Utilization of the license constitutes acceptance of the restrictions described on the back.

Why do these messages fail? What can we do to improve them? As we have seen, successful businesspeople think: Action! In both sentences, the action is blurred and ambiguous. We can improve them, first, by looking for the doer of the action. In sentence number 1, the likeliest candidate for the doer is "consumer."

Now we look for the action itself, expressed in a verb. Since purchasing is involved, let's try the simple word *buy*.

Next, what is being bought? Products, apparently.

At this point we have *consumers buy products*. After looking again at sentence number 1, we can fill it out to read: Consumers buy products for three major reasons.

Now to improve our second failed sentence:

We look for the doer of the action. It seems to be the person who receives the license. Since the message is coming from someone else, we can assume that the first action in the sentence involves you, the license holder.

What is the action, as put in a verb? Try *use*, as in *You use (something)*.

Start the sentence: *If you use this license* . . .

Then the rest of the sentence follows logically: If you use this license, you automatically accept the restrictions described on the back.

Observe that we have found two actions in this message:

- *You use license.*
- *You accept the restrictions.*

In each of the actions, you have a doer, followed by an action verb, which in turn is followed by a receiver of the action. This is a pattern that can be summed up in the formula *who does what*. Sometimes the action is a *what does what*. No problem; the principle is the same. Always look for the action in any situation you are writing about.

Do we have any more suggestions? Just one. We won't give it a number.

In 1962 Sir Ernest Gowers published a brilliant little book called *Plain Words: Their ABC*. In his book he suggested that every writer should remember four fundamental rules. The first three encouraged simplicity, brevity, and grammatical correctness: *Be Simple. Be Short. Be Correct.*

But it is Sir Ernest's fourth rule that should impress us most and echo in our heads as we end this Overview. *Be human.* This is a major point, well made by Daniel Rowland, District Sales Manager, Cahners Publishing Co:

> Actually, writing good business letters, memos, and reports is a lot simpler than most people dream. The language of business is the language of ordinary conversation. It isn't the language of poets, professors, playwrights, or novelists. Do you have any trouble talking to someone face-to-face or across a desk? If you can talk to people, you can write to people just as easily. Use the same words, the same sentence structure and you'll write an excellent letter. If you start getting self-conscious, stuffy, or pompous, you'll write a terrible letter.
>
> Whenever you write anything, read it back aloud. Does it sound exactly the way you talk? If it doesn't, change it until it does. Letters that sound like someone talking are great letters — the best letters. Letters that sound stuffy, bookish, or professorish are terrible letters. In your letters you should talk to people just the way you do in person. Look at the letters you receive. The ones that sound like someone talking in a relaxed, friendly manner are always the best. If you can talk well with people, you can also write to them. It's exactly the same thing. The trouble is that nobody in school ever tells us this and we get a lot of crazy, absurd ideas about what a letter should sound like.

EXERCISES

1. For each of the three following messages, prepare some notes for class discussion on the way the message follows Suggestions One through Five in this chapter. Is each message particularly strong in using one of the suggestions?

Note for Message A. The Council for Basic Education is a small, private organization with national headquarters in Washington, D.C. It deals only in educational matters, and its mission is to help public education by encouraging Americans to improve the teaching of basic skills and knowledge. Mortimer Smith was for many years its director; this letter is an example of one of his most successful attempts to gain from its members support for the organization.

Message A

Dear Member:

This year I have been seriously debating whether or not I should make my annual appeal to the membership of CBE for contributions beyond the membership fee.

My uncertainty arises from the fact that income from our principal sources of support — membership and subscription fees, publications, and foundation grants — has been up and we will end the year in the black. However, other circumstances persuade me that I should again seek your help. While there is no financial crisis of the sort that has faced us in the past, there is no certainty that next year will equal this year. Indeed, several grants received this year undoubtedly will not be renewed and there is a possibility that income from publications will fall off in 1974.

We must take up this slack and your contributions will be of great help. I know that many of you want to contribute on a regular annual basis, whether it be a feast or a famine year. I realize that in these days many of you have to be as watchful of income (and outgo) as we do, but if your circumstances permit, we will be glad to have your help. Contributions are, of course, tax-deductible.

The Council tries to live frugally without curtailing our effectiveness, and we keep constantly in mind the goal of long range survival. I am sure that most of you see the necessity for a continuing organization that works for rational (and realizable) change in the schools. This note of continuity and survival is often sounded in the unsolicited letters we receive. "There is no other voice around," says one recent writer, "that would take CBE's place should anything happen to it." Says another: "I am so glad you people exist. You do much good — please never quit."

CBE doesn't intend to quit. Your contribution will help us to continue the struggle on behalf of sound basic education.

Sincerely yours,

Mortimer Smith
Executive Director,
Council for Basic Education

MS:rb

Message B

Mr. and Mrs. John R. Farmer
R. R. 2
Champaign, Illinois 61801

Subject: *Estate Planning — Joint Tenancy or Tenancy-in-Common*

Dear Mr. and Mrs. Farmer,

Yesterday as you were leaving my office we briefly discussed planning your estate. I mentioned your and your wife's holding your property under either *joint tenancy* or *tenancy-in-common,* and you seemed a little confused. Perhaps this information will help clear things up.

Joint tenancy is a form of co-ownership of property that has advantages especially for smaller estates. Joint tenancy carries with it the "right of survivorship," which means that if one of the joint tenants dies, the other immediately assumes full ownership of all property under the agreement. It does not pass as part of the deceased's estate, so it isn't subject to the added cost and delay often involved in the administration of a will. This is an important consideration when the survivor is heavily dependent on the property for income.

Disadvantages of joint tenancy may outweigh the advantages, however, depending on the case. If a couple owns property jointly and has no children, property that has been passed down through one side of the family for ages may eventually end up on the other side. When family heirlooms are involved, this may be a consideration.

Inheritance tax laws also place joint tenancy at a disadvantage. If the estate is large, double taxation may result before the property is passed entirely to the children. Consider this example:

> Mr. and Mrs. A own all of their farm, valued at $150,000, in a joint tenancy. Mr. A dies, and Mrs. A immediately assumes full ownership. The entire $150,000 is taxable under the federal inheritance tax, but Mr. A's estate receives the full marital deduction and the tax will only be $1,050.
>
> Problems arise when Mrs. A dies. The marital deduction cannot be considered for her estate, since it was used when Mr. A died. The full $150,000 is taxable, and the total tax is $17,000.

Tenancy-in-common is the other method of property ownership. The major difference is that there is no right of survivorship. Each co-tenant has a specified interest in the property and can transfer it undivided by selling it, giving it away, or transferring it to persons of his or her choice at death.

The major advantage over joint tenancy is that the federal estate tax applies only to the fractional interest that a person holds at his death. (Remember: Under joint tenancy the entire property is taxable to the deceased tenant.) The total property is thus taxed only once. Consider our example once again:

> Mr. and Mrs. A now co-own their $150,000 farm under a tenancy-in-common agreement. Each holds title to half the total, or $75,000. Mr. A dies, and his $75,000 share is taxable. However, considering his allowable marital and other deductions, no tax is paid.
>
> Mrs. A has received the $75,000 share tax-free, so she holds title of the total estate, worth $150,000. When she dies the total tax will equal only $3,000, since she can also assume deductions.

Although it appears that the advantages of tenancy-in-common far outweigh those of joint tenancy, they do not in all cases. If the property of one owner is willed to someone besides the other owner, conflicts of interest may develop, and the estate may eventually be split up.

As you can see, whether to own your property under joint tenancy or tenancy-in-common depends on your objectives and your situation.

I hope this description helps you understand the issue a little better. In any event, by now you can surely see that the type of ownership you elect to use is important.

If you have any more questions please call in and we can set up an appointment. I'll be glad to help.

Sincerely,

Bradshaw T. Link
Attorney-at-Law

BTL:ss

Message C

September 18, 1986

Mr. John A. Smith
Personnel Director
Berkeley and Company
221 North 52 Avenue
Cicero, IL 60602

Subject: Product Recall — Biofeedback Equipment

Dear Mr. Smith:

I have received a recall notice on the Model A−1300 alpha wave monitors that your company is currently using. The manufacturer has discovered some faulty resistors that may result in false alpha brainwave signals in excess or deficit of actual alpha brainwave activity.

You should immediately stop using the A−1300 model because it may yield improper baseline readings, thus making progress into deeper stages of relaxation impossible. The A−1300s are powered by a nine-volt transistor battery, so no danger of shock is involved in this defect.

To insure that your training program proceeds as scheduled, we have arranged for you to receive twenty-eight ABTD−2000s, as replacement units, before October 14. The ABTDs have all the capabilities of your present equipment.

Since your staff will need instructions in using the ABTDs, Jennifer Maxwell, one of our technicians, will visit you to conduct a one-hour training session the day the replacement units are delivered. So that you can schedule this instruction time, we will telephone you forty-eight hours in advance of delivery.

Monolith Electronics has arranged with the Railway Express Company to cover all shipping costs resulting from the return of the defective machines. Please repack and ship the units by October 17, 1986. Packing and shipping specifications are enclosed.

Upon receiving the recalled monitors, Monolith will install and solder new transistors, completely eliminating any chance of improper baseline readings. Soldering will correct the design of the transistor-fed brainwave equipment across the industry. In addition to correcting the design, Monolith will clean and recondition your A—1300s. Your A—1300s will therefore be in excellent working order when Monolith returns them to you the first week of November.

Please feel free to call me at 555—492—2289 if you have questions. We appreciate your cooperation in this procedure. With your help, your biofeedback stress reduction program can proceed as planned.

Sincerely,

Jonas Webb, Manager
Specialization Supply Co.

2. Here is a good example of writing that works through action. The writer, William Zinsser, taught himself to use a word processor. How many action words can you find in the passage? Make a list of them.

Next, make a list of the doers of the action — the *who* or *what* that makes things happen. (In this passage, you will find that, since Zinsser addresses his readers directly, a number of the doers will be "understood," as in the first sentence of the second paragraph:

Doer   *action word(s)*
[you]   learn to play

> Here, again, a word processor encourages you to play. The English language is rich in words that convey an exact shade of meaning. Don't get stuck with a word that's merely good if you can find one that takes the reader by surprise with its color or aptness or quirkiness. Root around in your dictionary of synonyms and find words that are fresh. Throw them up on the screen and see how they look.
>
> Also learn to play with whole sentences. If a sentence strikes you as awkward or ponderous, move your cursor to the space after the period and write a new sentence that you think is better. Maybe you can make it shorter. Or clearer. Maybe you can make it livelier by turning it into a question or otherwise altering its rhythm. Change the passive verbs into active verbs. (Passive verbs are the death of clarity and vigor.) Try writing two or three new versions of the awkward sentence and then compare them, or write a fourth version that combines the best elements of all three. Sentences come in an infinite variety of shapes and sizes. Find one that pleases you. If it's clear, and if it pleases you and expresses who you are, trust it to please other people. Then delete all the versions that aren't as good. Your shiny new sentence will jump into position and the rest of the paragraph will rearrange itself as quickly and neatly as if you had never pulled it apart.
>
> — William Zinsser

3. Professor Daniel McDonald of the University of South Alabama calls the message below "the world's worst business letter." For class discussion, make some notes for a description of the specific flaws in the letter. Then rewrite the letter completely.

Anarda Bonding Co.
1501 Mirrabel St.
Locksley, Ala.

Attn: Mrs. Sally Hall

                                                Re: Truckstop Ranch Corp.
                                                     Mobile, Alab.
                                                     QAP # 958-254-8927

Dear Madam,

    Per our telephone conversation this date, please be advised of the fact that we are no longer insurance carrier for the above referenced company. We regret we cannot, pursuant to your request, transmit information in regard to the record of said account in the area of fire-protection viability. Enclosed please find documentation in reference to the referenced account. Be advised that during the month of January and subsequently, the above company and/or its personnel did not honor our requests to forward data describing interface between manpower and fire-protection hardware capability. Again, permit me to remind you that insurance was carried on the subject company only for the period from June 1963 to December 1980. Transition data relative to specific transactions prior to termination date are indeed available. In the event that you can utilize aforementioned documentation (in lieu of requested information), do not hesitate to contact me at your earliest convenience or at any point in time thereafter. Feel free to direct your request to the writer (at the above address), and we shall transmit required data by return mail.

    Thanking you in advance, I remain

                                                              Very Cordially yours,

                                                              Mitchell R. Shortfall
                                                              B.C.S.

MRS/em

(enclosure)

4. Below you see parts of two annual reports, both from the St. Paul Companies, Incorporated. Read them carefully and prepare notes for class discussion.

Which of the ten suggestions in the chapter apply best to the second report? (It is better-written than the first.) Be specific in your answer.

How many *who does what* sentences can you find in the St. Paul reports? Make a list of them — for example, in the first complete sentence of sample *two*:

Who	*Does*	*What*
we	carry	bonds

Sample one (1977)

Leasing

Full pay-out leases are accounted for on the financial method. At the time leases are executed, income is recognized to the extent of acquisition costs and estimated losses. The remaining unearned finance charges are recognized as income over the terms of the leases in proportion to the decreasing balances of the receivables. Investment tax credits on equipment leased are amortized over the terms of the leases. (See note 11.)

Less than full pay-out leases are accounted for on the operating method.

Investments in leasing joint ventures, which use primarily the operating method of accounting, are accounted for on the equity method. Accordingly, the Company's share of the ventures' operating results is included in income.

Title Insurance

Policy premiums are taken into income when the policies are issued. Provision is made for reported claims and estimated unreported claims and loss expenses based upon past experience adjusted for current trends. Costs of acquiring property title records are capitalized. Current costs for updating title records are expensed as incurred.

Sample two (1978)

1.2-2 *The year end fair value of bonds.* As mentioned, we carry bonds at their amortized cost. The amortized cost figure is based on purchase price and does *not* reflect current market value, which is what we might get if we had sold the investments at year end. However, if we feel that a bond is "troubled," that is that we may have trouble redeeming it, we will estimate how much we might realize and reduce the value of the bond on our books to its estimated realizable value.

We make a year end estimate of the fair value of our bonds so you can see how their current value differs from the value we carry on our books. At the end of 1978 our estimated value was $1,886,345,972. This figure is found in parentheses on the balance sheet.

5. At a small college, students must register their bicycles if they ride them on campus. They have to go to the Division of Parking and pick up a sticker for their bikes. Below is the set of instructions that the clerk hands them with the sticker. The clerk gives no other instructions.

For class discussion: Using the ten suggestions discussed in this chapter, describe specifically the errors in the message. Then rewrite the message completely, so that the reader will know exactly what to do. Try to use all the techniques you can think of to make the message clearer and the parts stand out visually. Your instructor may ask you to read Chapter 2, on visual effects, before you write this assignment.

Also consider whether you need a drawing to help the reader.

DIVISION OF PARKING (bicycle section)   El Wimpo College

This sticker must be properly affixed on the vehicle for which it was issued as explained before (improper affixation may result in a monetary fine — see Campus Code #37–B 14). This Code does not apply to handicapped students engaged in the use of three-wheel vehicles except when parking at the Learning Resources Center or when they ride on the Athletic Grounds. On 10-speed vehicles the sticker must be placed on the handle bar, left side; on mono-speed vehicles, place the sticker on the post beneath the vehicle owner's seat. There are two stickers to be accomplished. One is green in color; it is for students matriculated in the two-year certificate program. The other one (red) is applied to 4-year degree persons.

How to Affix Stickers

The sticker is printed on the non-gummed side which is not sticky. It does not require glue or paste. Put directly on the affixed spot by pressing with the fingers. Before affixing, you should separate the two parts of the sticker with the fingernail, throw the unnecessary part away and affix the numbered part. You cannot transfer the sticker to another individual or person. If vehicles are changed a new sticker must be obtained by applying to this office. One is required to surrender the pieces of the old sticker. No charge is made for the requisition of new stickers. Housing permit stickers must be displayed next to vehicle stickers. Only current stickers can be displayed on the appropriate vehicle.

6. You are the director of the Division of Parking mentioned in Exercise 5. The original instructions for handling the bike sticker were written by Fred Raisin, the assistant director. Write Fred a memo, asking him to rewrite the instructions, using certain suggestions that you will make in the memo. Don't rewrite the instructions for him, but do be fairly specific in your suggestions for rewriting.

7. Claire Wilson, working in the Student Loan Department of a college, received this letter:

Re: Student Loan Repayment (NDEA)

To whom it may concern,

I sincerely hope your computer bears no personal grudge against this insignificant alumnus of your illustrious institution. For some unknown reason, you have neglected to bill me for my October loan payment. Every month, I dearly look forward to that exquisite yellow card that arrives with such precise regularity. The schedule for my monthly existence is focused around its appearance, like that of Orestes and the Furies of old. Therefore, you can now empathize with my dismay at its unanticipated absence from my mailbox. Ah, but if homage is not duly paid to the computer, like the Furies it plans a rather costly revenge. It cries in a shrill way for more blood. The price of retribution it demands is a high price to pay. I thus humbly entreat you to look carefully into this matter on my mortal and lowly behalf so indeed my debt to your society can be resolved in a manner satisfactory both to myself and your divine representative.

> With all grace and speed
> please bill me,
>
> Jack Milburn

Claire Wilson answered as follows:

Dear Mr. Milburn:

Fear not, worthy borrower, our computer knows you to be a fair and equitable man.

Your apprehensions should be directed toward another mighty power. Your statement was sent upon its way with all due blessings from this computer's realm to another's.

Alas! Your exquisite yellow card is at the mercy of the Post Office — what fate it has met we know not.

But dismay not further; enclosed is another yellow card and its accompanying return envelope.

In our eagerness to appease our divine representative, we humbly entreat you to send homage of $60.99, the amount due for September and October.

> With all grace and speed,
>
> Claire Wilson
> Student Loan Department

A woman who works full time as a consultant in business writing uses these two letters as an example of one way to make communications more interesting and effective. What do you think she tells her clients about these letters?

8. You are a mechanic specializing in small-car repair. You work on any car, foreign or domestic; but most of your customers drive small cars, many of them old and rickety. A few drive big new American cars.

    a. Analyze in detail four of your customers. (Try to choose real people you know.) What types of personality do they have? What do they like or dislike, as people? What are their prejudices, politics, hobbies, interests? When you talk to them and want to make them like you, what do you talk about? What subjects do you avoid? If you want them to use your service regularly, what about them as people would you appeal to?

    b. Using this last question as a springboard, write a paragraph on each of the four personalities you have chosen. Examples: an aging hippy of the sixties who still drives a 1964 VW bug; an elderly woman who drives a full-size 1978 Plymouth; a college fraternity man who drives a new Corvette; a woman graduate student who drives a two-year-

Ten Basic Suggestions 25

        old Toyota. If you wish, pick your own personality and your own car. Be sure to make a point about each person you describe.

    c. Write an individualized letter to each of the four persons in part a. Or, if your instructor suggests it, write to just one of them. In the letter say that you have a sale on tune-ups. Try to encourage the reader to want to come to you for a tune-up right away. Assume that each reader neglects his or her car, that he or she thinks tune-ups cost too much money and should be put off until the car just stops in the street some day.

9. You are the business manager of a geological field crew, the first woman ever to hold such a post in your company. You have been on the job for fourteen months and have been doing very well.

Now you have an interesting problem. You have been directed by your division supervisor to move your crew to the town of Mesquite, a small mountain town in one of the western states. For two weeks every July, Mesquite goes on a rampage. It all started a decade ago when Mesquite had its centennial celebration and found it so much fun that it has the same celebration every July.

The trouble is that during the celebration this small town of 677 people goes mad. Everybody is either celebrating wildly or hiding in the cellar until the party wears itself out. When your crew was here last year, you had trouble getting gas and diesel fuel for the equipment (the two stations were closed most of the time), food for the workers, and safe shelter. One truck was damaged by celebrators and an engineer was attacked when he walked by a bar at ten in the morning.

You are afraid to base your crew in Mesquite. The closest town (Union Springs) is fifty-four miles away, so if you stay there you will have two hours of extra driving every day to get to the job near Mesquite. You consider the extra expense of travel and the lost time on the job. You have two women working on your crew in the field office (a trailer), one a geologist and the other a map maker. You wonder about their safety. If they stay in Mesquite, all members of the field crew will have to sleep and eat in the town's one motel and restaurant.

The Division supervisor in Denver is an old-time "dootlebugger" — a field man of twenty-five years' experience. The situation in Mesquite is the sort of thing he loves to tell as a great story about a great life: "Boy, let me tell you about the time we stayed in . . . !"

What are you going to do? You are responsible for your crew, its well being, its equipment, and its production schedule.

Make your decision and write to the Division supervisor in Denver.

10. You are a sophomore in a large university. Recently you were sick for two weeks with one of those illnesses nobody can quite diagnose — a virus, a physician at the Health Service called it.

During these two weeks, you went four times to the Health Service, seeing

Doctor A the first time, Nurse R the second, Doctor B the third, and Doctor A the fourth. You were more or less ambulatory, so you never got an official Sick Slip that would allow you to miss classes without penalty.

Professor Kerry has questioned your missing four of his classes. You were really too sick to make the four classes (you have not, in three months of the semester, missed any other classes of his). If you don't get an official Sick Slip, Professor Kerry is going to lower your grade in the course.

But you can't get a Sick Slip because you never asked for one, and the three people you saw in the Health Service did not offer to give you one. You are caught in the cracks of a big university system.

Now you decide to write a letter to someone (who?) at the Health Service, laying out a case and asking for something. Now you must decide:

    a. What exactly will you ask for (point)?
    b. What is your best role? How will you project the right image?
    c. What is the best way to handle the reader's viewpoint? (How many readers eventually might be involved?) Describe your reader(s) carefully.
    d. How exactly do you want to influence your reader?
    e. How will you anticipate and answer any questions your reader(s) may have?

Write a short paper that answers these questions in reasonable detail.

    11. Write the letter required in Exercise 10.

    12. After forty years of service, John Jix is retiring as second-in-command of accounting in your firm. He has been very effective as a manager so far as the technical side is concerned, but he has been unpopular with many people because he has been so picky about money — he has been very tight with expense accounts, secretarial supplies, and so on.

You have been put in charge of his retirement party. You sent out 120 letters, using a word processor, asking people to come to his retirement party to be held in the Zed Ballroom in the Smythe Regency Hotel. So far you have answers from only seventy people (fifty of whom are coming), and the date for the party is approaching. As your assignment, you have two messages to prepare:

    a. Write a memo to Jix, who wants to know how the preparations for his "wonderful party," which he has been so eagerly looking forward to, are coming. He wants to know everything you are doing to get ready for the festive occasion.
    b. Write a letter to the Smythe Regency, telling management in detail how you want the Zed Ballroom laid out, how much food you want and what kind, how much to drink and what kind, and so on.

In order to write the letter in part b, and perhaps the one in part a, you must ask around in your community and learn the details of what people in this kind of situation expect in the way of refreshments and surroundings. Your student union or faculty club may be of help.

13. For many years, we have given the following assignment as an end-of-term exercise. It has become well known and quite popular among students. The reason for its popularity lies apparently in its practicality: Students can practice business writing while trying to get something they want for themselves. One student actually succeeded in getting a change in the way state scholarships were handled in Illinois, a change that meant a couple of thousand dollars to him personally.

We are introducing the assignment now, in case your instructor might like to use it eventually, or modify it for his or her own purposes. It usually takes a couple of months to get your material and evidence together.

The "public medium" mentioned in part c(2) can be, for example, a radio station, a magazine, or a newsletter.

    a. Focus on a change that you want made in one of your so-called communities — university, state, local, hometown, housing, and so on.

    b. Investigate this situation, and interview, write, or call the people involved — get the facts concerning the change you want made.

    c. Write two letters:

        (1) Address one to the responsible official or person who has the most power to effect the change you want. Give the facts surrounding the problem; state your proposed change clearly and in detail. Be persuasive. About two typewritten pages are usually enough; sometimes more are necessary.

        (2) Address the other to a public medium, usually a newspaper. Persuade the general readership that the change you want is needed; ask the public to help you get the change made. Length depends on the newspaper.

        (3) Send both letters. Give your instructor copies of the letters.

    d. Examples of changes students have wanted in the past are: an end to block-busting in a Polish neighborhood in Chicago; an end to the use of ammonia as a cleaning agent in a women's dorm; a better method of training teaching assistants in freshman rhetoric; a change in the handling of emergency procedures in a local hospital; a change in a decision to close a Catholic school in an Illinois city.

PART 1

Planning Your Message

CHAPTER 1

Hang Your Message on a Hook

It is winter — cold, and there's snow outside.

The students come into the classroom stamping their feet, blowing on their hands. There is snow on their heads, books, coats. They blow snow off their books; they shake their coats and hang them on hooks along the back of the room, one coat to a hook. Looked at from the instructor's chair at the front of the room, everything appears neatly arranged in front of him: twenty students, one to a chair; twenty coats, one to a hook.

The class begins.

On this day the students and instructor are discussing report topics. A student says: "Look at all this writing I've got here: three, four pages, and I haven't even gotten into the subject. My problem is that I don't know where to begin."

"Meaning what?" says the instructor.

"Everything about my subject is too complicated," says the student. "There's too much of everything. I can't get started and keep going. Every time I do, I think of ten things I should say at the beginning."

The instructor says: "Look at your coat back there hanging on the wall. When you came in, you didn't throw your coat at the wall and hope it would miraculously stay up there off the floor. You hung it high and dry on a hook. You're trying to throw your report at a 'message wall,' hoping it will stay there; but your subject keeps falling down in a heap. Try some hooks."

"Glad to, once you tell me how to hook the entire Clinton Nuclear Power Plant. You remember that's what I'm writing on."

"No," says the instructor, "I don't mean that you should hook the thing all at once, just parts of it. You didn't spread your coat over ten hooks back there. You used one hook at a time. Let's make up some hooks for your report on the Clinton Power Plant; we'll put them on the board and underline them:

- The plant is <u>safe</u>.
- The plant <u>costs too much</u>.
- Some of the inspection is <u>undependable</u>.
- Illinois Power needs a <u>rate hike</u> in order to finish the plant.

"Each of these underlined words or phrases," says the instructor, "is a verbal hook to hang your report on, or to hang a part of it. Now you people suggest some more. Say anything that comes to mind."

In a few minutes, students suggest this mixed list of hooks (underlined):

- We citizens will never be <u>sure</u> that the Clinton plant is <u>safe</u>.
- <u>Union workers</u> have made the plant too <u>costly</u>.
- Nuclear power is <u>less expensive</u> than coal power.
- Illinois Power failed to realize how <u>expensive</u> the Clinton plant was to <u>build</u>.
- <u>Rates</u> will <u>go up</u> because of Clinton Power Plant.
- Clinton has not licked its <u>engineering problems</u>.
- Clinton used the <u>wrong nuclear design</u>.

The class we are describing continued in this vein. Each suggested hook or hooks again made the point that "hooking a topic" provides control in both planning and writing a message. Indeed, the chapter you are now reading is hooked on two words: *hang* and *hook*.

Writing is an enigmatic art, but you can find processes in it. One of these is the hooking process, which allows you to limit and define your topic. And it does not matter whether you are writing a report of ten pages or a memo of one paragraph: Your message will still be about one thing or cluster of things — a small hook, a big one, or a series of hooks used one after the other.

HOOKING A SHORT MESSAGE

Most memos and letters, of course, are fairly short. You usually write them to take care of one problem or one group of related problems.

This fact means that you can often inspect your situation and find the hooks in it. Example: You have a warranty for the typewriters your company sells. The warranty is satisfactory legally, your attorneys tell you, but it will not pass one state's readability laws. So when you plan a memo to your legal division, your subject line reads:

Hang Your Message on a Hook

Readability of typewriter warranty — XYZ model

Your main hook here is *readability;* your minor hooks are *warranty* and *the model number.* Just by looking at your own subject line, you have an idea of the point of your message, and you can write it quickly. In addition, when they see the subject line your readers will have an idea of the content of the message, and they can read it with the proper degree of attention.

For the same situation, other possible hooks (again in the subject line) are:

- XYZ model — readability of warranty
- Typewriters (readability of XYZ model warranty)
- The question of readable typewriter warranties

As you can see, each of these major hooks is different, and each implies that your message will hang on something different. The first is hung on readability, the second on typewriters, and the third on the abstract idea embodied in the word *question.* The first might apply to your situation, but the second and third probably would not. If they are irrelevant hooks to hang your ideas on, they might cause you to write a badly focused memo. Furthermore, they could mislead your reader.

HOOKING A LONGER MESSAGE

Most longer messages are complex enough to require breaking them down into parts. Suppose, for example, you are a consultant who has been asked by an absentee owner to investigate the slipping sales of her retail store specializing in designer clothes. As you look into the situation, you realize that the problem is more complex than you thought.

When you have finished your investigation, you start to write a report. But first you sit down with some scratch paper and doodle a bit. You write a list of problems and difficulties with the store:

- aisles too crowded
- too many part-time salespeople
- too many special sales
- customers confused
- too much stock
- cash-flow problems
- good merchandise mixed in with poor

You don't want to write a report that just throws all this together without proper emphasis. Furthermore, you need a unified idea for the entire report. What should you hang it on?

First, you think you might hang it on the phrase *manager's incompetence,* because everything points to the manager's not being on top of things. But the phrase appears a bit strong, and it makes a decision for the owner. Wouldn't it be better to make the same point somewhat more neutrally? So you decide to hang the report on the word *mishandled,* which is a fair description of the entire operation. The total problem is most evident in the mishandling of stock, special sales, displays, and so on.

Now you take a fresh sheet of paper and write *mishandling* on the top. But that is pretty negative. You change it to the phrase *handle things better.* But what things? Group the problems in a few words or phrases in the middle of your sheet of paper.

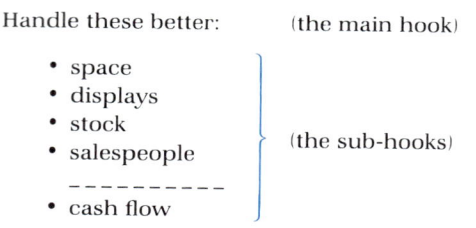

Handle these better: (the main hook)

- space
- displays
- stock
- salespeople

- cash flow

(the sub-hooks)

Each of these five items is a hook for a part of your report. Each involves the handling of something. As it happens, each of the hooks above the broken line is the responsibility of the store manager. (For reasons we won't go into here, the cash-flow problem is more the owner's fault.)

HOOKS PROVIDE CONTROL

Considering what we have just been saying, observe how much control your hooks provide in writing your report. You can introduce the report by pointing out that the store's problems are five in number, and that they are all related to handling something in the business. Sub-hooks one through four suggest the first four sections of the report. Each is a hook, or subhook, for its own section. But the cash-flow problem should be laid at the owner's feet, and you will say so in the later part of the report. The point of your report might be phrased as follows:

> If you and your store manager can agree to handle five things better [list them], then this store should stop losing money.

Before you have even started to write your report, you are in control of it. Your hooks not only suggest what you want to put in the report, they also suggest the order of subpoints. But if you don't like the order suggested above, change it to:

- cash flow
- - - - - - - - - -
- salespeople   ⎫
- stock   ⎬ Handle these better
- space   ⎪
- displays   ⎭

We can't tell you what an ideal order, or organization, would be, for these matters come out of the situation. Don't forget: Every situation is unique, and every message written should, if possible, fit that uniqueness.

STRATEGY — ONE HOOK AT A TIME

To return to the controlling hook for this chapter: If you hang your coat carefully on a wall hook, it will probably stay up there high and dry. But if you try to hang it over two or three hooks at the same time, it may slip and fall down.

Use one hook at a time. Hang your message on it. If your message threatens to fall off, look critically at the situation and see if you need several subhooks, each holding up its own section of the message.

We have known writers, by the way, who almost literally use hooks. One of our friends uses a board on which he tacks groups of three-by-five-inch cards containing information about the situation he is working on. When he is through tacking, he rearranges the cards and puts a title card on each group. Then he puts a big card in the center and puts a title on it. Now he has, in effect, a title hook and a certain number of sub-hooks, all of the latter tacked together in their own groups. These form the sections of his message.

Another friend uses little cubbyholes like the letter boxes in an old post office. She tapes a title slip over the top of each cubbyhole and organizes by shoving pieces of paper into the holes.

Regardless of technique, these systems all do approximately the same thing. They allow you to separate and classify your information. They encourage you to tell yourself:

1. what your main point is, and
2. what your subpoints are.

And they remind you to:

3. stick to the main point throughout, and
4. deal with your material one subpoint at a time (don't mix things up).

Chapters 4 and 5, on organization, are relevant to the message hook.

EXERCISES

1. In Appendix A you will find "extra problems." Read carefully numbers 1, 3, 8, and 18. For each of these, create two major hooks (for two different approaches) and as many minor hooks as you think are necessary. Prepare to defend your choice of hooks in class discussion.

2. Turn to the table of contents in this book. How do the chapter titles suggest hooks that we used to write the book? What is the hook in the title of the book?

3. As you plan your own messages in the course, write your hook(s) on scratch paper. When you turn in your message to your instructor write the hook at the end and circle it. Example:

(billing error not your fault, but ours)

For each of the situations below, create at least one hook. Write the message itself only at your instructor's request.

4. Plan to write home, asking for $100 (not a loan).

5. Plan to ask a bank for a $500 loan.

6. Write to your instructor in this course, giving your reason(s) for missing three classes and one assignment.

7. Plan a message to XYZ car company saying that its automobile, which you bought new three months ago, is unsatisfactory.

8. Plan a message to the dean of your college, saying that Assistant Dean X has been very helpful to you on three occasions. This is a letter of praise for Assistant Dean X.

9. Plan a message to the manager of a store in your hometown. Sell yourself to him or her as a summer employee (either part- or full-time).

10. Consider your favorite hobby or pastime. Plan a message to other people of your age "selling" this hobby or pastime; try to get them to do it or adopt it.

11. Plan an advertisement for a new tissue that people will use when they have colds or allergies. Why should people want to buy this tissue instead of other brands?

CHAPTER 2

"Listening to the Look": The Power of Visual Effect

One of our favorite people is a specialist in visual makeup and design. She will take various elements of a page (including illustrations and text) and place them on an oversized sheet, which she tapes to her desk. Or she'll have a page made up in its real size, using different type faces, arrangements of heading, employment of color, and so on.

You can find her standing over a page on her desk, looking down at it.

"What are you doing?" we'll ask.

"Oh, just listening to the look," she will answer.

Our friend is an expert in the visual effect of messages, that all-important, but often neglected, aspect of writing. So much of visual effect hits readers intuitively. They may know that they like (or don't like) something they see on the page, but they don't know why. That explains our friend's remark that she is "listening to the look" — to the appearance of the page. She is trying to sense or intuit what works, or doesn't work, in its appearance.

Before going further, let us turn over a couple of examples to you and your instructor. We will all save time if you have a class discussion of two sample messages, the first given in the following exercise.

EXERCISES

Read quickly the passage below and the questions that follow it.

It is ironic that, at a time when its audiences are growing dramatically, public radio is the victim of severe cutbacks. But WILL-AM/580 and WILL-FM/91 will survive if you, the listeners, choose to sustain them. Your two public radio stations are clearly an important resource for you and for our communities. WILL-FM continues to fill our days with programs like *Opus One*, *Nocturne*, and the Chicago, Boston, New York, and Los Angeles orchestras. There is no other radio station in our area devoted to classical music. WILL-FM just celebrated its sixtieth year on the air with programs like *Morning Edition*, *All Things Considered*, *Classics by Request*, and the *Noon Report*. It is the only source of in-depth news and information in east central Illinois. I assure you we are doing everything possible to keep costs down and to increase revenue: We have subscribed to newly available, high-quality programming services, thus reducing local production costs; we have not filled vacant staff positions; we have increased our corporate support efforts; we are taking measures to reduce power consumption; and we are involving more volunteers in the work of the stations.

We took the sample you just read from the middle of a direct-mail letter from a PBS radio station. For the complete real letter, see Figure 2.1. All we did to the sample from the real letter was to remove its visual effects.

1. For class discussion, make notes about two things: the contrast between the sample passage and the real letter in Figure 2.1, and the visual effects in the real letter. In your notes consider these questions:

    a. How, exactly, did we change the visual effects in the original letter when we took out the sample? List the changes.

    b. What do these changes imply about visual effect generally?

Questions 2 through 19 apply to Figure 2.1, the complete original letter.

2. How many different devices of visual effect can you find in the original letter? List them.

3. Where are the points of visual emphasis in the letter? Do these correspond to the points of organizational emphasis in the letter? What do you infer from this correspondence (or lack of it)?

4. How many paragraphs are there in the letter? Are there too many?

5. Why is the large heading placed in the left top corner instead of in the right corner, or centered on the top? Or somewhere else? Why is it tilted? Why is it big? Is it too big?

6. What is the effect of the underline in line 4?

7. Why did the writer use the spaced periods in line 13?

8. What is the effect of boldface type in lines 16–18?

9. Certain lines use italics. Why?

"Listening to the Look"

WILL Radio Priority Transmittal

Dear Friend,

This is a very difficult letter for me to write. In the midst of a critical economic situation affecting all of us, I must share our particular problem with you.

As you have undoubtedly heard, <u>public broadcasting is fighting for survival</u> all across the country. Here at WILL we are faced with a severe financial problem. To put it simply, WILL must raise significantly more money from the private sector than ever before and must do so before July 1.

WILL Radio relies on a combination of state, federal and private support. This year, 20% of our total revenue of $618,000 came from the listeners of the stations. Next year, because of the anticipated loss of almost $100,000 in state and federal support, 35% of our status quo budget must come from private sources. This translates to $219,000 ... an increase of 78%!

It is ironic that, at a time when its audiences are growing dramatically, public radio is the victim of severe cutbacks. **But WILL-AM/580 and WILL-FM/91 will survive if you, the listeners, choose to sustain them.**

Your two public radio stations are clearly an important resource for you and for our communities. WILL-FM continues to fill our days with programs like *Opus One, Nocturne,* and the Chicago, Boston, New York and Los Angeles orchestras. There is no other radio station in our area devoted to classical music.

WILL-AM just celebrated its sixtieth year on the air with programs like *Morning Edition, All Things Considered, Classics by Request,* and the *Noon Report.* It is the only source of in-depth news and information in east central Illinois.

I assure you we are doing everything possible to keep costs down and to increase revenue:

...we have subscribed to newly available, high quality programming services, thus reducing local production costs,
...we have not filled vacant staff positions,
...we have increased our corporate support efforts,

Figure 2.1. Direct mail letter

<pre>
35
</pre>

... we are taking measures to reduce power consumption,
... we are involving more volunteers in the work of the stations.

A Friend of WILL said recently, "We have lost control of so many things in our lives, but we can directly affect the quality of the radio programming that comes into our homes." **Your contribution now will make a difference** — whether it is an additional gift, a renewal of your current membership, or a first time contribution to the Friends of WILL Radio.

<pre>
40
</pre>

For your support — past, present, future — you have my deepest gratitude.

P.S. Remember, a contribution to Channel 12 helps WILL-TV only. If you have never before supported public radio, please consider doing so now.

Sincerely,

Donald P. Mullally
Director of Broadcasting
and General Manager,
WILL-AM-FM-TV

P.S. Remember, a contribution to Channel 12 helps WILL-TV only. If you have never before supported public radio, please consider doing so now.

WILL-AM/580 WILL-FM/91
Broadcasting Service of the University of Illinois

Figure 2.1. Direct mail letter (continued)

"Listening to the Look" 41

10. What is the "separating device" in the list, lines 30–35? Do you approve of this device? What other might be used? We have used a different one in this book. Where? Why did we use this different device?

11. How effective visually is the type face in the letter? Compare it to the type face in this book.

12. Would you suggest any other uses of type face in the letter?

13. The color in the letter is called "the second color." (The first color is the ordinary black of the black type.) Where is the second color used, and why?

14. Why didn't the writer use more second color? Why, in lines 38–39, is the second color used for only part of a sentence?

15. What other second colors might be used? Green? Orange? Red? Others? Why?

16. Why isn't the closing (signature, and so on) blocked along the left margin? For that matter, why isn't the whole letter blocked along the left margin? With double-spacing between paragraphs, do you need the paragraph indentations as well?

17. Attack or defend the postscript as a visual matter.

18. At the bottom of the page, you see what amounts to a letterhead, so-called because it is usually printed at the top of the sheet. Is the letterhead in the wrong place?

19. What has any or all the previous eighteen questions got to do with: the writer of the message? its point (what is it)?, its readers?

20. The editor and the book designer collaborated on trying to make this book visually attractive.
   a. Using a page as a sample for judgment, did they succeed?
   b. What techniques or devices have been used for visual effect?
   c. Can you suggest any improvements in the visual effects?
   d. Compare another of your textbooks with this one. In visual effect, which is better?

21. Write a letter to the publisher, evaluating the use of visual effect in this book. Say what is good and not so good. Offer suggestions for improvement.

THE LAWS OF VISUAL EFFECT

The first two laws of visual effect are so obvious that we never think of them.

Law One: We read from left to right. That is, we read from the left side of the page to the right side.

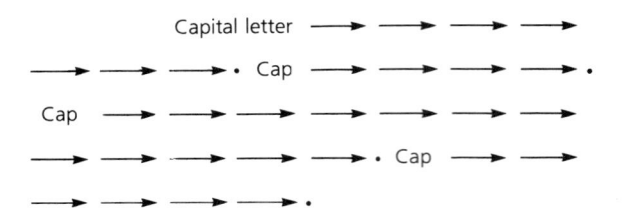

Law Two: We read from top to bottom of the page:

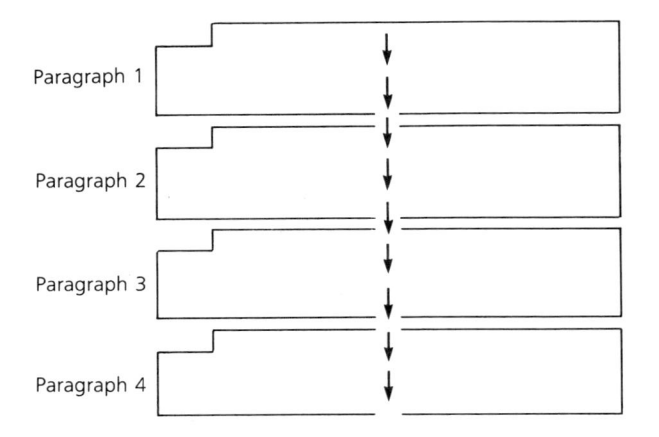

Law Three: We follow laws one and two at the same time:

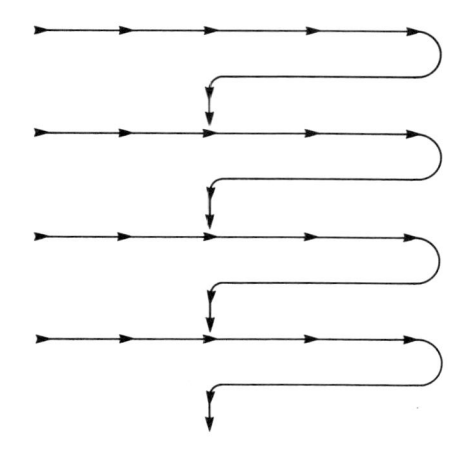

And here is where our problems come from. Reading is not easy. You only think it is because you have spent years learning to do it — left-to-right, DOWN, left-to-right, DOWN, etc., etc. That is hard work! It's like slogging through a great mud field. You get tired: "Oh, if I could only just stop and rest, but there's at least another mile of this."

Rest. A paragraph indention rests you.

A short paragraph rests you.

A second color provides a jolt of pleasure, and you feel a little better. A surprising type face comes out of nowhere and provides relief.

Law Four: The reader needs relief...and surprises. They help make reading more pleasurable.

Law Five: Visual effect and chunking go together. See Figure 2.2, which shows how the last 123 words in this section employ chunking and visual effect.

Perhaps you are thinking: All these laws are OK, but my typewriter has only one type face and no second color. All these fancy effects have little to do with me, or with business writing.

Well, let's see. In Figure 2.3, you will find a page from Transco Energy Company's Fourth Quarter Report for 1982. How many devices of visual effect are used by Transco? In Figure 2.4 you will see the second page of a typical business memo. How many visual devices can you count?

Visual effect can be as important as what you say. It can give your message a wonderful boost.

EXERCISES

1. Discuss the visual effects of the Transco report, Figure 2.3.

2. Discuss the visual effects of the page from a memo, Figure 2.4.

3. Inspect your typewriter. How many devices of visual effect does it have? Look at every key. Consider the possibility of spacing, and so on.

4. Go to any office on your campus that uses word processors. Talk to the operator and find out how a word processor can provide visual effect.

5. Consider your arsenal of pens, pencils, rulers, and so on. Can these help you improve the visual effect of your messages?

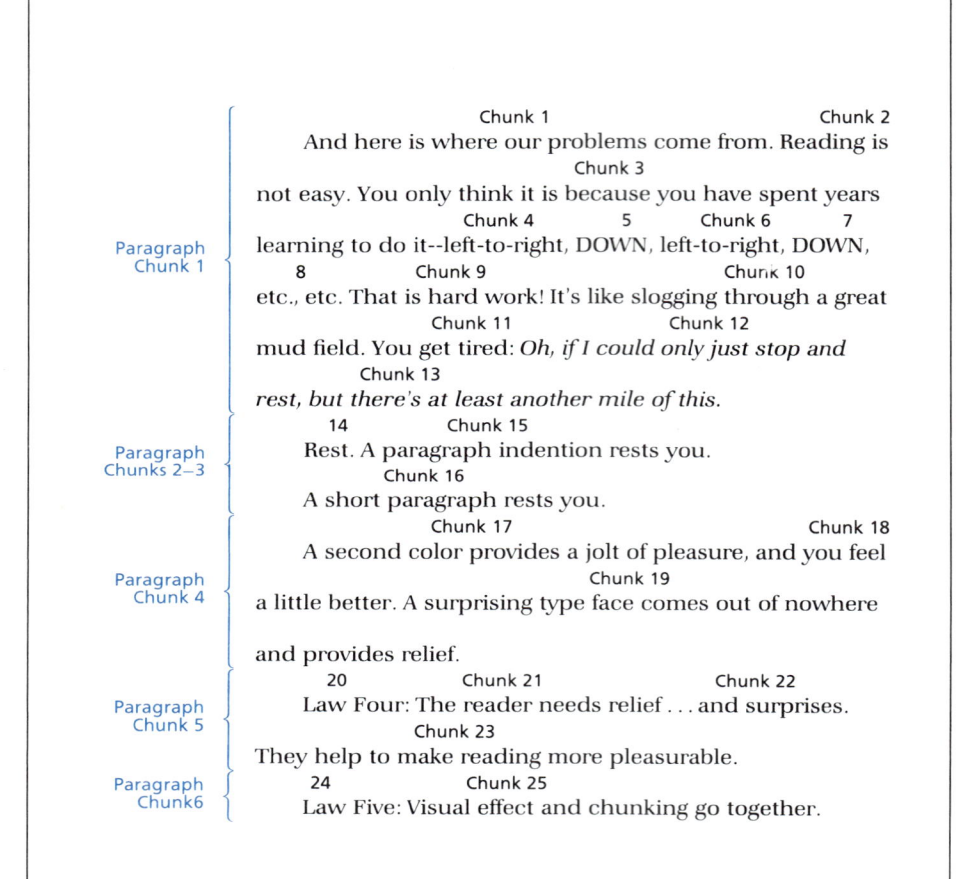

Planning Your Message

                            Chunk 1   Chunk 2

And here is where our problems come from. Reading is

                                    Chunk 3

not easy. You only think it is because you have spent years

                   Chunk 4   5   Chunk 6   7

Paragraph Chunk 1 — learning to do it--left-to-right, DOWN, left-to-right, DOWN,

        8   Chunk 9   Churk 10

etc., etc. That is hard work! It's like slogging through a great

                    Chunk 11   Chunk 12

mud field. You get tired: *Oh, if I could only just stop and*

             Chunk 13

rest, but there's at least another mile of this.

        14   Chunk 15

Paragraph Chunks 2–3 — Rest. A paragraph indention rests you.

                 Chunk 16

A short paragraph rests you.

               Chunk 17   Chunk 18

A second color provides a jolt of pleasure, and you feel

Paragraph Chunk 4 —   Chunk 19

a little better. A surprising type face comes out of nowhere

and provides relief.

       20   Chunk 21   Chunk 22

Paragraph Chunk 5 — Law Four: The reader needs relief . . . and surprises.

                 Chunk 23

They help to make reading more pleasurable.

       24   Chunk 25

Paragraph Chunk6 — Law Five: Visual effect and chunking go together.

Notes: 1. A *sentence chunk* is that group of words between punctuation marks.
            2. A *paragraph chunk* is created by indention.
            3. The passage above has 6 paragraph chunks and 25 sentence chunks — but only 13 sentences!

Figure 2.2. Visual effect and chunking

"Listening to the Look"

Fourth Quarter Report, 1982

Financial Highlights	Fourth Quarter 1982	1981	Change
(Expressed in $ millions except average shares and per share amounts)			
Operating revenues	$1,060.9	$ 897.2[1]	+18%
Operating income before income taxes	87.6	93.9[1]	−7%
Common stock equity in net income	20.9	41.3	−49%
Earnings per common share	0.88	1.66	−47%
Dividends paid per common share	0.45	0.40	+13%
Book value per common share	31.20	27.50	+13%
Average common shares & equivalents outstanding (000's)	26,527	26,447	—
Capital expenditures[2]	123.4	146.5	−16%
Funds provided from operations	144.5	150.2[1]	−4%
Total capitalization[3]	2,193.1	1,969.6	+11%
Common equity and convertible preferred stock, net	835.9	747.0	+12%

[1] Restated to reflect the effect of the Transcontinental Gas Pipe Line Corporation rate settlement agreement approved by the Federal Energy Regulatory Commission in April 1982.
[2] Net of allowance for funds used during construction.
[3] Excluding current maturities of long-term debt.

Financial Results

Transco Energy Company's preliminary unaudited net income available for common stockholders for the fourth quarter of 1982 was $20.9 million, or $0.88 per share, compared with $41.3 million, or $1.66 per share, for the fourth quarter of 1981. The decline in the fourth quarter earnings resulted from higher overall operating and capital costs, and Transco Exploration's (TXC) reduced gas sales and lower liquids prices. The 1981 fourth quarter earnings included an after-tax gain of $6.8 million, or $0.26 per share, from the sale of the present headquarters building.

For the full year 1982, preliminary unaudited net income available for common stockholders was $129.2 million, or $5.26 per common share, down slightly from the 1981 record net income of $132.3 millon, or $5.41 per share. Excluding the 1981 real estate gain, earnings were up 3% in 1982.

Transco's improved operating performance in 1982 resulted primarily from an increase in the profitability of Transcontinental Gas Pipe Line (TGPL) and initial recognition of investment and energy tax credits related to the Great Plains coal gasification project. These factors more than offset the decline in earnings of TXC.

TGPL contributed $115.0 million to consolidated earnings in 1982, an increase of 41% over the $81.3 million recorded in 1981. This earnings increase resulted from higher natural gas sales than in 1981 despite a generally weak economy and intensified competition from alternative fuels. Gas sales in 1982 were 936 billion cubic feet (Bcf), an increase of 4% over 1981 sales of 902 Bcf.

TXC contributed $8.6 million to consolidated net income, compared with $39.5 million in 1981. This decline reflects lower average oil prices, reduced gas production and higher operating costs.

Figure 2.3. Effective use of visual devices

Improving Our Publications, Page 2

The Barnhart book is the only one I can make this kind of comparison with because Judy and I are the only ones who worked on this book, and it is the only book where the tasks were so definitely divided.

As you know, the "in-house" operations have proceeded pretty well these past years in spite of the drawbacks of part-time help, and so on. But pressures have been considerable — especially on me. I don't particularly look forward to working overtime in order to keep us on schedule. Therefore, if we continue the present operation, I will need to hire a <u>full-time</u> typesetter when Judy leaves.

LOOKING TOWARD THE FUTURE

I think the time is right for us to start to explore some other options offered by the high technology available to us out in the marketplace.

<u>Advantages</u>. I am not proposing to save money; indeed, our publications may cost at least as much or even more than they do now. But ... there would be some compensations:

1. A possible reduction in size of publications from nine to ten percent (which may or may not result in lower printing bills, but certainly should reduce mailing costs).

2. Elimination of the time-consuming job of "paging" the publications in-house (the slowest operation we now perform).

3. Elimination of having the "heads" and "keylining" done outside.

4. A reduction in overall labor costs.

5. Improvement in appearance of our publications.

You're now thinking, "What is she talking about?" I propose that with a computer (and I am recommending the inexpensive, portable Kaypro with a dot-matrix printer) in the office to do our keystroking on — with a spelling checker program — we can greatly reduce the keystroking time, the output time, and the proofreading time that now goes into the <u>first</u> stage of getting the manuscripts ready for printing.

Those keystrokes (and their accompanying commands for heads, leading, type-size, and so on) would then be transported (by disk) to the printer, who would feed them into the computer in his plant and from there to the Mergenthaler CRTronic 150, which will magically turn our keystrokes into type. In effect, we will be out of the "book design" business.

Figure 2.4. Business memo, using visual devices

HOW TO CREATE GOOD VISUAL EFFECTS

Use Lots of White Space

Remember that your reader needs relief, relief from all those black crooked little marks marching across and down the page. White space (that is, vacant space on the page) reduces this dull, heavy blackness and relaxes the reader. Figure 2.5a shows a page that will wear a reader out. By contrast, Figure 2.5b shows the same material with white space.

Chunk Your Material

See Law Five for a discussion of this.

Vary Your Chunks

Don't use the same-sized chunks. Occasionally, for emphasis, use a one-sentence chunk–perhaps by itself as a paragraph.

Whenever Possible, Use Parallel Lists

Page after page of *running prose* (unbroken lines of type) puts some readers to sleep. So when you can, put your information in a parallel list:

- 6666666666666666
- 7777777777777777
- 8888888888888888

Those black dots are called *bullets;* you can make them on your typewriter by blacking in a small letter *o*.

You can number such lists if you want to:

1. 6666666666666666
2. 7777777777777777
3. 8888888888888888

Your readers should know where each item starts — it is very easy to jump a line. So if your items are long, consider using bullets (or numbers), capital letters, and indention:

- Cvnvnvnvnvnvnvnvnvnvnvnvnvnvnvnvnvnvnvnvnvnvnvnvnvnvnvnvnv nvnvnvnvnvnvnvn
- Xzxzxzxzxzxzxzxzxzxzxzxzxzxzxzxzxzxzxzxzxzxzxzxzxzxzxzxzxzxzx zxzxzxzxzxzx
- Yuyuyuyuyuyuyuyuyuyuyuyuyuyuyuyuyuyuyuyuyuyuyuyuyuyuyuy uyuyuyuyuyuyuyuyu

product combined with low prices has made Japan a formidable competitor, particularly in the automobile industry. Since my specialty is business administration with an emphasis on factory management, I need to know more about the Japanese system. I also need to know if what I have heard and read is accurate.

I may have to answer a question related to this subject if I am interviewed for a job; therefore I must be better informed than I presently am.

This is what I want to know: Is the Japanese managerial system one that could be adopted by American factories in order to improve quality control?

In your narrative, you have used a variety of terms. You will find some of these terms more important than others when you begin your search because they may be the ones chosen to index books and articles. In addition, certain combinations of these terms may be useful. Make a list of the terms (or combinations) you have used. Think also of synonyms that might be relevant.

- management/managerial
- factory/factories
- decision-making
- product
- quality control
- auto industry
- computer industry
- competitor
- Japan/Japanese
- United States
- manufacture
- industry/industrial

Since libraries and reference works depend upon a limited number of terms to index books and periodicals, you should probably check the *Sears List of Subject Headings* or *The Library of Congress Subject Headings* to see which of your terms, if any, are used in the library where you are doing your research. You will use many of these terms when you look for your subject in encyclopedias, the card catalog, and periodical indexes.

You will also find it useful to keep a copy of your subject terms with you any time you use the library. It is sometimes easy to forget important terms when you are scrabbling through many references and other card catalogs, trying to find information.

Step 2: Search Reference Works for General Information

The purpose of looking at reference works before using other resources in the library is to get an overview of your subject. Sometimes a general encyclopedia, such as the *Encyclopedia Americana*, can provide both information and bibliographies. Depending upon your own specialty, however, you may want to use encyclopedias that are geared toward your major. If, for instance, you are a finance major, you would probably find the *Encyclopedia of Banking and Finance* useful. Whatever encyclopedia you choose for your overview, you will follow the same procedure.

Figure 2.5a. Solid text

product combined with low prices has made Japan a formidable competitor, particularly in the automobile industry. Since my specialty is business administration with an emphasis on factory management, I need to know more about the Japanese system. I also need to know if what I have heard and read is accurate.

I may have to answer a question related to this subject if I am interviewed for a job; therefore I must be better informed than I presently am.

This is what I want to know: Is the Japanese managerial system one that could be adopted by American factories in order to improve quality control?

In your narrative, you have used a variety of terms. You will find some of these terms more important than others when you begin your search because they may be the ones chosen to index books and articles. In addition, certain combinations of these terms may be useful. Make a list of the terms (or combinations) you have used. Think also of synonyms that might be relevant.

- management/managerial
- factory/factories
- decision-making
- product
- quality control
- auto industry
- computer industry
- competitor
- Japan/Japanese
- United States
- manufacture
- industry/industrial

Since libraries and reference works depend upon a limited number of terms to index books and periodicals, you should probably check the *Sears List of Subject Headings* or *The Library of Congress Subject Headings* to see which of your terms, if any, are used in the library where you are doing your research. You will use many of these terms when you look for your subject in encyclopedias, the card catalog, and periodical indexes.

You will also find it useful to keep a copy of your subject terms with you any time you use the library. It is sometimes easy to forget important terms when you are scrabbling through many references and other card catalogs, trying to find information.

Step 2: Search Reference Works for General Information

The purpose of looking at reference works before using other resources in the library is to get an overview of your subject. Sometimes a general encyclopedia, such as the *Encyclopedia Americana*, can provide both information and bibliographies. Depending upon your own specialty, however, you may want to use encyclopedias that are geared toward your major. If, for instance, you are a finance major, you would probably find the *Encyclopedia of Banking and Finance* useful. Whatever encyclopedia you choose for your overview, you will follow the same procedure.

Figure 2.5b. Text with white space

Avoid Using All Caps

For years we wondered why, when our students tried to use capital letters or "caps" for variety or emphasis, the result seemed poor. In fact, the caps seemed almost to hurt readability.

Only recently, we learned from a publication of the Document Design Center that research shows the problem is one of differentiation. Caps are not different enough when you string them together. Here is the Center's example:

Poor:
> WORNOUT TIRES WITH LESS THAN 2/32-INCH TREAD RECEIVE A REPLACEMENT ALLOWANCE, OFF THE ORIGINAL PURCHASE PRICE, OF 50% DURING THE FIRST-QUARTER OF PERIOD.

Better:
> Wornout tires with LESS than 2/32-inch tread receive a replacement allowance, off the original purchase price, of 50% during the first-quarter of period.

The second version is visually much more distinctive. The Center concludes that you can use caps, but only sparingly — no more than three or four words at a time in a line.

You can use caps for headings when you type reports. Actually, though, an underlined heading is more distinctive:

- Not: A DISTINCTIVE HEADING
- But: <u>A Distinctive Heading</u>

Practically speaking, if you need two levels of heads in your message, and you have only an ordinary typewriter to work with, you will be stuck with caps for the first-level heads and underlining for the second level. Note the typical positioning in Figure 2.4.

Use Headings to Break Up Material

Headings are very important for visual effect, and they help organize your material for the reader. Keep your headings as parallel and specific as you can.

We don't want to beat the subject of headings to death, important as they are. The best way for you to learn about them is:

— Take a few minutes to look at the headings in a chapter of this book.

— Practice using them in several assignments.

(What do you think of our use of dashes, just above, instead of bullets?)

Use a Subject Line in Every Message You Can

See p. 19 for a sample subject line.

In many messages, a subject line is the first thing your readers see, so they are likely to remember it. It is also remarkably predictive; it tells your readers what the message is about and suggests why they should read it. Make your subject line specific, but don't (usually) make it longer than one line. A long, wordy subject line loses its sharpness of effect. What you want is a punchy idea that hits the reader right at the top of the message. Use the "three points of emphasis" to your advantage.*

Roughly speaking, a message has three points of emphasis: the beginning, the middle, and the end. We say *roughly* because the whole business of emphasis is too complex to make easy generalizations apply all the time. You will find that some messages have strong emphases where you won't expect them. But when that happens it is just a quirk of organization and visual effect that you will have to live with. It is also true that, if a message is long, it will have sections with their own three points of emphasis. These three points are, as you see in Figure 2.6, *weak, strong, strongest*.

You can put very strong points at either the beginning or the end. But rarely can you "hide" them at or near the middle. You will see them put there, but not often.

Your message
{
Beginning: strongest emphasis

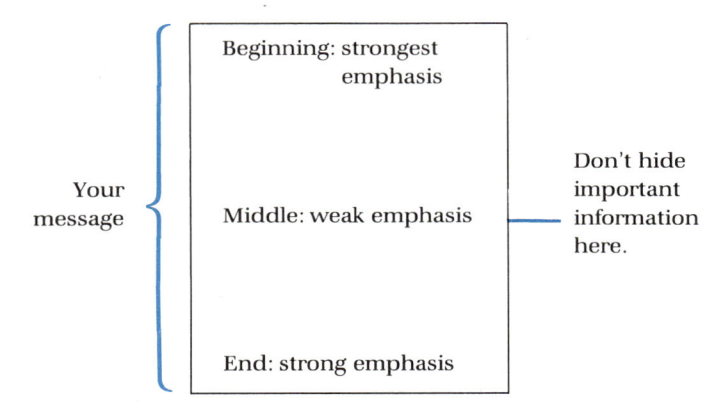

Middle: weak emphasis —— Don't hide important information here.

End: strong emphasis
}

Figure 2.6. Three points of emphasis

---

*This sentence is about as long as a subject line should be.

EXERCISES

1. The passage below is from David Bateman's book, *Business Communication Concepts.* In the original, Bateman used several devices of visual effect. Can you guess what they were? Except for omitting two phrases and one word, which were not a part of the text proper, we have not changed the original. But the original looked very different. And the order of the wording has not been changed either.

Can you guess how Bateman's original material looked? See if you can reproduce it.

> In an oral presentation, it is possible to use virtually any object to illustrate a speech. If the object is too large to bring to the room, videotapes can be used. The speaker is taped with the object, perhaps demonstrating it, and the tape is shown to a group. Some may think that the use of an object or model is applicable only to the oral medium and has no place in the written form. Actually, the object, or a model if it, can be useful in the written report. For example: An engineer is showing an improvement on a small lug nut. The old and new nuts can be included with the report. A secretary wants to show how the firm's telephone number and telex code can be placed attractively on the firm's new stationery. An actual example of the stationery will probably be the best form of communication. A marketing representative for a company sends a report to the marketing vice-president on a new gadget that can be left with clients to make a favorable and lasting impression. The actual object is appended to the report. On a separate piece of paper, describe a situation in which you would need to include a model or the actual object in a written or oral report. Explain how the item would be made part of the presentation and include the object with your explanation.

2. Rewrite an earlier message you wrote for this course. Concentrate on visual effect.

3. In Appendix A, read problems 7, 8, and 12. For class discussion, write some notes explaining how you might use visual effect in writing up these cases. How much does the particular case determine how you use visual effect?

4. Study the appearance of your standard desk dictionary. (Did it come with a dust jacket? If so, some of the questions here should apply to it.) Look at the introduction and prefatory materials, including any printing just inside the front and back covers. What devices of visual effect are used here? Are they used well? Now look at the text itself. What does the dictionary do to set off the various elements in a typical entry, starting with the word being defined and ending with the last word in the entry?

Are the pages of the dictionary thick enough? Explain.

Visually speaking, is your dictionary a successful job?

5. The dashboard of a car is an exercise in design and visual effect. Generally speaking, the more expensive the car the fancier and more attractive the dashboard will be. A dashboard is, of course, a collection of small messages, most of them meant for the driver. You have to know, for example, where and how to turn on the windshield wipers and what the oil pressure is.

Pick a car, preferably an unfamiliar one. Write a letter to the manufacturer evaluating the visual effect and "readability" of the car's dashboard. What is the quality of the total message of the dashboard?

6. Compare the editorial pages of your campus newspaper with those of the local city or town paper. What do these newspapers do about visual effect? How successful are they with it?

7. The company you are working for has asked you to select six first-class electric typewriters, all the same brand, to be used by the six people in your small branch office other than the secretary, who has her own typewriter and word processor. Drop by an office supply store and pick up literature on the standard electric typewriters they sell. For the purposes of this assignment, deal only with the visual effects that this typewriter can supply for the six people in the office who are not professional typists.

8. Design your company's new letterhead. The letterhead must have on it the following:

- company name
- company address
- company phone
- executive's name (each person will get his or her own stationery)
- a list of six board members and their titles
- the company logo
- the company motto

Notes: The paper must be colored. What color should you select? The letterhead must have a space for the date of each message. Where should it be?

CHAPTER 3

Should You Use Graphics?

The answer to the question in the chapter title is yes — whenever they will help get your message across.

Graphic aids — or simply *graphics*, as we'll call them here — are used to clarify and explain. Each of these, among other things, can be used as a graphic:

- pictures
- paintings
- drawings
- cartoons
- graphs
- charts
- designs
- plans
- maps
- tables
- photographs

One of us, working as an engineer, has written a number of reports that ordinarily used only two types of graphics. One type looked like Figure 3.1.

The other type looked like Figure 3.2. The wiggly lines in Figure 3.1 represent the effect of a tiny "earthquake" (created artificially by an explosion of dynamite beneath the earth's surface). Figure 3.2 shows a structure map of an underground hill 5,000 feet below the surface. By using only these two kinds

---

We are indebted to the Document Design Center for some of the ideas in this chapter. Figures 3.6, 3.8–3.14 are taken, with permission, from *Guidelines for Document Designers*, American Institutes for Research (November, 1981).

Should You Use Graphics? 55

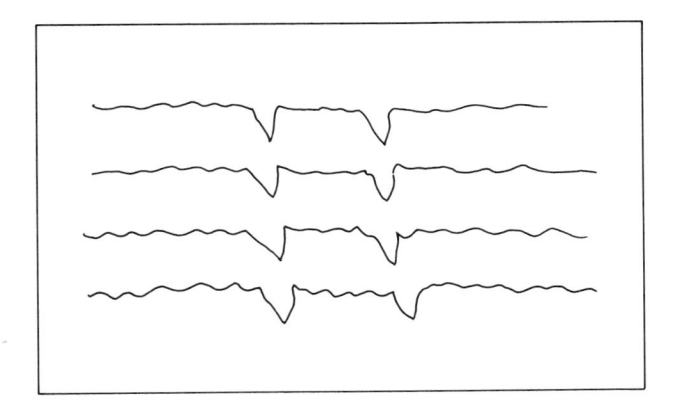

Figure 3.1. Earthquake pattern

of graphics, an engineer could save dozens of pages of painfully detailed explanation.

A graphic is designed to help readers, to save them time and trouble. In addition, a well-made and properly placed graphic adds to your discussion — it spotlights and supports it.

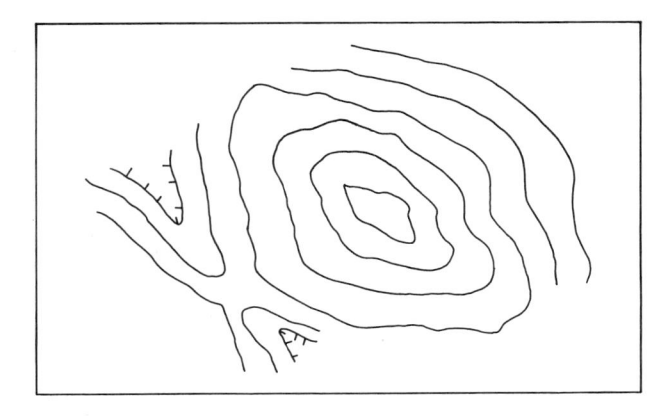

Figure 3.2. Structure map of a hill

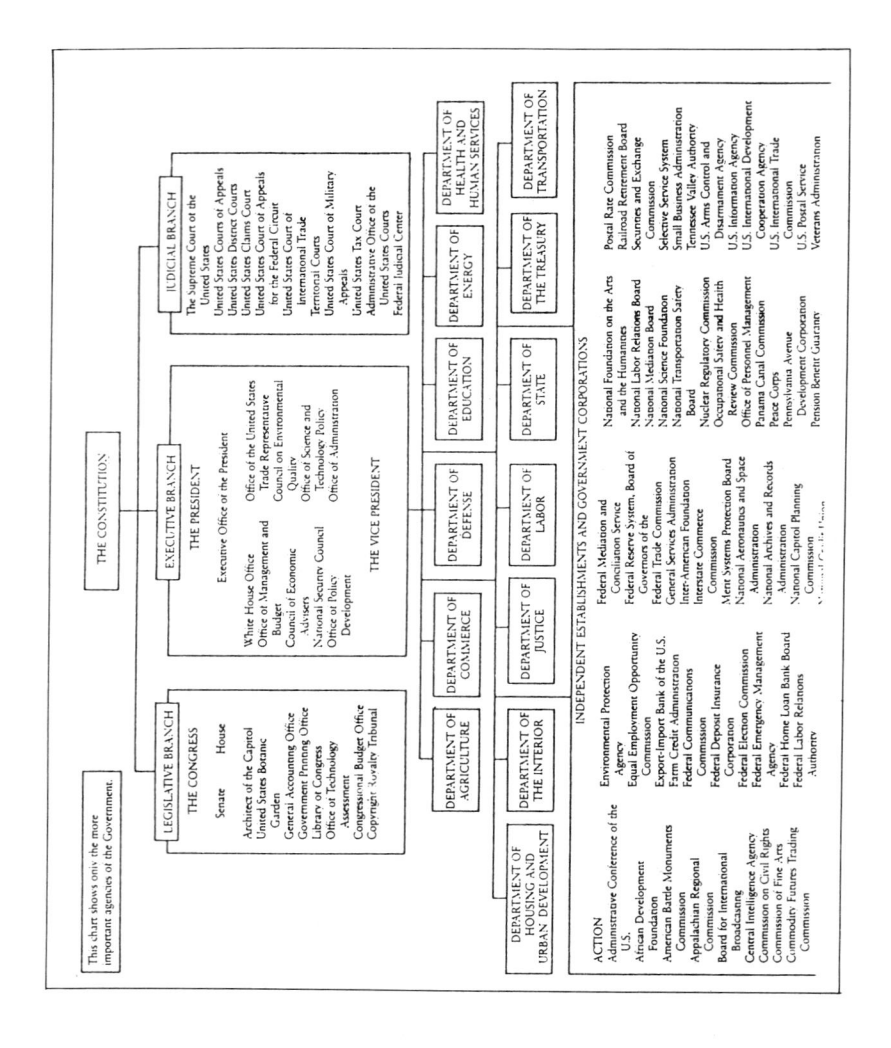

Figure 3.3. The organization of the government of the United States.

WHEN TO USE A GRAPHIC

A graphic should not be used as a crutch. Don't spatter the page with tables and drawings just to fill up space or because you can't think of useful things to say. Ideally, graphics should encourage a reader to understand, to remember certain important points, and to maintain interest in the material. Always apply this three-part test to a graphic:

- Does it help the reader understand?
- Does it help the reader remember?
- Does it create or maintain the reader's interest?

Do not use a graphic if your readers have to work hard to understand it, or if it is of poor quality. The graphic in Figure 3.3 has both these flaws. It is too "busy," has too much detail in it for quick understanding. And some parts of it are unclear. Always use good-quality graphics. If necessary, have them done professionally.

Fit the type of graphic to your writing problem. Make sure that your readers will understand the graphic — that it is within their range of experience. Look at Figure 3.4. For the trained geologist, this graphic is so simple as to be almost simple-minded (it represents a normal fault in sedimentary rocks). But for most educated readers, the drawing is meaningless without pages of explanation or a detailed caption.

Photographs are useful for maintaining your reader's interest and when you want to show something just as it is. They are, obviously, very realistic. Line drawings are less realistic. But because you can leave out irrelevant material, line drawings are often clearer (Figure 3.6). Diagrams, as in Figure 3.5, help explain complex situations or organizations.

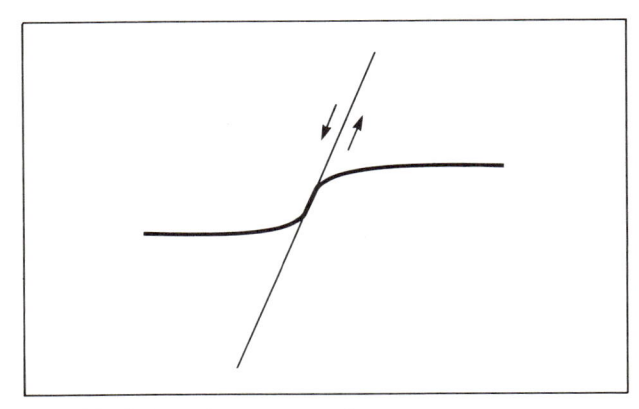

Figure 3.4. Normal fault in sedimentary rocks

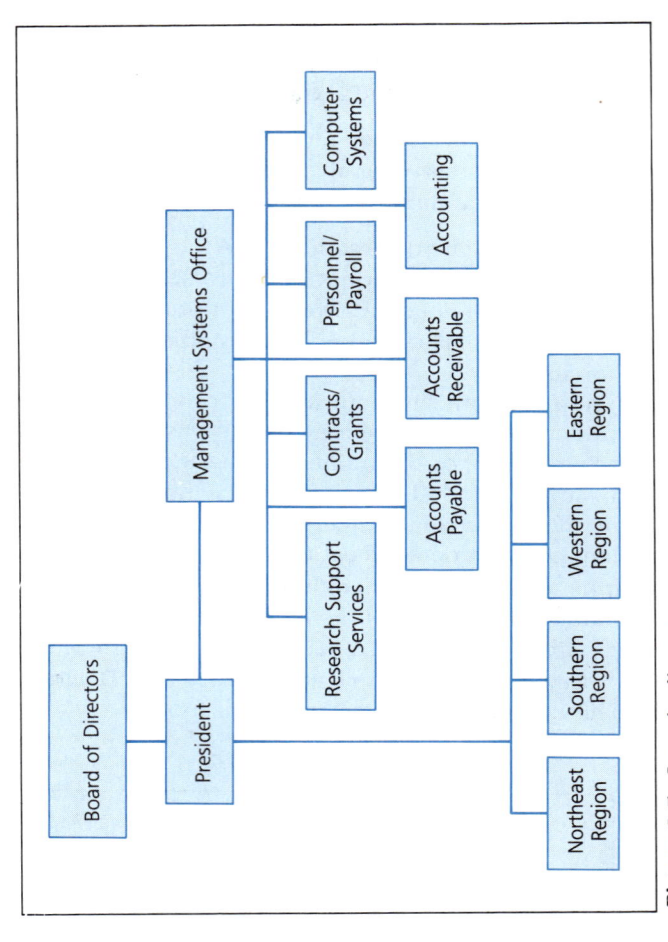

Figure 3.5. Sample diagram

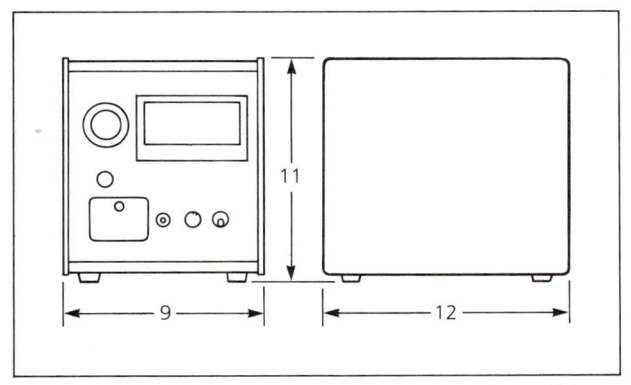

Figure 3.6. Outline dimensions of the Null Detector, Bench Model

TABLES

Use tables when you have to explain a lot of numbers. A table (Figure 3.7) consists of rows and columns.

Suggestions for Using Tables

1. Use enough white space (see Figure 3.9) so that readers can understand the table easily. But don't use so much that you get the so-called rowboat effect. (A rowboat floating in a large body of water is hard to see clearly from shore.)
2. Supply averages of rows or columns, or both. Averages help your readers evaluate the evidence in the table.
3. When you need to show an important comparison, use columns. It is easier to compare things by moving your eyes vertically. (You can get lost quicker in a row because your eyes tend to jump, thus putting you in the wrong row.)
4. Round your numbers off. Unless, for example, the last three places are significant in a number like 32.447, round it off to 32. The table in Figure 3.8 is inefficient, because there is too little white space; there are no averages for reference; the main comparisons are in rows; the numbers are carried to four decimal places (unnecessary in this case).

The table in Figure 3.8 should be revised, so that it looks something like Figure 3.9.

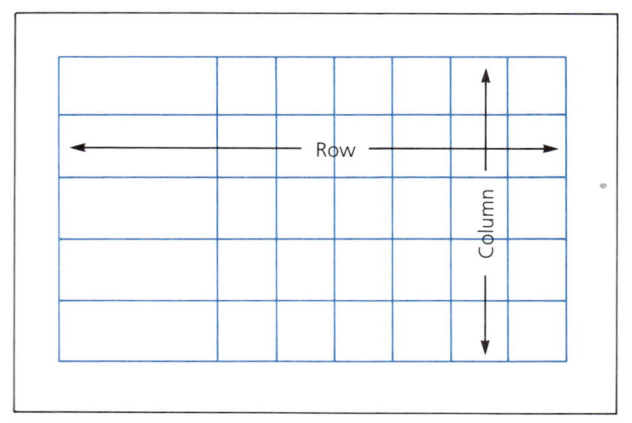

Figure 3.7. Rows and columns in a table

Changes in Air Pollutants
(In millions of short tons)

Pollutant	1970	1972	1974
Particulates	25.6664	23.1872	19.7476
Sulfur Oxides	32.8001	32.3651	31.4691
Nitrogen Oxides	21.9743	23.8619	24.0965
Hydrocarbons	31.2899	32.6437	29.9466
Carbon Monoxide	13.1526	15.0079	19.8347

Figure 3.8. Inefficient table

Changes in Air Pollutants
(In millions of short tons)

YEAR	Particulates	Sulfur oxides	Nitrogen oxides	Hydro-carbons	Carbon monoxide
1970	26	33	22	31	13
1972	23	32	24	33	15
1974	20	31	24	30	20
Average	23	32	23	31	16

Figure 3.9. Efficient table

A final note on tables. First, adapt them to your readers. Too often, a writer forgets that some readers aren't specialists and won't understand technical material in a table. Second, use your prose text to explain the comparisons in a table, unless they are self-explanatory.

BAR CHARTS

Bar charts are valuable:

- When you have fairly large contrasts in data;
- When you want to show these contrasts quickly and easily to your reader;
- When your prose explanation is relatively complete.

Generally, bar charts support your text better than tables. Having received your message in the text, your reader looks at the bar chart for the contrasts in it and then moves quickly back to the text. Note how fast you can inspect the chart in Figure 3.10 and move on to the text.

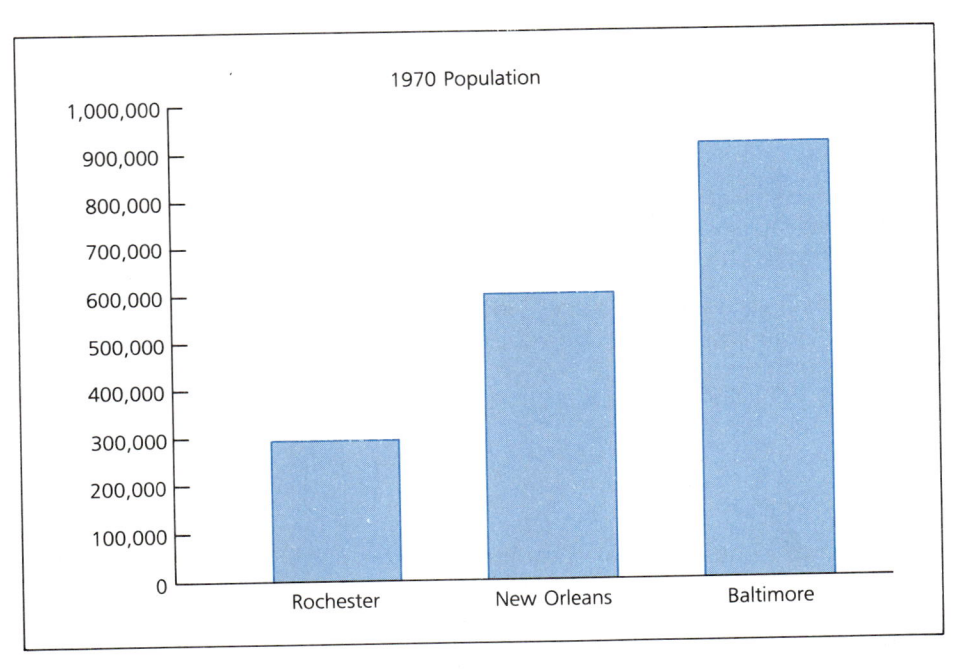

Figure 3.10. Bar chart

In a bar chart, you can show more than one relationship, as in Figure 3.11:

1960/1970 Population (in 1,000)

City	1960	1970
Rochester	~350	~290
New Orleans	~660	~590
Baltimore	~950	~890

Figure 3.11. Bar chart, two relationships

Bar charts can be arranged horizontally, but readers seem to prefer looking at them with the bars running vertically.

In summary, here are some points to remember when making a bar chart:

- Keep all your bars the same width.
- Don't force the chart to do your explaining for you. (Put sufficient explanation in the text.)
- Make your labels as clear as possible.

LINE GRAPHS

Line graphs, like bar charts, should be used carefully to support explanations in your text. Usually, you will employ a line graph to show a change over time or a trend, as in Figure 3.12.

If you take the line graph in Figure 3.12 and add more data, you can help your reader grasp a mass of information very quickly. (See Figure 3.13.)

Should You Use Graphics? 63

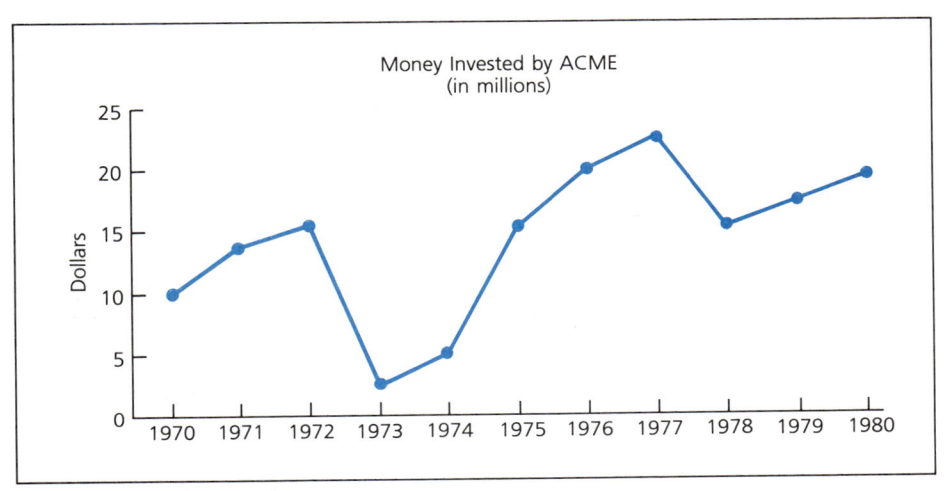

Figure 3.12. Line graph

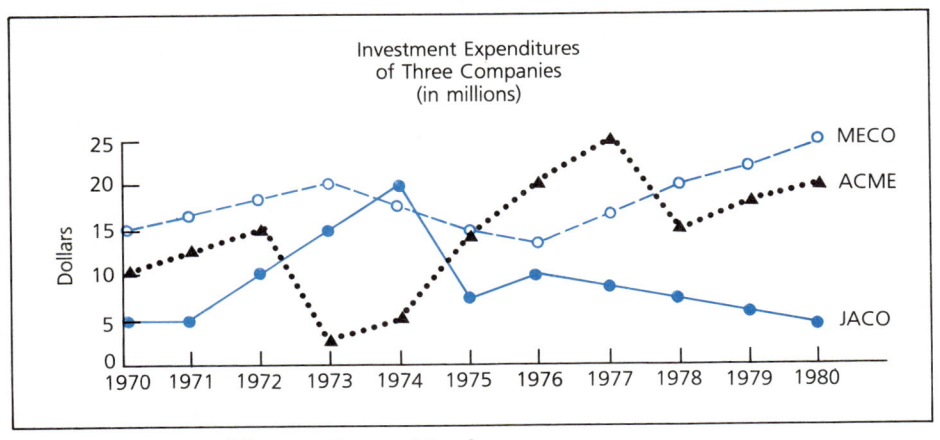

Figure 3.13. Several line graphs combined

Observe that in Figure 3.13 each line uses its own identifying characteristics:

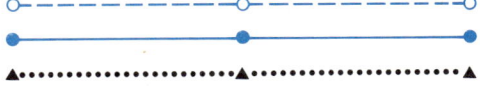

There is an obvious flaw in line graphs. They are so dramatic by nature that you can distort your data by manipulating the length of horizontal and vertical axes, as in Figure 3.14.

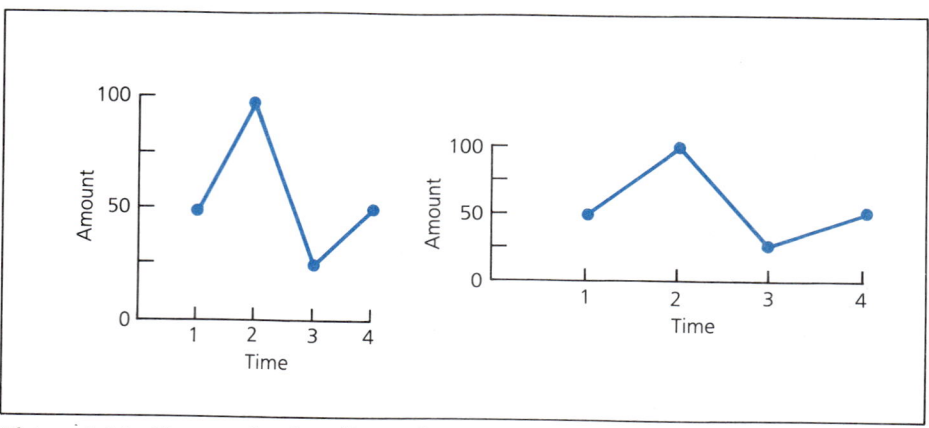

Figure 3.14. Line graphs that distort data

PIE CHARTS

Pie charts show how the parts of something are distributed. The parts are represented as slices of a whole pie.

If we take one of the components shown on the pie chart in Figure 3.15, we can also break it down into component slices. (See Figure 3.16.)

As these examples suggest, pie charts are useful in showing percentages as parts of a whole. When you make a pie chart, start slicing at the top, where the number twelve would be on the face of a clock. Then, moving clockwise, put the large slices, followed by smaller ones. (The smaller ones do not have to be graded by size.)

SOME CONCLUDING REMARKS ON GRAPHICS: AN INTERVIEW WITH AN EDITOR

You've been editing technical and business materials for many years. Can you give our students some tips on how graphics can best be used? And how they are sometimes misused?

EDITOR: I'd say that the major problem with graphics is failing to think carefully enough about the message and its reader. The writer should ask at the beginning: Do I really need graphics? Will ordinary prose carry the message? One should not ask, *How can I use graphics?* without first determining

Should You Use Graphics?

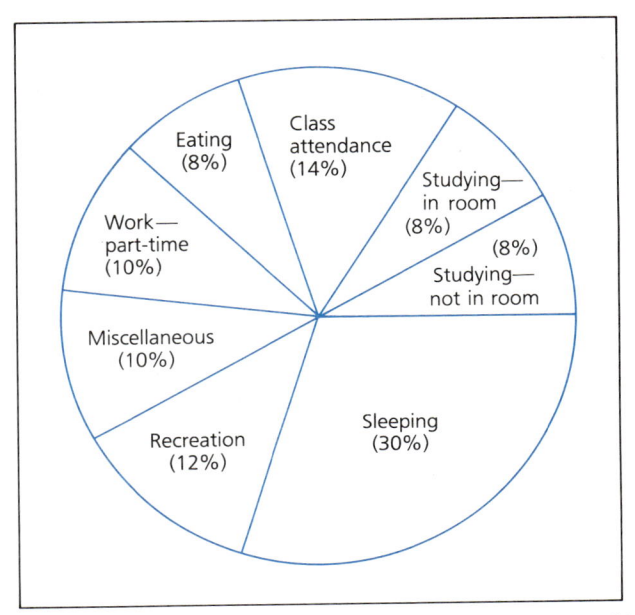

Figure 3.15. Distribution of time typical for a business student (1 week)

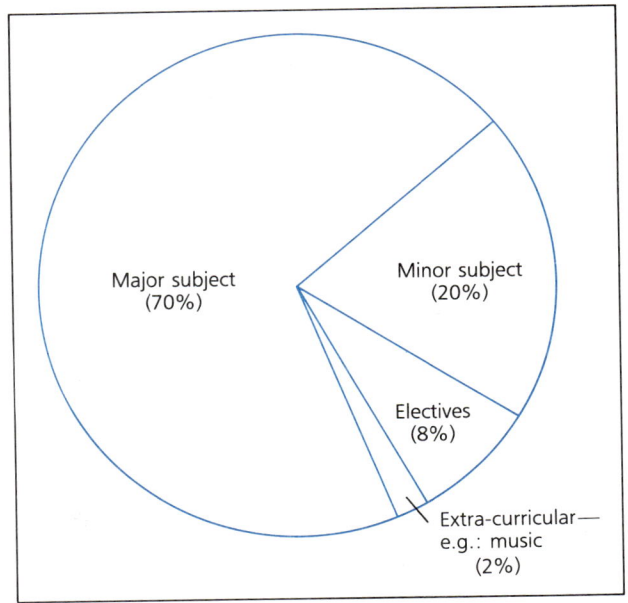

Figure 3.16. Distribution of study time (sophomore year)

that they are necessary to the message and the reader. In some reports I have to spend time ripping graphics out. Occasionally, they just get in the way.

Can you give us an example?

Well, if you tell your readers that in 1942 the price of corn was twice as high in South Nederland as it was in Nebraska, you don't need a bar graph on the same page showing one nice little bar that's twice as big as the bar next to it.

Do writers actually do that?

I'm afraid they do. Perhaps it's the result of Americans' reading too much fluffy journalism — newspapers and some news magazines showing the simplest ideas in cute little graphs and charts. Or a cartoon showing Mr. American Economy holding two weights with words written on them to symbolize, say, the balance of payments. One word is worth a thousand such pictures.

But while I'm on the subject, I'd like to make another point about graphics. This one may seem to contradict some of what I've been saying. Generally, a graphic should not be too complicated; let it make no more than a single point. A good graphic is meant for "quick study" — that is, it tells your readers something they can visualize quickly and retain easily as part of your total argument. Readers won't comprehend or retain an idea that doesn't stand out clearly.

To put it in a nutshell, don't clutter your graphics. Shape and limit each one so that your reader gets a single image and a single idea.

You sound rather negative about graphics.

I'm not, really. But they should serve a purpose and be carefully done. To come back to your question: I'm very positive, as are most readers, about graphics that support the written text or explain matters that are hard to describe in ordinary words. For example, thousands of times a day we Americans need to understand a process, a technique, or a special way of doing something. This may be repairing a carburetor, caulking around window frames, understanding a computer keyboard. Here is where graphics really work for the writer: pictures, diagrams, drawings — whatever will show more clearly than words alone can show. But there is no rule of thumb for telling the writer when to use graphics, or which ones to use. Writers must think this through for themselves.

But aren't there common-sense rules for handling graphics once you've decided to use them?

Oh, yes, there are, and I'll give some here.

Always say something in the text about the graphic before you show it. Don't just throw it in without warning. Say, for example: "As Figure 4 shows, the price for American wheat, compared to prices generally in the West, is . . ." Or: "To see the results of this comparison, look at Plate 7."

Can you overdo this?

Sometimes. Certainly, you don't want to explain anything in the graphic that is self-explanatory. A good graphic should shorten discussion, not lengthen it.

When do you number and title a graphic?

Every graphic should be titled. Number it only if you have more than one. Some authorities say that numbering is optional if the graphics are small tables or charts. I don't agree. I always suggest numbering them. With word processing coming on so strongly in this country, we are essentially publishing documents, and in the publishing process unnumbered graphics can get lost or put out of sequence. Numbering helps prevent that from happening.

Where in a message do you place a graphic?

A graphic has, generally speaking, two positions in a message. The commonest is in the text itself. If you put it there, place it as close to the mention of it as possible; in other words, don't separate text and graphic. Readers hate to hunt around for Table 14, only to find it three pages away from where they are reading.

The other position for a graphic is in an appendix. The appendix is the place for the graphic that is helpful but not immediately necessary. For example, photographs of a building site may be necessary to a whole report — or letter or memo — but unnecessary to any particular section of it, so you put the photos in an appendix and label the section as such. If you need to refer to the photos in the text, say "See Appendix for . . ."

Do you have any other words of wisdom for our students?

Sure, two of them.

1. Nowadays, messages are often sent out to many people. This means multiple copies, sometimes hundreds of copies. Make sure your graphics can be reproduced, by whatever reproduction method you have available. Check in your office to see what you need. If your message will be commercially printed, you may have to prepare camera-ready copy. By the way, many computer graphics can't be used because the printout isn't good enough, and photographs of such graphics are usually unsatisfactory.

2. Always check the graphics for pertinence and reliability. I can't tell you how many times I have found graphics that:

    a. don't fit the text
    b. fit the text only halfway
    c. contain material that is irrelevant to the text
    d. contain errors (misspellings, wrong numbers, misplaced decimals, and so on)
    e. contradict the text (!)
    f. are incorrectly copied from the source.

How do you keep such errors from occurring?

First, check every graphic individually. Adapt each one to the discussion in the text — or, if necessary, adapt each discussion to its graphic. Second, after you have finished the whole message, check the fit of text to graphic by considering each one separately — backwards. If you have ten graphics in the message, check number 10, then number 9, then 8, and so on, until you have finished all ten. By *check*, I mean check everything, including the fit between text and graphic.

EXERCISES

1. You are the editor of a campus magazine that is directed to the non-student population of your college — teachers, administrators, secretaries, and support staff (plumbers, carpenters, grounds workers, and so on).

Over a period of time, you have to make suggestions to your staff writers about graphics for articles and news stories. Examples:

    a. A story explaining the favorite (and unfavorite) foods in the dormitory;

    b. A sociological study of the TV programs, cable and otherwise, watched by the students;

    c. An analysis of the most popular, and least popular, courses on campus;

    d. An argument for moving a temporary building off the quad, planting new trees and tearing out others, and putting in new sidewalks — all part of a proposed beautification effort;

    e. An account of the effectiveness of the Pass-Fail grading system in four colleges in your state (including yours), broken down by department.

What specific suggestions about graphics would you make for each of these articles and stories? What type of graphic would definitely be helpful? What type should probably not be used?

2. You have been asked to be the writer of the new orientation booklet for freshmen at your college. The booklet tells new students how to find buildings; what they can expect from campus life; where to park their cars and bikes; how to fulfill freshman course requirements; and so on.

Write a report to the dean of the college proving to him or her that you need more money in your production budget in order to include certain kinds of graphics. Be specific: Mention the graphic types, and explain why they will help new students.

3. You have been chosen by a textbook publisher to be a student critic of your economics textbook. The publisher plans a new edition of the book and has asked you to write a short analysis of the graphics in the book's first edition. He wants to know how to improve them — from your standpoint as a student user of the book.

Look at the book carefully, and then write a short report for the publisher.

Be pointed and specific. When the publisher finishes reading your report, he or she should know exactly how to improve the graphics in the new edition of the text. Of course, if the graphics are flawlessly handled, say so, and give examples and reasons.

If you are not taking economics this term, or don't have an economics text, use any text you have that employs a good sampling of graphics.

4. The magazine *Direct Marketing*, "A Monthly Forum Devoted to Business Communications in Selected Markets," once ran an article called "98% Negative Database Holds Power of Expansion Benefits." On pages 42 and 44 of the article, the magazine used the graphics you see in Figures 3.17 and 3.18 on the next two pages. The article did not refer to the graphics in any way. For class discussion: Poll the class. What do you as individuals understand, or not understand, from the graphics? Who of you understand them completely? Who do not? Why? Ask a professor who teaches direct mail advertising in your college to comment on the graphics.

5. What kind of graphic would you suggest for each of the following? Write a short paragraph for each, explaining your decision.
- **a.** Average number per year of snow days in Montana.
- **b.** A comparison of population loss and gain in Illinois and Arizona.
- **c.** Changes in the United States' national debt since 1930.
- **d.** A method of preventing land slump on Lake Superior. The method builds up banks along the lake that regularly fall into the water; in some areas the bank is disappearing at the rate of several feet a year.

6. In your college town, you probably have zoning that sets aside areas in which people may rent out apartments. Call the zoning office and find out what the regulations are. Suppose that you must write a report on what you find. Explain what graphics you could use. (For example, would a simplified map of the city help?)

7. If you own a car, look at your car's owner's manual. What graphics are used? Why? Write a short explanation.

Optional: Look at a professional mechanic's manual for the same or similar car. What is the difference between the graphics in the two manuals? (Such a manual is not hard to find; any dealer has one, and any retail auto-supply store has semi-professional manuals that will give the contrast we suggest.)

8. Talk to anyone who has a business, preferably a relative (relatives are easier to get to!). Ask this person: What graphic material do you see or use most often? Which type of graphic fits your business best? Why? What weaknesses do you find in the graphics you use?

9. Consider displays in retail stores as a part of graphic use. Note, for instance, the number of graphic messages you see in any good-sized drug store. Write an analysis of such graphics.

10. Look through your city's phone book. How many graphics do you find there? Why are they there? How well are they done?

Group	Quantity mailed (000)	Number responding	Percent response	Response gain	Revenue generated (000)	Mailing cost (000)	Total profit (000)
1	600	20,250	3.37	2.25	$ 506	$ 240	$ 266
2	1,200	34,200	2.85	1.90	855	480	375
3	1,800	48,330	2.68	1.79	1,208	720	488
4	2,400	60,840	2.53	1.69	1,521	960	561
5	3,000	67,500	2.25	1.50	1,687	1,200	487
6	3,800	76,620	2.13	1.42	1,917	1,440	477
7	4,200	81,900	1.95	1.30	2,047	1,680	368
8	4,800	84,960	1.77	1.18	2,124	1,920	204
9	5,400	87,480	1.62	1.08	2,187	2,160	27
10	6,000	90,000	1.50	1.00	2,250	2,400	−150

Mailing cost: $400/M
Revenue: $25/RESP.

Figure 3.17. Gains chart

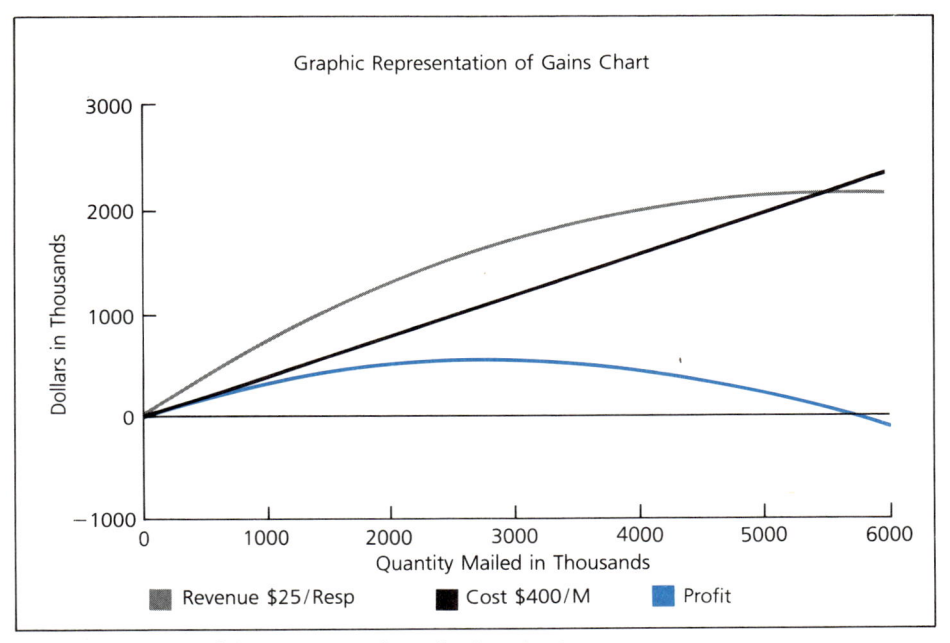

Figure 3.18. Graphic representation of gains chart

PART 2

Organizing Your Message

CHAPTER 4

Block Out the Big Picture

You have three choices. You can make organizing easy and simple; hard and not so simple — or just plain impossible.

Why not organize a message the easy way and use the time saved for other activities? Here's how.

First, we assume that you have decided on the point of your message and the hook you are going to hang it on. You have identified your reader. You have solved the visual problems of the message; you have considered how graphics will influence the whole affair. (All this we covered in The Overview and Chapters 1 through 3.) And you have the material you are going to communicate.

At this point, stop and see how much you have to write. If your message is short and sweet, write it and move on to other matters. If it is going to run more than a page or two, you had better consider organizing your material carefully before continuing.

SHOULD YOU WRITE AN OUTLINE?

Maybe.

If you poll successful writers and speakers on the subject of outlines, you may be surprised, for although they will agree on most standard techniques in communication, some of them will disagree about outlines. There are writers who swear by them — they wouldn't write a two-page memo without organizing it carefully and creating an outline that looks as though it came out of a textbook. You know the kind, with roman numerals and arabic numbers and letters, the whole affair in apple-pie order.

Then there are writers who swear *at* outlines. They hate the outline on principle. They say that it just gets in the way of planning and writing, that it even has a life of its own and causes writers to go off in a direction they don't want to go. I want to be boss, says such a writer. No outline is going to tell *me* what to do.

Something can be said for each of these extremes. Unquestionably, outlines can be more trouble than they are worth. It takes trouble to make them, and they can be hard to follow once you get started. On the other hand, many messages, particularly longer ones, will wander all over the map if you don't have some way to keep the parts in order.

On the issue of outlines, most of us should choose compromise .and common sense. If you like outlines and can make them easily, do so. Outline before you write, as you write, and after you write. After all, an outline is only a map, and you can make a map of a trip through a message any time you want — before, during and after the trip. Most outliners prefer *before*; then they know where they are going. But if they change their minds about the message as they go along, they aren't afraid to change the outline to fit. And outlining after you write is a good way to get a structural picture of the whole message, especially if it is a long one.

For a discussion of outline forms and ways they are used, see Appendix D of this book.

THE BLOCK METHOD OF ORGANIZATION

In order to practice good organization, we suggest a modified method of outlining. We call it the block method. All you need to use it is some ordinary full-sized sheets of paper and a set of three-by-five-inch cards. (We buy both in large quantities.) We'll start by discussing your use of the cards.

After you know what you want to say and to whom, determine the separate ideas in the message. Obviously, these are often determined for you; they are the data or evidence in the memo, letter, or report. Put these ideas on cards, one to a card. Emphasis: *one idea* to a card. If, for any reason, there are subordinate ideas involved in the message, create a subordinate entry on the card (see Figure 4.1). But as you can see, you still have one major idea to a card.

Even the most devoted of outline lovers will admit that outlines have a drawback in that they are rigid. For example, once you get point II. A. 1. in its proper place in the outline, it is terribly hard to dig it out and move it some-

Block Out the Big Picture   77

```
┌─────────────────────────────────────┐
│                                     │
│                                     │
│          Types of manager           │
│          Appealing style            │
│                                     │
│                                     │
│                                     │
└─────────────────────────────────────┘
```

Figure 4.1. A three-by-five card used in the block method of organization

where else. But in the block method (using cards) you can easily move ideas around.

When you have finished writing ideas on your cards, spread all the cards out on a flat surface. Most people use the top of a table or desk, but we've seen beds and even floors pressed into service. When your cards are out where you can see all of them individually, start putting them in a sensible order. Almost all messages have a natural order of some kind:

- Simple to complex
- Easy to difficult
- Evidence to conclusion or summary
- Cause to effect, or effect to cause
- Big to little, or little to big
- Statement of problem to suggestion of solution
- Comparisons or contrasts
- A breakdown of the parts of something (often called *analysis*)
- Chronology: first, second, third (in order of occurrence of events)
- Combination of two or more of these
- And so on.

We are not suggesting that you pick one of these orders for your message. Rather, we are saying that ideas and data tend to fall into patterns, some of which (like those above) have been known and studied for more than 2,000 years. Suppose, for instance, you have four cards with these terms on them: *types of training, appealing managerial styles, types of manager, unappealing managerial styles.* These four cards and their terms would naturally group themselves:

Card #1 types of manager   Card #3 appealing managerial styles
Card #2 types of training   Card #4 unappealing managerial styles

If you wish to discuss the material suggested by these four cards, which would you discuss first, the two cards on the left above or the two on the right? Most people would answer "those on the left," because it seems more natural to talk about styles of managers after you have talked about types of manager and training. But if you are typical of our students, a few of you will disagree.

When you have your cards arranged in the order you want, you can begin to create your blocks. A block is simply a grouping of ideas surrounded by blocks or squares and connected by lines on a standard sheet of paper. (See Figure 4.2.)

```
Block 1:  Types of managers
          Types of training
              ↓
Block 2:  Appealing managerial styles
          Unappealing managerial styles
```

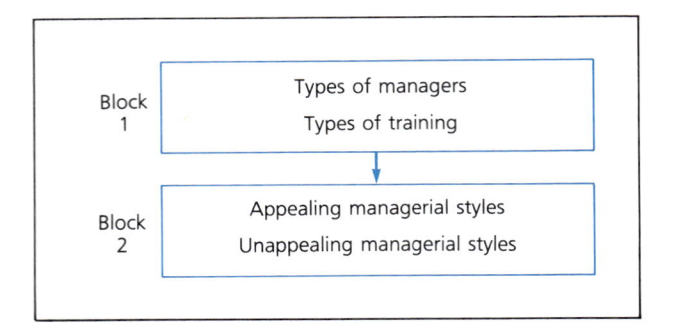

Figure 4.2. Typical blocks of organization

The blocks provide you a scheme for trapping your ideas and putting them in a certain order. When you have done this, you can start to write. If, after writing for a few minutes, you discover that you need to switch blocks or to switch the order of ideas inside the blocks, you can do it easily. Scratch paper is cheap.

Hint: Always use big, full-sized sheets of paper, typewriter paper measuring 8½ by 11 inches. This size gives you plenty of room to scribble and draw several blocks, if you need them.

EXAMPLE OF A PROBLEM IN ORGANIZATION

You are the operations manager of a good-sized firm that has successfully been manufacturing work shoes for men. Your company has decided to look into the market for women's work shoes, including heavy sportswear like hiking boots. You have been asked to write a report to the president on the outlook for the new line.

After looking at your data, you decide to hook your report on women's preference — specifically, "What kind of boot do women want?" In working on the shape of your report, you doodle two blocks on a sheet of paper (Figure 4.3).

Block Out the Big Picture

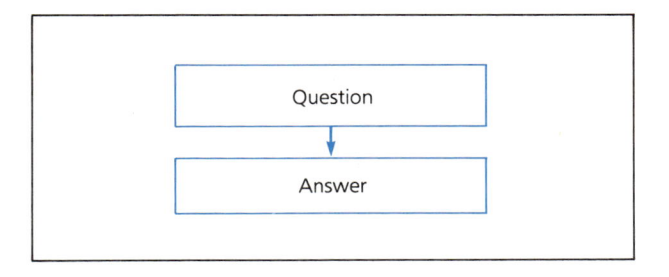

Figure 4.3. Two blocks for a question-and-answer organization

The Big Picture: Your Overall Message

The drawing in Figure 4.3 is important to you because you need to know the big picture, the overall picture of your message. And you need to know it early. If you are going to drive from Denver to Seattle, the first thing you want to see is how the whole picture looks: where roads go, where major cities are, where mountains will get in your way, where likely stopping places are, and so on. In other words, you want to know more or less where you are going before you consider the details found on state or city maps.

If you like outlines and prefer to use them, consider writing the big-picture items first and then the little ones — that is, write the roman-numeral information first:

      Introduction
   I. First big idea
  II. Second big idea
 III. Conclusion

Then fill in the supporting facts and examples under each roman numeral. (See outline forms in Appendix D.)

Your Completed Organization

Back to the blocks in Figure 4.3. You have decided that the overall organization of your message will be question-and-answer. Looking further at your material, you discover certain complexities. There are some irrelevant questions, and there are several answers to the main question. You need a more specific set of blocks to take care of these. After a period of wrestling with the problem, you draw the blocks in Figure 4.4.

Your irrelevant questions you set aside because you just don't want to deal with them at this time; they are insufficiently pertinent to the main question. To this question, you have three answers, one of which is more pertinent (or important?) than the others, so you leave it until the end, which is a point of emphasis.

Now you have completed your blocks with material in them (Figure 4.5).

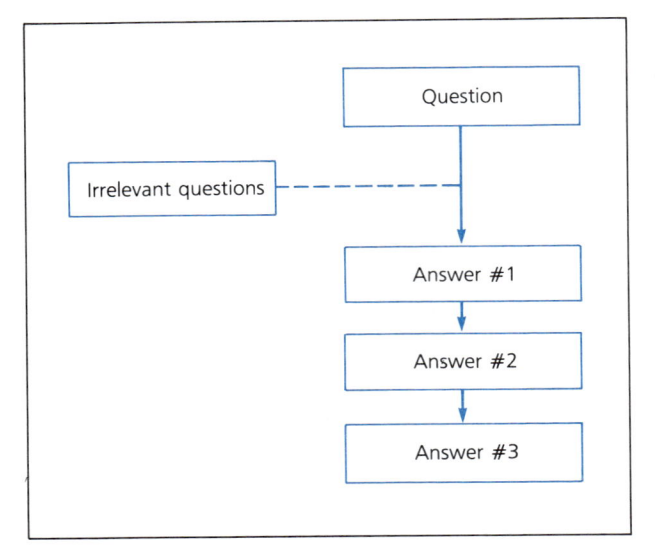

Figure 4.4. Basic blocks for question and answers

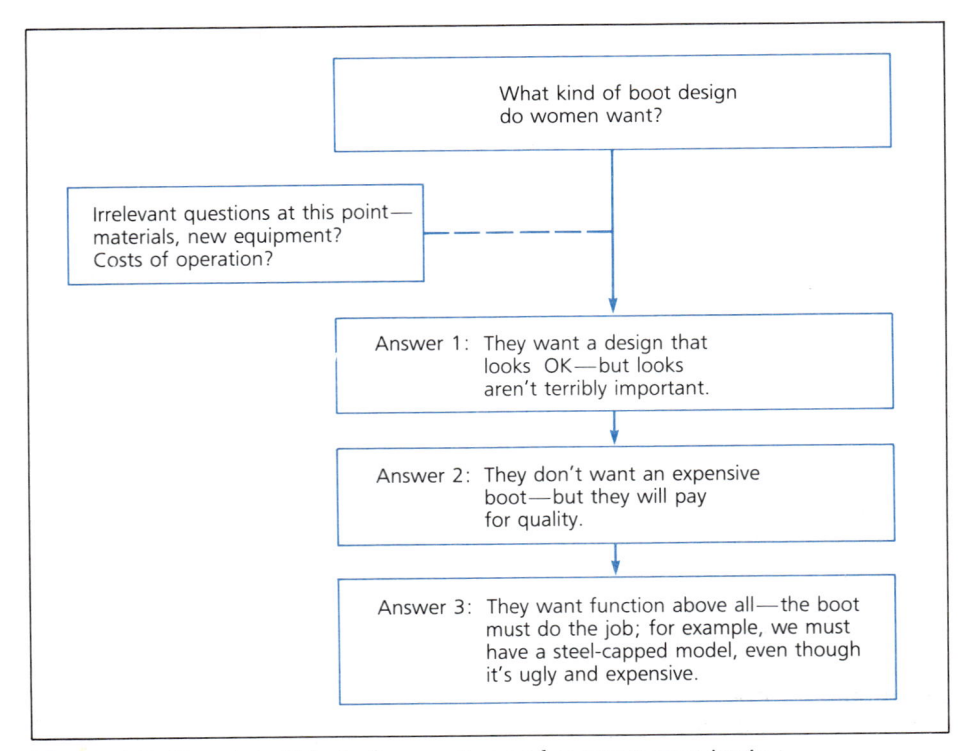

Figure 4.5. Completed blocks for question-and-answers organization

BLOCKING OUT OTHER ORGANIZATIONS

So far, we have emphasized the fact that the subject and its blocking have a special relation to each other. Now, let's look at the matter differently, and discuss the blocking of common organizational patterns.

Blocking an Action

Do you want your reader to do something, to take an action of some kind? Try blocking out an action (Figure 4.6). This type of blocking, invented by the ancient Greeks and adapted by every western culture since, does a beautiful job for messages that ask readers to do something. What follows is an analysis of Figure 4.6.

Describe the need for action.

Describe the action briefly.

Give details of the Action

Explain why the action is beneficial and practical.

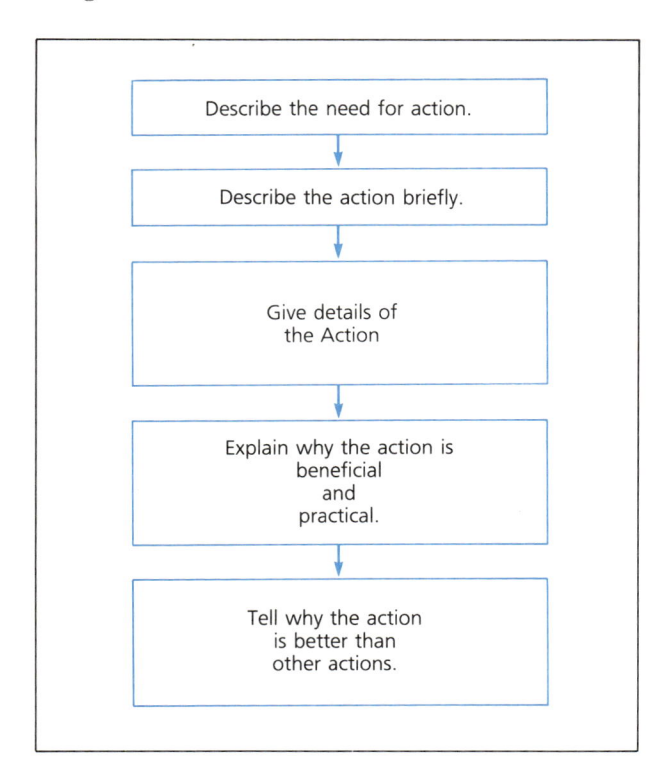

Tell why the action is better than other actions.

Figure 4.6. Blocking a request for action

The need — Sometimes your readers won't agree that action is needed. When this occurs, you may want to spend an entire message just laying out your case for something's being done — the background of the problem, its basic nature, its causes and effects, and so on. On the other hand, perhaps the need is so obvious that everyone sees it immediately and no further argument is necessary.

Description of the action — State specifically what you plan to do; don't leave your reader in the dark. This section may be rather long.

Why the action is beneficial and practical — Put yourself in your readers' place. They may agree with you about need; they may completely understand your proposed action. But they may be doubtful that it will work — or that, if it does work, it will do any good (be beneficial). In other words, you may have to prove to them that it will both work and do good. (Abolishing the federal income tax, for instance, might be beneficial to millions of Americans, but for the entire country would such an action be practical?)

Other possible actions — In many situations, you will be competing with other people who will have their own suggested actions. Bear this fact in mind as you organize your message. You don't want to make a good argument only to have others come along a short time later and say they have a better solution to the problem.

Anticipate. As you organize your arguments, consider other actions besides yours. If you think any of them might be relevant to your discussion, state them fairly and completely, and then state why your suggested actions are better. It's a lot easier to knock down a prospective opponent's argument before it is made than after.

BLOCKING THE TYPICAL REPORT

There are, of course, many ways to organize a report. But there are two ways that have worked so well they deserve special mention.

The Report That Gives News

This standard report is written for a particular audience that needs to be told some news on a subject that should interest them. Broadly speaking, the organization of this report can be used by both business and technical people. See Figure 4.7.

The *news* in this report is any idea or material that you organize especially for the message in question. Why can you think of it as news? Because by doing so, you remind yourself of the one characteristic that all of us human beings have in common: we are curious about things. We want to know the latest score in the World Series, the latest information on wars in the Middle East, the latest Dow Jones average, the latest development in the takeover of a company. In treating the point of your message as news, you tend to sharpen

Block Out the Big Picture

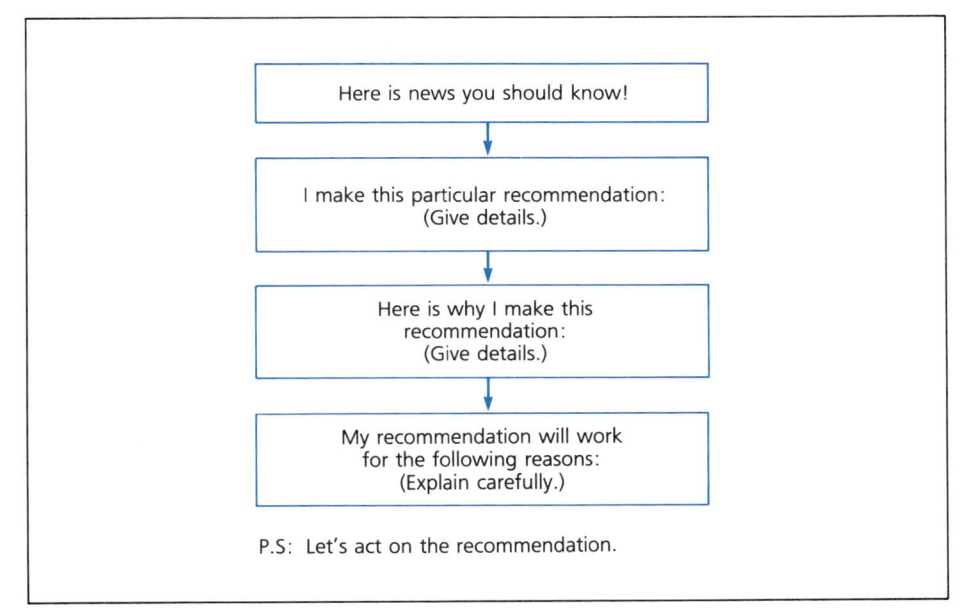

```
┌─────────────────────────────────┐
│   Here is news you should know! │
└─────────────────────────────────┘
                │
                ▼
┌─────────────────────────────────┐
│ I make this particular          │
│ recommendation:                 │
│      (Give details.)            │
└─────────────────────────────────┘
                │
                ▼
┌─────────────────────────────────┐
│   Here is why I make this       │
│       recommendation:           │
│        (Give details.)          │
└─────────────────────────────────┘
                │
                ▼
┌─────────────────────────────────┐
│  My recommendation will work    │
│   for the following reasons:    │
│      (Explain carefully.)       │
└─────────────────────────────────┘

   P.S:  Let's act on the recommendation.
```

Figure 4.7. Blocking a typical business report

that point and make it more precise, while at the same time you cannot help making the message more interesting and persuasive to your readers. Of course, you don't need to use the word *news* anywhere in the message.

The Report That Gives Results

Many reports are the result of "going to look." A supervisor tells you: "Go to Phoenix and find out why ten percent of the grummits Branch X makes are faulty." Or you decide to investigate a different system of handling health insurance for your group of workers. Or you are asked to evaluate the new contract with a union. So you "go to look" at the problem or issue, using whatever techniques of investigation seem appropriate.

When you start to write the report on the results of your investigation, consider using the blocking pattern shown in Figure 4.8. This pattern emphasizes two elements of the situation: the problem itself, which you may be free to define, and the results of your investigation. By keeping your eye on these two elements as you block out your report, you will write concisely and to the point.

The two arrows at the bottom of the blocking sheet remind you that many reports conclude in a certain way:

- By telling the reader what the material adds up to — what it means.
- By telling the reader what to do (recommendations).
- By combining these two in whatever way seems sensible.

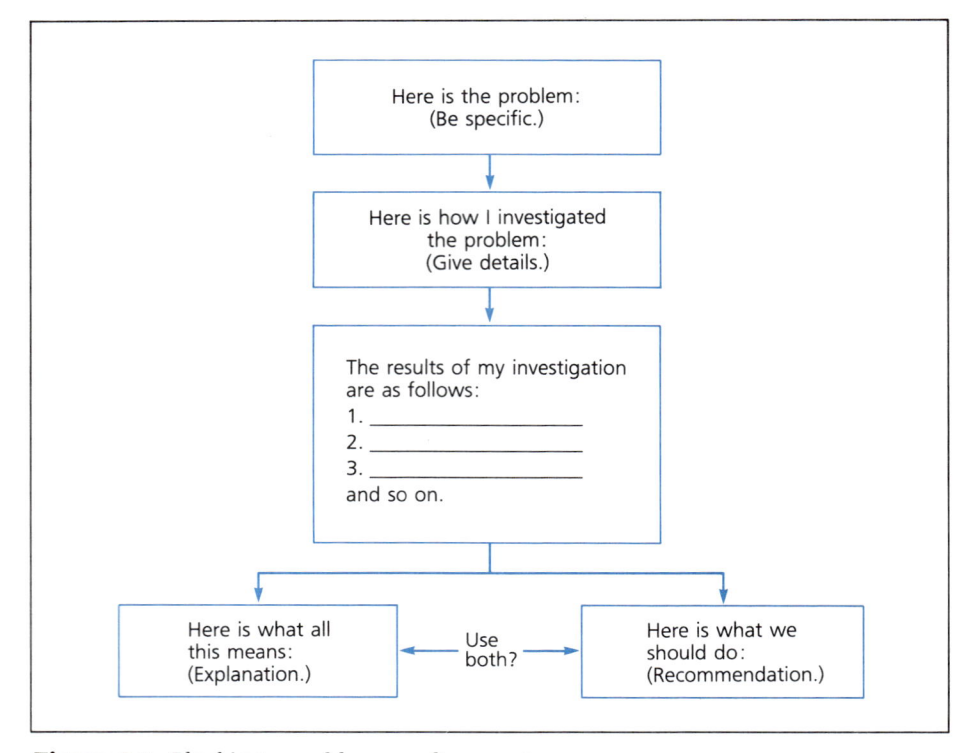

```
                    ┌─────────────────────────┐
                    │   Here is the problem:  │
                    │     (Be specific.)      │
                    └───────────┬─────────────┘
                                ▼
                    ┌─────────────────────────┐
                    │ Here is how I investigated│
                    │      the problem:       │
                    │     (Give details.)     │
                    └───────────┬─────────────┘
                                ▼
                    ┌─────────────────────────┐
                    │ The results of my investigation│
                    │      are as follows:    │
                    │   1. _____  │
                    │   2. _____  │
                    │   3. _____  │
                    │      and so on.         │
                    └───┬─────────────────┬───┘
                        ▼                 ▼
        ┌───────────────────┐   Use   ┌───────────────────┐
        │ Here is what all  │ ◄─────► │ Here is what we   │
        │ this means:       │  both?  │ should do:        │
        │ (Explanation.)    │         │ (Recommendation.) │
        └───────────────────┘         └───────────────────┘
```

Figure 4.8. Blocking a problem-results report

BLOCKING IS FLEXIBLE

As you may recall, the technique of blocking starts with arranging single cards, each with a single point or idea written on it. By doing this you gain great flexibility, for you can arrange the cards in any way that looks reasonable or logical. If you don't like one arrangement, you can quickly find another.

It doesn't matter how many cards you have, either — six or six hundred. It will take you longer to arrange six hundred, but that's the only difference. Once you get the cards arranged, you can start to block out the major elements of the message on a sheet of paper. We recommend just one sheet at first for the major blocking process — that is, try to get the major divisions of your message on one sheet rather than on two or three; you can see the overall pattern better. Fundamentally, blocking is a method of seeing the whole picture; and if you want to see the small details of the picture, you can use as many more sheets of paper as you need. And you can write detailed outlines, too, once you get your basic blocking done on the message.

TO CONCLUDE

1. Every message has an organization that can be blocked before you write. Blocking supplies the "big picture" for you. The actual blocks can vary considerably, but there are not many basic ones.

2. Your reader must have a hint, however slight, of the way you have arranged your blocks. (More of this in Chapter 5.) If you wish, you can describe your blocking pattern explicitly: "I will define the XYZ Process, and give three reasons why it is too costly to use at this time."

3. When you set up an expectation in the reader about the order of blocks in your organization, be sure you fulfill it.

4. Certain materials suggest, even demand, their own patterns of blocks. If you are writing a memo explaining a problem, for example, you will tend to get a set of blocks like those in Figure 4.8.

EXERCISES

1. What is the passage below about? Make some guesses for class discussion. After your class has decided on what the subject is, block out an organization for an improved version of the passage. Use a whole page for your blocks so that you have plenty of space to tinker with them.

> The procedure is actually quite simple. First you arrange things into different groups. Of course, one pile may be sufficient depending on how much there is to do. If you have to go somewhere else because of lack of facilities that is the next step; otherwise you are pretty well set. It is important not to overdo things. That is, it is better to do too few things at once than too many. In the short run this may not seem important but complications can easily arise. A mistake can be expensive as well. At first the whole procedure will seem complicated. Soon, however, it will become just another facet of life. It is difficult to foresee any end to the necessity for this task in the immediate future, but then one never can tell. After the procedure is completed one arranges the materials into different groups again. Then they can be put into their appropriate places. Eventually they will be used once more and the whole cycle will then have to be repeated. However, that is part of life.

2. Read the following letter and for class discussion make notes of its flaws in organization. Be specific. Create new blocks for an improved letter, and be prepared to put them on the board for discussion.

Rewrite the letter completely. Improve it in every possible way.

Ms. M.I. Urbanette
1204 Cornet Dr.
Champaign, IL 61820

RE: 502 West Oboe St.

Dear Ms. Urbanette:

This is supplementary to our conversation of Friday, January 23, 1987.
Additional inspections at this property, today a.m., revealed the following:
An important item, apparently overlooked in previous inspections, but still applicable and equally important is that the heating plant (boiler) must be enclosed in this same *fire-rated* separation from the rest of the house, including the ceiling. This requirement is extended to all residential buildings, other than one or two-family dwellings.

An alternative is the installation of water sprinkler leads in the immediate area to protect the floor joists above, however an approved walled enclosure is still required.

Further information on this requirement can be had from this office.

I am aware of your position, in that these requirements will represent additional expenditures, however, I must inform you that these are requirements of the Building Codes and cannot be overlooked.

Therefore, I must advise you that we must seek compliance with the same in a reasonable time in order to permit this property to be "Approved for Occupancy" and so as not to be forced to take more extreme measures to accomplish this.

At your request, you may appeal any or all of these requirements to the Building Code Board of Appeals, who will hear your appeal for variance from these requirements.

You will then either be granted a variance or be required to comply and be given a time limit in which to have completed same.

Therefore, I will require a reply to this letter within fifteen (15) days, and you may again discuss these matters, during which you may decide what actions you desire to take, and if you choose to appeal.

You may call this office, 367-6661, and arrange an appointment.

Respectfully,

Dick Sharp
BUILDING INSPECTOR

3. You are W. Foley, the manager of a large bookstore chain. Recently the chain's stores in the Midwest have averaged four bad checks a week. You decide that employees at these stores are not exercising enough caution in accepting checks; you want local bookstore managers to conduct refresher meetings in which they will go over check-cashing procedures with all employees.

Here is your list of the main points that you want covered in these review sessions:

- Don't cash checks for strangers unless they identify themselves properly.
- Don't accept these as identification: temporary driver's license, receipts, hunting license, lodge cards, social security cards, marriage licenses, pay stubs, or paid utility bills.
- Take your time in investigating each check presented. If there is a line of customers waiting, get another employee to run the register while you validate the checks.
- Examine identification for erasures or tampering. Remember that identification, like a check, can be forged.
- Make certain that names and handwriting match on the check. Check endorsements and items on the face of the check for misspellings.
- Don't cash any third-party, payroll, or cashier's checks.
- Always insist that the customer write his or her address and phone number, if these are not already on the check. Don't worry about being businesslike in cashing checks. It's your money!
- Please place your OK and identification information on the right end of the check; the bank places its sticker on the left end.
- Don't be bashful about asking questions concerning the check you are asked to accept.
- When a driver's license is used as an ID, take it in your hand and compare the description of the check-passer with that on the license. Note the expiration date. Write the license number on the back of the check yourself; the passer could transpose numbers.

Write a memorandum that presents the points listed above, reorganizing and rewording the points for coherence, conciseness, and clarity. Persuade the managers of the need for carefully conducted review sessions.

—Jim Fleming

4. Check the assignments in Appendix A. Pick one of these and block out the message that you might write for it.

5. Block out a message that uses a question-and-answer format. Employ a section on your blocking sheet that employs "irrelevant questions." Put a little of the content of the messages in each block so that your instructor can tell how the message will be organized.

6. Repeat the assignment given in exercise 5, but this time create blocking for a message that asks for an action on the part of readers.

7. Take an old paper or message of yours and create a blocking sheet for the paper exactly as you wrote it. Does the organization you see on the sheet satisfy you now? If you could, how would you change the organization of your old paper?

8. Criticize the blocking sheet in Figure 4.9. Write a memo, addressing it to the writer, saying what is wrong with the blocking and how it might be changed.

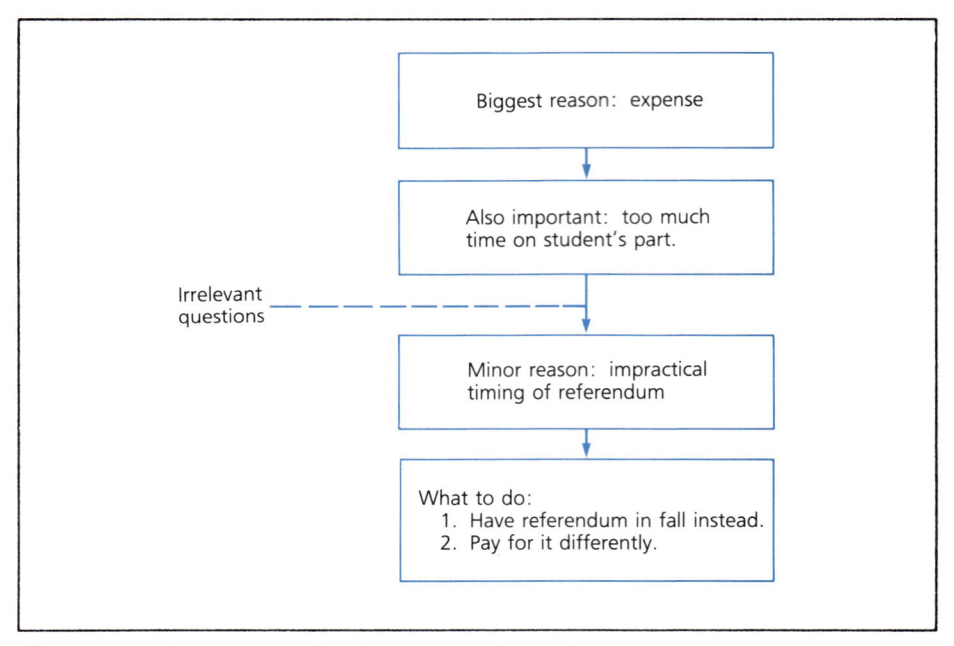

```
                    ┌────────────────────────────┐
                    │  Biggest reason: expense   │
                    └──────────────┬─────────────┘
                                   ▼
                    ┌────────────────────────────┐
                    │  Also important: too much  │
                    │  time on student's part.   │
                    └──────────────┬─────────────┘
  Irrelevant                       │
  questions  ──────────────────────┤
                                   ▼
                    ┌────────────────────────────┐
                    │  Minor reason: impractical │
                    │  timing of referendum      │
                    └──────────────┬─────────────┘
                                   ▼
                    ┌────────────────────────────────┐
                    │  What to do:                   │
                    │    1. Have referendum in fall  │
                    │       instead.                 │
                    │    2. Pay for it differently.  │
                    └────────────────────────────────┘
```

Figure 4.9. Three reasons for changing student-referendum procedure

CHAPTER 5

How *Not* to Lose Your Reader

We have been emphasizing the fact that your reader follows your words just as you wrote them. You write along a line like this:

Capital letter → → → → → → period.

And your reader follows you word by word.

When you develop paragraphs moving down the page, your reader follows you as you go from the top to the bottom of the sheet of paper:

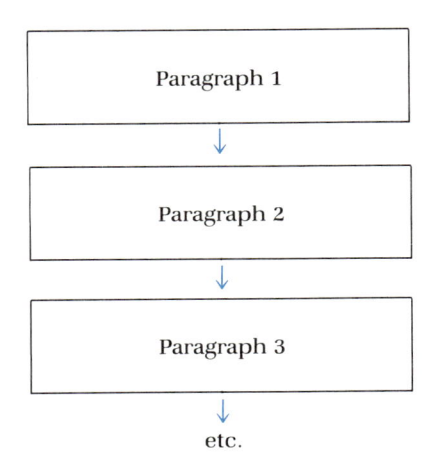

```
┌─────────────────────────┐
│      Paragraph 1        │
└─────────────────────────┘
            ↓
┌─────────────────────────┐
│      Paragraph 2        │
└─────────────────────────┘
            ↓
┌─────────────────────────┐
│      Paragraph 3        │
└─────────────────────────┘
            ↓
           etc.
```

As a writer, then, you are making two trips on the page: from left to right along a line, and from top to bottom down the page.

At any point in making these trips, you can lose your reader. For example, in this sentence there is a word left out.

> I remember the manager did that.

Should that sentence read:

> I remember that the manager did that.   (?)

Or should it read:

> I remember the manager who did that.   (?)

Or suppose (when beginning a paragraph) you omit the word *but:*

> [But] Mark said that the invoices were saved in a blue box.

By omitting *but*, you have failed to tell your readers that the sentence is an objection or a refutation. So your readers may stumble as they follow you across and down the page.

SIGNPOSTING

Always try to tell your readers where you are going. Give them signposts that point the way. One excellent type of signpost is the topic sentence that begins a typical paragraph. Example:

> Here is what you must look for when buying new tires for your car.
>
> ↓

This topic sentence provides a signpost that points down the page, one that suggests that readers will get information on certain important points about car tires. Having seen the signpost, readers are now ready for the information appearing just below it in a full paragraph:

> *Here is what you must look for when buying new tires for your car.* First, make sure that any tire you are considering is the same size as those that came with the car. Tires of the wrong size can be dangerous. Second, do not mix tires of different constructions or riding characteristics. And do not mix worn tires with new ones. Third, ...

A good signpost is a device of prediction. It prepares readers for the material they will see in a moment by pointing forward to it — by predicting certain ideas or facts. Note how much these topic sentences, acting as signposts, predict the ideas to follow:

Topic Sentence	*Signpost as Reader Interprets It*
There are two objections to the XYZ theory of management.	The subject will be the XYZ theory of management. I will learn two objections to it. ↓
If you will call her before Tuesday, Ms. Ramon will take you to meet the three people involved in researching the problem. They are . . .	Ms. Ramon is my source person. There are three people doing the research. I will learn who they are. ↓
Health authorities recommend regular activity that uses many parts of the body.	I will learn about the value of *regular* activity, and which parts of the body can be used. ↓

USE HEADINGS (WHEN APPROPRIATE)

Headings predict and explain your organization very well. Keep them as short as possible while being specific.

YOUR INTRODUCTION PREDICTS ALSO

After you have blocked out the organization of your message (see Chapter 4), you are ready to make predictions for your reader.

Observe how these introductory sentences predict:

- Gene Knolls, the Chief Auditor, suggested that we do three things to make his job easier.
- Gene Knolls uses a new method of installing the bearings.
- If President Gene Knolls wishes to improve his administration of affairs before the Board meets on April 1, . . .
- Gene Knolls's training program is the best in the company. Here's why.
- Clearly, Gene Knolls was ready for the promotion when it came.
- Dearly beloved, we are gathered here to join Gene Knolls and . . .
- The night watchman, Gene Knolls, was apparently murdered by a technique, it is alleged, known only to Southeast Asians.
- As the medical examiner assigned to the case, I performed a routine autopsy on the body of Gene Knolls.
- We will always revere the memory of Gene Knolls.

An introductory paragraph, even a short one, can promise and predict:

> Contrary to any news reports you may have read, our company will be producing the B Car starting in April of this year. For, make no bones about it, the B Car is back — it provides everything customers want in a big car.

What follows? As you might predict, several paragraphs of specific description of what the B Car "provides."

USE THE "DOUBLE SIGNPOST"

The double signpost occurs mainly at the beginning of a paragraph. It points back to where your readers have been reading and forward to where they are going to read:

You put the double signpost at the beginning of the paragraph:

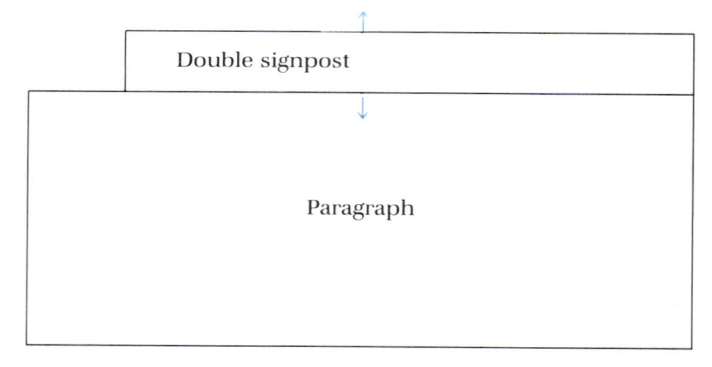

Double signpost

Paragraph

Examples:

1. This particular computer error we have been explaining is worth more discussion.

2. To the four problems I have just mentioned should be added two others. First . . .

The double signpost has one special advantage. Because it points two ways, it links or ties paragraphs together:

              ties ↑ back

1.	As you now see from the evidence,	the question of national economic policy is not nearly as simple as it appears.

                                              ties ↓ forward

              ties ↑ back

2.	This kind of bulky résumé	often produces simple boredom in the employer.

                                                ties ↓ forward

If you practice using the double signpost, you will discover that it will help you greatly in clarifying the organization of a message.

USE "ECHOES" AND REPEATED WORDS

Throughout this chapter, we have been emphasizing one main thing: As your readers scan your message, they need all the help you can give them to stay on track. If you start a new subject, they need to know it. If you intend to tell them three major ideas in the body of your message, they need to be aware of this fact early.

If you want to know how typical readers feel when they get in the middle of complex or confusing materials, imagine that you are driving through the business district of a city in the busy hour, and you are following a car driven by a friend who knows his way around the city. You are trying to follow him to his house, which so far as you are concerned might as well be in South Timbuktu. Your friend knows exactly where he is going. You do not. How do you feel as your friend darts through yellow lights, makes sudden turns when you least expect them, shifts lanes to turn left without warning you so that you are in the wrong lane when the turn comes up?

In a situation like this, what you need is careful signals from your friend. What your readers need is equally careful signalling from you, the writer, so that they know where you are in your message and where you intend to go.

An excellent method for keeping readers close on your track is to use so-called echoes and repeated words. Before we define these terms, consider the passage by W. Whyte below. Note carefully the words in **boldface** type:

Its signal characteristic, as the reader and all other critics of **businesese** will recognize, is its **uniformity**. Almost invariably, **businesese** is marked by the heavy use of the passive construction. Nobody ever *does* anything. Things happen — and the author of the action is only barely implied. Thus, one does not refer to something, reference is made to; similarly, while prices may rise, nobody raises them. To be sure, in **businesese** there is not quite the same anonymity as is found in federal prose, for "I" and "we" do appear often. Except when the news to be relayed is good, however, there is no mistaking that the "I" and "we" are merely a convenient fiction and that the real author isn't a person at all but that great mystic force known as the corporation.

Except for a few special expressions, its vocabulary is everywhere **quite the same.** Midwesterners are likely to dispute the latter point, but a reading of approximately 500,000 words of **business prose** indicates no striking differences — in the Midwest or anywhere else. Moreover, in sounding out a hundred executives on the subject, *Fortune* found that their views coincided remarkably, particularly so on the matter of pet peeves (principally: "please be advised," "in reference to yours of . . . ," "we wish to draw attention," "to acknowledge your letter"). The phrases of **businesese** are everywhere so **uniform,** in fact, that stenographers have a full set of shorthand symbols for them.

Because of this **uniformity,** defenders of **businesese** can argue that it doesn't make for misunderstanding. After all, everybody knows the symbols, and furthermore, wouldn't a lot of people be offended by the terseness of more concise wording? There is something to this theory. Since **businesese** generally is twice as wordy as plain English, however, this theory is rather expensive to uphold. By the use of regular English the cost of the average letter — commonly estimated at 75 cents to $1 — can be cut by about 20 cents. For a firm transmitting a million letters a year, this could mean an annual saving of $200,000. Probably it would be even greater; for, by the calculations of correspondence specialist Richard Morris, roughly 15 per cent of the letters currently being written wouldn't be necessary at all if the preceding correspondence had been in regular English in the first place.

Here, in a famous article written on its subject, you see William Whyte repeating and echoing words and their ideas. If he does not want to repeat the word exactly, he will echo it with a somewhat changed word. Thus *uniformity* is echoed by *quite the same*, and *uniform* is echoed by *uniformity*. *Businesese* is echoed by *business prose*.

Such echoes, along with simple repetitions, provide a splendid guide for the reader. If you put them in table form, you can see how they help the reader follow Whyte's message:

Paragraph	Mention of 1st term	Mention of 2nd term
1	businesese businesese businesese	uniformity

Paragraph	Mention of 1st term	Mention of 2nd term
2	business prose businesese	quite the same uniform
3	businesese businesese	uniformity

Not once since the publication of Whyte's three paragraphs has anyone ever complained that the passage is dull or repetitive. Readers are so grateful for the signals and echoes that Whyte uses to direct them through his writing that they don't even notice how much this direction depends on the repeated use of two terms. In addition, the slight shifts, as from *businese* to *business prose*, provide some useful variety.

USE TRANSITIONS

The typical transition says to your reader:

 Look out! I'm about to . . .

What you are "about to" do depends on the development of your message and the transition you choose at any particular point. If you are about to give examples, you may write *for instance* or *for example*. If you are about to give a list of examples, you may set up this pattern:

 For example, _____ .
 Second, _____ . Third, _____ .

If you are about to show an effect of something, you may write *therefore* or *thus*.

The word *transition* originally meant "to go across," and the word still suggests a kind of preparing to go from one thing to another. Almost any such preparation can help your reader:

- *It is certain* that fuel rationing is not now needed . . .
- *While this was occurring*, we tore down the punch press and found . . .
- *Moreover*, the two suppliers could not agree on the contracts.

Consider these transitional devices:

To separate or count ideas: *first, second, third, in addition, moreover, besides, furthermore, another, then, again, also, last, finally.* (*Finally* signals the end of your counted ideas.)

To explain ideas or give examples: *for example, for instance, indeed, such as, in particular, to illustrate, specifically, that is, thus.*

To show effect or cause: *accordingly, therefore, so, thus, consequently, because, hence, nevertheless, as a result.*

To contrast ideas: *on the other hand, even though, on the contrary, in contrast, though, yet, but.* (*Yet* and *but* are the signals most used for contrast.)

To make a comparison: *also, similarly, in the same way, likewise.*

Many expressions listed here can be considered transitional. For that matter, any term that helps your reader "to go across" from one point to another in your message is technically a transition. Observe how this writer, Robert D. Gieselman, a specialist in business communication, uses such terms to link sentences and ideas. (The emphasis is ours.)

> *Most college students* — who, *remember*, represent the very best of high school graduates — are not properly trained in the art of writing while in college. *Too often*, they are permitted to complete four years of higher education, even at our best universities, without extensive useful writing practice and criticism. *The key term is "useful."* By that I mean that much of the writing college students do is, at best, of limited value. *For example*, I think term papers on broad, general topics are not of much use in training students for the kind of writing they will be asked to do on the job. Term papers are of dubious value as training in writing; *they* are more valuable as training for the next term-paper assignment. Partly *this is so* because *they* are not written for real audiences to present solutions to real problems. Only in college will you be writing for readers who know more about the subject than you do. *In real life*, to be blunt, there is no such thing as a term paper.

EXERCISES

1. One of the great success stories in modern publishing is Paul Samuelson's *Economics*, for many years the most-used textbook in its field. There are many reasons for Samuelson's success, not the least being the superb organization of the book's ideas. Here, from the tenth edition, is a typical page of Samuelson's writing. For class discussion, prepare some notes on his organization. Consider his use of headings; the employment of prediction in the introduction to the passage; the double signposts; and the use of echoes, repeated words, and transitional words or phrases.

THE PARADOX OF THRIFT

Induced investment throws new light on the age-old question of thrift versus consumption. It shows this:

> An increased desire to consume — which is another way of looking at a decreased desire to save — is likely to boost business sales and increase investment. On the other hand, a decreased desire to consume — i.e., an increase in thriftiness — is likely to reduce inflationary pressure in times of booming incomes; but in time of depression, it could make the depression worse and reduce the amount of actual net capital formation in the

community. *High consumption and high investment are then hand in hand rather than opposed to each other.*

This surprising result is sometimes called the "paradox of thrift." It is a paradox because most of us used to be taught that thrift is *always* a good thing. Ben Franklin's *Poor Richard's Almanac* never tired of preaching the doctrine of saving. And now along comes a new generation of financial experts who seem to say that the old virtues may be modern sins in depressed times.

Paradox resolved Let us for the moment leave our cherished beliefs aside and try to disentangle the paradox in a dispassionate, scientific manner. Two considerations will help to clarify the whole matter.

The first is this. In economics, remember, we must always be on guard against the logical fallacy of composition. That is to say, what is good for each person separately need *not* thereby always be good for all; under some circumstances, private prudence may be social folly. Specifically, this means that the *attempt* of each and every person to increase his saving may — under the conditions to be described — result in a reduction in *actual* saving by all the people. Note the italicized words "attempt" and "actual"; between them, in our imperfect mixed economy, there may be a world of difference when people find themselves thrown out of jobs and with lowered incomes.

The second clue to the paradox of thrift lies in the question of whether or not national income is at a depressed level. If we were at full employment and always remained there, then obviously the more of our national product we devoted to current consumption, the less would be available for capital formation. If output could be assumed to be always at its maximum, then the old-fashioned doctrine of thrift would be absolutely correct — correct, be it noted, from both the individual and the social standpoints. In primitive agricultural communities, such as the American colonies of Franklin's day, there was some truth in Franklin's prescription. The same was true during World Wars I and II, and during periods of boom and inflation: if people then become more thrifty, less consumption means more investment.

But, according to statistical records, full employment and inflationary demand conditions have occurred only at intervals in our nation's history. Much of the time under laissez faire there were some wasting of resources, some unemployment, and some insufficiency of demand, investment, and purchasing power. When such is the case, everything can go into reverse. What once was a social virtue may then become a social vice. What is true for the individual — that extra thriftiness means increased saving and wealth — may then become completely untrue for the community as a whole.

Under conditions of unemployment, the *attempt to save* may result in *less*, not more, saving. The individual who saves cuts down on his consumption. He passes on less purchasing power than before; therefore, someone else's income is reduced, for one man's outgo is another man's income. If one man succeeds in saving more, maybe it is because someone else is forced to dissave. If one man succeeds in hoarding more money, someone else must do without.

2. The paragraph below has been taken from the middle of a student report. Read the paragraph and write a sentence or two stating what you think the subject of it is. Then look at page 494, where you will learn what the subject really is. Finally, rewrite the paragraph so that it flows properly from first sentence to last.

METHODOLOGY

It will first be determined precisely what format of study could be used in the examination and analysis of daytime TV soaps. Once a suitable format of study is chosen, a discussion of its appropriateness in the classroom will reveal the evidential information necessary to determine its effectiveness. Student interest will be canvassed. The discussion will look at whether or not the daytime TV soaps have the significant elements of drama for study. And lastly, it is appropriate to review other institutions who have had such a program.

3. The paragraph below is part of a memo to a senior executive in a company that has just bought a chain of night clubs located in college towns. Tell how and where the writer (the manager of one club, called "Mabel's") loses his reader. Be specific. Then rewrite the paragraph so that the reader can understand the material more easily.

The next step in promotional strategy is determining the budget. Such costs as advertising, promotions, and overhead must be estimated accurately. Overhead can be very exorbitant in the nightclub business. A good example of this is the average monthly electric bill for Mabel's, $1,700. The overhead cost of an "average" night is as follows: band, $800; employees' wages, $100; utilities, $100. This totals $1,000 per night just to open up and have a band play. The method Mabel's (and many other nightclubs) use to offset these costs is to charge a nightly cover charge. This charge is usually $2-3, but can go as high as $10 for an expensive band like Marshall Crenshaw. The hope is that the door (via cover charges) will be able to pay the cost of the band, some advertising, and some electricity. Mabel's joins advertising and promotions into one account. This figure can be anywhere from $3,000-$3,500 per month. Now in promotional strategy we deal with management of program elements, and the first element is advertising. The first segment of advertising deals with the analysis of media resources. Mabel's distributes the $3,000 monthly expenditures among many types of advertising, which I will now examine.

4. Below are four paragraphs on the subject given in the heading. Discuss in detail the problems a reader of these paragraphs might have in following the train of thought. Rewrite the first sentence of each paragraph, making it point more specifically toward the material that follows. What does each rewriting do to the second sentence in each paragraph? Does each second sentence now have to be rewritten? Why?

If your instructor wishes, rewrite all four paragraphs.

MARKETING THE COMMUNICATIONS GRADUATE

Various comments on the market situation revealed that job opportunities are not as good this year as they were last year, but the low peak of a few years ago is not upon us either. Fewer recruiters coming to the university this year than last from Chicago and New York indicate a definite need for more effort on the part of the student. Several untapped markets were suggested for investigation: government associations, trade unions, non-profit organizations, and research firms; for example, the College does not offer work experience with the school *Daily*, WILL-AM-FM-TV, WPGU-AM-FM, the *Illio*, local merchants, the communications library, and well-equipped newsrooms, photography darkrooms, radio-television broadcasting laboratories, a printing laboratory, and an advertising layout laboratory.

Agencies, large companies, newspapers, magazines, and broadcast stations seem to be the main focus of students in search of account executive positions, creative assignments, data analysis positions, announcing spots, and production assignments. For all of these kinds of markets the best qualification appears to be experience and grades in larger firms.

While interviewing Tony Smith (from the College Placement Office) several facts relevant to the individuals who actually are involved in the hiring process were disclosed. According to Smith, recruiters are usually men from twenty-five to thirty or from forty to forty-five years old, married, with very conservative lifestyles. The latter is dictated by the fact that they are in the personnel office of their companies, and this requires them to live up to the spirit and letter of company regulations.

According to a placement office survey, the job market is such that most communications graduates can find jobs prior to and immediately following graduation. The present starting salary of bachelor's graduates in communications averages between $800 and $1,000 a month, although some are below $500 and others as high as $2,000 a month.

5. Prepare class notes for a discussion of the letter below. Cover signposting, prediction, the double signpost, echoes and repeated words, and transitions.

Dear Susan:

Here's what I've discovered about buses for the company vacation trip.

It turned out that all of the ski areas still being considered were in one of two general locations. One location was southern Wisconsin and the other was the upper peninsula of Michigan. This made it easier when dealing with the bus companies because only two price quotes were needed from each company. The bus companies all agreed that because certain ski areas were so close together, there would be little, if any, price difference for transportation to these areas. The information received from the bus companies is summarized in the table below. The prices in the table are for a trip leaving on a Friday afternoon and returning on a Sunday night. The prices also include lodging, meals, and wages for a fully licensed driver.

BUS INFORMATION

Bus company	Cost to Wisconsin	Cost to Michigan	Alcohol Allowed	Washroom	Insured	Capacity of Bus
Coach Travel Unlimited	$1091	$1661	yes	yes	yes	47
Keeshan charter	$1210	$1772	yes	yes	yes	47
Munsen's Discovery Coaches, Inc.	$1150	$1730	yes	yes	yes	47

    All three of the bus-chartering companies I talked with were based in the southern Chicago area. The reason only three bus companies were contacted was that the people at the third one I talked with, Coach Travel Unlimited, impressed me immensely. First, the company had the lowest prices. Second, it would provide a place that the trip could depart from where the group members could leave their cars over the weekend. The other bus companies did not offer this; they required that I talk to people at local churches, hotels, and so on, to find a place of departure where the group could leave their cars. The final reason Coach Travel impressed me so much was that if we did not get the forty-five people we were expecting on the trip, Coach Travel representatives said they could almost always provide additional skiers. For these reasons, I decided to charter the bus from Coach Travel Unlimited.

                                                                     Yours in snow,

                                                                     Sam

PART 3

Writing Your Message

CHAPTER 6

Words — and the Problem of Bizbuzz

Despite its problems, American business is still the best in the world: the most pragmatic, flexible, and inventive. Its use of English, the primary medium of our communication with each other, should also be the best. We cannot be satisfied with vague, trivial, faddish, or jargon-ridden use of English.

ONCE AGAIN, KEEP IT SIMPLE

The best English for business writing uses plain, clear words — simple ones. They are practical. Simple words ordinarily work for everyone concerned. In their book on the success of excellent American companies, Peters and Waterman tell about a friend of theirs who chose IBM for a major computer-system purchase. (Italics are ours.)

> Many of the others were ahead of IBM in technological wizardry. And heaven knows their software is easier to use. But IBM alone took the trouble to get to know us. They interviewed extensively up and down the line. They talked our language, *no mumbo jumbo on computer innards*.

An executive at Hewlett Packard recently remarked that his company doesn't really know what type of organization works best for it. "All we know for certain is that we start with a remarkably high degree of informal communication, which is the key. We have to preserve this at all costs."

103

Keep It Simple

Strike three.
Get your hand off my knee.
You're overdrawn.
Your horse won.
Yes.
No.
You have the account.
Walk.
Don't walk.
Mother's dead.
Basic events
require simple language.
Idiosyncratically euphuistic
eccentricities are the
promulgators of
triturable obfuscation.
What did you do last night?
Enter into a meaningful
romantic involvement
or
fall in love?
What did you have for
breakfast this morning?
The upper part of a hog's
hind leg with two oval
bodies encased in a shell
laid by a female bird
or
ham and eggs?
David Belasco, the great
American theatrical producer,
once said, "If you can't
write your idea on the
back of my calling
card,
you don't have a clear idea."

Figure 6.1. Direct, simple messages.

Simple, informal words work for you in many ways. They make products and services attractive. Note the attractive simplicity of this letter (written by a CPA to a client):

> We would like to have you bring to our office your life insurance policies, Keogh plan contracts, tax-sheltered annuity contracts, and related papers. Using these, we can determine how these assets will be treated at death. It is fairly easy to have the contracts read so that all of the proceeds — or a portion of them — can be excluded from federal income tax. But it is almost impossible to have them excluded from state income tax.

One of the commonest misunderstandings about the use of words in business was illustrated the other day when one of us was doing a consulting job for a bank. As we were discussing some problems of communication, one man said: "I can see your point about keeping words simple when I write to 'outsiders' — nonspecialists. But simple words surely aren't necessary when writing to other specialists like me."

The evidence on the question shows that nothing could be further from the truth — for in the vast majority of cases the issue is one of communication between human beings. It does not matter what kind of specialist you are: whether you are in sales, purchasing, medical technology, engineering, marketing, personnel, research, support services, and so on. You are still a human being. You have the same mental, emotional, and basic verbal equipment you had before you became a specialist. Your eyes, ears, brain, voice box, knowledge of English and its usages — none of these has significantly changed. And you still have the same problems with communication (only perhaps more of them).

No matter who you are or how you make your living, simple words still work best in most situations.

As a test of this generalization, read the short passages below. Each is written by a specialist for other specialists. The words in each are mainly simple.

The first passage is written by a lawyer who is also a CPA:

> The will you've asked me to comment on is acceptable so far as I can see, although I expect some changes in state law by November. At the present time, the only items that would pass by will are their [the clients'] jewelry, personal articles of clothing, household goods, and (possibly) automobiles.
>
> Their joint tenancy property would pass by operation of law. And their life insurance, Keogh funds, and tax-sheltered annuities would pass by operation of the contracts.

Our second example is written by a business executive who was originally trained as an engineer:

> The data for one horizon are plotted and contoured on a map, in regular unmigrated form. A line extending down-dip is drawn on the map, perpendicular to the contours, anywhere that contours are nearly parallel for some distance. Contour values at intersections of contours with this line are plotted by hand on a cross section. Some migrating method is used to migrate this section. The computer methods described don't apply, because they need a record section as a starting point, but overlaying a diffraction chart will work. From the migrated horizon on the cross section, data are plotted on a new map. The process is repeated for other dip lines. When enough migrated points are plotted on the new map, it can be contoured. It is then a map with data in true migrated position.
>
> The process has to be repeated for other horizons. Note that the dip lines of one horizon are not necessarily dip lines on another, so a whole new set of cross sections may need to be plotted for each horizon.

In all of this technical discussion, there are only two unusual words: *diffraction* and *migrated*.

Finally, here is a medical doctor who is writing for other doctors:

> We know but little of the incubation period in acute lobar pneumonia. It is probably very short. There are sometimes slight catarrhal symptoms for a day or two. As a rule, the disease sets in abruptly with a severe chill, which lasts from fifteen to thirty minutes or longer.
>
> — Sir William Osler, the great physician

By contrast, consider the wonderful *un*simplicity of another physician writing on exactly the same subject:

> Symptomatology relative to impending or incipient onset of illness generally manifests itself initially via a marked chill, following which a rapid rise of temperature to the 103°-105° range is characteristically observed. Cutaneous palpation demonstrates . . .

These medical examples are taken from *Dx + Rx: A Physician's Guide to Medical Writing* by John Dirckx, M.D. Of them, Dr. Dirckx says: "I submit that anyone accustomed to reading literature, whether technical or not, of the tone and calibre of the first paragraph would be virtually incapable of writing rubbish like the second."

WHEN IS THE FAMILIAR WORD UNFAMILIAR?

One of the reasons that simple words work for you is that they are familiar. If we write words like *rock, please, stock market, baby,* and *profit,* you will have some idea of what these words might mean, particularly if we put them in a context.

But if I write *parameter, détente, trauma center, passive voice, cost-effec-

tive, you probably will not have a clear idea of their meaning. Yes, these words are familiar, so much so that to most people they are trite and worn out; but tests of them imply that almost no one understands them clearly, even in their contexts.

We have tested these and other pseudo-familiar words on several samples of people, all with at least two years of college, some with Ph.D.s. The results on the five words are typical of pseudo-familiar words in general:

Pseudo-familiar Words

- *Parameter* — Eight percent understood it in context.
- *Passive voice* — Four percent understood it in context.
- *Détente* — Twelve percent understood it in 1975, four percent in 1983. (The word has gone somewhat out of style in recent years.)
- *Trauma center* — Six percent understood it in context. (Since this phrase appears on hundreds of road signs in the United States, this low level of comprehension is alarming.)
- *Cost-effective* — ????

Cost-effective is puzzling. Very widely used, it also seems to be very ambiguous. People in our sample argued so bitterly over it that final agreement appeared impossible. About twenty percent said they thought they knew what it meant when they first read it in context, but after a few minutes of discussion, agreement among the twenty percent tended to decrease markedly.

For instance, we tried the word on one group of twelve graduate students. They were all in business or the sciences. They were given the sentence, "Gasohol is not cost-effective for the Illinois farmer." At first, most of them were sure that they knew what the sentence meant. But in a minute or two, consensus broke down, and they started firing questions at each other:

- What exactly *is* the cost problem?
- Do the original materials from which gasohol is made cost too much for the farmer to make it himself?
- Does the equipment to make gasohol cost too much?
- Does this equipment break down? Is it unreliable?
- Is the cost of gasohol too high for the farmer who buys it at the pump?
- Are transportation costs somehow involved?
- Does gasohol give less mileage?
- And so on.

We asked a specialist in agricultural engineering, a professor in the university, what he thought of the sentence.

He said, "There is no way of telling what it means for sure. But I can guess. It means, 'In Illinois, it costs the farmer more to make gasohol himself than it costs him to buy gasoline at the pump.'"

"Then," we asked, "why didn't the writer say that?"

"Who knows?" he answered. "Maybe he didn't know the facts and was just trying to hide his ignorance."

BIZBUZZ

Bizbuzz is the opposite of clear, simple, familiar language. It is made of jargon; tired, wornout expressions; empty (if fashionable) catchwords; and what someone has called "boneless abstractions." The boneless abstraction is a ghastly expression like *essentiality, attitude orientation, plethora, ambiance, facilitator, seminal* — words that have no more solidity than blubber cut from a whale.

Nothing can cause as much havoc in the writer's mind as bizbuzz. Use a word like *facilitator* in your first sentence, a phrase like *vital essentials* in your second sentence, and *more unique* in your third sentence, and you may be too unsteady to even write the fourth one.

As the examples just given indicate, bizbuzz is of various kinds.

Clichés

These are wornout, trite expressions that should have been put out to pasture years ago:

- at this point in time
- new avenues are being explored
- first and foremost
- bottom line
- more unique
- warrants further investigation
- in-depth study
- real challenges
- multifaceted problem
- in this day and age
- many and varied
- henceforth and hereafter
- cutting edge
- leading edge
- for all intents and purposes

Fadwords

These are words and phrases that come into fashion like new clothing styles. People pick up such words, work them to death, and then (usually) abandon them for something newer in fashion. They are also called *vogue words*. Examples:

- viable, viability
- vital
- resource utilization
- overview
- input, output
- hopefully
- dichotomy
- crisis

- orchestrate
- matrix
- longitudinal study
- simplistic
- orient, orientate, orientation
- ballpark figure
- ambiance

Redundancies

A friend of ours calls these "two-tailed dogs." The second tail is redundant — unnecessary. The verbal redundancy is typically a phrase wagging an unneeded second tail. In *absolutely essential*, for instance, *absolutely* is unneeded because its idea is built into *essential*. In *completely unanimous*, *completely* is unneeded because unanimity is complete. In *combine together*, you don't need the second tail of *together*; it is built into *combine*. Other examples of redundancy:

- true fact
- small in size
- obviate the necessity of
- join together
- red in color
- general consensus
- few in number
- complete absence
- audible to the ears
- continue on
- clearly evident
- positive gain
- vital essentials
- modern life of today
- for all intents and purposes

Observe that the last item on the list, *for all intents and purposes*, was also the last item on the list of clichés. *Cliché*, *fadword*, and *redundancy* are not exclusive categories. Many words can be classified as all three. Redundancies tend to be faddish. And fadwords tend to be cliché-ish.

Sometimes a perfectly acceptable word will become so overworked, even by good writers, that it becomes a fad and a cliché. One example is *controversial*. Editors at the New York *Times* got suspicious when the word began popping up often in news stories. So they tapped their Information Bank computer and discovered that reporters were working *controversial* to death. Here is only a partial list of what was controversial in the *Times* in a two-week period:

- The suffragist Lucy Stone
- A fumble by Allen Rice of Baylor
- Pet projects of powerful legislators
- A United States stamp honoring St. Francis of Assisi
- A tax-shelter case before the Supreme Court
- Glenn Gould's recording techniques
- The Bendix-Martin Marietta takeover battle
- The Vancouver Canucks' third-period goal

- The second half of the play *Sister Mary Ignatius*
- A proposed assault by Israeli paratroopers
- Banks' alliances with brokerage firms
- The conservative church body Opus Dei
- Osborne Earl Smith, Jr.'s, predecessor as shortstop
- An endorsement by the National Organization for Women
- Johnson/Burgee's A.T. & T. headquarters
- The umpire Larry Barnett's home-run call
- A no-first-user nuclear weapons policy
- The government's reclassification of drugs
- Canada's nationalist energy program
- Linda Ronstadt's "new wave" album

As one *Times* editor put it, "When all those things are 'controversial,' *nothing* is controversial."

BIZBUZZ AS A PERSONAL DANGER

It is clear enough that bizbuzz injures clear communication. Jeanette Gilsdorf, a professor of business communication, did a survey of business people chosen by their executive vice-presidents as being the best communicators in their organizations. All were from Fortune 1,000 industrials. More than half these "best communicators" said that bizbuzz bored them. Nearly eighty percent said that they sometimes did not understand a bizbuzz expression when they heard it. This lack of communication produced by bizbuzz is probably its most dangerous characteristic.

But there is another danger in bizbuzz that you may not recognize until it is too late. Arn Tibbetts discovered it on his first job.

The boss sent one of Arn's early reports back with the phrase *center around* circled in pencil. In a handwritten note the boss said:

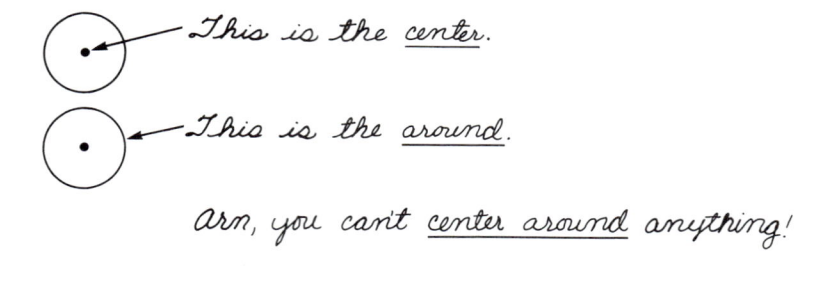

This is the center.

This is the around.

Arn, you can't center around anything!

Another time, Arn used the familiar *and/or* in a memo, and somebody circled the expression and wrote in the margin: "No such word." That memo went through every department in the building. One of the secretaries kindly pointed out to Arn that *and/or* was not considered standard English. This was news to him. *Hint:* In general, don't use the slash mark (/) to make compounds, as in *letter/memo, proposal/report, his/her.*

Laughing is pleasant. But not when people are laughing at you. Since 1949, we three authors have worked in many offices. In every office there was at least one person who enjoyed pointing out, often anonymously, examples of bizbuzz. The bulletin board is a common place for pointing it out.

Right now, to the bulletin board outside our office are tacked a dozen letters, memos, and instructions from various important personages. Each message has a circled word or phrase with !!! next to it, or some satiric comment written in the margin. Next to *hopefully*, for example, from the university president's last message, someone has carefully copied out a quotation from *The Harper Dictionary of Contemporary Usage:*

> Jean Stafford writes: On the back door of my house there is a sign which I had made by a gifted calligrapher. It reads:
>
> THE WORD "HOPEFULLY" MUST NOT
> BE MISUSED ON THESE PREMISES.
> VIOLATORS WILL BE HUMILIATED.

Pinned to a business letter on the same board is a cartoon from the *New Yorker*. It shows a minister marrying two people in church. The caption reads: "I now pronounce you interfaced." When you read the letter, you find *interface* misused three times. And the writer's name is there for all to see.

A GLOSSARY OF USAGE

This glossary is based on good contemporary usage — *standard* usage, as described in this chapter. The major authorities used in compiling the glossary are listed below.

Bernstein, Theodore. *The Careful Writer: A Modern Guide to English Usage.* New York: Atheneum, 1965.
———. *Do's, Don'ts and Maybes of English Usage.* New York: New York Times Books, 1977.
Copperud, Roy H., *American Usage and Style: The Consensus.* New York: Van Nostrand Reinhold, 1980.
Ebbitt, Wilma R., and David R. Ebbitt. *Writer's Guide and Index to English*, 7th ed. Glenview, Illinois: Scott, Foresman, 1982.
Evans, Bergen, and Cornelia Evans. *A Dictionary of Contemporary American Usage.* New York: Random House, 1957.
Follett, Wilson. *Modern American Usage.* New York: Hill and Wang, 1966.
Fowler, H.W. *Modern English Usage*, 2nd ed. New York: Oxford University Press, 1965.

Mellinkoff, David. *Legal Writing: Sense and Nonsense.* New York: Scribner's, 1982.

Morris, William, and Mary Morris. *Harper Dictionary of Contemporary Usage,* 2nd ed. New York: Harper and Row, 1985.

ALOT, A LOT. Use two words: *a lot.*

AD HOC. The phrase means "with respect to this [particular thing]." Commonly used in *ad hoc committee,* one that is created to consider a particular problem or issue.

AFFECT, EFFECT. *Affect,* a verb, means "to influence." *Effect,* as a noun, means "result"; as a verb, "make, cause to happen."

AFORESAID. One of the "worthless old words," according to Mellinkoff. Mellinkoff's list of such ancient legalisms to avoid: *forthwith, hereafter, hereby, herein, hereinafter, heretofore, aforesaid, whereas.*

AMONG, BETWEEN. Use *between* when only two persons or things are involved. Use *among* with three or more.

AMPERSAND (&). Stands for the word *and.* Use *and* unless & is a part of the official name of a company: *Jones, Smith & Wentworth.* Note that & takes no comma before it.

AND/OR. The expression is clumsy and unnecessary; no authority supports its use. Some lawyers believe they need it, but Mellinkoff says *and/or* is not only unnecessary but "it is still confusing readers and costing litigants money. Anything *and/or* can do, ordinary English can do better." Two better choices: use *or* by itself; otherwise use *or . . . or both.*

Examples: (1) You can rent *or* buy property. (2) You can rent *or* buy property, *or both.*

AS, BECAUSE. *As* is a joining word that does many jobs. But *as* does not mean *because* (it does not signal causation in a sentence).

> *Wrong:* I wanted you to address this group *as* you had some experience with the problem.
> *Right:* I wanted you to address this group *because* you had some experience with the problem.

BI, SEMI. These words are generally confusing only when used with time. *Bi* means "two" or "every two," as in *biweekly* (every two weeks). *Semi* means "half of," as in *semimonthly* (twice a month).

But note these usages: *Biannual* (twice during the year) and *biennial* (every other year).

Because so many people are confused by these words, it is best to avoid them. If you mean *every other year,* say so.

CENTER AROUND. As Follett remarks, an expression derived from geometry ought to make geometrical sense. A *center* is in the middle of a circle and cannot be *around* it. Say *center on* or *cluster about* or *group around*, depending on what you mean.

CHAIRMAN, CHAIRPERSON, CHAIRWOMAN, CHAIR. Of these, only *chairperson* is much frowned on in standard English. Like *Ms.*, *chairperson* was in vogue for a time, but seems to be losing out, except in certain academic situations. *Chairman* is the commonest word in the business world; *chair* is safer, though, and fairer to women. (See "Sex and the Language," in Appendix D.)

COMPLEMENT, COMPLIMENT. *Complement* means "to complete." *Compliment* means "to praise."

COMPRISE. The whole *comprises* (takes in) the parts: The Union *comprises* fifty states; fifty states *compose* the union.

CONCEPT. Has become a fadword for *notion, idea, theory, hypothesis, guess,* and so on. Avoid the word, if possible.

CONSENSUS OF OPINION. "Of opinion" is built into the idea of *consensus.* Just say *consensus.*

CONTACT. Careful writers avoid the word for two reasons. First, it implies touching:

> "Tomorrow, I'll *contact* your secretary—"
> "If you do, I'll tell your wife!" (Or husband, as the case may be.)

Second, *contact* is vague. Be specific, and say *call* or *write*.

CONTINUAL, CONTINUOUS. A *continual* action has breaks in it; the action stops occasionally. A *continuous* action has no breaks.

CRITERIA, CRITERION. Fadwords. They are just a fancy way of talking about a standard of some kind, and *standard* has the advantage of being pluralized with an *s*. Too many writers don't know Latin plurals and make themselves look ignorant by writing: "*This* criteria . . ."

DATA, DATUM. For a long time, people have told each other that *data* has a single form. Historically, it doesn't. *Data* can be singular or plural. In most instances, you'll be safer to avoid *data* and use *evidence, figures,* and so on.

DIFFERENT FROM, DIFFERENT THAN. The accepted usage is *different from*.

DISINTERESTED, UNINTERESTED. To be *disinterested* is to be impartial. To be *uninterested* is to be without interest.

E.G. Means *exempli gratia,* Latin for *for example.* Use the English phrase.
ENTHUSED. Nonstandard. Write *enthusiastic*.
EXPERTISE. A fadword. Use *expertness*.
E.T. Means "extraterrestrial."

FIRST, FIRSTLY. The *-ly* forms are unnecessary here. Use *first, second, third*— not *firstly, secondly, thirdly*.

FORMER, LATTER. Avoid these when you can. They force a reader to go back and reread to see which item is the former and which the latter.

FORWARD, SEND. When you start something on its way, you *send* it. When someone starts (sends) it, and you readdress or re-direct it, that is *forwarding*.

HE/SHE. See "Sex and the Language," in Appendix D.

HEREIN, HEREWITH. Legal jargon — avoid them.

> *Not this:* We are enclosing *herewith* a response to your request.
> *But this:* Here is a response to your request.

HOPEFULLY. When used as the first word in sentence, or to mean "It is to be hoped that . . ." it is incorrect grammar as well as a fadword.

> *Not this:* *Hopefully*, the newspaper will present our views on the subject.
> *But this:* *I hope* (or *we hope* or *the company hopes,* or *the engineering division hopes*) that the newspaper will present our views on the subject. (Make *somebody* do the hoping.)

I.E. Means *id est*, Latin for *that is.* Use the English phrase.

IMPACT. May be used as a noun: What *impact* will the new tax have on the economy? *Impact* may not be used as a verb: The tax will *impact* our economy. (Here the correct word is *affect*.)

INFER, IMPLY. If you say something indirectly, you are *implying* it. Your reader or listener, if alert, *infers* what you are implying. The words are direct opposites in meaning.

IN TERMS OF. Very clumsy, sometimes misleading: don't use.

> *Not this:* I'll see you *in terms of* next Thursday.
> *But this:* I'll see you next Thursday.
> *Not this:* *In terms* of radio advertising, our ad campaign was successful.
> *But this:* Our ad campaign was successful on radio.

INSURE, ENSURE. The usage panel of *The Harper Dictionary of Contemporary Usage* voted sixty-two to thirty-eight percent to support this distinction:

Ensure — "to make sure or certain."

Insure — "to guarantee against financial loss."

This is a reasonable distinction, but we wonder whether it might not be simpler to avoid *ensure* altogether:

> *Not this:* The court's decision will *ensure* the protection of voters' rights.

But this: The court's decision will require that the voters' rights be protected [if that is what the writer means].

    Ensure has a stiff, formal ring.
INTERFACE. Unless it is used to describe a physical plane between two surfaces, *interface* is bizbuzz.
IRREGARDLESS. Nonstandard. Use *regardless*.
ITS, IT'S. *Its* is a possessive pronoun. *It's* is a contraction for *it is*.

LEND, LOAN. *Lend* is a verb: I *lend* you money. *Loan* is what is lent (the money).
LESS, FEWER. In general, *fewer* applies to countables, *less* to things in masses: *fewer* dollars, *less* money; *fewer* particles, *less* energy; *fewer* widgets, *less* inventory. Note that *less* likes to attach itself to abstractions.
LITERALLY. Means the opposite of *figuratively*, and it should ordinarily be used only when you are telling your readers that they should not take your statement as metaphorical. If your friend is hanging out the third floor window — desperately hanging on by the ends of his fingers — you might shout: "Sam is literally hanging on by his fingernails!" But if you say, as Walter Cronkite did on national television: "New York is literally hanging on by its fingernails," then you have said something silly indeed. *Literally* does not mean *very:*

Not this: I am *literally* worn out.
But this: I am very tired.

MEDIA, MEDIUM. The words are bizbuzz when used for newspapers, magazines, TV, journalists, and so on.

Not this: The *media* are unfair to business.
But this: Some journalists are unfair to business.

    Medium is singular; *media* is plural. You can't say, "The *media* is attacking the president."
MS., MISS, MRS. See "Sex and the Language," in Appendix D.

ORAL, VERBAL. *Oral* refers to speech. *Verbal* refers to anything communicated in words. An oral agreement is verbal by definition; a verbal agreement can be oral or written. A clear distinction can be made between an *oral* (spoken) *agreement* and a *written* one (put on paper).
ORIENT, ORIENTATE. *Orientate* is nonstandard. (It is also British usage.)

PARTY. Sometimes used by lawyers to mean *person*, but Mellinkoff says that even that usage is unnecessary. Use *party* only to mean a group of people who are having fun, as in *office party*.
PER. Latin for "through." The word is hardly ever necessary, except in some formulas: *per capita, per diem*.

These usages are bizbuzz:

Per your request, here is the evaluation.
As per our agreement, I am sending a revision of the plans.

PERCENT, PERCENTAGE. Both of these are written as one word. If numbers are written out, use *percent: Seven percent.* If not written out, use the percent symbol (%): *38%. Percentage* indicates a generality: A large *percentage* of the employees attended his last rites.

PERSONNEL. Avoid this inhumane word except in formulas like *personnel office.* Refer to human beings as *persons* or *people.*

PRINCIPAL, PRINCIPLE. A *principal* thing is the main thing. A *principle* is a law or rule.

QUALITY. A fadword. Avoid it where possible. Except in formulas like *quality control*, never use it as an adjective. People are so accustomed to its being used dishonestly that if you say you have a *quality product*, they will automatically assume you are varnishing the truth.

RE, IN RE. Legalese. Don't use.
REGARDS, AS REGARDS, IN REGARD TO. Trite. Avoid if you can.

SAME. Should not be used as a pronoun in this way: "I received your suggestion and implemented *same.*"

SHALL, WILL. In modern English, there is no sharp distinction between these words. *Shall* sounds a little more formal. *I shall return*, said pompous General Douglas MacArthur as he left Corregidor. And he had a battery of photographers recording his return some time later. A man of more modest tastes might have said: "I will return," and have done it under cover of darkness.

SIMPLISTIC. A fadword. Use *simple* or *oversimplified.*

UNIQUE. Means "one of a kind." You cannot be *one-er* than one, so you can't write *more unique* or *most unique.*

UTILIZE. Bizbuzz for *use* (verb).

VIA. Bizbuzz for *by.* "Send it *by* (not *via*) plane."

EXERCISES

1. In your library, spend a few minutes reading *The Wall Street Journal.* Write down any examples of bizbuzz you find. Now spend a few minutes reading any academic professional quarterly in a business field—for exam-

Words — and the Problem of Bizbuzz   117

ple, a journal in economics in which professors publish the results of their research. Again, write down any examples of bizbuzz. What do you conclude from this exercise?

2. Rewrite each sentence below. Don't worry much about whether your rewrite changes the meaning. In fact, you may make up a meaning if you want to. In each case, try to write a new sentence that is interesting, reasonably specific, and human. Some rewrites may require two sentences, even three.

    a. We should be, hopefully, ready for an explain session on the parameters of the problem with financing.

    b. Cost-effective interpretations of the housing code are excessively judgmental.

    c. First and foremost, take time to orientate yourself to the situation before acting.

    d. It is vital that we develop a more clear concept of company resource utilization.

    e. We are on the cutting edge of the new technology, but the many and varied orchestrations of the funding problem require us to inspect the ballpark figures on production again.

    f. Before we continue on with this controversial aspect of negotiations, let's join together on a possible vote to obviate the necessity of more meetings futurewise.

    g. This multifaceted issue warrants further investigation because now there is a complete absence of general consensus on plant expansion.

    h. Your idea is simplistic, vague, fuzzy, and completely ignores the new avenues that are now being explored in media advertising.

    i. When a CEO can no longer continue on facing the true facts of failure, suicide is a viable option. (Check *viable* in your dictionary.)

    j. Try to see Ms. Kender and/or Mr. Wright, and contact the head of the secretarial pool for criteria information on who can use the dictating machines mornings.

    k. I am enthused about your proposal and hope you will forward your expertise to the committee chair; e.g., to Joan Isaacs, who is acting chair this year.

    l. On Friday, please interface with the Parts Department on the problem of why they aren't ordering more brake release units. The boss literally went up in flames over the lack of unit availability. He had made a verbal agreement with Division that this sort of quality breakdown in availability would never happen again.

    m. Utilize!

3. Discuss the bizbuzz in the following letter. The letter was sent to all the people (many of them from business and industry) attending the Charter House Conference sponsored by the Samson Foundation. Why did many of these people treat the letter with contempt and make jokes about it?

Dear Mr. Jameson:

We were pleased to learn from A. R. Wilson that you will participate in the conference on *Writing in America,* to be held April 11–13 in Sacramento, California.

The Samson Foundation is privileged to be your host for this conference. Over a year in planning, this Sacramento conference comes at a time when the initial reactions of alarm to the discovery of falling test scores on standardized writing examinations have abated, and thoughtfully seasoned, long-range responses are coming to the fore. The draft report of the Commission on Writing, to be read and discussed in Sacramento, is partial evidence that the current movement to improve the teaching of writing is maturing.

The cessation of crisis stories in the media and the realization that crash programs will not bring about quick cures do not mean that the problems inherent in improving the general level of writing have been solved. Nor is there evidence that the sharply divided opinions among authorities over the best methods to achieve this end have been resolved.

It is precisely because so many problems remain, and because approaches to date have seemed consistently unable to meet the realities and varieties of the situations in which teaching and learning take place, that the Samson Foundation continues to give priority to this vital educational matter.

It is hoped that the critical examination and open discussion at Sacramento will help focus the ongoing general discussion of the writing problem and sharpen the arguments on all sides of the debate.

Charter House, which will be your working home for the period of the conference, was designed by A. MacLean Hill and serves as a secluded, informal setting for creative thought and free discussion.

We look forward to greeting you at Charter House, and trust that your time here will be both productive and enjoyable.

Cordially yours,

John Smith
Vice President — Program,
Samson Foundation

4. Gerald Grow, authority on business writing, designed ten steps for creating bizbuzz out of normal English. Here they are:

1. *Start with a simple statement:* We quit. Why? Nobody knew how to program the computer.
2. *Put it in the passive voice, and dilute the responsibility:* It was decided to quit.
3. *Expand with terminology that does not add meaning:* It was decided to terminate.
4. *Build in noun strings:* It was decided to terminate project processes.
5. *Add a qualifier of uncertain relation to the original statement:* On account of the status of the computer, it was decided to terminate project processes.

6. *Add noun strings and terminology to the qualifier:* On account of the status of the computer program assessment planning development effort, it was decided to terminate project processes.
7. *Separate related words:* On account of the status of the computer program assessment planning development effort, it was decided to terminate until a later date project processes.
8. *Equivocate:* On account of the uncertain status of the computer program assessment planning development effort, it was proposed and tentatively accepted to terminate until a later date project processes.
9. *Obfuscate:* Due to uncertainties in the status of the computer program assessment planning development effort, proposals were carefully considered and tentatively adopted to suspend temporarily until a later date project processes.
10. *Cover your tracks, make yourself look good:* Due to unavoidable uncertainties in the status of the computer program assessment planning development effort, a number of contingency proposals were carefully considered and one was tentatively adopted to suspend on a temporary basis until a later date those project processes deemed unessential to the expeditious fulfillment of contract requirements.

Use Grow's ten steps to create bizbuzz out of these ordinary statements:
    a. After his company went broke, the president resigned.
    b. My car won't run. The carburetor needs adjusting.
    c. I like Spanish. It is an easy language to learn.
    d. *The Return of the Jedi* made back its production costs almost overnight.

CHAPTER 7

Style: Make Your Writing Readable

Americans first became interested in readability shortly after World War II. That interest has been growing fast, and it is now one of the major forces in communication. Hundreds of books and articles have been written on ways to make a message more readable. Many states have passed readability laws. If you go to work for a company that does interstate work, you may have to comply with the readability laws of one or more states. Some states require that a readability formula be applied to certain documents. The formulas work pretty well, but scholars are not generally in favor of them as tools to teach readable writing. The formulas tell you something about the product (your writing) but not much about the process (how you did it). And you should know the process, which is outlined in this chapter.

New York's law goes back to 1978. By 1983 it was pronounced a success. It has caused almost no litigation, and the cost of compliance has been low. Most of those people who were originally against the plain English laws, as they are often called, have changed their minds and now approve of them.

Why? Because they are practical, and because plain, readable English works — for everybody. When all the people involved (buyer, seller, client, supervisor, worker) understand what is being said in a message, everybody benefits. Time is not wasted. Disagreements and foulups tend to disappear. Work goes more smoothly.

In this chapter, we are going to let you in on the secrets of being a readable writer and give you some rules for becoming one. The discussion will not be difficult, but you will have to pay attention. When we are through, you will

Style: Make Your Writing Readable   121

know almost as much about readability as the experts. Of course, you will need practice in writing readably, but that is no problem. Here and there in the chapter we will supply some exercises. Be sure to do them carefully.

WRITE WHO DOES WHAT

Remember Suggestion Ten, in the Overview? Think Action — then write Who Does What!

This is a major strategy in readable writing. Practically speaking, it means that you use *action* statements.

- Sam hates fried eggs.
- Louise stopped dictating.
- The company made money.
- The new model broke down.
- Let's buy new equipment.

Look at every underlined word we just used: hates, stopped, made, broke, and buy.

Put such action words into every sentence that you can. Examine the situation carefully, find the actions in it, and then write action sentences.

Don't write: The bill was paid by Ms. Ardrey. (*What* is done by *whom*)
Do write: Ms. Ardrey *paid* the bill. (*Who* does *what*)

The first sentence is technically a *passive* construction. It tells you what is done by whom. Passives waste words. And they are often vague: "The bill was paid." (But who did it?) For some reason (no one really understands why), the *passive* attracts jargon and gobbledygook as a magnet attracts iron filings:

Passive: Verdict information in the matter of Lenz vs. Galway was promulgated in written form.
Who does what: In Lenz vs. Galway, the judge gave his verdict in writing.

Here is how you write *who does what* sentences:

1. Find the *doer(s)* of the action. Write it down: The *employees*
2. Use an *action* word (a verb): *demanded*
3. Write down the *what* (finish the sentence): The employees demanded *more benefits.*

More examples:

Who	Does	What
You	should take	more time with that report.
Many people	will read	the report.
What you say	involves	everyone in the company.

Who	*Does*	*What*
Management	has lost	its credibility.
No one	believes	our managers any more.

To show you how valuable *who does what* is, let's work backwards, avoid action, and write typically unreadable sentences. We will use the ideas in the five sentences just quoted:

- More time with that report should be taken. (*By whom?*)
- The report will be read by many people. (*Twenty-five percent wordier — typical of passives*)
- Everyone in the company will be involved by what you say. (*Ditto*)
- The credibility of management has been lost. (*Vague — who lost it?*)
- They are not believed any more. (*Not believed by whom?*)

You can see why the pattern of *who does what* is valuable to you. It not only saves words, it also tells your readers what the action is and assigns a responsibility for the action.

Don't write: The memo was intended for Ms. Barker.
Do write: I addressed the memo to Ms. Barker.
Or: I wrote the memo for Ms. Barker.
Or: I intended the memo to go to Ms. Barker.
Or: I wanted Ms. Barker to read the memo.

As you can see, there are many possibilities when you write *who does what*. Just decide on what you want to say, and then say it.

WHO IS WHAT?

Sometimes you can't write *who does what* because the logic of the situation won't allow it. This often happens when you must identify or describe something. In such a case, use the *who is what* pattern:

Jack is the one you want.
Marie will be your agent.
This is Mr. Parkway, the new assistant.
I am the former assistant.
That was a very good job.
The new design will be a disaster.

In the last two sentences, did you notice that the *who*'s are *what*'s? — that and *design*. No problem here. If the situation calls for them, you can easily write:

What does what (action statement), and
What is what (description statement).

Style: Make Your Writing Readable

Now you know the strong basic patterns of a readable style. They are:

| First choice | Who does what | (or, What does what) |
| Second choice | Who is what | (or, What is what) |

The most readable writing uses these patterns from eighty to ninety percent of the time. They are basic in the grammar of the English language.

EXERCISES

Using what you have learned so far, improve each of the sentences below. Try to start each sentence with a definite *who* or *what*.

1. It is specific and concrete that you want your writing to be.
2. The meeting was organized by Smith.
3. There are three arrangements to be made in working out an agreement with the officers of the corporation.
4. The motion to table the question was presented by Mr. Kelin.
5. On February 25, there was an inquiry made by you about our experience with Mr. Caluder.
6. We were confused by the computer manual.
7. We were told by the instructions in the manual to "delete."
8. It is necessary for you to use your imagination to rewrite these sentences.
9. The efficiency in the office was created by Wendell's hard work.
10. It is a possibility that these sentences may give you trouble.
11. The hiring of two full-time lab assistants was suggested by me.
12. There is a writing technique that you can use to make these sentences more clear and readable. The method requires a knowledge of sentence structures. (Make these two sentences one.)
13. Part-time assistants were wanted by the vice-president of the department.
14. There is discomfort regarding room temperature among your office workers.
15. It is a possibility that their discomfort is caused by excessive dryness of the air.
16. An hour of preparation is saved by use of Sarkon cutters.
17. It was felt that the cassette projector should be used by you in the presentation.
18. There is an enclosure with the report giving more data on your problem.
19. The specifications should be sent as soon as possible.

20. There is a definite usefulness in the XM MemoryWriter.
21. It's a definite truth that the MemoryWriter produces more words a minute than another machine.
22. New equipment has been requisitioned by the company.
23. After the job was finished, a bill was submitted.
24. There's a monotony-avoiding technique in using *action* statements.

YOU SAY YOU DRANK A MOUSE?

Once a semester, we draw the blinds in our classroom, turn on the projector, and project a few words on a screen. We project the words one at a time until a phrase or sentence is finished. After each word is added, we wait a second and quickly turn off the machine. Then we ask students to write what the phrase means so far and what they think it will say next.

Our favorite phrase for this exercise is one that we will now give you word by word, along with some of the students' reactions. The first word:

Drinking

The students respond:

"It tells us something about alcohol."
"Drinking is bad."
"Drinking is expensive."
"Drinking is dangerous to your health."

Now we add a word:

Drinking mice

(Remember that the words are flashed on the screen for only a second.) Laughter, followed by:

"What? What did that say?"
"Are *mice* drinking?"
"No, I read it *mousse*. Somebody is drinking mousse, that soft ice cream stuff."
"I know what, they're putting mice in a blender, grinding them all up, and then *drinking* them!"
"That's crazy — yuck!"

The exercise goes on:

Drinking mice slow

"No, I wasn't crazy; they are drinking mice *slow!*"
"Hey, are you putting us on?"

Style: Make Your Writing Readable 125

The sentence grows:

Drinking mice slow to mature

"Oh, now it makes sense . . . drinking mice don't mature as fast as mice that don't drink."
"But drinking *what?* It doesn't say what the mice are drinking."

Now we throw the last word on the screen:

Drinking mice slow to mature sexually.

"Well, I'm glad I'm not a mouse."
"You played a trick on us. That's not a sentence."

A READABLE SENTENCE PREDICTS

The words we threw on the screen appeared as a headline in a major newspaper. And headlines, like sentences, must predict in order to make sense, as they move horizontally across the page.

Every sentence has *motion* — that is, you read it from left to right:

In addition, every sentence you read or write is imprisoned in this small space. You can't move the words out of the space — say, put them in the four corners of the page. You have to read them in the order you see them, from left to right:

Drinking mice [are] slow to mature sexually.

Your brain — that computer inside your head — understands such a sentence because the parts of it *predict*. You can best understand prediction by looking at simple sentences that have missing words:

The _____ said something _____ when she hit her _____ with a _____ .
A man _____ us that he _____ that job.

Owing to the laws of prediction, there are only so many words that you can put in the empty spaces. For example:

The *woman* said something *angry* when she hit her *thumb* with a hammer.
A man *told* us that he *wanted* that job.

Of course, you could put other words in the spaces. But the point is that there are millions of words, phrases, clauses, and combinations you could *not* put in the spaces because they would violate the rules of prediction. In the first sentence above, for example, you could not put these words in the empty spaces:

> The *how do you like that* said something *participle of* when she hit *bitter gasoline* with a *management by objective.*

The word *the* predicts a noun:

the *cat*   the *manager*   the *speech*

The three phrases just given predict verbs:

The cat *meows.*
The manager *wants* (something).
The speech *was* (boring).

So, as you read a sentence from left to right, your brain is continuously predicting:

Predict . . . predict . . . predict . . . predict. . . .

The Most Important Prediction

For both writer and reader, the most important prediction is usually at the beginning of the sentence. A writer starting a sentence is rather like runners of a race when the gun sounds. If runners get a poor start they may stumble, and for ten yards or so may not really regain their footing. If you start your sentence in a stumble, you may never regain your verbal footing — until you start another sentence.

Now we discover a major reason that the *who does what* pattern works so well. It forces you to start your race through the sentence strongly; it requires you to predict clearly where your sentence is going.

The sentences below started wrong. They predict poorly:

- Functional microspace implies the . . .
- Symptomatology relative to . . .
- A conceptual relationship as a means to an end is . . .

Prediction occurs throughout a typical sentence until near its end. But the most important predictions usually take place in the first few words.

Bad prediction: Behavior problems act out . . .
Better prediction: When people behave badly, . . .
Bad prediction: Isolation stigmatizes . . .
Better prediction: Lonely people need . . .

Always start a sentence with the most specific subject and verb you can find. This will help your sentence to be predictable.

USE PARALLEL STRUCTURES FORCEFULLY

Parallelism refers to a listing of sentence elements. Parallel elements will be (1) roughly equal in importance or emphasis, and (2) written in the same form. Such elements can be anything from single words to full sentences:

- Short elements:
  planning and *working*
  sale or *purchase*
- Longer elements:
  planning for the sale and *working for profits*
  the sale of material or *the purchase of services*
- Full sentences using parallelism:
  I expect to plan for the sale, and *I will work for the profits.*
  I will think; I will organize; I will succeed.

Parallelism allows you to state ideas *quickly* and *economically* (the italicized words are their own example). In addition, it gives your prose a pleasant strength and musical rhythm. Many memorable sentences depend on the balance that parallelism encourages. Here are four examples, with the parallel items italicized:

Four score and seven years ago our fathers brought forth upon this continent a new nation, *conceived in liberty* and *dedicated to the proposition* that all men are created equal.
— Abraham Lincoln

Complexity and obscurity have professional value — they are the academic equivalents of apprenticeship rules in the building trades. They *exclude the outsiders, keep down the competition, preserve the image of a privileged or priestly class.*
— John Kenneth Galbraith

The secret thoughts of a man run over all things, *holy, profane, clean, obscene, grave,* and *light,* without *shame* or *blame.*
— Thomas Hobbes

Economics is an important subject. Economics can also be an exciting subject. How could it be otherwise, when it deals with the great issues of *unemployment* and *inflation, poverty* and *wealth,* and *possible exhaustion of material growth?* ... For we have in political economy not a *finished, embalmed* corpus of conventional wisdom — but rather materials for the great debate on *revolution, liberty, efficiency,* and *the endless quest for the good society.*
—Paul Samuelson

A writer can't stress parallelism too much, for it is a fundamental structure in the English language. In her computer study of parallelisms, Professor Mary Hiatt discovered that more than fifty percent of the sentences in her large sample of sentences employed them. Rather more than fifty percent, probably; her computer could not be programmed to catch them all.

Sometimes you will have to go back to the front of a sentence in order to make it more predictable *and* parallel:

> Bad: The quality of a business exists in relation to its people, its capital as well as the markets involved.

The problem begins with the subject and verb. What can the reader make of *quality exists?* Having stumbled over these words of his own, the writer fell flat, and so did the reader. So we fix the front of the sentence and nail down the parallelism:

> Better: A business is only as good as its *people, capital,* and *markets.*

Parallelism and Predictability

Parallelism works partly by being predictable. Suppose a sentence begins:

> The material included cloth, ____¹, ____², and ____³.

The reader will predict nouns in spaces 1, 2, and 3 because *cloth* is a noun. Another example:

> Those items should be wrapped properly and ____ on a conveyor belt.

Here the reader will expect a verb (like *placed*) because *wrapped* predicts a verb in the space.

USE STRONG SIGNAL WORDS

These are signal words:

when   because   also   but

We call these words *signals* because, like traffic lights, they give you a powerful warning of what is to come. Just as a flashing yellow traffic light signals something (*caution*), a word like *because* in a sentence signals something (a cause-effect explanation is coming).

A sentence signal is a type of prediction, and the more strongly it predicts the more useful it is. Below are phrases with typical signal words; note that they start a sentence and help to predict what the sentence is going to say:

Because credit is linked to a person's credibility . . .
When you refuse credit . . .
After giving credit . . .
But a bad credit risk can become . . .
If you must report unfavorable credit information . . .
Therefore, always be careful . . .
Yet there are cases in which you should . . .

To repeat: Signals usually start a sentence. Your reader must see them early or, like a red stoplight seen too late, they will be ineffective.

Perhaps the strongest short signals are words like *thus, yet, so,* and *but.* The great playwright George Bernard Shaw said that *but* is "the most important conjunction in the English language." Whether accurate or not, his remark shows how respectful the good writer is of signals and their power to predict.

Here is an incomplete list of the most common signals (there are many more available). Some of them, as you see, use more than one word to make up the signal.

- but
- and
- now
- so
- consequently
- when
- also
- for example
- first, second, third
- while
- then
- however
- because
- indeed
- before
- finally
- in fact
- still
- on the other hand
- during
- yet
- since
- as a result
- therefore
- thus
- after
- like
- unlike
- by contrast
- by

It is nearly impossible to overwork signals like these!

CHUNK YOUR SENTENCES

About forty-five years ago, David Ogilvy arrived in the United States from England with ten dollars in his pocket. By 1960, he was running an ad agency doing fifty-five million dollars' worth of business a year. He wrote a fascinating book about his experiences: *Confessions of an Advertising Man.* It was a national best seller for five months — an extraordinary run for a book with supposedly limited appeal.

We can learn a good deal about writing from Ogilvy, for his technique as a craftsman in words applies to every kind of business writing. Let's look at a typical Ogilvy paragraph:

> How long should your copy be? It depends on the product. If you are advertising chewing gum, there isn't much to tell, so make your copy short. If, on the other hand, you are advertising a product which has a great many different qualities to recommend it, write long copy: the more you tell, the more you sell.

One reason this is effective is that Ogilvy breaks his sentences into easily digested *chunks* (note punctuation):

> $\overset{1}{\text{If,}}$ $\overset{2}{\text{on the other hand,}}$ $\overset{3}{\text{you are advertising a product which has a great many different qualities to recommend it,}}$ $\overset{4}{\text{write long copy:}}$ $\overset{5}{\text{the more you tell,}}$ $\overset{6}{\text{the more you sell.}}$

A heavy-line diagram will dramatize the separation of Ogilvy's sentence chunks. Note punctuation, which tells you where the chunks start and stop:

```
chunk 1      chunk 2                          chunk 3
────────, ──────────,    ──────────────────────────────────,
  chunk 4       chunk 5        chunk 6
────────── : ──────────, ──────────.
```

Why is it so important for you to chunk your sentences?

First, we all read better (more efficiently) if sentences are broken into pieces that we can assimilate. The brain can assimilate only so much at a time. This sentence is hard to assimilate:

> (a) The readability of a sentence depends in most contexts and conditions upon its handling of syntax and word choice.

We must try to swallow that sentence in one big chunk. But suppose we rewrite and break the sentence into smaller chunks:

> (b) Usually, a sentence is readable for two reasons: good word choice and clear syntax.

When you diagram them, the contrast between these two sentences is dramatic (note the punctuation):

```
(a)              all one chunk
    ──────────────────────────────────────────.

(b)    chunk 1        chunk 2          chunk 3
     ────────, ────────────── : ──────────.
```

Sentence (b) is more readable: Your readers can assimilate it one chunk at a time.

Chunking is useful in yet another way. It allows for, and encourages, prediction. As readers move from left to right through a sentence, they are, of course, trying to predict what is coming:

? ⟶ ? ⟶ ? ⟶ ? ⟶

But a long sentence of one chunk is often weak in prediction. By contrast, chunked sentences usually predict much better, partly because the punctuation marks themselves tell your readers where the idea-chunks start and stop. Example:

_____ , _____ ; _____ .

If you avoid jargon while using chunks, you have an even better chance of writing readably. Sentence (a) below uses jargon and is written in one chunk:

(a) Failure to affix a signature to the form will result in disallowance of the claim.

Sentence (b), on the same subject, avoids jargon, and uses two chunks:

(b) If you don't sign the form, we will disallow the claim.

Using simple words and chunking go together.

THE CHUNK AS OPENER

An opener is a useful type of sentence chunk. It has these characteristics:

1. It starts the sentence, so it is the first thing your reader sees.
2. It often employs signals.
3. Because of points 1 and 2, it is high in prediction.
4. It is often used as a transition from the previous sentence or idea.
5. It cannot stand alone as a statement (it is incomplete).
6. It is usually set off by a comma.

Here are examples of opening chunks *(in italics)*. The signals are in capital letters.

1. *WHEN you see the results,* you will agree that the campaign was a success.
2. *ALTHOUGH we received your order last week,* we cannot fill it until Wednesday, April 4.

3. *BECAUSE we do not carry the Onion brand,* I am returning your request by special delivery.

When you inspect these opening chunks, you will see that:

- None of them can stand by itself as a statement.
- Each uses a signal, which predicts.
- Each is the first thing the reader sees in the sentence, and so tends to predict an idea coming up.
- Opener 3 supplies a transition from a previous idea or sentence.

Note: A good many openers do not have signals:

- *Adding up the figures,* she came to the conclusion ...
- *In their first years of profits,* the managers decided ...
- *With a good year under their belts,* they began to plan ...
- *In good economic days and bad,* the nation has always ...

The pattern of the opening chunk can be diagrammed as follows:

<u>opening chunk</u> , <u>second chunk</u> .

Research shows that this pattern is one of the most-used in readable prose. (By contrast, unreadable prose uses it little.) The opener is a regular workhorse: It predicts, chunks, and supplies transitions — all at the same time.

Combine the opener with a signal, and you have one of the best devices known for writing clearly.

VARY THE LENGTH OF YOUR SENTENCES

A major unit in writing, of course, is the sentence itself, which runs from capital letter (Cap) to period:

Cap _____ .

We readers don't like sentences to be of the same length. We are bored by them. We want variety and change. After a sentence of ten words, we don't want a second of nine words, followed by a third of eleven words. The pattern of similar lengths is boring:

Cap _____ . Cap _____ . Cap _____ .

Rather, readers prefer sentences like the last six we just wrote:

                        18 words
Cap _____ .

Style: Make Your Writing Readable

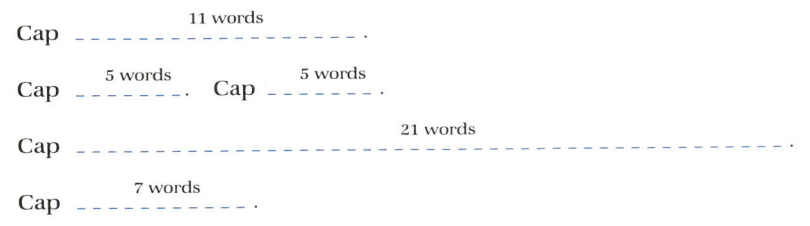

```
        11 words
Cap _____ .

     5 words           5 words
Cap _____ .  Cap _____ .

                          21 words
Cap _____ .

     7 words
Cap _____ .
```

Professional writers know how important variety is, and they apply the principle vigorously. (If they fail to apply it, they won't stay professional very long.) Consider this paragraph from *Fortune* magazine:

> Whenever an upturn is in prospect for the automobile industry, observers get bullish on the companies that supply it with parts. This time is no exception. The standard analysis goes as follows. The suppliers have closed outmoded facilities and pruned payrolls. They've pushed breakevens down so far that they're profitable operating far below capacity. When new-car sales turn up, a large portion of the additional revenues will go right to the bottom line. Maybe. But perhaps you shouldn't stop at your broker's on the way to the dealership to buy that new car.

You will find such variety in sentence lengths in almost every piece of writing that succeeds, and not just in journalistic prose. Consider this short paragraph from the *Harvard Business Review*. Note the effect of the short four-word sentence at the end, coming as it does after two fairly long sentences of roughly equal length:

> Many companies are undertaking oral interviews with significant people, conducted by an expert who asks focused and probing questions. Perhaps more important, however, is the development of ongoing methods of recording and preserving important facts. Historians can help here.

That last short sentence provides *relief*— which is spelled v-a-r-i-e-t-y!

FIGHT NOUNOPHILIA — *Kill a Noun Today*

Nounophilia is a common writer's disease. A nounophiliac is a noun-lover, a writer who loves to string together abstract nouns like these:

- ramification potentials
- resource use
- attitude myopia

A nounophiliac would call Satan a *devil figure religion representative*, a plan a *consequence determination*, and the chapter you are now reading a *readability utilization study unit*.

No one knows exactly why strings of nouns are dangerous, but they are. Kill them when you can. Cut them out ruthlessly. If you allow too many of them in a sentence, they will multiply like rabbits, both as plain nouns and verbal nouns. They will also invite in their best friend, the putrid preposition. When this happens, you get a ghastly sentence like the following, written in a sales brochure. It has ten nouns and five prepositions; the nouns are in caps and the prepositions are in italics.

> English TEACHERS agree that personal OWNERSHIP and USE *of* a good DICTIONARY is a prime NECESSITY *for* every STUDENT *in* OBTAINING the maximum RESULTS *from* the STUDY *of* ENGLISH.

With a simple rewrite, you can cut the nouns from ten to three, the prepositions from five to zero:

> English TEACHERS agree that a STUDENT should own and use a good desk DICTIONARY.

Whenever you feel an attack of nounophilia coming on, read the passage by Bruce Price below, and take two aspirins.

> Have you noticed the new look in the English language? Everybody's using nouns as adjectives. Or to put that in the current argot, there's a modifier noun proliferation. More exactly, since the matter is getting out of hand, a modifier noun proliferation increase. In fact, every time I open a magazine these days or listen to the radio, I am struck by the modifier noun proliferation increase phenomenon. So, I decided to write — you guessed it — a modifier noun proliferation increase phenomenon article....
>
> Abstraction is the enemy both of clear expression and easy understanding. And abstract is what these strings of nouns become. And very quickly the reader or listener doesn't know what the actual relationship is. Take "Reality Therapy," the name of a new book. Do you gather that the author uses reality as a means of therapy or that the goal of his treatment is facing reality or that he has worked out some sort of therapy which he applies to reality? Take a phrase puzzled over in *Newsweek:* "antenna television systems operation." Manufacture? broadcasting? consulting? The article said that somebody was going into that field and I still don't know where he's going. I suspect that the people who turn out these phrases might insist that they are seeking greater precision, as though each new noun pinned down the matter a bit more. Wrong. Another article like this one and we'll have a modifier noun proliferation increase phenomenon article protest campaign, but will you know what you've got?

USE PERSONAL PRONOUNS *(particularly* I, You, We*)*

To gain a readable style, you need to get nouns out of your sentences and action into them.

A good way to do this is to personalize your writing by placing you and your reader firmly into the message. Use pronouns and talk directly to your reader. This can easily be done in many memos, letters, explanations, and directions.

Here is a badly written message:

> The top portion of the statement will be used to mechanically process the payment to the user's account and its enclosure in the envelope supplied with the bill will aid in the accurate crediting of the user's account.

If you throw the sentence into action and use pronouns, you will write a clearer message — and a more human one:

> *We* will use the top portion of *your* statement to mechanically process *your* payment to *your* account. If *you* enclose *it* in the envelope that *we* supplied with the bill, *we* will be better able to credit *your* account accurately.

WRITE AS YOU SPEAK . . .
. . . *when you are speaking very well*

One significant fact about communicating we often forget is that we human beings have been writing for only a few thousand years. We have been speaking and listening for a million years, give or take a few weeks.

Our mouths, tongues, and breathing systems are all designed to produce speech. Our brains are designed to listen to speech.

Reading and writing are very late developments in human life. No part of us is designed specifically for the work of reading and writing. So it is unsurprising that writing works best when it fits human animals as they are, not as we might wish them to be. Writing works best when it fits the sounds and rhythms of speaking and listening. Perhaps that is why when we reject one expression for another as we write, we often say: "Oh, the first one didn't *sound* right."

Write as you speak — when you are speaking very well — because you will then write more clearly and humanly. And people will understand you better.

They will also like you better, because people hate the excessively formal, bloated jargon of bizbuzz, most of which cannot be spoken easily without twisting the tongue or huffing and puffing. Indeed, an excellent test for readable writing is: *Can you read it aloud easily?* Does it "breathe" well? (Can you find places between sentence chunks to take a breath?)

John DiGaetani teaches communication at Harvard Business School. In an article printed in the *Wall Street Journal*, DiGaetani proposes the following conversational test in business writing: "Imagine yourself speaking to the person instead of writing."

TECHNIQUES FOR REVISION

On one point about revision the research is very clear. Changing anything in a sentence changes the meaning — perhaps a little, perhaps a lot. The language is not like a brick wall, where it is possible to chip out a red brick and replace it with a white brick of similar size. There are no perfect synonyms in English. Replace one word with another, and you have a different communication. How much different depends on the words involved. Cut one word from a sentence — like the word *not*, for example — and you may change an idea one hundred percent:

> She is not the person we want.
> She is the person we want.

As you read the rest of this chapter, don't worry about "changing" meanings. Instead, think about making statements clearer and easier to understand. After all, in your own writing, you will be in control of meanings, and with practice in revising you will be able to express them accurately and attractively.

It might be added that there are people who are so smart they don't have to revise. As Mark Twain said of such people, they are not ordinary mortals and cannot be trusted. Anyhow, this chapter is not written for them.

Read Your Message Aloud

Read your message aloud is excellent advice. Your voice and ear will catch mistakes your eye will pass right over, particularly if the material is very familiar. But don't read or speak a message over and over; you will just memorize it, mistakes and all. Write it; let it cool off, preferably overnight. Then read it aloud, and listen carefully.

Business people sometimes tell us they don't have the time for this. We always ask them: "Do you have the time to save yourself a good deal of money? The evidence is that millions of dollars are wasted every year in messages that don't work. Take a little extra time, and you will save far more money in successful messages than you lose in time."

Translate Any Abstractions

By *translating* an abstraction, we mean put it into normal, plain, specific English. Examples:

Abstract:	The new Glitter 8 is a *road-plausible* car.
Translated:	The new Glitter 8 holds the road very well.
Abstract:	Business endeavors in regard to wages suggest *an upward pattern.*

Translated: We will have to pay more money to our hourly employees.
Abstract: The *availability of time* is an *important factor* in product development.
Translated: In order to develop this product completely, we need more time.

Note that the abstract parts of the sentences above require translation so that your reader knows what you mean. Don't worry if your translation uses more words than your original: use the words you need. In the long run, you will save time and money by doing so.

Cut Unnecessary Words

At first glance, our suggestion to cut words contradicts the statement in the last paragraph about using more words (if necessary). But there is no significant contradiction here because the situations you face as a writer are not all the same. Translating is necessary for vague abstractions, but cutting is necessary for simple wordiness. Examples:

Wordy: It occurred at a point when we needed help.
Cut: It occurred when we needed help.

Wordy: Somebody or other must in any case have performed the job.
Cut: Somebody must have done the job.

Wordy: The property appreciated in its basic value in the past decade of 1975–1985.
Cut: The property appreciated in the past decade.

Wordy: They embezzled the money by means of computerized fraud.
Cut: They used a computer to embezzle the money.

Check for Dangling Modifiers

The opening modifier is a very common construction. It is used for transitions and explanations:

Before calling the agency, ask me for its new number.
After seeing the condominium, she decided against buying it.
Warned by their lawyer, the residents tore down the temporary buildings.

Such opening modifiers must tie logically to the subject of the main clause. If they don't tie logically, you have dangling modifiers:

Dangler: Having drunk three martinis, the plane left.
Correction: After he drank three martinis, he left on the plane.

Dangler: After noting the interest-rate decrease, the property was bought.

Correction:	After noting the interest-rate decrease, the company bought the property.
Dangler:	When calling the vet, the dog should be described.
Correction:	(1) When calling the vet, describe your dog.
	(2) When people call the vet, they should describe their dogs.
	(3) When one calls the vet, he or she should describe the dog.

As you can see, there is more than one way to fix many dangling modifiers.

Readability—A Checklist

1. Use *who does what*.
2. Make your words and sentences *predict*.
3. Start your sentences *with a specific subject and verb*.
4. Use *parallel structures* forcefully.
5. Use strong *signal words* (*but, so, yet*, etc.)
6. *Chunk* your sentences — break them into short units.
7. Use *opening chunks* as transitions.
8. Vary the *lengths* of your sentences.
9. *Cut nouns*, particularly abstract ones.
10. Use *personal pronouns* (*I, you, we*).
11. Revise, revise.

Write as you speak (the conversational test).

EXERCISES

1. Imitation is a good technique for practicing the art of chunking sentences. There are only two kinds of sentence chunks: those that can stand alone and those that cannot. (Punctuation shows where the chunks start and stop.) In the examples below, the chunks that can stand alone are in **boldface** type. Read through them to get a feel for chunking.

Group I. Chunks that can stand alone (note punctuation)

a. **Jim went home at nine.**
b. **Jim went home at nine,** but **Louise stayed late.**
c. **Jim went home at nine; Louise stayed late.**
d. **This is the problem: Louise stayed late.**
e. **Jim** (he was tired) **went home.**

Group II. Chunked sentences that use both stand-alones and not-stand-alones (note punctuation)

Style: Make Your Writing Readable

   a. Whistling softly, **Jim opened the door.**
   b. Startled by the noise, **Jim opened the door.**
   c. To get outside, **Jim opened the door.**
   d. Jim opened the door, and was glad he did.
   e. Jim, an expert repairman, **opened the door.**
   f. These were the staples: bread, cheese, and wine.
   g. Curious about the noise, **Jim opened the door.**
   h. Slowly and carefully, **Jim opened the door.**
   i. After a while, **Jim opened the door.**
   j. His hands trembling, **Jim opened the door.**
   k. When he heard the noise, **Jim opened the door.**
   l. Jim opened the door, which had been sealed shut.

It is often helpful to imitate such patterns of chunking. Imitation will give you a feel for stylistic variation while learning how to manage the chunks and the punctuation marks that separate them.

Here are a few of our imitations, made up on the spur of the moment. Note that we follow the exact punctuation of the originals in Group I and II above.

Group I:

   b. The company earned more money, but it still did not make a profit.
   d. Here is the issue: We have too many managerial styles.
   e. The members of the repair crew (they were well trained) worked hard to find the leak.

Group II:

   a. Grumbling unhappily, they began to work on the project.
   b. Irritated by the constant bickering, Louise said "No!"
   c. To involve the audience, she told jokes.
   e. Susan, an excellent raconteur, entertained the audience for an hour.
   h. Eagerly and hopefully, E.T. phoned home.
   j. My brain wandering, I read the assignment.
   l. We finally started the interview, which had been delayed for an hour.

Imitate these chunking patterns.

2. Revise the sentences below. Don't be afraid to add or delete ideas, or to use two or more sentences. Treat the sentences as if they were yours and you were trying to revise them so that the reader could understand immediately what you were saying.

   a. The prosecution of our company's comptroller had much speculation to it.
   b. The nerve center of the office lies in its computer. The need for a reliable computer center is the bane of our working day.
   c. He only prefers cash discounts and neither does his partner.

d. The next point to make about idiom differences is one of the most difficult problems for Japanese businessmen.
e. It is not believed that the critics show complete rationality in their judgments when they criticize the automobile industry.
f. After explaining my job to me there was a car sent by the head of the department to take me to the plant in Aurora.
g. Our division has been really having huge difficulties with hard-core resentment on the company lawyers' part, who have been claiming that we play favorites for outside legal consultants.
h. Thus the continual success, interest, and the test of endurance are reasons racing is an important topic for the auto industry.
i. There have been several proposals that have since come forth about what to do with the dangerous crossing south of St. Louis.
j. What you need for this job is a group of managers labelled according to ability.

3. From each sentence below, cut any unnecessary words. Also revise the sentence, if necessary, to make it clearer and more readable.
a. During the year 1986, the clients were happy and pleased with our work.
b. We went to a meeting held in the great city of New York.
c. In response to your request of a week ago, we are sorry to have to tell you that the schedule you inquired about and wanted is not now circulated from this headquarters.
d. With regard to your idea, we do not believe it will work or be feasible.
e. The good-quality fine paper is to be used only for résumé-writing purposes.
f. The character of the offer from Xyz Company is not understood by us.
g. Ms. Sharp is now engaged in an ongoing discussion with consultants on the practicability of no longer supporting United Way mandatorily.
h. The city of Portland could not produce an actual reason for not giving or supplying us with a tax break.
i. We had awaited Portland's decision in great anxiety of mind.
j. All those interested in the question of tax breaks should plan to attend the meeting on Wednesday concerning same.
k. After investigating the facts in the case, the cash order was filled and sent out immediately.
l. I am in receipt of your report of the 17th June revising your figures for August upward, and I want to thank you for this information.

4. Below you see the first draft of a memo. The writer, Pete Jarvis, has decided that he needs to revise it before sending it. Write a brief memo, using a list form, telling him what kinds of revision the memo needs.
Then rewrite the memo completely. Make it succinct and to the point.

September 13, 1986

To: Robert Sherwood, Vice-President Personnel

From: Pete Jarvis, Kankakee Plant Manager

Subject: Recommendation for Formal Instruction for Mr. Comstock

    As you are aware, continuing education is important in developing the potential of our employees. Mr. Chris Comstock is a well qualified candidate for additional training. As Maintenance Engineer at the Kankakee Plant, he continues to do an excellent job. He is energetic, ambitious, and very dependable. With the proper mixture of time, experience, and training, he is capable of advancing to the level of Plant Engineer.
    Mr. Comstock's present abilities are visible in his work record. Responsible for overall performance and effectiveness of the plant maintenance function, he shows good judgment and stability when under pressure. He successfully keeps the plant operating efficiently even though his crew is too small for the scale of our operation. He understands the cost and payment system, our manufacturing methods, and our quality standards. Responsible for meeting the maintenance budget, he always stays within it! He is an outstanding worker.
    With this background, Mr. Comstock has the potential for promotion as he further develops the qualities of a successful Plant Engineer. However, he needs your assistance in obtaining authorization to attend formal instruction.
    One area in which Mr. Comstock needs concentrated instruction is the fields of labor management and personnel behavior in organizations. He cooperates very well with fellow workers when he understands the problems, but sometimes he is slow to realize that a worker has a problem. Furthermore, Mr. Comstock needs more experience in developing new supervisors and workers. His ability to plan, control, and delegate authority is already improving with time and experience. A two-day seminar at the University of Illinois' College of Commerce would provide him a good theoretical and practical foundation for his development.
    A second area in which Mr. Comstock should have a better understanding involves knowledge of (1) Company policies, rules, and regulations; (2) Union contracts, and (3) labor laws. He has some familiarity with these policies, but he needs a more complete understanding. A training program as offered by your office in Detroit would provide the knowledge necessary for his successful advancement.
    Mr. Comstock is a valuable investment of C.E.C. His value will continue to increase as he gains experience. Time is one factor, but additional education is especially important for our employees like Mr. Comstock who has already proven his ability and willingness to work hard. For these reasons, I recommend that Mr. Comstock receives the formal instruction that he needs for future promotions.

PART 4

Typical Messages

CHAPTER 8

Goodwill

Many goodwill letters are, or seem to be, an exercise in friendliness. "I like you," says such a letter. "Moreover, I like your service — or your product — and the way you do business. (Or: I like you as a customer.) So I am writing a letter to tell you, no strings attached."

Of course, people being what they are, strings are always attached. When you write to your Chevrolet dealer telling him that the shop manager found the vibration in the front end that three mechanics in another town could not find, and tell him how happy you are about the whole thing, you'll probably hear a small secret voice in the back of your mind. This voice says: "The happier I make the dealer and the shop manager, the better the service on my new Chevy is likely to be. Then I'll be happy, and they will be happy, and the whole world will dissolve in a sea of bliss."

Which might remind us again that goodwill letters should not be overdone. We are not really after bliss but a cementing of relationships, an offering of friendship, and possibly a look to the future. In the future of the goodwill letter can lie increased business and profits for everyone concerned.

Goodwill letters take a number of forms. They can be invitations, welcomes, offers of information and services, messages of sympathy, and expressions of appreciation. The main problem with all of these is that they have a tendency to sound hackneyed and phony:

> Welcome to our suburb! — the finest and most progressive in all the northeast! Where people are cheerful and untiring! Where the Ninth National Bank serves with unstinting pleasure. . . .

When writing the goodwill letter, avoid such clichés, particularly any mush-and-gush words: *happiness and pride, the soul of courtesy, well-earned, highly deserved recognition, heartiest greetings, genuinely pleased,* and so on. Be quick and quiet; just state your case:

Dear Home Owner:

Not much hot weather left and we're having
A PAINT SALE!

Our best outdoor Bluebird latex — any color.
Five dollars off every gallon.

Easy to pick up. Just drop in . . . turn left as you come in the front door, and you will see the Bluebird paints on sale stacked up in neat rows. We'll have a special salesperson to handle your order and help you carry it out.

The sale starts August 15 and ends August 29. Hot weather and the best paint available for your house . . .

At 25% off!

REMEMBER THAT WE HAVE A FULL LINE OF PAINT AND PAINT SUPPLIES. YOU CAN BUY ANYTHING WE STOCK WITH YOUR BLUEBIRD CHARGE CARD.

That goodwill (direct mail) letter worked for the store because it offered clear value, promised good service, and did not look like an attempt to revive an account, although it was. The letter was sent only to those customers who had not used their accounts for a specified time. And it was successful in part because it did not whine about the missing customers and their failure to use credit in the store.

Let's consider another example. The repairman who worked on the heating system in one of your buildings took the trouble to tell you:

(1) that the burners were fairly clean and did not require the usual amount of time on his part (he's charging you less);
(2) that the main floor furnace had a defective pulley, which he replaced; and
(3) that the heat transfer unit outside, for cooling in the summer, did not appear to be dirty and so could miss its annual inspection and cleaning in the Spring.

You are happy about this for several reasons, all of which can be found in the goodwill letter you write:

Dear Ms. Bandfield:

I really appreciate your repairman's dropping by Thursday afternoon after he had worked on the units in Building C–6.

Two years ago, a pulley broke in a heating unit in another building. We were using the building only for storage at the time and didn't realize that valuable materials were freezing. We could have bought a thousand pulleys for what that cold spell cost us.

Thanks too for the information about the heat transfer unit.

We will be opening up three storage buildings next Fall. I'd like to contract with your company for heating and cooling maintenance of all our buildings, if you think you have enough people to handle the work. When you get some time, why don't you take a look at our situation and give us your best bid on the work we are likely to have?

Thanks again.

If your situation does not call for the material in the last paragraph, you could end your letter with:

Thanks too for the information about the heat transfer unit. I appreciate your repairman's helping us out as he did, and I'll be sure to call on your company when we need maintenance work in the future.

In the next few pages we give some samples of goodwill letters, along with questions for discussions for each.

Thomas Campbell and Sons
122 South Ridge Parkway
Ervin, Minnesota 43434

May 13, 1987

Dear Christine:

    Today you have been with the company for eight years, ever since the company started up.

    In the seven years I have worked here myself, I have passed by your desk every morning. And you were always there!

    Not just there, but working away — and you always had a smile and a cheery hello.

    I know you have had rewards from the company. (I'm looking at your salary record right now, and your last raise was three months ago.) What makes me write this letter is to tell how pleased we are that *you* have been rewarding us for these eight years, and how we hope that the situation will continue — for a very long time indeed.

                                    Cordially,

                                    Jack Campbell

Figure 8.1. Goodwill letter

Discussion Questions for Figure 8.1
This letter was written by the junior partner in the firm.

1. Why does Campbell omit the inside address?
2. Is this a form letter? How can you tell, and how sure are you of your answer?
3. Do you approve of Campbell's calling the employee by her first name?
4. How much detail about Christine is there in the letter? Do you approve of using this detail? this *kind* of detail?
5. Comment upon the paragraphing in the letter. Is it effective? Were you surprised by it?
6. How successful is the letter?

Millikan, Frye, and Associates
General Practice of Law
P.O. Box 7655
Bartlestown, Missouri 65432

June 21, 1986

Dear Tony,

    I can't tell you how sorry I am to hear of Sally's death. I had not seen her since she was taken ill, and I'm relieved to hear that she went without pain.

    I know that your work at Gillette is a great help to you at this time. With the company growing so fast you will have much to occupy your mind.

    I called your son in Jackson. He seemed cheerful and told me some wonderful things about your new grandson!

As ever,
Margaret

Figure 8.2. Goodwill letter (of condolence)

Discussion Questions for Figure 8.2

This is a letter of condolence written by a business acquaintance of the person who has suffered a personal loss.

1. Why didn't Margaret type the letter, or have it typed?
2. Why didn't she use a signature line and her full name?
3. What is the purpose of sentence 2 in the first paragraph?
4. Why did Margaret write paragraph 2?
5. Can you explain the tone of the last paragraph? What does the paragraph tell about the writer? About the relationship between reader and writer?
6. Do you think that Tony will appreciate the last sentence of the letter? Would you, if you were Tony?

SOUTHERN MANUFACTURING CO.
1744–46 Mirado St.
Atlanta, Georgia 30361

Ms. Caroline Joyce
General Manager, XYZ Company
1313 Kamath St.
Bellflower, Georgia 30892

August 21, 1987

Dear Ms. Joyce:

Congratulations!

Not only is your company one of our top customers, but your record of payment for the seven years that you have ordered from us is PERFECT in promptness. We appreciate that, and we most appreciate having you as a steady customer.

Accordingly, we are designating you and a small number of other companies as *preferred* customers for the rest of this calendar year. All items in our catalogue, without exception, are now available to you — until January 1 — at a full ten percent off.

We hope you can take advantage of your preferred status during the remainder of the year. Also call us on our toll-free number (see p. 2 of the catalogue) if you have any questions about our merchandise.

Thanks for everything these last seven years!

Cordially,

Andrew Nathan
Vice President

Figure 8.3. Goodwill letter

Discussion Questions for Figure 8.3

1. Could you put this letter on a word processor? Why or why not? Is the letter designed for a word processor?
2. If it were put on a processor, where would the operator have to "intervene" to make changes in the letter?
3. Attack or defend the one-word paragraph at the beginning.
4. Explain the content of paragraphs 1 and 2. Consider each sentence in its turn. Do these paragraphs work for Southern Manufacturing? Could these paragraphs have been reversed? Explain.
5. What does the reader get out of this letter? How many times is the word *you* employed? How and why?
6. Why is the word *preferred* repeated?
7. If you were writing this letter, would you use the last one-sentence paragraph? Would you end the letter differently? Explain.

EXERCISES

1. You are the adult coach of a Little League baseball team. Like the other teams in your league, yours is sponsored by Washoe Center, a large shopping mall. Washoe Center buys your team's uniforms and supplies various services and sports items. The manager of Washoe carries equipment and some players to the game, using his own station wagon. Another person working for Washoe supplies soft drinks for the team after every game.

You are indebted to Washoe Center for its kindness toward you and the other players, and also for a certain amount of specific help in managing transportation and other matters. And don't forget those great uniforms.

At the end of the season, your team placed fourth in the league. All your players got their allotted playing time, no matter how badly they played. Your team likes and respects you and your coaching.

But the manager of Washoe Center wants a winner. And his son, not a very good player, wants more playing time. (He's a fumble-fingered second baseman.) The manager is not going to bounce you as a coach; he likes and respects you, too. But he is getting a bit restive. Now, at the end of the season, write him a goodwill letter. Put into it everything you can think of that will make him and Washoe Center know how much you appreciate their support — and will make them continue it willingly.

2. You are the manager of a large clothing store situated in a shopping center close to many large organizations who employ women in executive positions. Your store has previously carried only men's business suits and clothing. You will soon open a department aimed at working women, particularly those high up in the businesses surrounding your store. You call your new department "Tailored Lady" and stock only expensive hand-tailored suits made of tropical weight all-wools, poly-wool blends, and all-year wools. You will also issue a free catalogue, describing the specific models you will stock and have on order. The catalogue will be useful for women who may live in neighboring cities where there is no store like yours but who may wish to order from you. The catalogue might also be useful for organizations wanting to place group orders.

Write a goodwill letter describing your new department. Aim the letter at the organization woman who is interested in executive apparel.

3. During a recent storm there were many power outages in your community. The power company worked with remarkable speed to make repairs and restore service. This was particularly important to you because without power your business simply closes down.

Write two letters, one to the power company expressing your gratitude for their round-the-clock efforts in clearing out fallen trees, repairing lines, and so on, and the other to the local newspaper saying much the same thing. The second letter should be written to a general audience, of course.

4. Write a memo to all the people you supervise (about twenty of them working throughout a large building). Christmas is coming, and you want to thank them for the good work they have done preparing for the Christmas rush. You decide on the type of business involved.

5. Write a letter to one of your instructors, saying how grateful you are for the course given last semester (or year). Give details on how helpful the course was in preparing you for your major or minor.

6. You read in a newspaper about a bill being sponsored in Congress. You have a strong interest in the bill (either positive or negative). Write a letter to the sponsor(s). Try to give a reasonably detailed argument for your position on the issues while gaining goodwill.

7. You manage a restaurant in your college town. You have a very good business, most of which depends on students coming to the restaurant. Lately, however, other businesses that compete with you have been opening up. Write a letter to new students suggesting that your food and service are the best and that they should patronize your restaurant (give it an interesting name!). This will be an open letter that will be published in the college paper as a paid advertisement.

8. A friend of yours has accomplished something rather unusual. Write a letter to the friend praising him or her and giving congratulations.

9. You belong to an athletic club that recently traveled to Toledo for a tournament. You stayed in the dorm of Tarryton College, a private school. All the accommodations were splendid. The food was excellent. The people working in the dorm were most helpful. Write a letter (to whom? — pick the person) expressing gratitude for all this. You would like to come back there for next year's tournament.

10. A friend of yours has lost a job that he or she needed badly and liked very much. The loss was not due to any error on this person's part. Write a letter saying how sorry you are about the situation. Be positive about the future, and try to persuade the person not to blame himself or herself.

CHAPTER 9

Selling a Product or Service

In selling a product or service you must decide on the answers to several questions.

First, what are you trying to sell? What is it good for? Why would anyone want it? Is there anything negative about it? — is it dangerous, for example, when wrongly used, or applicable to only a few situations?

Clearly, these are questions that apply mainly to a product, but similar ones should be asked about a service. What does your service do (how can it be described)? Does it require anything of the buyer other than his or her money? For example, Brian Miller was sold a small service for his lawn a few years ago. The seller neglected to tell Miller that he would have to water the grass right after a chemical was applied to it. Miller thought watering might be a good idea, but he was going to be out of town and did not want to impose on neighbors and ask them to spend their time moving a sprinkler around for an eight-hour period. He never bought that service again. The seller should have analyzed it better and warned Miller about his part in it.

Second, what is the cost of your service or product? Higher or lower than the competition? Can your prospective buyer afford it? Are you going to have to overcome a good deal of price resistance?

Third, where and how is your service or product available? If customers want it, how easily can they get it? Availability is important.

Finally, how will you encourage your potential customers to buy? Let's consider that problem.

STEP ONE: GET THEIR ATTENTION

Examples of attention-getters:

- Ten of your neighbors have bought new Washrite washing machines recently. Would you like to see why they are happy with their purchase?
- Is there anything more precious to you than your eyes? When you use your precision shop equipment, are you protecting them completely? Shasta Shop Eye Protectors have been used by more than . . .
- The Blare Beeper Service is not just for anyone. Frankly, we cost a little more than our competitors. But we offer *much* more than they do . . .

STEP TWO: MAKE THEM WANT IT

Examples:

- Our new backhoe will get your store parking lots cleaner than ever. No more unsightly mounds of snow piled right on top of valuable, needed parking spaces.
- With our Beeper service, you can be reached anywhere at any time in the prescribed area. No wall too thick, no building too high. No shielding can prevent your call from getting through.

STEP THREE: GIVE THE FACTS

Examples:

- With our new Money Bank Account, you will get more interest — on a $10,000 deposit this can be worth as much as $200 a year!
- Last year, Insbruck Insurance Company provided more than two and a half billion dollars in additional coverage to our regular policyholders. And we did this without raising the cost of the policies.

STEP FOUR: SUGGEST ACTION

Examples:

- Why don't you try Jordan's Jiffy Glue yourself? Just fill out the enclosed order card and send it to us (no postage necessary).
- While the weather is still bad, bring in your mower. We'll put it back in running condition for spring mowing and give you a 20 percent discount on parts — until March 1!

SUMMARY

Focus your thoughts on two aspects of your product or service: (1) what you've got to sell, and (2) whom you're going to sell it to. Know exactly what it is and how it works. Know who manufactures the product or gives the service. What materials are used? Are specifications important here? Can you get testimonials about the product or service from users? What is unusually good or even outstanding about it? Will it require any special attention from you, the buyer, or the service people?

What does it cost, and why? Many of us will pay a little more if we can get good quality. On the other hand, if your product or service can be sold at a substantially lower price than the competition's, say so. Explain in detail.

In what specific ways will your product or service help your customer? Remember also that pleasure itself is one of the strongest motivators in human beings. We have seen mature people go into ecstasies over things as different as a beautifully designed car, a lovely wedding cake, and a display of jade plants. If you can sell pleasure to your customers, say so.

If customers buy from you, what's in it for them?

Following is a series of sales letters written for various purposes. Read them and use the related questions for discussion.

Discussion Questions for Figure 9.1

Page Airways is a small company that has lost business to its sole competitor — business that it is trying to get back.

1. The sentence above suggests one purpose of the letter. What is another major purpose? How clear is that purpose? Should it be clearer?
2. What exactly is Page trying to sell? How can you tell this from paragraph 1? What is the purpose of the four words in parentheses?
3. In paragraph 2, why does Page use the allusion to United?
4. Discuss the tone of paragraph 2. How effective is it?
5. Does this letter use all four steps discussed in the beginning of this chapter? How strong, for example, is the action step? Is the action step outlined explicitly in the letter?
6. Does this letter sell pleasure to its potential customers?

Page Airways
Levon, Nebraska 68855

March 10, 1987

Ms. Sandi Snyder
Manager, Fort Levon Hotel
Levon, Nebraska 68855

Dear Ms. Snyder:

We have just added two NEW aircraft to our fleet and two new schedules. We are now flying twice a day to Omaha and also twice a day to Denver, with stops in between (see the attached schedule).

As you know, we have only one competitor flying from Levon, and it runs only single flights to both cities daily. We will thus be able to serve you twice as often and, we hope, twice as well! The two aircraft we have added are brand-new, with all the amenities you have come to expect from Page Airways. No inflight movies (our skies are friendly enough, although our planes are not as big as United's — *yet*). But we do have stereo tape equipment for every seat, lunch between here and Denver, and plenty of fine service from our flight attendants.

We will be happy to have travellers picked up from the Fort Levon Hotel. Just call Marvell Cab, and we'll pay for the trip to the airport (special arrangement with Marvell).

See you in the air!

Rena Mitchell
President, Page Airways

Figure 9.1. Sales letter

AGRICHEEN, INC.
122 Michigan Street
Cartwright, Missouri 59642

March 17, 1987

Mr. Will Penchel
RR 5
Benson, Missouri 59640

Dear Mr. Penchel:

You asked for information about our line of agricultural equipment. Here is our latest brochure!

Notice that we have added a line of Dismek plows, plows that have proved revolutionary: inexpensive, hard-working, and virtually indestructible. We have a special on these plows until April 1, and would be happy to supply you.

Also note that we have added a great new line of pick-up accessories. We have scoured the country for these... and we GUARANTEE that anything you might want for your pick-up — from special power takeoffs to add-on tool chests — you can buy from us at THE BEST PRICES.

I have included a special page with questions about your business, along with a self-addressed stamped envelope. Could you please take a minute and write us about your equipment needs?

We would be PLEASED to hear from you. Perhaps you can help us help you — if we can add something to our line that you need, we'll both be happy.

Cordially,

Frank Millins, Manager, Sales

Figure 9.2. Sales letter

Selling a Product or Service

Discussion Questions for Figure 9.2

1. Obviously, this company sells many different things, but its letter draws attention to only two, plows and pick-up accessories. Is the letter therefore badly balanced? How does the writer, Frank Millins, try to balance his material?
2. What is the purpose of the next-to-last paragraph? (This company sells only by mail; it has no salespeople who visit customers.)
3. How well does this letter appeal to the reader? What benefits does the letter suggest directly to the reader? Indirectly?
4. Why does the letter use so many paragraphs? Do you object to any of the paragraphing?
5. If you were to describe the personality of the writer in a word or phrase, what would it be?
6. Would you change anything in the letter?

XEROX® NOW YOU CAN OWN ONE OF AMERICA'S FAVORITE
ELECTRONIC TYPEWRITERS
— THE XEROX MEMORYWRITER —
FOR HUNDREDS OF DOLLARS LESS THAN EVER BEFORE!

Take advantage of our limited time trade-in offer and
SAVE AN ADDITIONAL $325.00!

Dear Executive:
If you've been waiting for the best time to purchase one of America's best-selling electronic typewriters, that time is now! Xerox has just announced the greatest Memorywriter offer of all time: Now you can own the Xerox 610 Memorywriter for the lowest price ever ... under $1000!

And when you buy through this direct-by-mail offer, you pay just $965. That's less than the nationally advertised single-unit commercial list price. At $965, you can easily charge the Xerox 610 to your company credit card. Or, if you qualify for Xerox Flexible Financing, you can pay for your Memorywriter in affordable amounts ... *as little as $29.00* a month* — with no down payment!

*Save $325 more when you trade in
your current typewriter!*

For a limited time only, you may be able to trade in your present typewriter for the Xerox 610 and receive an additional $325 off the already reduced price! You pay just $640 for a *new* state-of-the-art Xerox 610 Memorywriter! Xerox will even make arrangements to pick up your old typewriter. (Almost every brand name typewriter qualifies — no matter how old it is! Call us toll-free today to confirm your trade-in eligibility.)

You can also take advantage of Xerox Flexible Financing along with this trade-in offer and, if you qualify, own the Xerox 610 for just $25.00 a month*! But keep in mind this is a limited time offer. To receive your $325 trade-in allowance, you must order by March 31, 1985!

*You get a free Memorywriter Starter Supply Kit
through this offer!*

*Payment may be lower depending on local sales tax.

Figure 9.3. Sales letter

As an extra bonus for buying the Xerox 610 through this offer, we'll send you a Starter Supply Kit FREE! Your supply kit is complete with everything you need to put your Memorywriter to work right away — correctable ribbons, lift-off correction tapes and two advanced daisywheel print elements.

With an unbelievably low price and a great offer like this, there's absolutely no reason for you *not* to have the Xerox 610 Memorywriter in your office. And you can be sure that the time and trouble-saving features of the Xerox 610 are every bit as outstanding as this offer!

The Xerox 610 "remembers" words...
phrases...sentences...
that makes typing easier!

With the Xerox 610, your typist can easily store text that will be used again and again (up to 1,150 characters), then recall that text in an instant. That lets your typist complete repetitive elements with the touch of a key.

The Xerox 610 lifts off up to 180 characters
at a time!
That helps assure you of error-free documents!

While self-correcting electric typewriters lift off just one character at a time, the 610 makes corrections much faster. It can remove up to 180 characters with one touch of a key!

It makes everyday typing go faster — automatically!

The Xerox 610 does automatically what standard electrics require the typist to do manually. It underlines automatically at the same time the word or character is typed...automatically centers text so there's no need to count or guess...returns the carriage automatically so there's no slowing down at the end of the line.

It even lines up numbers by their decimal points or percentage signs...sets a temporary left margin so your typist doesn't have to tab in to type indented text...and makes it easy to set up tables and charts.

Best of all, the Xerox 610 is upgradable!
It grows along with you!

Later on, you may find you want more text-storage capacity or additional text-editing features. You'll be glad to know we can upgrade the Xerox 610 right in your own office. You don't have to trade in your Xerox 610 to buy a more advanced Memorywriter.

(In fact, if you're ready right now for a Memorywriter with more advanced features, call us toll-free at 800-828-9090 and ask about our other Memorywriter models...their capabilities...financing options...and new LOW PRICES!)

You have everything to gain through this offer!

Direct-by-mail buying may be particularly suited to your office needs. You save time when you order — no lengthy meetings are required. Best of all, you get a special direct-by-mail low price!

There's nothing to risk...nothing to lose!

When you buy through this direct-by-mail offer, you get every benefit you'd get if you bought in a "traditional" face-to-face method. Namely, you get Xerox' 90-Day Limited Warranty on your Memorywriter...and you can purchase a Xerox Full Service Maintenance Agreement at an affordable cost.

You also get THE XEROX PROMISE OF FULL SATISFACTION. You may take 15 days to make sure the Xerox 610 is the right machine for you. Then, if you decide it's not what you need or expected, simply return it for a full credit or refund.

Just mail the enclosed No-Risk Order Form today!

Or, if you prefer, call us toll-free at 800-828-9090. We'll enter your order immediately and ship your Memorywriter and free Starter Supply Kit to you. But do it now. You don't want to miss out on Xerox' greatest Memorywriter offer ever! Put one of America's favorite electronic typewriters to work for you...and save hundreds of dollars!

Sincerely,

Terrance B. Ahern
Manager, Direct Marketing

P.S. Remember...for a limited time you may be able to own a new Xerox 610 for just $640 if you trade in your present typewriter... an additional $325 savings! See the enclosed insert and call us toll-free today!

Figure 9.3. Sales letter (continued)

Selling a Product or Service   165

Discussion Questions for Figure 9.3

For many years, authorities have told us that length is not the major issue in good letters that sell a product or service. "Long copy," as it is called, works if it does the job. People will read long copy when they are interested in what it says, when they get benefits from doing so.

1. Why is the Xerox letter so long?
2. Refer again to the four steps listed at the beginning of this chapter. Exactly where in the letter do you find these steps being used? How? And in how many places in the letter?
3. For discussion, prepare an analysis of the physical appearance of the letter. Is there anything unusual about it? Would you call the letter elegant? Why or why not?
4. One authority calls this letter "a fine example of the use of repetition." Do you agree? Where is the repetition? Why is it used?
5. Can you suggest any improvements in the letter?

EXERCISES

1. Exercises 1.a and 1.b give you a chance to analyze two kinds of readers who by nature will have some important similarities, but there are also some important differences in such readers that you must take into account. Your instructor may want to assign only one of these exercises — or all four as a package.

Your company has just introduced a new metal alloy for use in making partial plates for people with missing teeth. You call the alloy NO-BREAK.

NO-BREAK has many possibilities for commercial use, but right now you want to sell it to those small companies that specialize in making partial plates (to order) for dentists. This is a good, steady market. The world is full of people, from football players to grandpas, who are missing several teeth. The metalwork (alloy) in a plate holds the false teeth together and also curls around the permanent teeth to hold the plate in place. A partial plate lying out on a table looks a little like a large metal bucktoothed spider. The biggest problem with such plates is that they bend and become loose in the mouth, or suddenly break when one is halfway through a meal at a favorite restaurant.

In no particular order, here are some facts and judgments about the situation.

Most companies that make partial plates for dentists are satisfied with their present metals. These companies are conservative. The dentists they work for are conservative also, and they like to order materials they are familiar with.

Some facts about your NO-BREAK alloy:

- It is harder than other alloys.
- It "works" (can be shaped) at a lower temperature.
- It is completely inert; that is, it does not interact with other matter (but, then, neither do the competing alloys).
- It works out smoother than other alloys (why might this be important?).
- It is stronger than other alloys.
- It bends less easily than other alloys. (Why might this be a detriment? Consider the problem of fitting the bridge in the mouth.)
- It is about the same weight as other alloys.

a. Write a sales letter to be sent to a wide sample of the companies that make partial plates for dentists.
b. Write a sales letter about NO-BREAK to a broad sample of dentists.
c. Consider the two types of reader involved in this situation. Write an analysis comparing and contrasting them in detail.
d. As the maker of NO-BREAK, are you supplying a product or a service?

Put yourself in the place of the kinds of readers involved. What do they think you are supplying? What do they think *they* are supplying?

2. Complete surprise! You have inherited a small TV repair business from an uncle you hardly knew. The business is strictly service; no sales. It made a small profit last year. It is located in Fenokee, a southern town of 35,000 people. (You are a college student in Michigan.) The area is prosperous, with a number of farmers and small businesses. An Air Force base is nearby.

All you know about TV repair is what you can find in books. You can't work on sets, but you know another student, a brilliant fellow with his hands, who can. You decide to go run the business; your friend says he'll help.

Off the two of you go to Fenokee and the sunny South in your ten-year-old car. Along the way, you plan a campaign to sell your services. Here's what you have learned from reading and some other sources:

- By 1974, black-and-white sets were not as popular as color sets. People buying new sets in recent years tended to buy color, even for a second set. By 1978, the ratio of new purchases was about two to one in favor of color.
- Color sets are somewhat more expensive to repair.
- The town of Fenokee has cable network facilities, and the cable company contracts a certain amount of work to local repairmen. The cable company has been successful in Fenokee.
- Fenokee has only one large chain store that both sells and services TV sets. Other stores contract out their service work.

The only comparative TV color-reliability measures you can get are from 1977:

Calls per set

Made in Japan	Made in US	Made in United Kingdom
0.09–0.26	1–2	1.2–3

Before you left the university, you called a local TV store and got typical prices for typical services. (You will have to do this yourself; or have one person in the class do it; it is part of the problem.)

Now you are riding through Tennessee on your way to Fenokee. To pass the time, you and your friend begin to plan a campaign to sell your service. Bearing in mind that all this is tentative, what do you decide to do?

Make a set of clear readable notes that you can start with when you get to Fenokee.

3. Here is a very delicate situation. You have gone to work for an adoption service in a major city. You have been asked to write a sales letter for the service, a letter addressed to unmarried pregnant mothers who would prefer to put their babies up for adoption. Your supervisor wants this to be an open letter that will run in the classified section of one of the world's great newspapers.

You will include these facts in the letter:

- Your adoption service is nonprofit.
- Its only job is to place babies with couples who want children but can't have their own.
- Your service provides a physician (by contract) and, if necessary, a home for the mother until birth.
- Appointments with the physician, and transportation for appointments, are taken care of by the service.
- The service pays all fees, including prescriptions, medical and hospital fees, and housing expenses.
- Someone from the service will stay with the mother during birth.

NOTE: What kind of benefits should you emphasize?

4. You are selling what is essentially a weight-control service in a medium-sized city that has a fast-growing community college. You know that college students form a distinct part of the market for your service. You have all the standard workout equipment, a new building, and several exercise programs designed especially for young people. Write a sales letter for your service that is directed just to college students. Be as specific as you can (given your knowledge of such students) about your service. Offer a thirty percent cut in rates for those who sign up during the next thirty days for the service.

NOTE: Emphasize the benefits of your service.

5. Your medium-sized company sells and installs floor coverings of all types. It is an old company in the area with a very fine reputation — a reputation that you and your fellow workers have earned by using superior materials and "perfection" workmanship. The problem is that your rates are about ten or fifteen percent higher than those of your competitors, who are gradually eating into your business. You decide to target an area in your city (upper middle-class) and write the homeowners in that area a letter that says, in effect: "Yes, we are more expensive, but we do better work." Examples: *superior materials; experienced, careful workmen, who have been doing the job for many years; very careful underlayment procedures (particularly with tile coverings); superior cleanup procedures. Satisfaction guaranteed!*

Write the letter using the four steps discussed early in this chapter in the order they are given. Try doing this mechanically in your first draft. How well does the letter work? Will you have to rewrite it for a final draft?

Assume that you are sending with your letter a complete brochure that describes materials and costs.

6. Consider your major or minor college subject. Write a sales or service letter based on the work you can perform in the subject of your major or minor. Pick your audience carefully, and give your instructor a specific description of its members.

7. You are asked to rewrite sample letter 9.3 and get it onto one page. What material will you keep? What material will you discard? Rewrite the letter as best you can, and include some notes for discussion with your instructor about your selling strategies in the rewrite.

8. Consider a ballpoint pen or mechanical pencil that you own and use. You manufacture and sell this product, and you need a new sales letter for it. Study the product carefully and write the letter, which will be addressed to business managers of companies. You will be dealing in orders of 500 to 1,000 only and putting the buyer's company name on each pen or pencil. You will also be including a sample of the product in the letter. Give all pricing information in your letter.

9. You are starting a new automobile service station in your suburban area. Write a flyer that you and your employees will deliver by hand to each house in the neighborhood. Describe your service completely. Strive for a clear appeal to reader benefits: What will the car owner get from changing from another service to yours?

10. Step one, as described in this chapter, is *Get their attention.* For problem 9, above, write four different attention paragraphs, along with an explanation of each. What does each paragraph try to do specifically? (Think of what you, as a car owner, might want in service and in attention to your needs.)

CHAPTER

10

Inquiries, Orders, and Replies

INQUIRIES

An inquiry is a question relating to your business. Subjects for inquiry are obviously almost unlimited. In a normal year, you may have dozens of questions about personnel, products, services, operations, credit, and so on.

Most inquiries can be straightforward and brief:

> Please send me information on your Calcupal pocket calculator, Special Size, Printer. I am not interested in other models.

In such inquiries, say what you have to say and stop. If you need special information, say so:

> Please send me information on your Calcupal pocket calculator, Special Size, Printer.
>
> I have a special requirement for your calculator. The person who will use it is a senior citizen who is bedridden. The numbers on the tape must be large enough to be read easily by such a person.

When you answer an inquiry, be sure you respond to its main point. Before you respond to the request for information on the calculator, for instance, note exactly what the writer is asking for. A good practice is always to mark such messages in the margin with a felt-tipped pen, so that as you

Inquiries, Orders, and Replies 171

dictate or write you can check off the points you will respond to. In the case of the calculator, you would mark, first, the model the writer is interested in and, second, the fact that the numbers on the tape should be large enough for easy reading. As a third point you could add any special characteristics of the calculator that might sell it to the customer.

ORDERS

Depending on whether you are dealing with a product or a service, an order usually starts with:

Please *send* something . . ., or
Please *do* something . . .

Products

In your message, give all pertinent information:
- How much (quantity)
- How big (size)
- Color
- Model number
- Catalogue number
- Costs
- Other requirements

Then say how you are going to pay, and say where, when, and how you want the product delivered.

Services

You will usually know what a service costs before you order it. Even so, it is wise to include the cost in a prominent place in your message, just in case anyone involved has made a mistake of some kind in the quotation. An order for service usually also includes a description (on occasion, very detailed) of the service wanted. If necessary, add your method of payment. Sample message using a memo form:

To: Sunrise Motel
From: Henry Dorn
Subject: Order for (1) Motel reservations (two single rooms), August 27
      (2) Meeting-room space and equipment for presentation, August 27, 9:00–11:30 A.M. Two presenters, and an audience of 25.

On August 15 I phoned your Mr. Clemson about the two requirements listed above, and he assured me there would be no problem with either of them.

Note that there will be two of us presenters, which means that we must have a reasonable amount of space open in the front of the meeting room. We will not, however, need an extra lectern.

Here is a list of *necessary equipment:*
1. Big card on meeting room door saying:
   "Executive Development Session: *Writing*"
2. One overhead projector and screen
3. One movable blackboard with chalk
4. A room that can be darkened

I will be paying the bill myself, by Certa Charge Card. Thanks very much for your help.

Why did the writer use the memo form? One answer is given in the Overview to this book: This form is efficient. In the memo above, note how everything that is important stands out.

REPLIES

When an order comes in, you will try to fill it as soon as possible. Quick service, quick profits. Ah, but look at the pile of incomplete orders on Smith's desk, a pile that seems to grow by the hour. Orders, for instance, that say: "Send me something right away," but that:

- don't give an address
- don't give a model number
- give an imaginary model number
- ask for a model that is out of stock
- ask for two models that don't work together (they do work with other models)
- and so on.

Many of these problems can be solved with form-letter replies or cards. Those that can't be solved in this way will call for special treatment in the reply. An example:

Today we are sending you your new Carpenter's Model bench saw. It will arrive by Maileze Express.

We are temporarily out of stock of the Lite Router, which you ordered at the same time. We will send it to you immediately when we get it.

May I make a suggestion about the Lite Router? As its name implies, it is designed for light work in a shop that handles, say, balsa modelling, or work with relatively soft or thin stock.

Your new bench saw, though, will handle just about anything in any size shop. So the router and saw don't fit each other in performance or capability.

Inquiries, Orders, and Replies 173

If you think you might need it for your work, I would suggest our Carpenter's Router which, like your new bench saw, will handle heavy stock easily and efficiently. Of course, the Carpenter's Router is more expensive (twice the cost) than the Lite model. But it might be far more useful to you in the long run and make up for its extra cost many times.

We'll send you the Lite Router as soon as we receive it from the factory.

You have been a good customer of ours for many years, and we would like to serve you in the best way we can.

Observe the method of this reply. It begins with the very short positive statement, "Today we are sending you . . ." This is followed by the first negative part of the reply, that the Lite Router is not presently available. Later comes another positive remark: "We will send it to you immediately when we get it."

The second negative part is the difficult one. Whether he did it through mistake or ignorance, the buyer ordered a machine he probably can't use, one that may well break down when he tries to couple it with the heavy-duty bench saw. If it does break down, he will be unhappy with you and your company.

So you decide to tell him in advance facts he would rather not hear. The router is too light, and a more suitable one would cost twice as much. You explain this carefully and neutrally.

After this, you end positively: You'll send the Lite Router as soon as you get it from the factory, and you tell your reader that you appreciate his being a good customer.

(This letter worked; the customer cancelled his original order for the Lite Router and ordered a heavy-duty machine.)

What follows is a series of sample letters and questions to use in discussing them.

31 Easter Lane
Marmon, Pennsylvania 21922

April 2, 1986

Richard Brooks
Director of Sales
Wentford Manufacturing
Townville, New Hampshire 35811

Dear Mr. Brooks:

    I am writing about the installation and use of your Model D-224 humidifier, which can be added to my Burnkleen furnace, Model No. 333592.

    I need the following information:

    1. My furnace front is set 31 inches from a permanent wall. Is this sufficient space to install the humidifier?

    2. There is no drain available in my basement that is close to the furnace. How will this fact affect installation, if at all?

    3. How much of a cycling effect does this unit have? In other words, can we depend on setting the unit humidistat at (say) 50, and keep the house humidity within two points either way of that level?

    4. If I order on the first of the next month, when might I expect delivery?

    Thank you for your help.

                                Sincerely,

                                Dolores Muniz

Figure 10.1. Inquiry letter

Discussion Questions for Figure 10.1

1. Explain the use of specifics in the first paragraph.
2. Explain the format of most of the body of the letter — that is, what has the writer done to make her reader able to answer her inquiry easily?
3. Is there any possible problem of confusion in the writer's mixing questions and statements in the letter?
4. If you were writing the letter, is there anything that you would do differently?

Amdex Weather Stations
9874 Partridge Street
Seattle, Washington 98101

November 12, 1986

Bardwell Instrument Company
Box 555
Bardwell, North Carolina 27501

Sir:

    Please send us the following:

    1. Three hundred and sixty-five aneroid barometers, no. 36202. Diameter: 72 mm. These barometers are listed in your special catalog no. 74 at a special price of $2.64 each for 100 units or more.

    2. Two hundred and seventy-nine hygrometers, no. 36302. These are not listed in your special catalog no. 74, but we would appreciate any help you can give us on prices.

    3. Six hundred and fifty brass bezels for items listed in 1 and 2 above. Bezels are no. 36903 in catalog no. 72 and are priced there at 79 cents each.

    Please charge our account, as usual, and deliver by UPS.

    Sincerely,

    A. R. Guthrie
    Manager

Figure 10.2. Order

Discussion Questions for Figure 10.2

1. Check the early part of this chapter for information on how to make a complete order. Is this order complete?
2. Why does Mr. Guthrie use a numbered list in the letter?
3. Is there anything omitted in item 2 that was in item 1? Should this not have been omitted?
4. Do you find anything odd in the arithmetic in point 3?
5. Why is 72 underlined in point 3?
6. Do you see any problem with the order — that is, is Amdex going to have any difficulty filling it? Why or why not?

Performance Sports Supply
P. O. Box 4494
Ft. Savage, Oregon 97702

October 12, 1987

Susanna Opper
Manager, Delta Sports, Inc.
2223 South N. St.
Susquehanna, Pa. 18922
Dear Ms. Opper:

    We appreciate receiving your order for 30 Mi-tex jogging suits, 16-1000 and 16-1002.

    As you know, these are for *pants* and *hood* only, with the jacket excluded. Since this is a new line for us and for everyone else, so far as we know, we were wondering if you meant to order only pants and hood.

    Retail customers tend to buy jackets and hoods together, if they buy more than one unit at a time.

    Right now, we are filling your order but holding it and sending this letter special delivery. When you get it, why not give us a toll-free call and tell us if you want the Mi-texes sent as ordered? If you want to change the order with your call, we will be happy to do that, of course.

    We wouldn't want you to be stuck with paired units of Mi-tex that don't sell well together!

Sincerely,

Michael Tenise

Figure 10.3. Reply letter

Discussion Questions for Figure 10.3

1. Taking each paragraph of the letter in order, state the purpose of the paragraph.
2. Paragraph 2, second sentence: There is an idea omitted here. What is it? Why was it omitted?
3. In paragraph 4, sentence 2, why did Tenise put this in the form of a question? Would you prefer the idea expressed as a statement?
4. Why does Tenise put the last paragraph in its position? Why wouldn't it be better as the first paragraph?
5. What is the total strategy of the reply?
6. Describe the tone of the reply.

EXERCISES

1. You manufacture a line of aluminum ladders. The longest ones have a special attachment at the top that allows the ladder to be held away from the wall of a house in order to scrape or paint a surface. Because this ladder is very long and the worker will be high off the ground, you also make a safety locking device (SAFLOK) that prevents swaying or bending of the ladder when extended. SAFLOK is built into each ladder of more than twenty-five feet in length (when fully extended). The special *top attachment*, which has no other name, is not built into the ladder and must be ordered separately.

You have an order from North Rental Agency for five thirty-foot aluminum ladders. The order specifies these numbers:

- five 30-foot ladders — #1-601987
- four top attachments — #1-601988
- five SAFLOK attachments — (no order number given by North)

There are some problems about the order, which is accompanied by a check that covers payment for the merchandise but does not cover shipping, which must be prepaid. In addition, the number given for the top attachment is wrong; it is a number for safety pads, a special item for use on slick floors inside a building (for example, hardwood floors in a basketball gym). The correct order number for the top attachments is 1–601989. And why did North mention the SAFLOK?

Write a letter to North Rental Agency about this order. Make up your own title and responsibility.

2. *Part A:* You are about to expand a small business that specializes in all kinds of wood refinishing. You would like to buy an exhaust fan (commercial size) for the new shop you are building. You use many chemicals in your refinishing, some of which are dangerous to breathe and others which are explosive in vapor form.

Write an inquiry to Addison Electric, a wholesale company. Cover these questions and problems:

- How many models of fan are there?
- What are the costs of fan models?
- Is special wiring needed? How much current does it draw?
- Is special installation needed?
- You need a "combination" fan, one that will exhaust a large volume of air, and also one that will not "spark." (All ordinary fans "spark," causing lacquer vapor to explode like gasoline vapor.)
- What sizes (dimensions) of fan are available? The space you want to put it in is restricted.
- Can the fan be turned off by a switch that is *on* it? (Does it have a built-in switch?)
- Are there any guarantees of average fan life under heavy usage, and so on?
- Is there any literature for best fan employment? Where in a room should the fan be placed for best movement of air?

Part B: Now you have received information from Addison Electric on fans. Write an order to Addison that includes this material:

- I want Fan #2–556–3498.
- Do not send adapter switch AS–453 (ordinarily used). I want AS–21.
- Send me a three-foot cord.
- I need a case for the fan (#9008).
- Send mounting and baffle (#4).

Inquiries, Orders, and Replies 181

- The literature sent me is confusing on one point. Given room volume of 20 x 20 x 8, how far from the floor should the fan be mounted? Can this information be sent separately from the order?
- As per phone call of August 9, I will pay full amount for fan and attachments within 90 days.

3. It is July, and you are worried about paying expenses for college next year. You would like employment in the nonacademic side of your college, perhaps working for cash part-time in a dorm. (That is, you don't want a "food job," which gives you free meals but no cash.) Find out whom to write to in your college, and write an inquiry asking specific questions about possible jobs.

4. Look in the yellow pages of the local phone book. Find a service that, under ideal conditions, you might like to have performed for yourself. Write an inquiry about the service.

5. Using a standard catalogue for a large firm (like Sears and Roebuck), write an order for an item that has several parts to it. Many pieces of machinery, for example, come with add-ons that can be ordered with the main unit. Make your letter very complete, giving all necessary information.

6. You have saved enough money to go to Florida for a week's vacation during the Spring semester break. Pick an imaginary hotel or motel in the city or area where you would like to stay and write an inquiry regarding rooms, prices, meals, and so on. Make your inquiry complete.

7. Answer the inquiry in exercise 6 as if you were the manager of the motel or hotel. Give a complete reply, and also make it clear that your establishment is somewhat conservative; it is not a place where wild student parties are welcome. How can you say this indirectly without being offensive?

8. You are the assistant manager of Weatherwise Windows, a wholesale maker of replacement windows. On your desk you have a large order from a Minnesota company that specializes in installation of replacement windows. (When their old windows go bad, homeowners have Minnesota Replacement Service rip out the old and put in new ones — in effect, replacing frame for frame.) The order that you have is handwritten and gives so little specification that you are not sure how many units and of what kind are being ordered.

Write a reply that mentions the following: insulated or uninsulated windows are available; so are solar or tinted glass, as well as plain glass; windows can be custom made, if specs are given; standard windows are also available; there is a choice of aluminum or vinyl; six colors are available; Model 4D windows are tilt-in and take-out for easy maintenance; Model 6F windows are standard sash windows. Mention a price list that you can send with the letter.

End the letter on a positive note.

CHAPTER 11

Claims

A claim is something you ask for, something that is rightfully yours. If a product is unsatisfactory or a service does not do what the seller said it would, you can write a claim. And your claim will ask for the service or product to be set right.

Claims are useful for both buyer and seller. They give the buyer a chance to improve his or her situation and the seller a similar chance to correct flaws that he or she may even be unaware of.

About claims, the first thing to do is: Wait a minute. Look the situation over carefully. Are you sure you really have a claim? George Parker bought a shirt at an outlet store that specializes in seconds. The left sleeve, he discovered, was slightly shorter than the right. Horrors! He decided to write a stinging claim to the store. But the store deals in seconds; that is its business. Parker wouldn't find perfect shirts there, unless someone made a mistake. Ergo: He probably has no claim.

We will assume that you are sure of your claim. First, make a list of everything you know about the product or service on a sheet of scratch paper. Next, circle every item in the list that is factual. Don't circle "This shirt looks bad." That is a judgment, not a fact. When you are sure of your facts, try this outline:

- *History* of the problem in detail
- *Description* of the problem in detail

Claims

- Your *judgment* (here's where to say that the shirt looks bad)
- Your *request for action*

Following this outline, a business person wrote this letter on behalf of her company, Whynar Manufacturing:

> Could you please check the Whynar Manufacturing account for the months of January through April for this year? Each month we have been billed for services to the 721AR computer, which we bought last year from you. Obviously, our service contract should have taken care of any service on the 721AR. Unfortunately, we can't find our file on computer service, and so can't check to see when your serviceman was here.
>
> I am guessing that your bill for the months in question is possibly for our older computer (608A), which we sold in February. But it could not have been the 608A that you worked on in March for an April billing.
>
> If you can uncross these wires for us, I'll be very grateful.

You can see that the woman who wrote this letter blended the history and description of the problem. She also used a pleasant, light tone throughout, as did the man who responded to her claim letter:

> After receiving your letter of November 3 about the discrepancies in your computer-service account, I checked the Whynar records.
>
> First, you were absolutely right about the service on the two computers, the 721AR and the 608A.
>
> Here is how the account now stands. You owe us nothing on the 721AR because your service contract is still in force. And you are paid up on the 608A; our April billing was a computer error. And they say computers can't make errors!
>
> We're sorry this happened and will double-check our billing in the future to see that it doesn't happen again.

In the outline, the typical seller's response to a claim letter looks like this:

- Reference to your letter and problem
- Discussion of what I found out about the problem
- What, if anything, I am going to do about it

If, as the seller, you can't do anything about the problem, then say so as nicely as possible:

> I am sorry about the problem with the shirt. But you must realize that we sell such merchandise from twenty to thirty percent below the typical retail price. The shirts are clearly marked as seconds, both on the counter and on the tag. In every "second," you will find imperfections.
>
> And these shirts *are* a bargain at their price!

The little boost for the product there at the end doesn't hurt the seller's case a bit.

A & F Electronics
P. O. Box 9812
Dayton, Indiana 47903

May 12, 1986

Lloyd Jarvis
Publications Department
National Media Corporation
9576 N. Fredricks Ave.
Chicago, Illinois 60607

Dear Mr. Jarvis:

    Over a period of about two months, we have placed a dozen orders for Maynard Clarke's *History of the Most Successful American Companies*. Orders, I am afraid, have not been centralized, but have come from several divisions in the company.

    When we were billed recently, you noted that your original advertisement said that orders were to be sent to Southern Publishing in St. Louis, because they were the originating publisher.

    At this point, you have several checks (I am not sure how many) from a number of our executives, who ordered directly from you. They did not get the books, nor did they get their money back from you. Instead, A & F Electronics received a credit memo from you for $232.17.

    We are apparently at fault for most of this problem. We should have made one order and asked for proper billing.

    I suggest that we now order directly from Southern Publishing and that you send us a check for $232.17. In addition, if you will keep sending your brochures to the present listing of people here at A & F, I promise that any more orders we send you will be coordinated here before they are sent.

    Thanks very much for your trouble.

                                            Sincerely,

                                        Don Will, Office Manager

Figure 11.1. Claim letter

Discussion Questions for Figure 11.1

1. Near the beginning of this chapter we give a sample outline for a typical claim. Does sample letter 11.1 follow this outline?
2. Explain the purpose of each paragraph in order. Why are there so many paragraphs?
3. Is the situation that Don Will is writing about clear? If you were a new employee of National Media, could you tell from the explanation what was going on?
4. What technique is Will using in the last two paragraphs? Do you think it is successful?

Diefer Insurance Co.
Mente Road
Phoenix, Arizona 85002

January 18, 1987

Mrs. Kathleen Shapland
23 Snyder Lane
Phoenix, Arizona 85021

Dear Mrs. Shapland:

After receiving your letter of January 5, I have looked into the problem you describe.

When you made your claim on the damage to your station wagon, I sent the claim forward to Southwestern Insurance. At about that time, the company started checking by photograph all damage over $1,000. That is why the company representative showed up at your door asking to take pictures of the back of your wagon. I realize that you weren't aware of this new policy of Southwestern's, but at the time I sent forward the claim, I wasn't aware of it either. The policy was changed as letters crossed in the mail.

After checking the photos of your station wagon and reviewing your claim, Southwestern reduced the amount it would pay on the damage for the car. This is why you received $200 less than you thought you would get.

At this point, I am afraid, there is nothing I can do about the situation with Southwestern. As you can see, nobody in the entire situation did anything wrong or underhanded; we all just got caught in a time warp during policy changes.

I can, however, change insuring companies for you. For about the same rate that you are now paying, I can get you the same coverage for your car with a company that has no photo requirement.

Would you like me to make this change?

Cordially,

Sam Diefer

Figure 11.2. Reply to claim letter

Claims

Discussion Questions for Figure 11.2

1. Make an outline of the letter. What does the outline suggest about the reply?
2. Does Diefer spend too much time explaining what happened? Give reasons for your answer.
3. Discuss the strategy of paragraph 4. Defend or attack the strategy. Is the paragraph put in the proper position?
4. Put yourself in Mrs. Shapland's place. Are you satisfied by the letter — and, most particularly, by the last two paragraphs?
5. Can Diefer do anything else to make this sutuation better? Or say anything else?

EXERCISES

1. How do you think the following claim should be handled?

You hired the Christie Demolition Service to knock down and clear away a building next to your company's main office building. The job was a difficult one because the neighborhood is old and the buildings were placed too close together. Your written agreement with Christie reads, in part, that it will "remove the building described as follows ... and level the ground...." Your company owns the lot involved.

Christie did a good job of removing the building, and the lot was levelled to perfection. The problem lies in the row of excellent crabapple trees on the lot line next to your main office building. These are attractive trees and flower beautifully in the spring. The company brochure has always run a color picture showing your office building and the trees in bloom.

Now the chief executive officer is very angry. Two trees near the front of the lot were damaged by Christie workers. The trees were not killed or knocked over, but large branches were torn off by the moving about of heavy equipment. The CEO wants something done about this.

You call a large nursery and learn that through careful pruning, the trees can be encouraged to grow out to something approximating their former shape (encouraged by nursery professionals at a cost, of course). Or the trees can be replaced with half-size trees put in place by special heavy equipment. Since such trees grow fast, the line of crabapples will look normal in about three years.

You have been told to handle the matter — now. And deal only with Christie Demolition Service. They'll have to take care of everything themselves. Write the claim to Christie.

2. After a death in your family, you had to leave college in mid-semester. You had shared a good apartment with three other students; and, in order to save money, had sublet your "quarter" of the apartment to a student we will call Lee Braxler.

You went to the trouble of asking Lee to sign an agreement for subletting, which included:

- No partying or noise after midnight Sunday through Thursday.
- No "sleep-overs" — that is, no students not living in the apartment to stay the night.
- A hundred-dollar breakage deposit (which you received).

Here is what happened in the last two months of the semester, the time that Lee was in the apartment:

Claims

- Lee did not keep to the agreement about partying and noise.
- On two occasions, Lee did let students sleep over.
- One of Lee's friends broke the color TV in a rock-and-roll session.
- Lee's check for the breakage deposit bounced. You got another from good old Lee (for $50), which did not bounce, and a promise of $50 more. The second check never appeared.

Lee Braxler graduated and got a good job with the Baremont Corporation. You are now back in school. Write a claim letter to Lee. (Lee can be male or female, as you wish.)

3. You are director of music at a large suburban high school in what is known as the Golden Ghetto, where even the servants have servants. Recently you bought two fine new French horns from Manheim Music, 5599 Portage Street, Philadelphia, Pennsylvania 23599. These are horns that you use with young students (usually freshmen) who are training for places in the school band and orchestra. (When the students "make" band or orchestra, their parents usually buy new instruments for them.) The students, eager to start work on the school's new French horns, unpacked the instruments themselves from the box they came in and started tooting on them. The students are fourteen-year-old girls, nice but spoiled.

What ensued reminds you of the horrors surrounding the often-told tales of dead mice supposedly found in cola drinks. There aren't any mice in the horns, but there *are* mice droppings; the girls shook the horns upside down to remove traces of the packing, and the droppings came out — the biology teacher on the faculty has identified them. Moreover, traces of nesting material that is not packing also came out of the horns. The girls got hysterical; worse, their parents are raising the roof and are threatening a lawsuit. ("Who knows what diseases the mice might have carried; how long have these vermin been making their home in the French horns!?," and so on).

To keep the peace, you have decided to write Manheim Music and ask for replacement horns. The lawyer for the parents got the serial numbers off the horns, so you can't merely clean them up and pass them off as different horns. And you can't stick a valuable instrument in a pan of hot water and boil it.

Write the claim letter.

4. Write a response to this strongly worded letter:

Dear Manager, Shopworth Inc.

You've got my account all screwed up out there. In the first place, I don't buy out at the Mall, but from your downtown store. I have an account number at the paint store that I use for any clothing for personnel here and my own personal account number that my family and I use. It's your business to keep these accounts straight, not mine. Up until May everything was straight. Then my family got billed for $103.44 worth of clothing that the paint store bought, and the store was billed for everything my son bought for his wedding; Jack Samuels was the salesman. I paid the former with check number 7785 and the latter with check number 7792 on June 1 and June 3 respectively. This should have paid us all up for the June billing. Then I got a July bill with $657.88 on it, which must have included both the paint clothing and my son's things.

Could you straighten all this out?

Ron Beldon
BELDON PAINTS

You have checked the Beldon account, and it is as Ron Beldon says; he is the owner of Beldon Paints. Everything is paid for, but the accounts are confused, with the wrong stores involved, and so on. Write a detailed answer to Ron Beldon, and say how you are going to handle things in the future.

5. Look back into your own life and recall a situation in which you might have had a valid claim. Write it up as clearly and specifically as you can.

6. You think you and your company have a claim against Giant Airways. The airline bumped you off a flight to Dallas that you badly needed to make. Your company flies a great deal with Giant. Write a claim to Giant, stressing the inconvenience of its bumping you; for the details, use your imagination. Let the details carry the weight of your argument.

7. Rewrite the following letter for tone and content. Make the reader feel that you are interested in his or her problem and that you will do what you can to solve it. *Be positive.*

Dear Optician:

You really waited too long to write about the problem you have had with our lens grinding over the past few months. We have never had any trouble before, and in fact you are the first optician to bring the matter up. We can hardly believe that all seven orders were defective, as you say they were. Did you check to see that the lenses may have been damaged in transit? In any case, you failed to notify us early enough after locating the problem, and it is too late for us to do anything about it now. It is unreasonable to expect us to grind new lenses at this late date when we are full up on work for a long time ahead. Why didn't you send us the defective lenses immediately when you found they were not done right?

Lightner Lens Service

CHAPTER 12

Credit

Credit is essentially confidence — confidence on the part of everyone involved that A will pay B at some time in the future.

You get credit by asking for it, which is why so many letters involving credit are more or less standardized. Of course, asking for it is not necessarily getting it; but that fact does not change the standardized quality of many credit requests and approvals.

FOUR QUESTIONS CONCERNING CREDIT

Credit is given after certain questions are answered (we'll use the word *company* to stand for either an individual or a group asking for credit):

1. Does the company have a good reputation? Does it pay its bills on time? What is its general record of performance?
2. What is the company's financial position? its net worth? How much does it owe, and to whom?
3. How good is the business that the company is in? Is it stable? Is there a reasonable demand for its product or service?
4. Is the company well organized and equipped to do its business? Does it have the proper machinery and personnel?

When these questions are answered, credit can be given — assuming there are no extra factors that might influence the decision.

STANDARDIZED CREDIT LETTERS

Here is an example, written on company stationery, of a credit request from one company to another:

> Will you please open a charge account for Zark Lumber Co.
> We have accounts with the following local companies:
> Caro National Bank, 31 Shippen Street
> Odel Oil Company, P.O. Box 236
> Dawsom Moving and Shipping, 186 Carter Avenue.
> Note the information on the enclosed financial statement. If you need more information, please write or call me.
> We will probably be buying about $1,000 worth of merchandise every month. (This is a rough average.)
> Thank you.

In turn, the Smith Fastener Company, to whom the credit request was written, writes to one or more of the companies mentioned. For efficiency, the writer uses a subject line on a standardized fill-in-the-blanks form. But the form is typed on a word processor so that it looks like an original letter:

> SUBJECT: Request for Credit Information on Zark Lumber Co., 1900-06 Handers Way
>
> The Zark Company has given Odel Oil Company as a credit reference. Would you fill in the blanks below for us? At the bottom of the page, please add any comments pertinent to allowing credit.
> Credit limit: _____
> Time credit has been used: _____
> Balance due at this time: _____
> Are paying habits reliable? _____
>
> Additional remarks: _____
>
> Thank you for your assistance. Your reply will be held in confidence.

APPROVING CREDIT

Letters that approve credit range from the simple statement "You've got it" to longer messages that approach salesmanship: "You've got it — and now use it and buy something from us."
The simple statement is:

> We are happy to open a new account for you. Come visit us when you can.

With selling added:

> We are happy to open a new account for you. Note the attached brochure that tells about our special sales — when you can expect them and what they offer you as a homeowner.
>
> P.S.: Our new wing is crammed full of bargains right now. We are open Tuesday and Friday nights until 9:30. Why not drop in and browse?

The postscript, placed in a position of emphasis, gives a nice casual touch to the selling aspect of the letter.

APPROVING CREDIT (THE FORMAL LETTER)

In many instances, particularly when companies rather than individuals are involved, you will need to cover the approval of credit in a more full and formal way.

A formal letter approving credit may use a pattern like this:

- Your credit has been approved.
- We are happy about this and welcome you.
- Here are the terms of credit.
- Here is how you will receive the product or service.
- Again, we are pleased (you can sell a little here, if you think your reader won't mind).

Here is a sample letter to a company that has asked for credit:

> Your credit rating is excellent, and we are very happy to approve credit for you.
>
> Here are the terms:
>
> (1) Please pay the full balance of the account within 30 days from the date of your monthly statement. If you pay within 10 days, you will get a 2 percent discount on the full amount.
>
> (2) Each month you have credit up to $2,000. If you think you need to go over that amount, please *write* Ms. Margaret Samson (Credit and Accounting). Note: Extending credit over $2,000 is done only in unusual circumstances.
>
> We will be shipping your orders by UPS within 24 hours after receiving them. We will be glad to take phone orders: call 216-333-4490.
>
> Just now we have an unusually large range of Suntar Winterware available (see the enclosed descriptions). And we can take special orders on these until November — at TEN PERCENT OFF!

REFUSING CREDIT

Refusing credit is a sticky business. When you refuse people credit you are commenting on them as well as on their financial condition. The refusal is essentially a negative message, so we discuss it under that heading in Part Five.

Following is a series of sample letters relating to credit and discussion questions for them.

Discussion Questions for Figure 12.1

1. Sentence by sentence, explain the detail in the first paragraph.
2. Paragraph 2 moves in a particular way from its opening statement. Could the paragraph have been written backwards, with the mention of the phone call coming first?
3. Could paragraphs 2 and 3 be reversed? Why or why not?
4. Describe the tone in paragraph 3. How is the command in the main clause of the first sentence softened?
5. The last paragraph is somewhat formulaic. Is this bad or good? Neither?

Lowrie Supplies
Main and Westby Avenues
Lincoln, Nebraska 68732

February 23, 1987

Charles Lyons
Purchasing, Thersa Company
2284 Timm St.
Kansas City, Kansas 66222

Dear Mr. Lyons:

    Thank you for your order of Feb. 17. We will be packing all of it in a day or so, with the exception of the magnetic couplings, which we can no longer get from Germany. You should be able to order them from J. M. Marck Co., 22 Powers St., Houston, Texas 79333.

    We will delay shipping your order because it is company policy to establish credit on so large an order as yours. Could you please forward to us the names of two firms and one bank with which you have recently done business? If you can call these in to us, this will speed the process greatly.

    If you need the supplies right away, let me suggest that you instruct us to send them C.O.D. The prices will stay the same, of course.

    It will be a pleasure to do business with your company, and I look forward to hearing from you.

                                 Sincerely,

                                 Debra Conerly
                                 Assistant Manager

Figure 12.1. Credit information letter

New Mexico Wholesale Jewelry
P. O. Box 9812
Albuquerque, New Mexico 93501

November 11, 1987

Ms. Mary Longhorn
112 E. Bush St.
Chilton, New Mexico 94422

Dear Ms. Longhorn:

    We are happy to approve credit for you, up to $3,000 each month.

    Around the first of the month, we will send you an itemized statement for the purchases made during the previous thirty days. Please make payment by the fifteenth of the month and keep a record of everything you buy and of your payment.

    You asked about stone setting graver sets. We have a good set of six sharpened setting gravers, each complete with a hardwood handle, and a metal plate showing four important steps in preparing a modern mounting. There are instructions with the set. Set order number is DI882; cost is $31.30. This is a very good value for the money.

    While I'm on the subject, let me mention two other items that are not in our present catalogue. These are <u>sale</u> items (while they last):

    --Market safety clasps, durable yet dainty. Order no. 41000, a dozen for $2.00.

    --Jeweler's saw frame, with hardwood handle, thumb screw, and holding clamps for keeping the blade tight, for $5.25. Order no. is 061337.

    Let us know whenever New Mexico Jewelry can be of help to you.

                                        Sincerely,

                                        Roberta Lucas,
                                        President

Figure 12.2 Approval of credit letter

Discussion Questions for Figure 12.2

1. At first glance, the letter seems overbalanced with selling. Do you agree? Discuss the issue.
2. Is the last sentence of paragraph 2 necessary?
3. Do you approve of all the detail in paragraph 3? Why might Ms. Longhorn appreciate knowing such information in detail?
4. Explain the function of the first five words in paragraph 4. Do you approve?
5. In paragraph 4, the word *sale* is underlined. Explain this, and also the purpose of the whole sentence.
6. Why did Roberta Lucas break down the information on the safety clasps and saw frame with dashes instead of weaving it into the paragraph?
7. Does the final paragraph seem too abrupt?

EXERCISES

1. Your company deals in technical equipment for doctors specializing in radiology. This material is expensive; setting up a lab can cost a third of a million dollars, and that does not include a CAT scanner.

Young Dr. Draper has decided to leave Goodson Hospital, where he is head of radiology, to set up his own private lab. (*Young* means that he is only forty years old.)

He has applied to you for credit for about half the cost of the equipment. You do give credit, but only after you have looked very carefully into the situation. Here is what you know about Dr. Draper:

- He has an excellent reputation as a radiologist.
- He is known to be difficult to work with.
- He is very ambitious.
- He lives high on the hog — fancy house, expensive vacations, children in private schools, and so on.
- He comes from a wealthy family. He has written you that half his new business will be financed by his father, also a physician.
- The last new private radiology lab that opened in a comparable city (400,000 people) succeeded.
- There is one private lab now in Dr. Draper's city, but it is owned by a doctor who is close to retirement age.
- Most radiologists nowadays work for hospitals and clinics, either directly for them or under a special contract to them. Sometimes two hospitals will disband their radiology sections and contract the service out to another hospital or a private lab.
- Dr. Draper has no business record — that is, he has never run a business, and has always worked for a salary and a percentage of the profits. He *has* made a lot of money as a physician.
- Dr. Draper is socially very popular in the city and mixes with the "in" crowd of the wealthy.

Dr. Draper has asked you for credit to help him get the basic equipment for his lab. Reread "Four Questions Concerning Credit" at the beginning of this chapter and write an answer to his letter of request.

2. You are the credit manager of a wholesale flower company. Frane Florist, a small business in a town of 50,000 people, has asked for credit. The information you have received on Frane is (you think) somewhat questionable. Without going into the situation in detail, you have decided you can give credit but only on a limited basis. You decided on credit up to $500 a month. The full amount on each bill will be due within thirty days, and you will allow a two percent discount if payment is made within ten days.

You also want to leave open the possibility of raising the credit limit after a certain time. What time will you choose? What, in your judgment, will determine whether the credit limit can be raised?

Write to Frane Florist, allowing credit and laying everything out clearly. Be very specific. Remember that you are after goodwill, and that there are other wholesalers in the area that Frane can buy from.

3. Write to a firm in your college town, one from which you would like to buy merchandise on a fairly regular basis. Consider carefully your assets and business transactions of recent years. Write a letter to the firm asking for credit and giving all the information about yourself that you think might be pertinent. Sell yourself, in other words. Mention your bank, and also your bank in your home town, if you think the information might be useful. Give all the detail you can that might help you gain credit. (Recheck "Four Questions Concerning Credit" at the beginning of this chapter.)

4. As a new employee at the Citizens' Bank, you are acting as a special assistant to the first vice-president. This is essentially a training job in which you learn many operations of the bank. A good customer of the bank, a large hardware firm in Oklahoma, has asked the vice-president to prepare a form letter (for the company's word processor) that can be used for most situations when responding to credit requests. Prepare a draft of the form letter for the vice-president.

5. Marie Janis is trying to start up a decorating and painting business, specializing in interiors. The community is prosperous and well able to handle another business of this kind; besides, she would be the first woman to run such a business locally, and ought to get customers simply because the other decorating firms are run by men. She has ten years' experience with a decorating firm in another city, and her husband has experience painting and wallpapering interiors. Her financial condition is satisfactory; her husband, who will work for her, appears reliable. But she has no definite character references — her previous employer has died, his second in command has retired to Florida, and the firm has gone out of business. She would have to get all (or nearly all) her supplies from you, Allstar Decorating Supplies. If you gave her credit, you would have to give her a credit limit of $5,000. Make your decision about whether to give credit to Marie Janis, and write the letter.

6. Rewrite this letter for greater effectiveness:

Dear Mr. Pardy:

We look forward to a mutually helpful situation and long-term association.

Let us know whenever you wish to reorder cameras — those you ordered or those of another brand.

Our usual terms are two percent discount if paid by the tenth of the month; total amount is due within thirty days.

You will find that all our cameras are popular with customers. They are well built and strong, and all cases are guaranteed for one year. We sell nothing but brand-name products, and all warranties are honored.

We are pleased to note that your financial record is excellent, and we are glad to have you on board. Your references were likewise excellent.

Your order of the 25th will be shipped immediately and you should receive the ten cameras shortly.

Don Lynn, Jr.

7. You are Marie Janis, the woman in Exercise 5. Allstar Decorating Supplies turned you down for credit, but you know through the grapevine that the turndown was close and could easily have gone the other way. Write to the manager of Allstar and appeal the decision. Point out that you have much good experience, that you worked for one company for ten years, leaving only when the company went out of business; that your husband, who will work for you, has years of experience in interior work, and so on. You are at present completely solvent, with no debts, $10,000 in the bank, with a serviceable van truck and a perfect credit rating in Elk City, where you came from. You need the $10,000 to buy a home and for starting materials on the business. Recheck "Four Questions Concerning Credit" at the beginning of this chapter, and write a letter to the Allstar manager appealing his decision.

8. Your large department store chain wants to encourage the return of customers who used to charge at the stores but have since either disappeared or pay cash. Create a form letter to be sent to each of these former customers. Emphasize the value of credit to them, and explain your terms carefully. Add some comments about your merchandise (standard department store items).

CHAPTER 13

Collections

Essentially, debtors pay when they think they should. Collection letters should therefore be so powerfully persuasive that debtors find themselves irresistably drawn to virtue and end by deciding (seemingly on their own) to send you the money they owe.

It is this decision to send the money more or less freely that you strive for in collection letters. And therein lies their difficulty. For debtors live in a great range of moods and degrees of honesty. Some — a few — won't pay if you approach them with a baseball bat. Many others are merely forgetful, and are truly embarrassed to have forgotten your due date.

Two things must be mentioned. First, federal law won't allow you to threaten or harass people in the process of collecting money. You can sue, of course; but the amount had better be worth lawyers' fees. And you can't legally tell a debtor you are going to sue if you don't follow through. Second, there is seldom, if ever, any reason for encouraging debtors to dislike you. Your strategy should be to avoid bad feelings as long as possible. If you can't spread happiness around, try not to spread misery — at least, not until the very end of a collection series.

You can consider a series of collection letters as an example of "graded series." With such a series you go by degrees from sweetness and light to (if necessary) darkness and damnation.

EXAMPLES OF A COLLECTION SERIES

First letter: "We know you meant to pay." Send a copy of the original bill, with a note:

> Sorry to remind you, but your bill is overdue. If you have already mailed your check, disregard this note.

Instead of the note, you can use a rubber stamp or a colorful sticker attached to the bill. Some people prefer the sticker because a note can get lost or separated from the bill.

Second letter: "Regret for everyone concerned." Send another copy of the bill with a note or sticker, or rubber-stamped message:

> We are sorry to bring this up again, but we still don't have your payment. *Please* help us keep our records up to date!

Third letter: "Is it our fault?"

> If you haven't paid because we did something wrong (that is, if the goods or services are inferior) let us know, and we will straighten the matter out immediately. We want to be fair to you, of course; and we know that you wish to be fair to us. If there is no problem, please remit as soon as you can.

This has to be in letter form, and should look like a personal message to the debtor.

Fourth letter: Put on a little pressure.

> You will recall that we have written you three times about your overdue payment.
> Please send us your payment immediately. Otherwise, we will have to turn your account over to our Collection Department.

Fifth letter: The Collection Department now writes, putting on more pressure.

> You will recall that we require payment within ten days after you receive our monthly bill.
> It has now been 90 days since we mailed our bill dated April 1.
> Please make payment immediately. We would very much prefer not to have to take further action.

At this point, we may assume that the chain of letters will be broken off. You can keep on writing letters if you wish, but probably the collection issue should now be turned over to your company's legal department or to other legal counsel.

The letters shown above are typical of the collection process, but they provide only its bare bones, and you should deviate from the suggested sequence when you think the circumstances warrant. Whatever you do, try to walk softly and hide the legal stick as long as possible. If your debtor pays something on the bill, act grateful and look hopefully to the future. For example:

> Thank you for sending us your check for $225.00. As you know, this leaves you with a $137.13 balance on your bill.
>
> We appreciate your paying a part of the bill and look forward to your sending us the remainder soon.

So far there is one device we have not mentioned. If your debtor is a company (or even a person) who clearly needs a good credit rating to stay in business, you can use a sentence like the one below:

> ...turn over your account to our Collection Department. I am sure you don't want this to happen, since it can have a negative effect on your credit rating.

Such a sentence might be most effective at the end of the fourth letter. Following are two sample credit letters and related discussion questions.

Discussion Questions for Sample Collection Letter 13.1

The letter opposite is probably as old as the century, and at least a dozen versions of it are known to exist; the author is unknown.

1. What is the basic technique of the letter?
2. When do you recognize what the technique is — in which sentence or paragraph?
3. Would you call this an aggressive collection letter?
4. If you received the letter, what would your reaction be?
5. What kind of audience would you suggest might receive this sort of form letter? What kind(s) of audience do you think the letter should not be sent to? Why?

A Very Old Collection Letter

A few weeks ago we sent a letter to several hundred readers reminding them that their subscriptions were in arrears and gently hinting that an early remittance would be appreciated.

A percentage of them promptly paid up. Some replied that they would pay "next week" or "next month" but two of these died within the week. Another said he would pay the "next time" he saw us. He went blind. And yet another telephoned that he would "run down and pay sometime." He has rheumatism now and can't even walk. Jim said he would "see us in h—— first." He got religion that night and will not be able to keep the appointment.

We have had no word from the others and you happen to be one of them. We have not taken your name off the list as yet because it seems "sorter" natural to see it there.

We have been pretty good sports to leave it there all this time. Won't you be an equally good sport and see that it stays "put." We can't carry you indefinitely.

From the London *Free Press*, reprinted, with permission, from ABWA *Bulletin*, September, 1939, p. 4.

Figure 13.1. Collection letter

Wright Milling Co.
1634 S. Joplen Ave.
Tulsa, Oklahoma 74122

November 10, 1986

Dear Mr. Gordon:

It is most unusual for us to turn an account over to our lawyers for collection. Indeed, it happens so seldom that our legal-collection file is the smallest file in our records. So when we do have to turn to the law, we feel it is only fair that we state exactly what the situation is and what may happen to the customer.

You will recall that for six months you have owed us $766.20, the original billing being sent to you on June 28, 1986. Each month thereafter, we sent you the bill again. On September 1, we sent you a personal letter. This was followed by two more personal letters, dated September 29 and October 25. We have not heard from you about this bill.

We believe that we have done whatever we could to help you make payment.

Since we have not heard from you, we have no choice but to turn the bill over to the firm of Fernandez and Wright, who will be in touch with you. We regret taking this step, partly because once the machinery of the law starts to turn, we will have no further say in the matter. There is nothing *we* can do about the inconvenience and embarrassment that the customer may suffer under these circumstances — not to mention the cost to the customer of defending himself in court.

Our lawyers have suggested a deadline of December 1 for you to pay us $766.20.

Let us hear from you — note the self-addressed, stamped envelope.

Sincerely,

Joseph Barker

Figure 13.2. Collection letter

Discussion Questions for Figure 13.2

1. Discuss the psychology of the first two sentences in paragraph 1. Is sentence 2 necessary? What does it do for the image of the company? for the feelings of the customer?
2. Is the last sentence in this paragraph necessary?
3. Describe the tone and attitude set by paragraph 1.
4. What is the strategy or purpose of paragraph 2? Would it be possible to start the letter with this paragraph?
5. Defend or attack the third paragraph.
6. Explain the psychology of the big fourth paragraph. In effect, what does this paragraph say? Does it say more than one thing? Why doesn't it come right out and say such things explicitly? Explain the italicized *we*.
7. Imagine the letter with the last two paragraphs placed elsewhere in the letter. Where might they go? Why?

EXERCISES

1. You work for a large company with retail stores in forty-eight states. You have been asked to draft a series of form letters to be used throughout the company for collection of overdue credit-card bills. The form letters now used, you have been told, are too negative and threatening; yet you are also told that the new series of letters must not be vague or ambiguous. Customers must *know* that they are asked to pay up. Here is the other information you have been given.
    a. All letters will be typed on word processors so that they will appear to be individual letters. Information for individuals will be inserted by the operator.
    b. You will supply a coding system for the letters so that the Collection Department will know what to do; that is, you will provide such information as: "When account is three months overdue, send Letter Three, and so on."
    c. This, your final instruction from the company, asks you to design the letters "from the paper up." You are the complete designer of this important series. You will take a blank sheet and decide upon placement of company logo and address; placement of message; paragraphing; use of decoration; type of complimentary close, and so on. (Check the table of contents in this book for material that may be relevant to this assignment.)
2. You handle both credit and collection for a large national company

specializing in building materials for home builders. You sold $19,820 worth of aluminum siding to Hardcase Roofing and Siding on March 3, 1986. Your terms were two percent off for payment within ten days, the net to be paid in thirty days.

Hardcase did not pay within thirty days — nor within sixty or ninety days. After 100 days have passed, you have already sent your first three form letters in the collection series.

Now you are ready for the fourth letter, which, according to company rules, must be written by you.

You wrote letter number 4.

Hardcase Roofing and Siding ignored you. So now, on day 115, you write a letter number 5. You decide to use all your skills of selling and persuading, hoping to get the money and keep the customer. Housing starts are increasing nationwide. They are booming in the Hardcase area, where aluminum siding is popular on new houses. You know that Hardcase is expanding its business and is probably overextended. J. J. Hardcase needs a good local credit standing. You are 500 miles away and he is probably paying off his local creditors first.

Accordingly, letter number 5 should try for two points: getting the money out of J. J. Hardcase while keeping the door open for more business from him. Hardcase does have a fifteen-year record of good if not perfect payment practice, so surely there is some future for financial dealings between your company and his.

Write both letters number 4 and 5. Tailor them specifically to the situation.

3. Karl Faust owed your company $2,034.55. Six weeks after you first billed him for this amount, he sent you $1,500, along with a detailed letter giving his reasons for not paying the whole amount. His business was flooded out and much of his stock ruined. He has been getting back on his feet as quickly as possible, paying each of his creditors as much as he can. He asks for an extension of a month to pay the rest of the full amount. Make your decision, and write him a letter outlining exactly what agreement you and he will come to.

4. A travel agency, Wainwright Travel Service, owes you, the manager of Twin City Office Furniture, $489.04 for office furniture purchased several months ago. You sent a bill, then a first collection letter, then a second one. You are surprised at Wainwright's problem because it is an old firm, the oldest and proudest in the region in the travel field. The grandson of the founder now runs it, but about his reputation you know nothing. The founder was famous as a person interested in charities and good works generally; the community hospital bears his name. Write a third collection letter.

5. You are the Wainwright grandson in Exercise 4. Frankly, you have been playing too much golf and living off the fat of the Wainwright name. You are, however, not a bad fellow basically, and have suddenly come to understand that if you don't get to work and pay attention to business you may not have a business. By putting in seven-day weeks for a couple of months, you think you can square away your finances. Write a letter to the manager of Twin City Office Furniture telling him what he can expect from you by way of payment.

6. Companies can on occasion make up a series of stickers that are put on bills to encourage customers to pay. Dr. Linda Torrez, a chiropractor, has asked you to create a sticker series collection, four stickers in all, that will:

> **a.** Act as payment reminders at four levels of collection, starting with the very first bill.
>
> **b.** Be tied in with the work of chiropractic — that is, related to bones, muscles, x-rays, exercise, heat treatments, manipulation of the body (particularly the back) to make it feel better and to eliminate pain, and so on. The tie-in should be lightly humorous and relevant, not macabre; encouraging, not pushy.
>
> **c.** Start with the original bill, not a later notice of nonpayment.

Write the sticker series.

7. Write an angry, mean, violent last-in-a-series collection letter to Jose von Zandt, a used car dealer who owes you $45.77 for hubcaps. (You gave him a very good deal on the hubcaps.) Von Zandt has ignored every attempt you have made to collect the money. Now write a second version of the same letter that eliminates every hateful, mean thing you said the first time. Finally, write a note, in list form, to your instructor explaining each change you made in the first letter.

8. You work for the monthly magazine *Bride and Groom*. Your supervisor has decided that, in order to save collection costs, the magazine will try using only one collection letter per delinquent account. All accounts in question have to do with subscriptions. You will allow the customer six weeks for payment, and then the account will be sold to a collection agency. You have been asked to write the letter. The subscription list indicates that most individual subscribers are women, while a large number of business subscribers are small firms specializing in wedding gifts, gowns, and so on — a mixed audience. Write the letter for it.

CHAPTER 14

Letters of Evaluation and Recommendation

A common inquiry, particularly for managers, is one made about someone you may wish to hire. When you write the inquiry for a recommendation, always be pointed and specific:

> I am writing to ask about Mr. Jackson Clay, who worked for you for two years, 1982–1983. We have an opening on our permanent staff for a serials librarian, and would like to know whether you think Mr. Clay would do well in such a job.
>
> I should mention that, since our library is large and employs dozens of student part-timers, we are looking for someone who can direct younger people in their work without seeming authoritarian. A person with two years' experience would be satisfactory for our needs.
>
> We need to make our decision by February 21, 1987.
>
> Thank you for your help.

Observe that the writer of this letter carefully describes both the job opening and the special problems surrounding it. The writer reminds the reader of how long Mr. Clay worked in the earlier job. He also describes the opening, stating that it is permanent and explaining some of the job's requirements. The reader can answer such a letter with the reasonable assurance that he or she is supplying all the information the writer asked for.

Here is a typical response (a letter of recommendation) to the inquiry about Mr. Jackson Clay, librarian:

Letters of Evaluation and Recommendations 211

> You ask about Mr. Jackson Clay and his qualifications for serials librarian.
>
> As you noted, he worked here during 1982 and 1983. He did an excellent job for us, spending about twenty percent of his time in serials. Our library is much smaller than yours, so our people must split their time among several departments.
>
> Jackson's work in serials was excellent, and I would recommend him for full-time employment in a serials department. He had no part-time help here, student or otherwise. My guess is that he would supervise student helpers very well because he is even-tempered and got along well with all the members of the library staff.
>
> I was sorry to see Jackson leave us, and I do recommend him for the job you describe.

At the heart of the recommendation is the question of fairness and truth. You have to be fair to yourself, to the company you represent, to the company and the person you are writing to, and — surely most of all — to the person you are recommending. And don't forget that there are legal issues here. Nobody wants to get tied up in lawsuits, even for the best of reasons. See "Legal Issues in Communication," in Appendix D.

In writing a recommendation, we suggest three C's: *care, caution,* and *candor.* Tell the truth, but be reasonably careful and cautious about telling it, particularly if you have anything negative to say about a person.

As part of your job, you may well have to write routine periodic reports on the activities of subordinates. These are essentially progress reports that evaluate and recommend. Here is a typical periodic recommendation; it is made on a form provided by the company:

Yearly
Evaluation and Recommendation

> Name: <u>Sasek, Jean Marie</u>   Date: <u>May 1, 1987</u>
>   Last,   first,   middle
>
> For period ending <u>April 31, 1987</u>
>
> Jean Sasek is ending her second year as supervisor of the assembly section in Electronics. She has worked for the company for three years and two months.
>
> Mrs. Sasek reports directly to me. I have checked her work regularly, usually once a week, for the past year. In addition to seeing her once a week, I talk to her about assembly problems as they arise.
>
> Mrs. Sasek is a good supervisor. She works well with her subordinates and treats equally the men and women working for her. We have had no complaints from assembly workers, with the exception of one older man for whom she had to write a reprimand in March. The man charged age discrimination, but the charge did not stick.
>
> Mrs. Sasek has an excellent quality as a supervisor. She does not wait for

problems to develop seriously or become chronic. She stays on top of the work, and has been able to keep her section ahead of the production schedule.

    My rating for Jean Sasek this period is EXCELLENT. I recommend her for a weekly raise of $25.

Joe Horton, Plant Manager

    The typical order of information in a message of this kind is as follows:

1. What the person does.
2. How long she has done it.
3. What she does well.
4. What she does not do well, if it is necessary to state this.
5. Any necessary explanation of number 4.
6. The evaluation and recommendation.

Give the necessary details on each point.

    In the report on Jean Sasek, a bit of negative information is sandwiched into the middle. Putting it either at the beginning or the end would make it stand out. Particularly, if you favor the employee, you don't want a negative judgment, or anything that can be taken negatively, as your first or last point; in that position it may influence your readers excessively.

    Following are sample evaluation and recommendation letters with related discussion questions.

Discussion Questions for Figure 14.1

1. Is there an outward purpose of the letter, as well as an unstated or underlying purpose? Explain your answer.
2. Do the first three paragraphs take too long to get to their point? If you were Ms. Krause, would you prefer that the letter get started faster?
3. Pearl says that his questions are "a bit pointed and negative." Do you agree? Why or why not? How might Ms. Krause feel about this?
4. To you, what is the most important paragraph in the letter? The second most important?
5. Do you approve of the last short sentence? Why or why not?

Letters of Evaluation and Recommendations 213

St. Charles Services, Inc.
P. O. Box 334
St. Charles, Missouri 63301

May 1, 1987

Ms. Erika Krause
Manager, Food Service
101 Barkham Hall
University of Illinois
Urbana, Illinois 61801

Dear Ms. Krause:

    Jean Goetz has applied to us for a job in sales starting next fall. If we hire her, she will be given a two-week orientation period of training and then will go "on the road." Her territory will be all of Missouri and the southern part of Illinois.

    Since Ms. Goetz worked for you for three years as part-time assistant in food service, I am wondering if you could answer some important questions for us about her.

    If we hire her, Ms. Goetz will be the first woman to sell on the road for us. Do you think she can handle being the only woman in a sales force?

    Most of the time she will be dealing with male customers. Has she had the kind of experience with you that has prepared her for this work?

    She seems to be very steady and sure of herself. Is this how you judge her?

    As I look over these questions, they seem a bit pointed and negative. Yet they are meant to help Ms. Goetz — and us. We want whoever we hire to be *successful*, and we want to be prepared to help that person toward success.

    Do let us know what you think.

                                           Sincerely,

                                           Jonathan Pearl
                                           Director, Sales

Figure 14.1. Request for evaluation

Erika Krause
205½ Indiana Street
Urbana, Illinois 61801

May 5, 1987

Dear Mr. Pearl:

I just received your letter (asking about Jean Goetz) on Friday. I didn't want to wait until Monday to answer it, and so will write you today (Saturday) and get the letter in the mail.

Jean Goetz was a student here for four years, during three of which she worked in food service. She was a part-time assistant to me for two years, not three as you said in your letter. I asked her to do this job — in fact created the position for her — because I needed her energy and ability, and the university could not finance a full-time assistant.

In her time with me, Jean performed just about every duty imaginable connected with food service, from ordering to supervising to taking care of personnel problems as they came up. Despite the fact that she was only a student, she managed to supervise people three times her age with a minimum of friction or bad feeling. Her "people skills" are truly remarkable.

If Jean has one flaw, it is that she is too energetic and too interested in doing everything that might need doing. On occasion, people in the office resented the flurry of activity that surrounded her wherever she went. But I always considered this a sort of positive flaw.

It seems to me that your basic question is: Will she fit in? I believe she will. Moreover, if she senses any problem, she will make herself fit in by special attention to the people involved.

Jean Goetz is a remarkable person, and a fine, solid worker. I recommend her very highly.

Sincerely,

Erika Krause

Figure 14.2. Recommendation letter

Letters of Evaluation and Recommendations 215

Discussion Questions for Figure 14.2

1. Reread the list of items in the typical order of information for a recommendation given just prior to these sample letters. Does Erika Krause's letter follow this list? Explain.
2. Put yourself in Jonathan Pearl's place. How do you react to Krause's first paragraph? (Was it a mistake for her to write on Saturday instead of waiting for Monday and getting the letter typed on university stationery?)
3. Consider paragraphs 2, 3, and 4. How effective are they in recommending Jean Goetz?
4. Is the next-to-last paragraph accurate? In other words, is the italicized question the right one? Does the paragraph do its job?
5. If you were Pearl, would you hire Ms. Goetz? Do you have any reservations?
6. In this recommendation has Erika Krause been *fair* to everybody concerned?

EXERCISES

1. Read this recommendation and answer the questions after it:

Confidential Evaluation of Louis Romeoli

(made by request)

Mr. Romeoli worked in our Legal Division from May 25, 1982 to June 13, 1984. Since our Legal Division is very large, he tended to specialize, as most of the people in the division do. He was assigned mainly to problems in Leasing and Production, although he was occasionally called to help out on other matters.

Romeoli had no administrative responsibility, and most of his cases were routine.

He was very quiet and did not socialize with other people in the division. He preferred not to work on cases directly involving persons outside the Legal Division; he did not, for example, like long-distance telephone interviewing. He enjoyed the theory of legal work but not some of its nuts-and-bolts applications.

In a limited way, Romeoli's performance was satisfactory, but his sort of work tends by nature to involve people of all kinds: engineers, landowners (big and small), those who know a great deal about leasing law and those who know nothing. He had trouble dealing with anyone outside his field of expertise.

We did not let Louis Romeoli go. He just seemed to "wind down" and let himself go. When he resigned we did not try to keep him. He was a pleasant and well-mannered professional; but as I said in my response to his resignation:

"You probably belong more in a legal library than on the fifth floor of a Houston skyscraper."

My own feeling is that Romeoli has good training and a good mind. He needs a different kind of job, probably, than the one we put him in.

Lee Macchiello

    a. What kind of evaluation is this? In a sentence or two, describe it: "This evaluation tries to . . ."
    b. Make two columns, one headed Good News; the other, Bad News. Write down all the good things said about Romeoli in the first, all the bad in the second. Which column is longer? Which might carry the most weight?
    c. What do you think Macchiello's "true" attitude is toward Romeoli? Is the attitude fairly stated in the evaluation?
    d. Would *you* hire Romeoli on the basis of this evaluation? For what kind of job?
    e. If you were evaluating Romeoli, would you write a different kind of evaluation? Why?

2. You are office manager for a professional association that frequently needs part-time help. During a particularly busy season, you decide to hire a fifteen-hours-per-week "permanent" part-time helper to ease the load of the regular staff.

The woman you decide to hire is a bright, intelligent young woman with a pleasing personality and extraordinary enthusiasm — at least on first impression.

After only two weeks on the job, however, you discover that this young woman is still bright and intelligent and still very personable, but that's where *your* enthusiasm stops. She is frequently late for work (without explanation); she sometimes doesn't come to work at all (but doesn't phone to say that she won't be in); when she does come to work she takes frequent breaks, even when the work is heavy and she is needed in the office.

You finally are forced to let her go.

A few weeks after she has left your employ, you get a phone call from her asking if she can use your name as a reference. You explain to her as gently as you can that you do not feel such use would be fair to her, since her work for you was unsatisfactory. You thought she understood.

Now, three months later, you are surprised to get a letter in the mail asking you for your candid evaluation of this young woman as an employee. What will you say? Write the letter.

3. Assume that Jonathan Pearl did not like his own letter (Figure 14.1), and did not send it. He asks you to rewrite it for him. Write a new draft, and also a set of notes explaining what you changed and why.

4. You are asked to write a recommendation for J. B. Williams — *good old J. B.*, anyone in your firm would immediately say. J. B. was named by his parents John Birch Williams, but for fairly obvious political reasons he would not use his first two names. In college he had read the play *J.B.*, a modern version of the Book of Job in the Bible. A curse on the professor who assigned the play, because J. B. would never let you forget that he was the most unfortunate of men. He was a walking comedy of errors. Around him nothing ever went right. He could miss a train as easily as a bus or a plane or a doctor's appointment. He was late for his own wedding.

His work was good but cursed by accidents and plagued by glitches. He tried harder than most people in the office, came to work earlier and left later, wrote longer reports, thought deeper thoughts, and in general was the most serious and ambitious of managers — only to miss glorious results by inches because of bad luck, fate, what have you. He was the sort of fellow who could take a multiple-choice test (machine graded) and have every answer right — but miss the sequence numbering and fill in the wrong lines in the answer booklet.

Write a recommendation for J. B. for a managerial position.

5. You have just finished interviewing Miss Selma Kleinsasser for an entry-level job in your firm. She says that she prefers *Miss* to *Ms*. You paid for the interview — had her flown to your city at your company's expense. Miss Kleinsasser has an average of 4.96 (5.0 is perfect) from a top business college in a major university. She has glowing recommendations from her professors, one of whom is internationally known. To the interview she wore a dress that was grotesquely out of style. The interview itself went strangely. To most questions, she answered in monosyllables. She volunteered almost nothing. She seemed tense and awkward and afraid. What does all this mean? From her recommendations she should be a first-class prospect for your firm. You decide to write to her recommenders (there is plenty of time to do so; you won't be hiring for two months). Write a letter to be sent to three recommenders. Try to find out diplomatically if there are any problems with her. She won't have to meet the public, so you are not worried about a possible speech problem, but she will have to get along with other members of the office staff.

6. Allen Galico came to you two years ago with two degrees, one in theology and one in business: an unusual academic background. As it happens, the theology degree was from a very strait-laced small college in one of the minor strait-laced denominations. Allen is personable to the point of sweetness. He can get along with almost anybody, the exception being anyone who uses bad language. Allen does not swear. For two years, his propensity for clean language made no difference, and Allen shot up in the company, with one fine success after another. All was rosy until a new vice-president came on board, a gifted man with an approach of hail-fellow-well-met, and have you heard the one about the farmer's cow and the steam engine? This man and Allen Galico mixed like oil and water. Finally one day Allen got so angry at the new vice-president's latest joke — a scurrilous affair involving sex, minorities, and a religious parody — that he simply quit on the spot.

A week later, you received a request for a recommendation for Allen from a firm similar to yours. Write the recommendation.

7. Write a recommendation for a famous person in the world of entertainment or athletics.

8. Write a recommendation for a real person whom you know fairly well, someone that you don't like very much — perhaps something in his or her personality "puts you off." You do, however, respect this person's work and professionalism. Try to be fair and positive while indicating delicately the possibility of a personality problem.

PART 5

Negative Messages

CHAPTER 15

Negative Messages

INTRODUCTION

A negative message is one that the receivers would prefer not to read. They may be greatly disappointed, or even enraged, when they read it. So you can see why the negative message has become one of the commonest problems in business communication. Lately, we have been hearing more of this kind of comment from both the public and private sectors:

> Right now we have many bad things to tell people. Somebody's got to tell the vice-president we lost a contract; tell a customer the part for her ten-year-old washer is unavailable; tell a woman we can't hire her because we don't have the budget we thought we had; tell the paving inspector we are going to be six weeks late getting our entry to Vine Avenue finished. We've got an endless number of things like these going out.

To solve the problem of the negative message, authorities in communication have suggested six techniques for shaping it. We'll assume here that the *it* is a letter, although of course it can be almost anything from a phone call to a long memo.

As you consider these techniques, remember that the negative message is going to provide a shock, sometimes a big one, to your reader. In most forms, it is a turn-down. You are forced to tell your reader that he or she won't get the job, the loan, the approval of an application for gas heat, the timely delivery of goods, the adjustment of imperfect service. Although there is little you can do to avoid disappointing the reader, you should try to make your message as courteous as possible. Here are the six techniques:

1. Consider using a buffer at the beginning of the letter. The buffer absorbs the shock of the turn-down; or, to describe it another way, provides a touch of human sympathy at the outset. These are typical buffers as they appear in letters:

> We have read your application carefully, and are impressed by your qualifications . . . However . . .
>
> Your proposals for a new water system have many obvious merits. Among them . . . Yet . . .
>
> I have talked with all members of the committee about your situation, but . . .

Authorities on business writing disagree about the use of a buffer. Some even argue against using it at all, believing that it tends to be an unthinking cliché. Sometimes it is. Yet you will often notice the unhappiness of readers about a negative message that starts out bluntly: They feel hurt, resentful, or put off. When they do, bluntness is a mistake. You should probably try (in your own way, using your own words) to provide a shock absorber in the negative message — assuming always that the message in question calls for one. It is true that some do not, and in those a buffer just gets in the way. One of us, for example, recently received this letter:

> March 5, 1986
>
> Dear Professor Tibbetts:
>
> I am sorry that we can't provide the graduate assistant for paper grading in English 438. Right now, the department budget just doesn't have the money for graders.
>
> Sincerely,
> William Brown, Chairman

There's no real buffer in that letter, unless you want to say that "I am sorry" is one. *I am sorry* is a ritual expression, rather like *Sincerely* at the end of the letter. As such, it is better than nothing and keeps the letter from seeming curt and unfriendly.

Returning to the issue of the buffer, suppose the chairman had started his letter this way:

> I know how much you have wanted to expand the offerings in English 438 — to offer more sections and allow more students to learn the material in this very popular course. And of course *you* know that the department would like to set aside money for these fine educational purposes. . . .

Despite the positive tone and you-attitude here, such a buffer fails to work. As the receiver of the letter, what Professor Tibbetts wanted was *information* — right now and without the empty talk. Now for the second technique for shaping the negative message.

2. Make your turn-down as early as you can. Don't make readers wait too long for the turn-down; waiting may make them quite angry. We once saw a businesswoman rip up a long letter and throw it on her office floor. What angered her was a two-paragraph buffer that made her think she was going to get something, when actually it was just the preparation for a turn-down.

Many good textbooks in business writing disagree with us about putting the turn-down early. They recommend putting the facts early — that is, the reasons for the turn-down. Our experience is that in many cases this does not work. Consider carefully your situation and reader. If you believe that placing the turn-down late will help, place it there. Be flexible!

3. Make your turn-down clear. Don't mince words, and don't be ambiguous. Your readers want to know the worst, and they should know the worst in the clearest way possible. Be as polite as you can, but don't be so diplomatic that the effect of your turn-down is lost on them. There is no getting around the fact that your message is essentially a negative one.

4. Be factual. After the turn-down, explain in reasonable detail why you cannot give the person what he or she wants. A reasonable and factual explanation will make the recipient feel better because it indicates that you took the time to deal with the person's problem. In addition, by giving the facts you may well open the way to more negotiation of the problem.

5. If possible or practical, leave hope for the future at the end of the message.

> ...Ms. Ryan, although the Recreation Committee did not accept your proposal at this time, why not submit it again in January? As you know, the company will have another $2,000 in the Recreation budget after the first of the year....

Or:

> ...We are sorry your sander motor burned out. As a hobby model, however, it was not made for the sort of heavy work you tried to do. If you would try our carpenter's model, you will find that it can do that work easily; and we can guarantee the motor for heavy use.

Warning: Don't leave hope if there isn't any!

6. Use a friendly tone throughout. Don't be flippant, too casual, or humorous, however. Attempting to soften the impact of a negative message by a light-hearted tone and attitude can infuriate the receiver more than the turn-down itself.

EXERCISES

1. Discuss the effectiveness of this negative message.

LONGCHAMPS APARTMENTS

January 2, 1987

Mr. John Garst
505 N. First
Ross, Illinois 61880

Dear Mr. Garst:

    I am very glad you have decided that Longchamps Apartments would be the ideal place for you to live. We are proud of the building and the reputation that it has earned over the years.

    This year has been rather unusual because we are only midway through our renting season and yet are already full and have been forced to turn people away for the past two weeks. As a rule, we seldom have all twelve of our apartments available for renting, since we always give priority to our present tenants and allow them the option of staying on before we even consider new ones. Many of them do stay — in fact, next year half of the apartments will be occupied by tenants who will be staying on, leaving only six apartments to be rented. In addition, the large number of students who are always interested in living at Longchamps contributes to our high occupancy rate so early in the season.

    I wish you good luck in your search for housing for next year. I'm sure there are still many other apartments available. If you think you would possibly be interested in living here the following year, feel free to drop by our apartment any Saturday afternoon, when we would be happy to answer any questions you might have. Next spring, then, you should see us in mid-February to assure yourself of an apartment. You can stop by in person or write. As before, we can be reached by phone at 344-7996.

    I hope you will keep us in mind. We are always ready to welcome students who will contribute to a graduate study atmosphere.

Very truly yours,

Horace Grundlich
Manager

2. A short writing exercise on the negative message:

Let's consider a personal catastrophe. What is the worst thing that could happen to you, as a student, in a business or economic sense? Examples: losing (for good) your transportation to college, your scholarship, your excellent and inexpensive room and board.

How would you prefer to be told about this calamity? Imagine that you are the person who has to tell you, and write the letter explaining the situation completely. Consider again the six techniques for writing negative messages discussed in this chapter.

REFUSING REQUESTS

When people make a request, they usually believe that it's a sensible one, or they wouldn't make it in the first place. So at the beginning, a request puts you in a double bind because your reader has high expectations of getting what he or she wants. To refuse such a request you must say *no* while retaining a reasonable amount of the requester's goodwill.

Here is a typical problem. You chair a committee that evaluates appeals for real estate tax relief for private homes. Mr. Alois Item, who owns a house in a middle-class part of town, has filed a request every year. Each year he is turned down, and each year he gets angrier. Your committee has just asked you to inform him of its decision to turn him down — again. They suggest that you write a letter that might pacify Mr. Item, for a while at least. Here is your letter, with your comments (in parentheses) on the problems of the negative message in question:

(Although Mr. Item has a tendency to lose his temper, he is very intelligent. I must not only tell him the complete truth, but I must also avoid any obvious tricks in doing it. First, a short buffer.)

"The committee has just met on your request for property-tax relief. We took up your request very early this year because we know you are anxious to get the matter resolved."

(Now the turn-down.)

"The committee has voted unanimously to maintain your tax evaluation without change, so this year you will be paying the same tax as you did last year. Members of the committee have asked me to explain their reasoning."

(I could have put the turn-down in a not-form "... voted unanimously not to allow you a lower tax...." But I thought that sounded too negative. I now quickly introduce the idea of reasons for the action's being taken.)

"First, there has been no change in any of the standards for judging the issues surrounding property taxes. The state multiplier is the same as last year's. The rules made by the local authorities are the same.

"Perhaps more important, the market evaluation of your house has not decreased. The average price of a house sold in your neighborhood in the

last twelve months was $78,000. Your house is evaluated for tax purposes at $25,500 (a third of the market value) times three for a total of $76,500.
(I might have said to Mr. Item that he is really $1,500 to the good; but he is undisposed to take such comments as anything other than unpleasant irony. The best thing to do now is to get out of this letter as quickly as possible. Any "hope for the future" I might give him would probably be taken the wrong way.)

"If I can give you any more information on the question of your tax, please call me."

Cranston Chavez

REFUSING CREDIT

You refuse credit, ordinarily, in order to get something else: You may want to get more information (so that credit can be allowed), or to encourage the person or group of people to buy in cash. In other words, you usually aren't just trying to slam the door.

You build a credit-refusal letter on a foundation of facts about the situation. Here is how one letter was designed to respond to the credit request of a new small-volume retail store specializing in miniature reproductions.

> Thank you for your order of twenty assorted animal statues, and also for your request for our Credit Account.
>
> As you know, on the receipt of such requests we have to run a credit check — which we did, using the information that you sent. The information we received was all positive, but we note that your assets-liabilities ratio is dangerously low. So we can't — *right now* — allow you purchases on a credit basis.
>
> We both know, however, that matters can change very fast. If your situation changes significantly, would you please let us know? We hope you can qualify for a credit account soon.
>
> At this point, do consider buying our statues for cash — and getting the standard discount that goes with buying for cash!
>
> Hilary Morten

We said a moment ago that you build your credit-refusal letter on a foundation of facts. But this does not mean that you state all those facts in your refusal. In the letter above, for example, if you stated what your accepted assets-liabilities ratio was, your reader might well note this figure and call you the moment her store reaches it. Do you want this result in this case, where flexibility is important to you? The new store appears to be in an unstable condition generally, and perhaps you would be better off dealing in cash until the little firm gets on its feet. If you don't make promises, you don't have to break them.

Here's a different example of a credit refusal, one that, taken altogether, is somewhat more positive:

> Welcome to Venture City!
>
> We appreciate your asking Goodenough Department Store for credit. We checked the references you gave us, and are pleased to tell you that the report is excellent.
>
> Our problem is that you are a brand-new graduate on a brand-new job. And you have practically no money in the bank.
>
> So we suggest that instead of buying from us on a credit basis, which might put an unforeseen strain on your budget, you use cash. We can serve you best if you buy from us on a cash basis, a little at a time.
>
> In a few months, when you have settled in, and you can see better where you are going financially, try us again for a credit account.
>
> In the meantime, watch for our sales. They often present bargains, and in them you may find inexpensive items to help you get started in Venture City.

This letter is positive throughout. The beginning short sentence, "Welcome to Venture City!" is set off in its own paragraph and is a pleasant way to begin. You tell the reader that the credit report is "excellent." The reminder that the reader is young and has almost no money is positively done.

The turn-down is in the fourth paragraph. Originally, in a first draft, the turn-down read: "So we suggest that you don't try buying from us on a credit basis...." In the final draft of the letter, this was changed to: "So we suggest that instead of buying from us on a credit basis, which might put an unforeseen strain on your budget, you use cash."

The next-to-last paragraph gives hope for the future, suggesting, "Try us again for a credit account." And the final paragraph makes an attempt to sell the reader on sales and bargains.

Perhaps you have noticed that the turn-down in this letter does not come right out and say, "We won't give you credit." Yet the letter has a record of success. Why? What is your opinion of the technique used here? Would you argue against using it in most negative messages?

REFUSING ADJUSTMENTS

A friend of ours bought an expensive American car, the biggest one made by the company. He liked the car, which gave him no trouble. One day, when he was waiting to pick it up after routine service at the dealer's, he idly asked the chief salesman what the warranty covered on a certain part of the car.

The chief salesman, who had been quite affable up to that moment, said: "Read the manual on the car," and turned and walked away.

Our friend picked up his expensive car, drove it out of the dealer's lot, and never went back.

Here was a case of mishandling an adjustment — but one that was never even asked for! The story shows just how sensitive people can be about adjustments and everything surrounding them.

When refusing adjustments, consider these three truths:

1. People don't like to be accused, even when they are guilty of something. Try not to tell them directly that they did not handle your service properly or that they abused your product.
2. People will often respond to the facts of the case if you can present them attractively enough.
3. "Hope for the future" is especially important because your customer already has your product or service. Try to make the customer feel better.

Here is a rather unusual set of circumstances that required a carefully written letter. A physician had a patient with a heel spur. (The typical spur extrudes from the bottom of the heel bone so that it becomes painful to walk.) The patient had visited the doctor three times in one month for treatment of his heel spur; each time he emerged unhappier than before. Incidentally, he was a jogger, and he told the doctor that he continued to jog even though she had advised him against it. On the fourth visit, he threatened her with getting a second opinion and "putting on some pressure at the clinic to see why I'm not getting any help with my problem." He also complained bitterly about her fee in relation to "the service you're not giving me."

The doctor thought this over. She wasn't getting anywhere talking to her patient, so she decided to write him a letter:

> I'm sorry that your heel spur continues to plague you as it does. Under any circumstances, a spur is unpleasant; if one is as active and athletic as you are, it can be frustrating.
>
> Now here is what we face about your heel spur. It is not likely to disappear. As time goes by, if you are careful in the way you use your foot, it may get used to the spur and you can walk about normally. I have even known spur victims to be able to resume hiking after a while.
>
> But the great majority of spur victims are unable to jog any more; the motions involved in jogging pound all the leg joints and are particularly hard on the feet. For you, jogging is like driving a spike right up through the bottom of your foot.
>
> You mentioned a possible operation. On the basis of the x-rays I don't recommend one. Dr. Blazar concurs with me in this opinion. Such operations are done in only one in ten cases — and these are severe cases. Remember also that the operation typically requires several months of recuperation, and during most of this long period the patient is on crutches — not a pleasant prospect for someone as active as you are!
>
> I am very much encouraged that by using the plastic heel cup I gave

you, you are able to walk normally for a mile a day. At this stage, that is very good. After a while you may be able to walk more.

May I suggest that you continue to wear your heel cup and to walk a moderate amount every day. When it's painful, don't walk.

Don't give up! With any luck, you can exercise more than most Americans ever think of doing; but jogging, I'm afraid, is out.

The doctor's letter is another example of ways to modify a writing formula for the occasion. First, she recognized that she was dealing with the typical middle-aged jogging enthusiast. Exercise was a religion to this person, and she had to push for a conversion to common sense.

She decided to try a combination of flattery and what might be termed "*we*-attitude." Flattery: "if one is as active and athletic as you are." *We*-attitude (that is, we are all in the same boat): "Now here is what we face about your heel spur."

In the second paragraph the physician begins lining up her facts about heel spurs and what victims can do by way of exercise. She emphasizes what jogging does to a spur — pounding it. She gives the facts about the spur operation.

The last three paragraphs combine hope for the future with win-one-for-the-Gipper. (This physician ought to be a coach.)

All things considered, her letter is an excellent example of positive material and tone. Then why the negative remark at the end? Well, her reader seems to need to have facts repeated, and she's got to re-emphasize the fact that if he jogs, he hurts.

Now for a letter on a more common problem, in which a customer wanted to return a supposedly faulty room air conditioner six years after purchase. The seller could find no reason for giving the customer her money back. The seller writes:

I am sorry you are having trouble with your air conditioner. Before going any further, let me outline the history of the air conditioner since you bought it.

You purchased it on June 12, 1980. We performed warranty work on July 17 and September 22. On October 1, we winterized the unit. As you can see from the enclosed service record, the last time you called us for service was six years ago.

We have no record of the air conditioner needing service after the September 22 date six years ago. The warranty carries a five-year limit, of course — a matter over which our store has no control.

The air conditioner is made by a reputable company, and it is a well-engineered model. I'm only guessing, but probably its problem could be solved by our repair people. At least we could try.

If you'd like, we would bring the unit into our shop and then give you an estimate on repairs. The estimate would cost you nothing, of course.

What do you think?

We liked this letter the first time we saw it. The writer slid the turn-down by the reader so smoothly she probably never noticed where it was in the letter. Yet it is there. And so is the offer of specific help — and in addition a possible service sale for the store.

EXERCISES

1. A couple named James and Karen Regnier stayed at the Riverfront Resort, a high-class hotel on the river in St. Louis. Just before checking out, the Regniers learned that they were paying $35 a night more for their room than the people right next door. The people next door had asked for a family rate when they phoned for a reservation. The Regniers had assumed that if the Riverfront Resort had had variable rates for the same room, they would have been told this when they phoned for their own reservations.

Mrs. Regnier wrote to the resort to complain. Below is the manager's answer. As a negative message, how successful is his letter? Make a few notes for class discussion.

**KLEM'S
RIVERFRONT RESORT**

Dear Mrs. Regnier:

Recently I had the opportunity to read over your comments regarding your recent stay at Klem's in St. Louis. First of all, I would like to thank you for picking our hotel during your stay, and also for the kind words concerning your previous visits here.

In response to your inability to receive a discounted rate, let me assure you that our package rates are not kept secret. In fact, Klem's, like many other hotels, spends thousands of dollars each year advertising various special packages.

As was explained to you, a few requirements must be met in making reservations for our different packages. The purpose of advance reservations is to insure that each guest receives all amenities and services promised with the package. I am sure you can understand how last-minute additions leave room for disappointment to all concerned.

I am sorry to read that you may not be staying with us in the future. I hope you will reconsider, with renovations now taking place, that we are within a few short months of becoming one of the finest hotels in the country.

If you do decide to stay at Klem's again, please contact me personally. You have my assurance that I will do all within my power in offering you the best available rate, and a most enjoyable stay.

>Sincerely,
>
>Frances Rossi
>Front Office Manager

2. You have just started to work for a company that sells office furniture. The company has no retail outlets; the salesmen sell directly to firms, usually not to individuals. Your predecessor, who has gone to another job in another company, approved a sale of an oak desk to a vice-president of a bank after she had retired and started a part-time consulting business.

The first time you are aware of a problem is when the vice-president writes to you on her new consultant's stationery, saying that she is unhappy with her new oak desk and everything related to it.

In her letter to your company, she makes these points:

- the desk is not solid oak, as promised;
- the salesman told her that she would get a standard discount for firms, but she was charged full price;
- the desk is not big enough for her to manage her new word processor as she wants to;
- there is a stain of some kind (water?) on the top;
- in shipping, the desk was scratched;
- the salesman told her that if the desk was not completely satisfactory, she could return it at the company's expense.

You must operate within your company's rules covering cases like this. In addition, there are certain facts and judgments that must be dealt with:

- The price she paid for the desk is that for the standard veneered model. The solid oak desk costs $105 more. It is the same size.
- You would not have approved the sale to her if you had been in your predecessor's position.
- Any damage as a result of shipping should be taken up with the mover, the Jarbix Company.
- Any damage as a result of manufacture should be taken up with you.
- The salesman's comment was not made in writing, and you are not sure what he said; but he has a reputation for being expansive with customers and promising more than he can deliver.

Write a letter to your angry customer.

3. You are responsible for writing your company's annual report, a publication that has been outstandingly successful since you took it over.

The company president has written you a memo making a strong request for major changes in this year's annual report. Here are the relevant paragraphs of his memo:

> First, would you please rearrange the financial information so that the auditor's statement comes first? Any added data can be put in an appendix. Second, the charts in last year's report seemed to get in the reader's way. Could you reduce the number of charts in the text? Third is the problem of public relations in the report; can we increase this aspect of our presentation?
>
> Fourth, we had a complaint from Samuel Withins — as you know, he is a board member — that the style of the last report was too casual. Can you do something about this? Fifth and last, please put all pictures of executives inside the front cover.

You know, of course, that the president is asking for some inappropriate changes. Write a memo refusing his request as firmly (but pleasantly) as you can. Explain carefully why you are refusing.

Perhaps you will want to give in on one or two points, just to gain acceptance of your other points. If you think you must give in on a point, which would you choose?

Write the memo as if your job depended on it.

4. You own the Smyth drilling company, a small outfit that specializes in drilling water wells.

On October 18, 1986, you started drilling a well on Jake Stacy's farm. Your arrangement with Stacy was to drill to whatever depth was necessary to get a good supply of water for farm use. The location was settled on by both of you: a point 120 feet from the farm house and 75 feet from the nearest barn.

You drilled 80 feet without getting enough water to provide for Stacy's needs. You called Stacy by long-distance phone; he had left on October 15 for a Florida vacation. He was reluctant to let you drill deeper, but said on the phone that you could go ahead.

You drilled to 118 feet and on October 20 twisted off the drill pipe in the hole — something that does happen, but not often. Ordinarily, this is no problem; you just move the drilling equipment, get annoyed about the cost of the lost pipe, and start a new hole a few feet away.

But at 118 feet, you also hit the aquifer of all time, and up came the water gusher. Your driller was panicked by this Niagara in his face (which is why he twisted off the drill pipe).

By then you had a small river of water shooting out of the ground and heading straight for Stacy's barn, which is down-slope. This went on for two days until you could get the well capped. You managed to divert the water away from the barn into the fields, but not before the barn was flooded. You opened up the barn, aired it out, and trucked off the ruined produce and hay.

All this time, Jake Stacy was vacationing in Florida with his family. You are going to have to write him a letter on October 25 to inform him of everything

Negative Messages   235

that has happened, and also try to get a decent well completed before he gets back, in two weeks' time.

Write your negative message.

5. You are the manager of a retail store in one of America's largest midwest cities. The store is part of a nationwide chain. You recently interviewed four candidates for assistant manager — a good position, one that many aggressive young men and women applied for. You hired one of the four top candidates, the one you and your staff rated (from the interviews and other evidence) as number one. Applicant number four was turned down (not unanimously) by you and your staff. Here is some information (relevant and not so relevant) about applicant number four, in no particular order:

- He has two years' experience in retailing.
- He presented three recommendations from previous supervisors, two of them superior and one lukewarm.
- He holds a B.A. in psychology and an M.B.A. from a university with a weak reputation in business.
- He dropped hints that he came from a wealthy family.
- His undergraduate grade average was 3.4 on a scale of 5.0.
- Two of your staff rated him as number one or two; three of the staff said "Don't hire." One wrote you a note saying, "I can't work with this man."
- When questioned by you about your kind of retailing, he always had very smooth answers but was never specific or detailed.
- In the interview, he kept remarking about the "structural psychology of retailing." He said at one point that "a store must be structured to maximize the psychology wants and desires of the customer," but he could provide no details to support this observation.
- He dressed very well and drove a Porsche.
- He was charming to everyone, particularly the secretaries and salespeople, who clearly would have hired him if they could.
- He has a heavy mustache.
- He is married (his second marriage, he said). He was not asked about this; it was volunteered.
- His hobbies are Japanese art and music, and he has a fair knowledge of Japanese. Eventually, he said, he would like to work in Japan as the company's American representative.

On your desk is a letter from the company's senior vice-president, its rising star. Your number four candidate, as described above, is his nephew, a fact concealed until now. In a very pleasant letter to you, the vice-president wants to know why his nephew did not get the job, "since he appears to be extremely well qualified."

Write an answer to the vice-president. Assume that there was little difference in the paper qualifications of the four candidates. Exception: Candidate four's B.A. grade average was lower than that of the others.

6. This has not been a good college term for you. First, you broke your leg playing your favorite sport. Second, you got a case of the flu that refused to go away and was followed by a serious chest cold. Later, your instructor in math was called home to India and never returned, so you missed important material on the math department's general final that all students in all sections had to take. If this wasn't enough, you also broke up with your boy (girl) friend — an event that supplied a miserable few days. In addition, the heating system in your dorm acted up and for ten days alternately froze and roasted you and the other students.

Your uncle is paying for your education, and when he sees your grades for this term he is going to hit the ceiling. He is a strict and short-tempered person who never had a piece of bad luck in his life ("You make your own luck," is his favorite motto). It is a part of your agreement with him that you will send him your official college grade report every term.

Send him the (bad) report and also your negative message explaining the situation.

7. An important charity in your area, the Good News Fund, has asked your company to join its program for giving. The program entails setting up a system inside the company for collecting money from employees either through cash gifts or withholding from paychecks. Last year, when you were in charge of the Good News Fund campaign inside the company, there was a good deal of complaining from employees about giving money. Some felt that they were being forced to give. Others said that for political or religious reasons, they could not give money that might end up in the coffers of subgroups in the Good News Fund that they did not approve of. The president of your company has decided that a Fund campaign inside the company would be more divisive than helpful. He told you to tell Good News Fund that while employees are certainly free to give on their own, they could not be solicited on company property or use the company's communications system for a campaign.

Write a negative letter to the Good News Fund.

8. You work full-time for the athletic association in your college or university. The association is responsible for coordinating all intercollegiate activities at your school. The college basketball coach is very successful. He is also personable and a good speaker, much in demand around the state, particularly at alumni dinners and high school athletic banquets. He gets about ten times the number of requests for speeches that he can accept. Your supervisor has asked you to draft a form letter that can be sent (with perhaps a few changes here and there) to most of the people he must turn down.

Write the letter. Assume that all copies of it will be typed on a word processor.

9. You are the general manager of a firm of electricians that specializes in wiring new and old houses. Your firm did a small job for Mr. Clay Mable, wiring an addition he put onto his house. The addition has a good-sized unfinished attic; following local and state electrical codes, you ran wire along the roof trusses and stapled it to the wood of the truss. Mable uses the attic as storage. One day he took up to the attic some old clothes kept on hangers. Finding no convenient way to store the clothes, he simply hung them on one of the wires. The wire pulled out of its staples and also out of its connection at the nearest box. Then it shorted out and started a small fire that was put out with a small amount of damage. Mable wants you to fix his wiring, which he said was "not put in right."

Write a letter to Clay Mable.

10. You are up against your annual problem: Ruth Ayers, long-time principal of Bardeen Grade School, has written asking you for permission for her third-grade class (a total of fifty students) to visit your plant, which makes heavy machinery. Every year, for as long as you can remember, Miss Ayers troops fifty or so eight-year-olds through your plant, and every year you and your supervisors are scared to death.

Why? Well, just visualize fifty children accompanied by one elderly principal. What might happen to children in a plant that makes heavy machinery if she should lose control of them?

Use your imagination and write a turn-down to Miss Ayers, who has been making this visit to the plant since before you were born.

PART 6

Report Writing

CHAPTER 16

Reports in General

A report is meant to be a lasting record of your thoughts on a subject or problem. You may spend a week or several months working up a report, and it may be read by many kinds of people: accountants, scientists, lawyers, technicians, laymen. Identifying your reader is very important. Never write for too narrow a readership. Experience shows, as a matter of fact, that the better the report the wider its possible audience. One writer had the embarrassing experience of writing a report on a scientific problem, only to have the division supervisor, a scientist in a different field, ask him some pointed questions about his technical jargon. The writer learned then that even though they work on the same projects, specialists in different fields don't necessarily use the same terms for technical matters.

A good report, like a good movie, gets a word-of-mouth reputation, and out of curiosity people outside your field may want to look at a report of yours even if it touches only indirectly upon their professional lives.

By their very nature, reports use the strategy of persuasion because they ask the reader to believe something or do something (or both). No matter how much exposition the writer inserts for evidence, the main strategy is that of persuasion: the writer wishes to convince readers that the facts, evaluations, or calls for action in the report are valid.

A report differs from some other types of written persuasion in that it relies more upon what is called the weight of evidence. In effect, the report-writer often seems to say to readers: "Here is a problem, and here are the results of my work on it. Don't you agree that my results show (1) that the facts clearly indicate a particular situation or condition, and (2) that certain action should be taken?"

Points one and two represent the writer's conclusions that are based on the available evidence, and it is one of the major characteristics of a report that the evidence may often support conflicting conclusions. Indeed, a report should be written so clearly and honestly that a reader can say, "I understand everything that you have done, but I question your conclusions. Isn't it possible that your conclusions should be as follows ... ?"

Two questions arise here. First, what is a report problem? It is any problem that requires a detailed explanation and, usually, a call for action of some kind. You may be asked to find a new method of manufacturing large amounts of brass cheaply. Or, on your own, you may decide to find out exactly why physicians are quitting your college's Student Health Service. Regardless of where the problem originates, it is up to you to narrow it down and define it. The Overview of this book is helpful in this regard, as is Part IX, "Using the Library."

A second question is: What form do I use? Reports can take many forms. There are business reports, technical reports, scientific reports, progress reports, feasibility reports, proposal reports, and reports on reports. We suspect that some of the elaborate classification of report forms are made up by textbook writers on the subject. Anyhow, if you have a report to write on the job, don't begin by checking a textbook (even this one). First, go to your organization's files and see what forms the standard reports take, and use those, unless you can see room for definite improvements.

HOW DOES THE BUSINESS WORLD THINK ABOUT REPORTS?

One answer can be found in this story. An important businessman was speaking at an open seminar attended by fifty or sixty students and a few instructors. One student rose and asked a question:

What does your company look for most in a report?

"Clarity and brevity" was the answer.

Brevity? How brief can a report be?

"As brief as possible — one sentence, if you can make it that short. I ask my people to see to it that no report more than two pages long comes to me. If a report runs longer than that in its original version, they boil it down for me."

But surely some reports have supporting material that requires greater length?

"Oh, yes. I have seen useful reports packed with information that required fifteen to twenty pages. Mind you, I am talking about text. Supporting material, particularly if it is technical, can usually be put in an appendix.

"Remember, our company is successful partly because we want to spend more time thinking and working than writing and reading. We have two questions about a report: (1) What can it tell me that I don't know? and (2) What can it tell me to do — and why? Most business problems aren't so complicated that the writer needs from twenty to thirty pages to answer those two questions. Reports are written to satisfy the needs of readers. If readers need many pages of text to understand a problem, then you should give them a long report. But I will tell you honestly: I don't see such needs every day."

How formal are your reports?

"I don't understand the question."

When do you require a formal, and when do you require an informal report?

"The question doesn't arise with us, and I haven't heard of it arising with other companies either. It's like the question of length. We don't ask for formal or informal reports for the same reason that we don't ask for long or short reports. In other words, these aren't report categories. We simply want a report that does its job and then stops, one that is clear and brief and covers its subject. But that's where I started a moment ago, isn't it, with clarity and brevity?"

HOW SHOULD YOU THINK ABOUT REPORTS?

Essentially, you should think about the report as you think about other messages. The suggestions in the Overview apply. There is one other thing to consider. Over the years, writers of reports have developed an outline of the typical report. This is a standard full outline that you should consider using — if you need all the parts in it. Here are the parts:

- PREFATORY
    Title page
    Transmittal letter
    Table of contents
    Abstract
- BODY
    Introduction
    Body of report
    Conclusions
    Recommendations (sometimes Conclusions and Recommendations are combined)
- SUPPLEMENTS
    Appendix(es)
    Bibliography (only if necessary)

In the next few pages, we will consider these outline parts one by one. A series of examples and comments about them follows.

FINAL EXPLORATION REPORT ON <u>EAGLE PROSPECT</u>

Prepared for

The Opel Oil Company

2443 Devon Road

Tulsa, Oklahoma 74120

Prepared by

A. L. Patterson

Party Chief, Crew 68

Pasadena Exploration Company

242 Schindler Street

Pasadena, California 91100

August 14, 1986

Figure 16.1. Title page

Comment on Figure 16.1
Title pages are designed to tell readers:

1. that the report has a name (describing the work that was done)
2. that the work was done for somebody
3. that the work was done by somebody
4. that the report on the work has a date.

The sample title page is typical. It gives all the information listed above. The title tells readers that it is an exploration report and that it covers an area named the Eagle Prospect, the latter phrase being underlined to make it stand out. Two blocks of information are given under *prepared for* and *prepared by*. The date stands out near the bottom of the page.

It is usually unwise to give much information on a title page because it creates clutter. Make sure you give enough, however. Here the adjective *exploration* in the title is important because it limits the report material. Other reports on the same Eagle Prospect might read:

- FINAL *GEOLOGICAL* REPORT ON EAGLE PROSPECT
- FINAL *DRILLING* REPORT ON EAGLE PROSPECT
- FINAL *RECOVERY* REPORT ON EAGLE PROSPECT
- FINAL *FUNDING* REPORT ON EAGLE PROSPECT

One other thing worth noting is that reports are filed. Make sure that your title is easily filable. This report will be filed in two places, under "Eagle Prospect" and under "Exploration Reports."

Pasadena Exploration Company
242 Schindler Street
Pasadena, California 91100

August 14, 1986

Mr. Dale Gordoni
Coordinator, Exploration
Opel Oil Company
2443 Devon Road
Tulsa, Oklahoma 74120

Dear Mr. Gordoni:

    Here is the final report on Eagle Prospect. It outlines the result of our work done from April 16 to August 1, 1986.

    I also include a summary of the old geological and geophysical findings that you gave us in January of 1985.

    We have made the report as complete as possible. If you have any questions on the project after reading the report, don't hesitate to call me (or Dan Fingal in Pasadena).

    As usual, I am sending five copies of the report.

Cordially,

A. L. Patterson, Party Chief

Figure 16.2. Letter of transmittal

Comment on Figure 16.2

The letter of transmittal goes to the person most concerned with the material in the report. Often this is the person who ordered the report done.

Such a letter tells:

1. What the report is,
2. what (in a general way) the report has in it, and
3. any added information.

Fundamentally, the letter of transmittal answers questions asked by the person it is addressed to. Typical questions are:

1. What is this thing in my IN box?
2. Why have I got a copy of it? (Should I read it?) If Mr. Gordoni himself had ordered the work to be done, Patterson would say so, but the work was ordered by someone else.

This report was bulkier than Gordoni expected, and so in his second and third paragraphs Patterson explained why it was so bulky.

CONTENTS

LETTER OF TRANSMITTAL i

ABSTRACT iii

INTRODUCTION 1

FIELD PROBLEMS IN EAGLE PROSPECT 2

DESCRIPTION OF THE "CALICHE PROBLEM" 4

    Geology 4

    Seismic results 4

NEW INSTRUMENTATION PATTERNS TRIED 5

    Star 5

    Cross 5

    Combinations of stars and cross 5

SHOTHOLE CHARGES 6

SHOTHOLE DEPTHS 7

    Above caliche 7

    Below caliche 7

    Below caliche with star-cross patterns 8

    Above caliche with star pattern alone 9

CONCLUSIONS 10

RECOMMENDATIONS 10

APPENDIX 11

    Table 1 — Costs of work related to field problems 12

    Table 2 — Breakdown of total costs 12

    Graph 1 — Reliability functions — instrumentation
            patterns 12

Figure 16.3. Table of contents

Comment on Figure 16.3

It is a good idea to plan your report with its total effect in mind — that is, organize it so that you can visualize the report as it will appear to a reader who looks at it for the first time. How will the words in the title fit the report? How will the table of contents reflect the material in it? How easily can your readers find their way around in the report?

In your report try to use headings that can be reflected in the table of contents, as is done in Figure 16.3. Pick your headings carefully. In your text, you can number the major headings (with Roman numerals if you wish, those that are capped on the page opposite). It is better not to number other headings because they may become confused with any numbered lists you decide to use in the body of the report.

When paging the prefatory material (anything before the introduction), use lower-case Roman numerals, as in Figure 16.3. Start using arabic numerals with the introduction.

ABSTRACT

In April and August of 1986, we ran a two-week experiment in Eagle Prospect (Nebraska) to see whether the caliche problem could be solved. We tried (1) new instrumentation patterns, (2) different shothole charges, and (3) differing shothole depths. We concluded that the caliche problem, for the moment, is unsolvable, and we recommend no further experiments. We suggest that the data we collected in the experiment be sent to Oklahoma Instruments.

Figure 16.4. Abstract

Comment on Figure 16.4

An abstract is a summary of the main ideas in the report. It should be clear, brief, and highly readable. Observe here the numbering of three ideas; these numbers help to break up the ideas in the second sentence.

Where possible in the abstract, use *who does what* patterns and simple language.

Final Exploration Report on *Eagle Prospect*

INTRODUCTION

Eagle Prospect lies in an area that no one has ever been able to explore using seismic techniques. The beds of caliche that lie near the surface diffuse seismic waves so completely that all attempts to analyze them using standard procedures have failed.

Accordingly, we determined to try a number of nonstandard methods. Among these were:

1. Differing arrangements of instrumentation patterns on the ground.
2. Widely differing charges in the shotholes.
3. Widely different depths of charges, both above and below the thin, shaly surface layers found in Eagle Prospect.

By using these variables, we hoped to get some computerized results that could be filtered electronically and so arrive at useful evidence on the Cretaceous rocks that Opel Oil Company is interested in mapping.

We ran this experiment for two working weeks, starting on April 16, 1986, and again for three days, ending on August 1, 1986. During the three-day segment, we were able to refine some data that we obtained in the first trials in April.

Figure 16.5. Introduction

Comment on Figure 16.5

The standard introduction deals, where necessary, with these questions: *who, what, where, when, why, and how?* Not all these questions, of course, are relevant in every report.

In the first two paragraphs of this introduction, the writer gives some background that answers the question: *Where* and *why* was the work done? The second paragraph, with its listing of nonstandard methods, tells the reader *how* and *what*.

The next-to-last paragraph gives more information on causes and effects in the experiment, and the final paragraph answers the question: *when?*

By the time readers finish this introduction, they have all the information they need to start reading the body of the report.

Eagle Prospect is in the heart of the Nebraska sandhills. It is 75 miles from the nearest community of any size (Lillian Springs), which means that field crews are 75 miles from water, gasoline, and supplies. Local ranchers will not allow drillers to use water from their pumps, and so all water for drilling must be transported by tank trucks from Lillian Springs, a round trip of 100 miles on paved road plus fifty more miles in the sandhill country itself. Four-wheel drive trucks are necessary, and we had to bulldoze approximately two miles of road over country impassable by four-wheel drive vehicles.

All these field problems contributed to the cost of the work. (See Table 1, Appendix.) Note that overtime payments increased costs considerably. We had to increase workdays to 12½ hours each in order to get in a full working day because travel times from Lillian Springs were so long.

LEGAL ISSUES ON THE JOB

All permits* were made locally, and were successful. But one hitch occurred when a driller could not cap a deep hole, and the water flowing from it eroded a rancher's access road. This permit was withdrawn by the rancher. We repaired the road using the contract bulldozer, and the rancher was satisfied. He signed a release exempting us from damages.

―――――――
* <u>Permit</u>: jargon for legal permission given by a landowner for experimental purposes.

Figure 16.6. Page in body of report

Comment on Figure 16.6

The writer uses headings, one of which is shown here, to indicate the organizational divisions in the report.

Note that the discussions are fairly complete without being wordy or excessively detailed. The details given are designed to answer any questions in the reader's mind: What were the field problems? What sort of equipment was needed on the job? Why were overtime costs high?

Generally, reports like this are designed for a very wide readership — taking in accountants, lawyers, engineers of several kinds, technical people, some without college degrees, and others. In addition, such reports will be filed permanently. Years later, people may come back to this report for information on the area known as Eagle Prospect, and the writer of the report wants to be sure that they will have their questions answered in the year 2000.

CONCLUSIONS

The problem of the caliche beds appears at this time to be insoluble. Every attempt we made to reduce the scattering effect of the beds on seismic waves was in some way unsatisfactory. No pattern of instrumentation produced usable recordings. The best pattern appears to be a star arrangement of geophones, but this pattern still produced only scattered effects, and we were unable to map any bed in the Cretaceous consistently.

Varying the amount and depth of shotholes produced no effective recordings.

With the possible exception of our results with the star pattern, we must conclude that the experiment was unsuccessful.

RECOMMENDATIONS

We recommend:

1. That, for the foreseeable future, experiments in Eagle Prospect be abandoned.

2. That Opel Oil Company allow us to send our test results to Oklahoma Instruments with a request for its technical analysis. Perhaps O.I. has instruments in its pipeline that could apply to the caliche problem, which is typical in several areas Opel has worked in the past few years.

Figure 16.7. Conclusions and recommendations

Comment on Figure 16.7

As sections in a report, conclusions and recommendations can be handled in two ways. First, you can separate them as the writer did here. This makes for clarity and precision of statement. But in some reports, the materials in the two sections are really blended, and in those cases we suggest that you put them under one heading: Conclusions and Recommendations.

Note the careful paragraphing in the Conclusion section, each paragraph having its special job to do. Report writers tend to write paragraphs that are too long; most reports need all the white space and paragraph breaks you can supply.

Recommendations are typically given in list form, as done here. This makes them easy to understand and discuss, because people can refer to individual recommendations by number.

PAGING THE REPORT

1. Title page: Do not number this page.
2. Prefatory material: Start numbering the first page after the title page. Use lower-case Roman numerals. Center each number in the bottom of the page, about an inch from the bottom.
3. Body of the report: Start numbering with arabic numerals, and number consecutively throughout all other pages.

THE STYLE OF WRITING IN A REPORT

For some reason, a few students believe that a report is not a report unless it is written in a heavy-handed, pedantic style full of long words and convoluted sentences. A report is no different from any other standard business message: It requires clarity, precision, and simplicity.

Use the *who does what* pattern in sentences. Avoid the passive construction: "In this report, three instrument patterns are considered."

And don't hide your authorship. Use *I* or *we* to identify yourself as writer(s). Not even in scientific reports should you avoid *I* or *we*. In the most authoritative book now published on scientific writing, Robert Day says:

> I herewith ask all young scientists to renounce the false modesty of previous generations of scientists. Do not be afraid to name the agent of the action in a sentence, even when it is "I" or "we." Once you get into the habit of saying "I found," you will also find that you have a tendency to write "*S. aureus* produced lactate" rather than "Lactate was produced by *S. aureus*." (Note that the "active" statement is in three words; the passive requires five.)
>
> You can avoid the passive voice by saying "The authors found" instead of "it was found." Compared with the simple "we," however, "the authors" is pretentious, verbose, and imprecise (which authors?).

A SAMPLE STUDENT REPORT

Now we present an entire sample report, written by a student named Mickey Stein. It is a typical student paper done for a typical assignment in a business writing class. The assignment read:

- Write a brief report of from eight to ten pages.
- For your source material use any job experience you have had. No job is too slight or too unimportant to supply useful material.
- Pick a specific reader or group of readers, and write directly for that audience. Do not write merely for a general audience.

- Use specific detail in your report, so that your reader understands clearly the ideas you are putting across.
- In your report, make at least one clear persuasive point — that is, argue that your readers should believe a certain thing, or that they should agree to make a certain change, or both.

Before you read the report, we suggest that you read the discussion questions that follow it (pp. 270–271). These will give you some idea of what to watch for and help you evaluate the report as you read it. The paragraphs in the report have been numbered for convenience in referring to them in discussion questions.

SETTING UP AND SELLING TOUR BIKES FOR THE

FORGOTTEN CUSTOMER

Prepared for Taylor Cycle Shops, April 16, 1986

Mickey Stein

Business Writing 251

Mrs. Marmody

Figure 16.8. Student report

INTRODUCTION

(1) Tour bikes have become Taylor Cycle's best-seller in the so-called specialty lines. Even in a college community, this is a little surprising. But if you look at the publicity on bicycle touring, you can see why our sales of the touring line are increasing every year. Time magazine recently ran a full news page on bike touring; in April the Gazette-Times had a long story on our local touring club; successful movies, such as Breaking Away and American Flyers, are giving a tremendous boost to biking in general. (Even though Breaking Away is several years old, it is still being shown at bike rallies around the country.)

(2) But selling touring bikes is not the only factor in the profit equation. No bike we sell has more possibilities for "add-ons." Typically, people who buy touring equipment have money to spare, and they often add new components within weeks or months of purchase. In addition, we sell tourers thousands of dollars worth of tour bags. One day last winter, a sixty-year-old Lutheran minister came into the campus store and bought a $600 Jugata, put seventy-five dollars' worth of different derailleurs on it, and then added more than a thousand dollars' worth of special equipment (mainly bags) for a week-long spring tour he was going to take in the California wine country.

(3) When the minister returned from the tour, he came into the store to complain. He loved his new equipment, but he had developed muscle spasms in his neck, and his doctor advised him to get off the bicycle and stay off it.

THE PROBLEM: The Lame, the Old, and the Short

(4) As a member of several touring clubs, I have heard many stories like the minister's. In fact, next to the familiar stories about "how far Fred and I ride each year," complaints about problems with touring bikes and their equipment are most common.

(5) We are dealing here with what may be the <u>forgotten customer</u>. What is he (or she) like? First, he is older and more mature than the average bike buyer who is buying a bike for himself. Second, he often has less experience riding the standard ten-speed than an average college student would have. In my experience, he is usually shorter than the freshman (a different generation is involved). Quite often he has been forced to give up jogging or handball because his bones and muscles won't take violent exercise any more, and biking has been recommended to him.

(6) If the forgotten customer is a woman, this description

Figure 16.8 Student report (continued)

will not apply so neatly. But one generalization does apply; women tour bikers are almost always five feet eight or under and have relatively short legs.

(7) At one time or another, all of these bikers complain of the pain of riding from forty to seventy miles a day on tours. A seventy-to-one-hundred-mile day may send them into paralysis. The main cause of their pain — apart from lack of practice — is that their bikes and their equipment do not fit them. A bike that works fine for a twenty-year-old like me turns a fifty-year-old lawyer on a Vermont tour into a mass of aches and pains. I am six feet one inch tall. He is five feet eight and weighs more than I do. His wife is five feet three inches tall, and she walked most of the steeper hills in Vermont.

(8) Finally, I should mention the question of maintenance. When the bike tourer is in the middle of Vermont (or Montana or Virginia), if something breaks he can't just drive two miles to the nearest friendly bike shop. On tour there may be nothing out there but cows. More is involved than just fixing flats, and we can help when we sell the tourer his bicycle and its equipment.

(9) The solution to the problem is to combine selling and setting up the bike so that these problems don't occur, or are minimized.

SELLING THE BIKE

(10) The rest of this report emphasizes mainly a point I have already made: "The forgotten customer" is a special case — and not just because he or she has more money. As we all know, many of the more expensive bikes, components, and add-ons really <u>are</u> better; they work better and last longer. If we sell these more vigorously, we are doing the forgotten customer a favor because he or she will enjoy touring more and have fewer breakdowns.

(11) <u>Type of bike</u>. The standard ten-speed (at whatever price) is not a good choice for this customer. I have had many customers buy one, and then say later — when they come in to buy tubes or something else — that they had trouble on steep hills, like those on the famous Hilly Hundred ride out of Bloomington, Indiana. I always recommend the fifteen-speed bike. The gearing gives no trouble, even to the beginner. For the exception, see below.

(12) <u>Make of bike</u>. In touring bikes, we sell three makes: Jugata, Mekin, and Robb. Generally, I do not suggest the Robb bicycle to this customer. It has the longest top tube of the three, and this fact means that the rider has a longer reach to the handlebars — which means, in turn, neck or back pain and an unhappy rider. The Mekin is a good bike, but it does not come in a 19-inch size and it will not fit many women. The Jugata is the

Figure 16.8. Student Report (continued)

best all-purpose choice. It comes in all sizes, has the shortest top tube in the nineteen-inch size (an inch and a half shorter than the others), and is extremely stable when loaded. It is nearly impossible to make the Jugata shimmy, even with a badly balanced load.

(13) <u>Components.</u> All the components that come with the Jugata are worth keeping, with the exception of the rear derailleur, a Shido. The Shido is only a fair touring derailleur; it shifts poorly under load. The forgotten customers are generally not the most expert shifters in the world, anyway. In a pack of forty riders toiling up a hill, you can identify them by the noise of grinding and chain chatter. I automatically recommend to this type of buyer that we replace the Shido with a Parvin, widely noted as the best of the touring derailleurs. We can do this for only about $4.60 and are willing to absorb the mechanic's cost of from five to ten minutes' time.

(14) <u>Touring bags.</u> The best bags are made by Winston. They cost more, but they are worth it. I show the customer the special advantages of the bags: their construction, their light weight, and the ease of mounting and dismounting them. The rear bags are especially easy to get on and off. I try not to sell these customers more bags than they need. The Lutheran minister sent half his equipment home by UPS; he just didn't need all we sold him. Two

rear bags, a carrier bag, and one handlebar bag are enough for most tourers. These people do not go on camping tours; at the end of a day they want a motel and a shower.

(15) Extras. Generally, I sell this customer the following:

1. Two tires and four tubes
2. An extra derailleur cable
3. An extra brake cable
4. Two extra spokes
5. A free-wheel remover
6. A Condor tool set

(16) Advice for the customer. The advice to give this type of customer depends on how much the customer knows about biking. If he or she knows a great deal, I try not to insult with unwanted advice. The extras I suggested just above were advised for the Lutheran minister, and they worked well for him. I suggested he practice changing tubes and tires. He did, and ruined two tubes, but at least he had them to ruin. I advised him to take an extra tire on tour (not on his bike but on the sag wagon). Sure enough, he needed it when he ruined a tire on a broken bottle in the San Juan Islands. I sold him the Condor tool set — the cheapest we carry — because that is all one really needs on most tours.

(17) Incidentally, the forgotten customer breaks more

Figure 16.8. Student Report (continued)

derailleur cables than all other types of customers combined. Why? He shifts more. Watch him on a tour; he is always running through the gears, trying to find a comfortable one as the angle of the hill changes or the wind comes up.

FITTING THE BIKE TO THE CUSTOMER

(18) For this customer it is particularly important to follow carefully all routines for seat height and handlebar geometry.

(19) Beyond this, I have found that two things should be done for this customer.

(20) <u>ONE</u>: Always change the saddle to a Blixocet, the best of the touring saddles. Exchange it for free with whatever saddle comes on the bike.

(21) <u>TWO</u>: By whatever means, try to raise the rider on the handlebars. Neck and back pain are the worst problems the forgotten customer has. Both are essentially problems of muscle spasm, and so cannot be cured by aspirin or muscle relaxers. In fact, if muscle spasms become chronic, as they tend to do in riders over thirty-five (or in riders of any age whose bikes don't fit them), the rider may be unable to ride at all — ever.

(22) Raise the rider by raising the handlebars both horizontally and vertically. (Don't go past the danger mark on the

stem.) Ask the rider to check back with you if he has neck or back pain. There are good standard stretching exercises, explained in several biking books; I make photocopies of these and give them to the customer.

(23) If nothing else works, flip the handlebars upside down. This raises the rider to a position roughly similar to that of the old child's balloon tire bike. You will have to remove the brake levers, take off the "cheaters" if the bike has them, and re-position the levers like this:

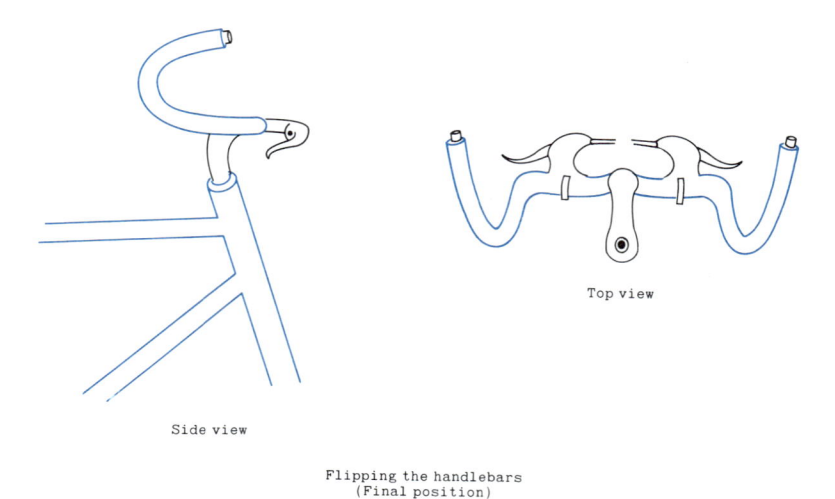

Side view

Top view

Flipping the handlebars
(Final position)

Figure 16.8 Student Report (continued)

(24) Make sure that the cables are not twisted, and that the right cables extend to the right wheels. (I got them mixed up once when we were busy and I was in a hurry.)

(25) Flipping the handlebars upside down is a last resort, but it really works in avoiding serious neck and back problems. It can mean the difference between being able to ride four or five thousand miles a year and not being able to ride at all. A physician told one fifty-year-old professional man here in town that he was through riding forever. I flipped his handlebars and gave him a copy of the stretching exercises, and he now rides more than four thousand miles a year.

(26) I have sold him and his wife a total of four bikes and many hundreds of dollars' worth of extra equipment, including full Gore-tex sets of rain gear.

CONCLUSION

(27) Whatever can be done for the men and women in the forgotten-customer category should be done. They are the most reliable customers we have, the ones with the most money, and those with the most desire to be repeat buyers.

Questions for Discussion

In his report, Mickey Stein chooses for his audience the owners, managers, and personnel of three stores known as Taylor Cycle Shops. They are located in three different parts of a city of 125,000, which has a large state university.

Since he was in high school, Stein, a junior, has been working as a part-time mechanic and salesman in these stores. In summers, he works full-time.

1. As you read the report, look for organizational devices and techniques. How clearly organized is the report? Should Stein have used any organizational techniques that he did not use?
2. Do you approve of the title? Is the term *forgotten customer* an accurate term?
3. What does the introduction do for the report?
4. Is the anecdote about the Lutheran minister (paragraphs 2–3) useful?
5. What is the function of paragraph 3 here?
6. Comment on the heading above paragraph 4.
7. What is the purpose of paragraphs 5 and 6?
8. Explain why Stein used the word *finally* in paragraph 8.
9. Explain the relationship of paragraph 9, first to the whole report, and then to the heading just beneath the paragraph.
10. Why did Stein make paragraph 9 just one sentence long?
11. How do the subheads in paragraphs 13–16 help to support the major heading "Selling the Bike"? Would you suggest different subheads? Why?
12. So far as the readers of this report are concerned, what is the purpose of paragraph 10?
13. Is the last sentence of paragraph 11 a good idea? Why or why not?
14. In paragraphs 12–14, how many different facts, details, and judgments can you count? What does your answer suggest?
15. Why does Stein use a list in paragraph 15?
16. Is the heading in paragraph 16 necessary? Why is the material in 15 separated from the material in 16?
17. Explain the visual device in paragraphs 20 and 21.
18. Are the drawings in paragraph 23 necessary? (Stein insists that they are — but do *you* think so?)
19. Stein has what he calls a "political" reason for including paragraph 25. Can you guess what he means?
20. What is the purpose of paragraph 26?
21. Stein says that the biggest problem with writing this report "lies in convincing my audience." What does he mean? How can you tell — from the facts included, the organization, the "slant" of the material — that Stein thought he was facing an audience not automatically ready to agree with him?

22. Are *you* convinced by this report? If you owned Taylor Cycle Shops, would you implement the suggestions in this report?

TOPICS FOR STUDENT REPORTS

In preparing a report, you must decide on the way to express your topic. Some ways to express it are:

- As a question: Which grocery store (X or Y) is preferable for the student shopper?
- As a phrase (non-question): Assessing Blank Bank's Image
- As a phrase (question): Make or Buy Oboe Reeds?
- As a two-part phrase: Component Depreciation — Trends and Guidelines
- As a full statement: Z Method Irrigation is Better for a Wisconsin Farm than Y Method

Below is a list showing a mixture of these ways of expressing a topic. Each topic has proved successful for a student writer. Note that the topics are meant only to be suggestive. It is a good idea to shape your own topic to fit your personal interests or academic field, or both.

- APB #15 and Earnings Per Share
- Evaluating Comparative Rhetoric Instruction Approaches
- Component Depreciation — Trends and Guidelines
- Branch-rooted vs. Tap-rooted Alfalfa
- Egg-laying Positional Preferences of the Block Cutworm
- The Image of Our Town's Downtown Mall
- Evaluation of the Illini Union's Travel Service
- Evaluation of American National Bank's Check Cashing Policies
- Comparative Patient Education Programs in This City's Hospitals
- Analysis of Program Preferences of Student Members in AMA Chapter
- Analysis of Non-Academic Employees' Participation in Campus Activities
- Alternative Methods of Presenting Information to Junior High School Band Members
- Designing the Optimum Wheel-Axle Combination for Concrete
- Comparative Methods of Two Manufacturing Processes
- Which Vehicle Should the Police Department Buy?
- Comparison of Two Home Computers: Apple vs. IBM
- Analysis of Low Attendance at the Monday Night Bridge Club
- Comparative Heating Systems for a Southern Illinois Home
- Snow Removal Efficiency, City A vs. City B

- Planning a Promotional Campaign for VIP
- Selecting the Best Computer Model
- Grade Inflation: Comparisons of Five Colleges
- Educational Alternatives for the Mentally Retarded in This County
- Test and Evaluation of a Paper-Money Identifier for the Blind
- Should FASB #8 be Repealed?
- Alternative System for a 600-acre Central Illinois Farm
- Testing a Merchandising Machine
- Evaluation of the Alumni Association's Reunions
- Which Pistol Should FBI Agents Carry?
- Comparison of Three Salary Plans for UI Non-Academic Personnel
- Readability of Computer Newsletters
- Should Mercy Hospital Install Vending Machines?
- Inventory Model for Potatoes, UI Central Food Stores
- Legal Liability of CPAs
- MAS and Auditor Independence
- Alternative Methods of Drying Ear Corn
- Which Videotape Machine Should WILL-TV Buy?
- Assembly Hall Concessions — Customers' Preferences
- Which Readability Formula Is More Accurate?
- Selecting the Best Tax-Sheltered Annuity
- The Job Market for Writers
- Which Car Should the U of I Motor Pool Buy?
- Improving Bike-Path Safety on Campus
- Customer Usage Patterns at a Local Delicatessen
- Broken Appointments at McKinley Health Service
- Selecting a New Shade Tree for the Quad
- Alternative Methods of Soil Sampling

The two cases that follow can be used in various ways in the three chapters on report writing. Using the material in them, your instructor may suggest that you write proposals, progress reports, or a combination of these.

Case One

Word Processing Case Study — An Opportunity for Improving Production of Messages and Documents

By Fran Weeks & Louise Steele

Your role in this case study is that of your university's "in-house consultant" in matters of Word Processing and office automation. Word Processing is defined as "new, sophisticated techniques to transform the written, oral, or recorded word into typed or printed form for distribution."

Reports in General

You have been asked by the head of the Veterinary Economics Department to study the production of the department's office support staff and to see if there are ways to improve production and quality without hiring more workers or using more space.

Preparatory to analyzing the department's problems, you conducted two surveys. You surveyed the office support staff (there are 30 secretaries, typists, and clerks), and you surveyed the professional and academic staff (44 research scientists and teachers). There are also 70 extension workers throughout the state, but you did not survey them. They are supported by the office staff to the extent that rough-draft manuscripts are mailed to the office for typing. Seventy-five percent of the typing done in the office is of handwritten rough drafts which break down this way:

25% — Technical
25% — Statistical
50% — Everyday narrative

Three typists specialize in technical/statistical material. Fifty percent of office staff time is allocated to typing. The manuscripts run from 40-150 pages, and long jobs are sometimes shared. If the load gets too great, temporary help is brought in from the university's temporary help bureau. All the typists have IBM Correcting Selectric typewriters. These are electric typewriters, but they do not have built-in memory features. They make correction of typographical errors easy by means of a correcting ribbon which "lifts off" the error. A "memory" typewriter records the typed message. Errors can be corrected; revisions made; and then the machine can type out the stored, final copy.

Some material is typed in special formats — 20 percent of that typing is tables and 3 percent is figure captions. Footnotes occur in most documents with need for superscripts.

The input from the professional staff is 48 percent longhand drafts. Eleven percent is machine dictation, and two percent is taken down in shorthand.

During your 10-day survey, 138,000 lines were typed, and you estimate that for a year over 3,000,000 lines are typed.

The document breakdown shows:

Correspondence — 20%
Narrative manuscripts — 24%
Technical manuscripts — 23%
Classroom materials — 8%
Statistical reports — 6%
Special-format reports — 6%
Various fill-in forms — 4%
+ Miscellaneous typing

Correspondence is the most frequent category of typing. It takes 30.7 percent of the office staff time. Manuscripts from 29 authors take 37.9 percent of the time. Eighteen of the support staff do classroom materials accounting for 28.9 percent of the time. All 35 authors claim to have rush work which happens about 38 percent of the time, and the typists think that is too much.

When it comes to revisions made in original drafts, word changes account for 42½ percent; sentence changes account for 22½ percent; paragraph reorganization accounts for 16.3 percent; format changes account for 4.2 percent of the changes; and "massive" revision accounts for 17.7 percent.

The office staff reports that principal areas of concern are typing backlog (10 say major area of concern; 18 say minor) and typing quality (8 major, 15 minor). They say they need help with telephone answering, mail handling, and filing. They think more people are needed. Eight consider that a major matter; nine a minor matter. More space is desired by some. Fifteen consider that a major matter; 6 a minor matter. More dictation equipment is needed.

All report that reproduction of reports is a bottleneck, that there are delays in getting publication series out on time. They have one publication called "Alternative Veterinary Futures for the Eighties," consisting of two manuscripts which have been sitting for five months.

The office staff would like an opportunity to rate the faculty and think that the faculty ought to rate the office staff. They think the faculty could do more work on their own, that some of the projects could be "do it yourself" projects.

The average number of people served by any one typist is three, although one person serves nine people and another serves eight. For most office workers the highest priority activity is typing. The changes desired by typists are (1) more typist positions so there's less pressure, (2) more help in proofreading and assembling, (3) fewer people in the office so that there would be more room for files, (4) elimination of needless repetition — standardization of more documents, (5) a more easily available photocopier (the one they use is on the next floor up), (6) a better way to handle repetitive letters, (7) less retyping of the same manuscript, (8) decrease in rush jobs — workflow needs to be managed better so that it will even out and that all requests don't come in at once, (9) with better scheduling of work, let support people know the schedule that has to be met, (10) have machines maintained regularly and repaired faster, (11) keep office supplies up to the need so that they don't run out all the time, (12) let graduate student TA's run the ditto and collate the class materials (As a consultant you are not going to recommend letting anyone run the equipment except the office staff. That's a sure way to have equipment constantly in need of repair.), (13) need better typewriters.

Your author survey shows that the authors want more support with telephone answering, mail handling, and filing. Eight authors think that more support personnel are needed, and fifteen say more space is needed. They think that the operations need more control.

A breakdown of documents produced showed that correspondence (unique typing) accounts for 25 percent but that revision typing accounts for 60 percent and repetitive typing, 8 percent.

What you have observed and determined from your surveys is a production situation which cannot keep up with the demands of the professional and academic staff. It is noteworthy that some respondents to the survey want more people but at the same time want more space for files. Space is at a premium at your university, and there's no way that you're going to recommend that they try to find room for expansion of the operation using its present equipment and methods.

There are several areas that need discussing. One of them is the "input" into the secretarial area. Entirely too much time is spent in revision typing and repetitive typing. With the equipment they have, a document has to be completely done over even though only a few corrections need to be made in it. There is newer equipment available which eliminates repetitive typing — the "memory" typewriters, the mag card typewriters, and the CRT (cathode ray tube) typewriters. With this equipment the typist need only make the corrections or enter the additional material, and the original material, stored in memory, is typed automatically by the machine after being corrected and revised. That one change alone would substantially reduce the 60 percent figure given to revision.

You do not want, in this report, to recommend types and brands of equipment. Many manufacturers are in the market. There's a wide range of models and prices. Telephone access to a Word Processing Center is possible. A staff member in the field could pick up the telephone, dial a number, and dictate a letter or whatever needs to be typed, thus eliminating the time spent in hand-drafting and mailing the report in to be typed. Of course, the office would still have to mail the final copy back to the person in the field.

This is how modern text editing equipment works. At the touch of a button, the recorded text can be displayed on a CRT display (cathode ray tube, a TV-like screen) which will show as much as an entire page at a time. And at the touch of another button, a page of text can be automatically printed out by the typewriter at a speed of several hundred words per minute, depending on the kind of equipment. At that speed, it is quick work to produce a draft for an executive to edit, then to make corrections and changes before producing a final typed copy.

The text-editing typewriter offers some additional advantages that might become important in the work of the department. For example, it can produce multiple original copies of letters and reports nearly as fast as they could be duplicated by other processes. This will not only allow the department's reports to come out looking sharp, but more important, it allows form letters to be produced quite cheaply — each one looking like an original. This is done by storing the addresses of recipients in one recording and the text of the letter in another. (The technique for storing such information varies with the equipment in use and it is not important for you to know.) What is important is that once the information is properly "coded," all the operator has to do is to push a button and the machine will coordinate the information in the two sections and produce "original" letters, each with a different inside address.

With new equipment, more personnel and more space would not be needed.

Acording to information obtained from IBM, the operator of a CRT typewriter can do three times as much work as the operator of a Selectric. Of course if Vet Ec bought CRT typewriters, the work assignments would have to be changed — 50% usage might be all right for Selectrics but CRT's should be used almost constantly to earn their keep, so to speak. Typing which is now done by 30 people, typing 50% of the time, could be done by 6 or 7 CRT operators.

You checked two departments — Business Administration and Life Sciences — which have phone-in dictation (i.e., writers can dial a special number and be connected to a Word Processing recorder). Of the memos and letters they write, 80% in Life Sciences are dictated and 90% in Business Administration. Only a few writers dictate articles and journal papers. And some of them read their handwritten copy into the phone. That's not the way to take advantage of new, advanced equipment.

The area of management will require study. Somebody needs to be responsible for routing work and supervising the workers.

[*Note to Student:* No doubt much of the above will be very confusing to you if you have no acquaintance with a modern Word Processing Center. The best way to resolve the confusion is to find such a center, talk to the supervisor, and observe the workflow.]

Main Points to be Considered

You are not yet ready to make specific recommendations concerning what equipment to buy, how to re-design the work space, how to re-assign the duties of the office support staff. Nevertheless the facts you collected lead you to believe that it is time for the Vet Ec department to reorganize its message and document production facilities. A modern Word Processing Center is probably the most desirable solution to the problem of doing more work with fewer people in less space.

Do not ignore the importance of helping the faculty, the scientific and research staff, and the extension workers throughout the state. Like everyone else, they would like to do more work in less time with less effort . . . and, if possible, work of better quality. It will not be easy to persuade these people to use modern dictation methods. Some will never give up pad-and-pencil drafting despite the time and effort it consumes. Yet, many are already using cassette recorders for dictation. A dictation input system using telephone lines would be a great time saver. If useful, some orientation meetings could be held to "sell" the new system and demonstrate how to use it.

Right now the paramount problem is not dictation, it is the amount of "do-it-over" typing, repetitive work which could be eliminated with modern equipment, and you have the data to support a recommendation in that area.

Another consideration is staffing the office, relationships within the office, and morale of office workers. If your recommendation for a Word

Processing Center is implemented, the Department will have to hire operators for the new equipment. Most of your office support staff are classified by university civil service as clerk-typists. The people who use the new equipment will be classified as word processing operators. The department will want to hire experienced operators, and no present employees have WPC experience.

Bringing in new employees in new classifications at higher rates of pay may cause unhappiness among present employees. Furthermore, word processing operators are not always happy either, since they feel they are underpaid in view of the fact that they operate such sophisticated and expensive equipment. The word processing operator's "typewriter" costs about $8,000. The clerk-typist's Selectric costs about $900. Needless to say, the clerk-typist has a different point of view about fair play and fair pay.

Your Assignment

Prepare a formal report for Professor John Doe, Head, Department of Veterinary Economics.

The data for this case study, and the original descriptions of office methods and procedures, were provided by Susannah Ganus, Systems and Procedures Planner, Administrative Information Systems and Services, University of Illinois at Urbana-Champaign.

Case Two

CANDIPOP, INCORPORATED: A "CASEBOOK" EXERCISE
by Bonnie Brothers York

Company Background

Candipop Incorporated is a national franchise system, specializing in retail sales of popcorn, candy and other confections. With corporate headquarters in Dallas, Texas, the company franchises 111 locations, seven in the state of Colorado. Mr. John Drummand, a former real estate developer, owns two of the Colorado shops. He opened the Central Plaza Mall (Denver) store in April 1981, and the Gatestone Mall (Greeley) location in October of the same year. Mr. Drummand, his wife and four employees operate the two stores. Mrs. Drummand spends most of the day at Gatestone, while Mr. Drummand drives fifty miles daily from their home in Greeley to oversee the Denver operation.

Mr. Drummand feels his sales depend on the mall traffic flows, since popcorn and candies are impulse items. His best sellers are regular buttered popcorn, caramel corn, and cheese corn; the balance of his sales are candy confections and eight other "flavors" of popcorn. Mr. Drummand has not noticed any distinct pattern of purchasers based on age or sex, but feels that a high degree of repeat customers do exist. Competition is minimal at both locations; the only real competition comes from the mall theatres.

The Central Plaza store is located on the third (and highest) floor of the Denver mall, directly in front of the escalator. Twenty-three other stores are open on this floor, but there are still some vacant locations. A planned overpass with the Colfax Mall across the street should increase foot traffic to this level, but to date Drummand has been disappointed with the traffic he is pulling at Central Plaza.

The Gatestone store is in a relatively new mall in suburban Greeley. As yet, few stores are in the mall, but the Gatestone Candipop has a good location near the center of the mall. Several developed stores and a theatre are nearby, and the traffic potential for this area is excellent.

Current Status

Two overriding problems faced these Candipop locations: Declining sales and increasing prices of ingredients have resulted in operating losses and inadequate cash flows. At the Central Plaza store, gross sales averaged $6,200 monthly from mid-April through December 1981. From January to March of 1982, monthly sales fell to $5,200. April to June results were again lower, averaging only $5,000. The Gatestone Mall location averaged monthly gross sales of $13,450 for the period October-December 1981. From January to March 1982, monthly sales plummeted to $5,270. From April to June, however, sales improved slightly to $5,475.

As can be seen from the table below, during the same periods the cost of goods sold and operating expenses increased as a percentage of gross sales. With declining sales and increasing costs, the net profit before owner's draw and taxes understandably declined.

Status of Candipop

Location	Cost of Goods Sold as % of Gross Sales	Total Operating Expense of % of Gross Sales	Average Net Profit (Loss) Per Month
Central Plaza			
Apr–Dec 1981	15.6	78.7	355
Jan–Mar 1982	12.0	85.1	148
Apr–Jun 1982	33.4	107.8	(2,065)
Gatestone Mall			
Oct–Dec 1981	10.5	66.1	5,406
Jan–Mar 1982	16.7	81.1	114
Apr–Jun 1982	31.0	87.0	(988)

In addition to the declining profitability and cash flow problems at both franchises, Mr. Drummand is currently facing debt in excess of $388,000 (see Appendix 1). These obligations were incurred in establishing the Candipop operations, as well as from the economic downturn of Drummand's previous construction business. Much of this debt has been assumed at the high-interest rates of the past three years. The losses in the Candipop franchises and the compounding interest are increasing this debt and, of course, precluding its repayment. Current debt payments cover only some of the interest due and none of the principal.

Because Mr. Drummand is delinquent in his Small Business Administration (SBA)-guaranteed loan payments, you as an SBA consultant have been assigned to review his operations and recommend the best alternatives available to him.

Company Objectives

After touring the Candipop locations and reviewing Mr. Drummand's financial statements, you meet with him to discuss his feelings about this situation. Drummand describes the following as his objectives for the company:

- to increase his revenues and cash flows
- to repay his debts
- to make a living for his family from the business

Mr. Drummand assures you that he wants to "make a go" of the business; he views bankruptcy as a last resort. He says he has worked for other employers, but would rather be in business for himself. He also tells you that he has contemplated selling his Central Plaza location, but will not consider any bids unless they are as high as his SBA loan. Drummand mentions that he cannot use his Candipop packaging except for direct sales to customers at his mall locations. He could, however, wholesale his product to other vendors under a private label. He has facilities at his Gatestone location for filling wholesale orders, but has no idea how to start, or whom to approach for orders. Mr. Drummand concludes that the best solutions for him would be for the economy to turn around, and for the SBA to extend him an additional loan.

You ask Mr. Drummand to give you his best estimate of expected revenues at each location for the next six months. You then develop a pro forma income statement for that period, using his sales estimates, and his 1981-82 financial statements to estimate variable cost percentages and average fixed costs. Your pro forma statement is in Appendix 2.

Assignments

1. Write a report to Mr. Drummand, outlining the problems facing Candipop that have been revealed by your analysis. Your memo may reference the Appendices, or other materials or financial analyses you create.

2. Prepare a cover letter and a report to Mr. Drummand, recommending alternatives for increasing the Candipop revenues and cash flows. Specify the recommended order of implementing your alternatives, and describe the benefits envisioned for each.

3. Assume that Mr. Drummand has successfully adopted the recommendations in your report and is beginning to show a *modest* profit. Compose a letter to Mr. Drummand's creditors, outlining his current status and his plan for repaying his debts.

Assignment 1 is a relatively brief assignment, requiring you to analyze the client's situation, and to summarize the facts clearly and to him. This analysis could also be the "Critical Issues" section of a comprehensive report. Problems that might be addressed include:

- Falling revenues and profits, break-even points
- Increasing cost of goods sold, operating expenses
- Inadequate cash flows
- High rent and insurance at Central Plaza Mall
- High interest expense
- Two separated locations, which require Drummand to drive nearly two hours daily, and to divide his time between them
- The burden on the franchises to repay the debts of a previous business
- The effect of the economy on the business

Assignment 2 is a longer assignment that probes for creative and realistic solutions for increasing the client's revenues and cash flows. This would constitute the "Recommendations" section of a comprehensive report. You should convey the relative importance and sequence of the alternatives recommended as well as the reasons they should be implemented. Possibilities for increasing revenues and cash flows include:

- Seeking outside employment (either Mr. or Mrs. Drummand), to bring in additional revenues and to assure the family of living expenses and insurance coverages
- Decreasing expenses of the business, for example: buying in larger quantities, switching to cheaper suppliers, deleting unnecessary items
- Refinancing some of the loans at lower interest
- Selling one location (Central Plaza is the least profitable and accessible), and using the proceeds to pay off some loans and to finance a wholesale business
- Developing a wholesale business to vendors outside of the mall. Prospective customers could include: sports arenas, schools, vending firms, catering route vendors, bars and private clubs, health food stores, large companies (gift packs for clients, employees).

Assignment 3 requires you to balance the temptation to tell the loan-holders that they will soon be paid (which is what they want to hear) with a realistic plan for repayment (which, given modest profits, may be longer than they want to wait!). A loan repayment plan would be part of the "Implementation" section of a comprehensive report.

Your instructor may make these assignments separately, as steps in a comprehensive report, or to several students writing the case as a team.

Appendix 1   John Drummand Debts as of August 1, 1982

Candipop, Incorporated	$165,000 *
Bank of Colorado	2,500 *
Mountain West Credit Union	2,500
Consumer Loans, Inc.	30,000
Ace Finance Company	28,500

Builders Savings and Loan 48,000
Harrison Scott 7,000
Greeley Plumbing, Inc. 3,000
White Furniture Shoppe 1,100
Green's Carpets... .450
Christopher James 5,150
Sheet Rockers 2,500
Candipop Shoppers Homart 7,000
WLY Brickyard 8,000
Tom Drummand... .395
Denver Escrow, Inc... 5,600
Colorado Box Company .... .800
Mastercharge .... .750
VISA .... .650
First National Bank .... 5,500 *
Candipop Rent — Gatestone Mall 5,000
Colorado National Bank (Residence)......................... 54,820
IRS — Payroll Taxes 1,400
State of Colorado — Sales Taxes 3,200
$388,815

* SBA-guaranteed

Appendix 2 Candipop Pro Forma Income Statement
August 1982–January 1983

	Aug 82 CP	Aug 82 GS	Sep 82 CP	Sep 82 GS	Oct 82 CP	Oct 82 GS	Nov 82 CP	Nov 82 GS	Dec 82 CP	Dec 82 GS	Jan 83 CP	Jan 83 GS
Estimated Revenue	$6200	$6300	$5500	$5300	$5800	$6500	$6000	$7000	$8000	$8000	$4200	$4200
Cost of Goods Sold @ 32% of Rev	2000	2000	1750	1700	1850	2100	1900	2250	2550	2550	1350	1350
Gross Profit	4200	4300	3750	3600	3950	4400	4100	4750	5450	5450	2850	2850
Operating Expenses (Variable)												
Labor & Payroll Tx @ 26.5 of Rev	1650	1700	1500	1450	1550	1750	1600	1900	2150	2150	1150	1150
Royalties @ 7%	450	450	400	400	400	450	450	500	550	550	300	300
Operating Expenses (Fixed)												
Rent	850	200	850	200	850	200	850	200	850	200	850	200
Insurance	250	50	250	50	250	50	250	50	250	50	250	50
Utilities	400	400	400	400	400	400	400	400	400	400	400	400
Travel/Auto	150	50	150	50	150	50	150	50	150	50	150	50
Interest	800	950	800	950	800	950	800	950	800	950	800	950
Depreciation	900	850	900	850	900	850	900	850	900	850	900	850
Other	350	350	350	350	350	350	350	350	350	350	350	350
Income	(1600)	(700)	(1850)	(1100)	(1700)	(650)	(1650)	(500)	(950)	(100)	(2300)	(1450)
Draw/Debt Repayment	—	—	—	—	—	—	—	—	—	—	—	—

CHAPTER

17

Proposals

The first question to consider about a proposal is: Why write it? To help answer the question, let's consider three characteristics of a typical proposal.

First, it is a request for action, one that usually involves a service of some kind. Sometimes you will perform the action; at other times you will hire someone to do it for you or your company.

Second, there are two benefits inherent in a proposal. One, of course, should be yours. You should make money or gain recognition from the work described in the proposal. The other benefit is similar to those in many business transactions. The people who adopt your proposal do so because they believe there is something in it for them or their organization.

The third characteristic of a proposal is that it solves a problem for somebody, perhaps for many people. It doesn't matter whether the idea for writing the proposal came originally from you, from your supervisor, from a long-term client of yours, or from a disinterested bystander; the nature of the proposal remains the same. A proposal is a problem-solving device, and it will be accepted by your readers only if it fulfills the "contract" you make with them: "Here is (1) how I analyze the problem of X, and (2) how I think it can be solved" (to our mutual benefit, it might be added).

DEFINE THE PROBLEM

Consider the problem very carefully. Ask other people about it. Don't be afraid to ask obvious or seemingly silly questions. Check with people, regardless of rank in the company, who might give relevant information. What do they think the problem is? Make a list of their answers.

When you are sure that there is a problem and that you can define it, sit down and do just that. Define and describe it in the most exact terms you can. Use whatever is necessary: words, schematics, drawings, photographs, mathematics.

Keep defining the problem until you are certain that you know what it is and (if possible) what caused it. Here, many writers go astray. Proposal writing intoxicates. Often involved in many problems are money, power, and, of course, promises. You can become persuaded by your own promises and begin to believe them whether they are any good or not. But the aftermath can be awful, as are the bellows of rage from the promisee: "Who proposed this thing? Seventy-five thousand dollars down the drain! Find out who suggested we do this and...."

So keep a cool head in the defining stage. Take time and make an effort to nail down the problem completely. Remember "Murphy's Law Perfected": That a poorly defined problem always has one more variable than you anticipated — and this variable is the one that will wreck your solution.

Proposals are easy to write. What is not always so easy is the necessary hard thinking to make them dependable ways of solving problems.

PREPARING TO WRITE YOUR PROPOSAL

In the following discussion we'll assume that you will both write the proposal and do the work described in it.

A good way to prepare is by asking yourself questions:

1. Have I defined the problem sufficiently?
2. How clearly can I explain the point of my proposal?
3. How can I show my readers that I am qualified to do the work? What evidence do I have of my qualifications?
4. How much money is needed?
5. How many people are needed for the work, and of what type? Will I need to get outsiders? Consultants?
6. What kind of materials will be necessary?
7. How much special equipment will I need?
8. How much space?

9. Where will the money for my project come from?
    a. Can I get it from the company?
    b. Is state or federal money available?
    c. Is grant money available?

If you want to look into questions a and b, call on a specialist. Most of us know too little about the complexities of getting public and private money, and we need expert help.

The next step is to make a scratch list of questions that will help you organize your proposal:

1. What do I want to do? (What is the point of my proposal?)
2. Why do I want to do it?
3. What is the value of doing it? Think carefully about this.
4. How long will it take me to do it?
5. What is the cost of doing it? the cost to whom?
6. Who will help me do it?
7. What sources (books, periodicals, reports, studies) can I use to show that my proposal is feasible?
8. Important: What are the questions of my enemies — those who might wish to see me fail?

Make a list of everything that might go wrong:

1. List every attack that a dear enemy might make on your proposal.
2. List everything that might go wrong when your proposal is implemented.

DESIGN YOUR PROPOSAL

Many textbooks give a set outline for the proposal. We object to the set outline because it may restrict your thinking too much. So our design of a suggested proposal will be tentative only. For your own purposes, change it where necessary.

As a subject for the proposal, we will use a real-life example, one that can be described briefly and clearly.

Sandra Mason (not her real name) is the new plant manager for a company that specializes in making several kinds of expensive furniture. Her plant makes only grandfather clocks out of top-quality walnut. The brass clock movements, along with fancy clock faces and pendulums, are imported from Germany. The beveled glass for the long front door and sidepieces of the clocks are made in the United States and shipped to her plant.

Sandra's plant is the oldest in the company, and the most prestigious. The company has always jealously guarded the quality of the clocks it turns out, and has refused to sell any but the most expensive line using the finest materials.

The plant has made little money in years, but until last year it lost none. Last year, its losses were significant. The executives of the company are having trouble agreeing on how to attack the problem. The long-time president, still proud of his "flagship" plant, wants to raise the prices of the retail clock. The general manager wants to hold the line on prices and cut quality by using cheaper hardwoods and clock movements from Japan. (No American-made movements are available.)

Sandra is caught between the president and the general manager. Moreover, since she came up the hard way (through ten years of work on the assembly line, four years studying nights to get a junior college business degree, and five years as foreman of the wood shop), she has a certain sentimental attachment to the company's classic walnut clock, the best product of its kind in America. In addition, as the company's first woman plant manager, she is facing jealousy and hard looks from men who were passed over for her job.

Sandra gets a phone call from the general manager. He tells her somewhat grudgingly that the president has decided she should study the problem thoroughly and make the decision about what should be done. After all, says the president, she is closest to the problem. When she has come to a decision, she will write a proposal addressed to the general manager, who will make his own recommendation and then pass the whole thing on to the president.

Sandra studies the problem for a week. She consults the workers in the plant, talking with all levels and specialities, from the men who apply the lacquer to the finished wood, to the case designers, to the bookkeeper. (The plant, by the way, is not unionized.) She calls long-distance to the suppliers of the American walnut and the German clock movements. She makes one phone call each to the president and the general manager.

After a week, she assembles her notes under these headings.

   I. The major problem
  II. The minor problems
 III. The possible solutions
  IV. The facts we must face — the "invariables"
   V. The variables
  VI. Possible solutions
 VII. Arguments against each possible solution

Rather than continuing to look over Sandra's shoulder, following her train of thought as she considers her options, let's jump to her proposal. It will tell you much about the way she thought through the problem. Each section of her proposal is followed by some discussion questions related to it. Paragraph numbers in the proposal will help you answer the discussion questions.

MAYERLING FURNITURE COMPANY

To: Mr. F. Q. McConnell, General Manager

From: Sandra Mason, Plant Manager (Clarksdale)

Subject: Proposal to improve the profits of the Clarksdale Plant for 1988

Date: May 2, 1987

...

Figure 17.1. Beginning of proposal

Discussion Questions for Figure 17.1
1. Is the subject line specific enough? Why or why not?
2. Before reading any further, check through the report and read the headings. Put them on a sheet of paper. Do they provide a good outline for the report? Would you suggest any changes in them at this point, before you have read the rest of the report?

BACKGROUND OF THE PROBLEM

(1) Until about 1970, the Clarksdale plant showed regular if small profits. These profits tailed off in the middle and later 1970s until, by 1980, the plant was no more than breaking even. Last year we showed our first big loss since the depression of the 1930s.

(2) Why did this happen? We cannot point to increased labor costs. These have risen, but only in line with inflation, and they have been offset by our increasing wholesale prices to retail dealers. Nor does it appear that the plant is as a whole less efficient than it was in the 1950s and 1960s.

(3) After studying our costs, I conclude that there are three sources of the problem:

(a) Our clock movements, made by Kinzlsee of West Germany, are much more expensive than they were ten years ago. The average movement now costs us $875.

(b) The movements no longer come to us set up. It presently takes an average of three and a half hours to set up and test each Kinzlsee movement — before it is placed in the case. The three men who do this are our highest-paid workers. Ten years ago, the only setting-up they did was to put the movement in the case and adjust it in place — a five-minute job.

Figure 17.2. Proposal (continued)

Discussion Questions for Figure 17.2

1. Explain the purpose of the first sentence in paragraph 2. Why is this sentence important to both paragraphs 2 and 3?
2. How do the first three paragraphs deal with the problem the writer is trying to explain? How are they important to her eventual proposal?

(c) The price of walnut has skyrocketed. The price of wood is our second greatest cost, after movements.

(4) But an additional hidden cost should be explained here. The walnut we are now getting from Tennessee Supply is different from the old wood we used to get. It is hard, "stringy," rough-textured. We lose a good bit of it from splitting. Many pieces with large knotholes have to be thrown away. I estimate that we spend twenty percent more time on the floor than we did ten years ago just dealing with wood flaws of one kind or another. In addition, our costs of cutting, planing, and sanding have risen out of proportion to other costs because we must replace saw blades and finishing materials more often.

PROPOSAL

(5) I propose that we:

    a. Replace our West German supplier, Kinzlsee, with Saarbrück, also of West Germany.

    b. Transfer two of our most expensive setup men to other duties in the plant.

    c. Replace our walnut stock with WW walnut stock.

DISCUSSION

(6) I talked with Kinzlsee managers by phone and asked them if they could give us already-set-up clock movements at a

Figure 17.3. Proposal (continued)

Discussion Questions for Figure 17.3

1. Where does the specific information in paragraphs 3 and 4 come from?
2. Count the number of specific examples and details in paragraphs 3 and 4. How many are there? What does this number suggest to you?
3. Count the number of action verbs in paragraphs 3 and 4. Count both verbs and verbals; for instance in the first sentence of paragraph 3, you would write down and count *studying* and *conclude* — but not *are*. Forms of *be* (*are, is, am, was*) do not show action. From your total count, what do you conclude about the quality of writing in this proposal?
4. Explain why the first sentence in paragraph 4 is a classic type of paragraph lead, one that every writer should practice.
5. Paragraph 5 uses a standard device of parallelism. What is it? What kind of word does each element of the parallelism start with? Why?
6. Why does the writer use a, b, and c in paragraph 5 instead of numbers?
7. Paragraph 4, unlike the paragraphs before and after it, has no breaks — just sentences, one after the other. Take each sentence individually and explain its length and emphasis. In addition, say something about the subject of each sentence: What is it, and why is it there?

slightly lower cost if we bought in larger bulk. They said absolutely not. In addition, they plan to raise prices beginning the first of the year.

(7) Last year, my predecessor, Wilfred Rupert, tried out six Saarbrück movements in our standard cases. They have worked well and require no setting-up. Saarbrück's American representative says that he can supply movements at a ten percent discount if we buy in larger bulk. This will result in a twenty percent total saving over the cost of the Kinzlsee movements.

(8) Since the Saarbrück movement requires no setting-up, I can transfer wage lines to other parts of the plant. One supervisor is retiring, and Brian Kemmel (in set-up) can take his place in wood finishing. The other set-up man, Jack Winchendon, can help out wherever we need him on a day-by-day basis. Both Brian and Jack have experience with the company in several parts of the plant.

(9) Our greatest saving should come from switching to WW walnut stock. Tennessee Supply will sell us this wood at a figure five percent higher than the present cost of walnut. We will have to buy slightly more at a time, but with our present production we can use the extra wood.

(10) The main point here is that we can effect a <u>considerable</u>

Figure 17.4. Proposal (continued)

Discussion Question for Figure 17.4

1. Read carefully paragraphs 6 through 9. Imagine that you are a hostile reviewer of this proposal. List the things the writer has said that are designed to answer any objections you might have to this proposal.

saving with the WW walnut because there is practically no waste in it. It does not crack or chip in the planer; the knotholes are firm enough that they can be used as they are with only occasional filling. And since the wood is relatively soft, we should save on sanding and cutting equipment. By using this wood, I anticipate a large saving in equipment and supply costs: at least twenty percent.

BREAKDOWN OF COSTS

(11) I'll give only the relevant figures here (estimated for the year following July 1).

Gain from switching to Saarbrück movements:	$252,000
Gain from transferring two set-up men:	30,000
Gain from using WW stock:	176,000
TOTAL	$458,000

SCHEDULE FOR MAKING THE CHANGES

Switching to Saarbrück movements .... by July 1, 1987

Switching to WW walnut .... by July 15, 1987

Transferring two workers .... by July 1, 1987

CONCLUSION

(12) On the basis of the information I have given you, I conclude that making the three major changes will save the company about $458,000 in the year following July 1. This saving should put the plant in the black by the end of this calendar year.

Figure 17.5. Proposal (continued)

Proposals

Discussion Questions for Figure 17.5

1. In paragraph 10 there are devices of emphasis and visual effect. Explain them, and defend or attack them.
2. In paragraph 11, the writer uses tables but does not identify them as such. Why?
3. Would the conclusion paragraph (paragraph 12) be better placed at the beginning of the report? Defend your answer.

OUTLINING A PROPOSAL

Sandra Mason followed a classic outline for her proposal:

I. State the problem.
II. Give your solution to the problem.
III. Answer these questions:
   A. What does the solution cost?
   B. What are the requirements in people, equipment, and material?
   C. When can the solution be completed?
IV. Restate the proposal (but not specifically, unless the proposal is complex or very long).

You can modify or add to this classic outline if the situation calls for it. Perhaps you will want to have a "benefits" section that spells out exactly how your solution will help matters. A "will-it-work?" section can be added to help convince your readers if your solution seems unusual or particularly debatable. You can also cover such matters as available facilities, breakdown of tasks, time and work schedules, and personnel and their qualifications.

If you are making a proposal from outside the company, you might include a section selling *you*. Give a brief account of your successes with similar projects, along with a list of companies and persons who know of these successes.

What you include in your proposal depends on the situation. Analyze it!

For practice in writing proposals, your instructor may wish to use one or more of the problems in Appendix A.

CHAPTER 18

Progress Reports

Whether or not you wrote a formal proposal for the job you are doing, someone — your company or client — may want to know how you are spending money, time, and material. Just how well is the solution to your problem going?

HOW TO REPORT PROGRESS

The type of report we are discussing here is well named. Imagine that you have been progressing along a time line, as your company builds a tunnel:

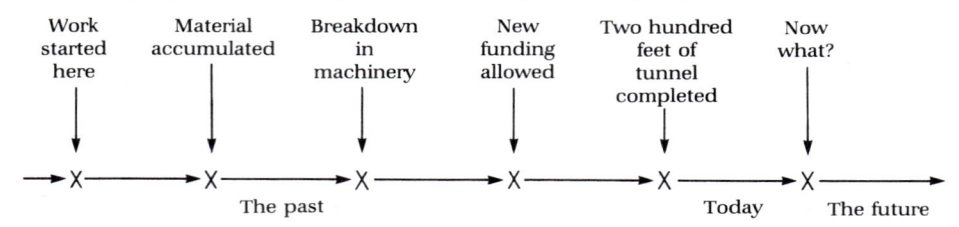

```
Work          Material       Breakdown      New            Two hundred    Now
started       accumulated    in             funding        feet of        what?
here                         machinery      allowed        tunnel
                                                           completed
   |             |              |              |              |             |
   v             v              v              v              v             v
—→X————————→X————————→X————————→X————————→X————————→X———————→
                      The past                                Today      The future
```

TIME LINE

Along the time line, you are at the point called *today* when you are asked to write a progress report. Some companies require regular reports; some ask for them only when there is trouble on the project. A few companies never ask for them; others require weekly fill-in-the-blank reports. Whatever the type or time interval, a progress report generally calls for answers to certain "reader's questions," for example:

- What have you been doing? (And for how long?)
- How have you been doing it?
- Has anything unexpected happened?
- Are you now on schedule?
- What is your future schedule?
- Do you anticipate any problems?
- What is your conclusion? Do all of us involved in this problem have hope for the future?

Your situation may call for other questions, but these are ordinarily the major ones on a reader's list.

Let's look at a progress report written in memo form. The memo is addressed to the vice-president of a university who is in charge of planning and building. The vice-president asked for the report because the university has experienced a crisis in funding. Originally, the school had planned to renovate the inside of a handsome old classroom building (the outside was in excellent shape) instead of building a new one. Now, after the contractor has almost finished Stage II (part of the second floor and the basement), the money for finishing the project has been withdrawn. The end point of the present contract is for completion of Stage II, so no legal problems are anticipated if work is stopped at the end of that stage. The vice-president obviously wants to know exactly where everybody stands right now so that he can plan for the future. His superiors are breathing down his neck, and he is leaning in a friendly way on the contractor. There is no bad feeling here, but the vice-president wants information in writing, as briefly and clearly as possible.

Here is the contractor's memo:

December 21, 1986

To: Carl Schofield, Vice President, Planning and Building
From: Robert Berger, RB Construction Co.
Subject: Progress Report, Renovation of Education and Arts Building to date

WORK COMPLETED

Basement. All work has been completed, with the exception of three of the following jobs:

1. The water-damaged new molding along the east corridor will be replaced according to specifications (at our cost).
2. The duct work above this molding will be redone to prevent condensation.
3. All necessary painting will be done.

Second Floor. All the office suites are completely finished except for the final coat of paint. The west corridor is unfinished. We are waiting for our sub-contractor to break up the old flooring there.

WORK SCHEDULED (with dates)

Basement. Replace molding and repair ductwork (to be finished by January 1, 1987).

Second Floor.

1. Finish all painting (to be finished by January 1, 1987).
2. Begin work on west corridor on December 28, 1986.
3. Finish work on west corridor by approximately January 8, 1987.
4. Clean up this floor by January 10, 1987.

SPECIAL PROBLEMS ANTICIPATED

1. The heaviest snow of the season is forecast to arrive in a few days. We have only one access to the building, and a big snow could slow us down by a day or so at the most.

2. The special molding for the east corridor has been back-ordered for weeks. We are supposed to get it tomorrow (December 22, 1986). Our work could be held up if it doesn't arrive on time.

CONCLUSION

<u>All work should be completed by January 12, 1987.</u>

In his progress report, the contractor has done his best to explain exactly how the work is progressing. There are no frills or unnecessary remarks in the memo, just the facts. And to make for easy reading, the parts of the memo are clearly signalled with headings, and the various pieces of information are separated by numbers so that they can be easily understood.

Why, then, is there a small amount of repetition, as in the sections under WORK COMPLETED and WORK SCHEDULED? Because the contractor knows from experience that busy people often read only parts of messages, and they don't want to jump from place to place looking for information. This is one of those occasions when a little repetition can save a reader's time. Note also the visual effect of the underlined sentence in the conclusion.

For writing problems, refer to Appendix A.

PART 7

Job Hunting
(Selling Yourself)

CHAPTER 19

Your Job Campaign

A few years ago we worked with a young woman who wanted to be a lawyer. She later became one. She wanted to get a job with a large, prestigious firm specializing in corporate law, and she got the job. There she was, twenty-six years old, at the peak of her youth and powers, doing exactly the kind of work she had yearned for since she was sixteen.

But she was unhappy.

"I'm bored," she said. "I never see anybody. I keep my nose in books and papers all day long. I never go into court; it's not my job to. I never *will* go into court."

"But," we said, "you knew what your job was like before you took it. Remember that you described it exactly?"

"I knew," she said. "But I didn't want to believe it. That job wasn't what *I* wanted. It was what my father and mother, my aunt — my whole family — wanted and made me think I wanted too. Their ambition became mine: the law, a famous firm, a big salary."

"The law," she continued, "is fine. No problem there. But I wasn't cut out to sit in the company's library and do research for other people!"

"I wasn't cut out," she said. In those four words lie the heart of this chapter's message. Every one of us is "cut out" to do something, or a group of somethings, a little bit better than other things. You need to find what it is — early. If you know what you *can* do and blend it with what you *want* to do, you are ahead of the game in finding a job that suits you best.

GIVE YOURSELF A COOL LOOK

Take paper and pencil. Describe yourself, listing good and bad points and indifferent ones. Don't start by telling fibs. Show yourself warts and all. If you sometimes don't get along with people, say so. If you are willing to work very hard to learn to get along better, say so.

You are the product you are selling. Learn more about yourself.

We suggest that you don't write a self-evaluation in neat paragraphs of prose. It takes too long and smooths off too many rough edges. Instead, make lists with headings:

Attitudes Toward People
- Don't like irreligious people
- Don't like salesmen
- Enjoy small groups
- Enjoy being someone's only friend

Emotional Strengths
- Seldom get rattled
- Secure with the opposite sex
- Good with money
- Always pay bills on time

The list (a real one, started by one of our students) told him a good deal about himself. He said: "I never realized I was so illogical. Look at the shift in column 2 from *emotion* to *money!*"

"But is that a real shift?" we asked. "Doesn't everybody get emotional about money? Whole novels, like Dickens's *Nicholas Nickleby*, have been written about the relationship between money and emotion. Don't worry about a little thing like that. Keep on listing. And don't think about the process; just put down what comes into your head."

He finished his list; he put it away; a week later we talked. He said: "I am shy, quiet, reliable, I don't mind being alone, and I am best at doing a job someone asks me to do on my own."

"Does that mean you can't be a salesman? You say on this list: *Don't like salesmen.*"

"No, I think that means that I don't like a type of salesman — pushy, loud, life-of-the-party. I think I can sell, but it should be a one-on-one type of job. I've overheard professors talking with textbook salesmen; I think I could sell books."

You see how the procedure goes. Look into yourself and put down what you see. Conclude by saying: "I can do X job or Y job best, but probably not Q, R, or T jobs."

For your scratch-paper inventory of yourself, here are a few suggested headings, arranged in no particular order:

- Jobs you have had
- Favorite recreation
- Likes
- Dislikes
- Favorite weather
- Least-favorite weather
- Hobbies
- Places you would like to live
- Places you can't stand
- Best course grades
- Worst course grades
- Type of person you like best
- Type of person you like least
- Favorite objects
- What you like to do most on a date
- What you most like to do indoors or outdoors
- What you most dislike to do indoors or outdoors
- Political strengths
- Major weaknesses
- Minor weaknesses

You may find this inventory revealing. Now put down a new heading: *If I had all the money in the world, what would I do? (How would I live?)* Why might this question be the most important?

Find another sheet of paper and list quickly any ideas you have under this heading: What others really think of me.

Do all this, and then put your scratch paper away overnight. While all your heated opinions are cooling off, we can go to the next steps.

These involve making an inventory of your work experience, education, and activities.

WORK EXPERIENCE

"You did that?" we found ourselves saying to a student. "Then why isn't it in your résumé?"

"I didn't think it was important. After all, who cares whether I was a male babysitter all through high school?"

The answer is that an employer might care. Just by itself it is interesting. How many boys have had a part-time babysitting business? And it tells people something about you as a person. You are as important as your credentials.

Start by analyzing your work experience by listing everything you have done, from delivering papers to working in a fast-food restaurant to caddying on a golf course. After each item, write down what you learned from this experience. Be candid. Make sure you include any learning that shows you are reliable and honest and can organize your work.

At this point you can also list those supervisors who may be willing to act as references. Find out if they are willing. Don't wait. One student waited too long to write a professor for permission to use her as a reference. As he frantically tried to fill the last space on his résumé, he learned that she had died the week before.

EDUCATIONAL EXPERIENCE

First, in a résumé nobody uses high school education; forget about it. Employers are interested in college or technical school education. For self-analysis, you need information about your:

- Major and minor
- Electives
- Professors (are any of them well known?)
- Grade-point average (GPA)
- Other useful information about your college career

Is GPA important? Thirty years ago, we could have answered confidently that in many business fields, social ability was more important to the average employer than grades. Most students then had B and C averages. When we graduated from college, we didn't know anybody who had an A or A- average. (Maybe we knew the wrong people.)

Nowadays, straight A averages are not uncommon, and employers don't usually consider students who have them as weird or bookworms. Yet informal surveys suggest that some employers are still looking for social ability more than high grades. One manager said: "If candidates got through reasonably well in their degree program, I assume they can handle their subject. What I need to know is, can they work with people and push a project through to completion?"

On the issue of educational experience, consider this advice. Go to your strengths. If you have many hours in your major, stress that fact. If you have a high GPA, and if you think it will impress employers in your field, mention it. If you have taken some interesting and relevant electives, mention them.

Arn Tibbetts teaches an elective, an advanced grammar course, taken by students from many parts of the university from engineering to law. Many times he has been told by students that a prospective employer was more interested in the fact that they had taken a grammar course than in the other courses in their program. It was a great ice-breaker in the interview. "What did you take *that* for? Did you learn anything?"

ACTIVITIES

List what you have done and what it meant to you. (Enough said.)

GO AND GET HELP

Talk to your favorite instructor and ask him or her something like the following: "What do you think I should put in my résumé to sell me to an employer?" Don't ask your parents; they love you already.

Where else should you go? Consider these sources for help:

1. *Your college or university placement office.*
   Talk at length with the people there. They are in constant touch with the market for jobs. If they have job literature, read it.
2. *A representative of your professional organization in your major field.*
   Every college major has such an organization, and it will almost certainly have a journal or newsletter in which jobs are listed. Moreover, the organization will have meetings in which job interviews are scheduled. If you have time, join the organization; it's a good move.
3. *Publications and directories in the library.*
   These are useful:
   Encyclopedia of Associations, National Organizations of United States, Gale Research Company, Detroit, Michigan.
   Dun and Bradstreet — Million Dollar Directory and *Middle Market Directory*
   Standard and Poor's Corporation Reports
   Thomas Register of American Manufacturers

ON TO THE APPLICATION!

You are now completing the first stage of your job campaign. And you should complete it; don't let it drag on. Keep your eye on your goals. Now that you know yourself and the kind of job you want, you can begin to write your job application.

As part of one application, a student was asked to answer briefly this question: "What are your most valued accomplishments?" The student, Andrew Wisniewski, answered as follows:

My Most Valued Accomplishments

The University of Illinois provided a challenge. Four years ago, I was determined to attain three distinctly different goals, without compromising my personality and values. My most valued accomplishment is achieving these three goals: success in athletics, development of leadership qualities, and performance in scholarship.

Athletically, my accomplishments included completing two twenty-six-mile marathons. I also ran 500 miles during my freshman academic year, and I continue to run regularly. Regular running and weightlifting provided a physical challenge and a series of measurable and attainable goals. Because I am not particularly strong by nature, I have had to work hard for my athletic achievements. This perseverance has kept me from just coasting through semesters with relatively easy classes — I always have some goals to achieve. Furthermore, the internal competition relaxes me, allows me to think more clearly, and gives me an opportunity to understand the difficulties that contemporaries have in other fields, such as academics. Now I receive the same type of exhilaration from a long run or heavy lift as I do from solving a challenging academic or social problem.

Beyond athletics, I developed my leadership skills in two directions: through social organizations and through technical societies.

As a social leader, I coordinated the campus-wide Illini Guide program. Through it I experienced the political and bureaucratic processes of a large corporation (the University) through the Guides' affiliation with the Dean of Students' office and through Residence Hall activities.

My leadership was also experienced in a more professional setting when I served as president of the student chapter of the Association for Computing Machinery. In this organization, in addition to working with professors and department heads, I developed a committee style of organization. Prior to my term, ACM was inactive. Through the work of my officers and committee chairmen, however, we developed a working organization, with definite goals and tangible rewards. I learned about motivation, persuasion, and group behavior. This knowledge has also been important to me.

I found that I could manage and organize highly intelligent and ambitious fellow students. Furthermore, I developed techniques for managing a group of enthusiastic volunteers determined to succeed. I also learned the art of speaking with

> important people, such as the Vice-Chancellor and the Dean of Students.
>
> Academically, I have integrated friends, communication, part-time employment, hard work, and luck to achieve a strong technical knowledge base. Additionally, my grades have been good.
>
> Finally, my part-time employment at Digital Technology Incorporated has provided me with essential experience, not only with technology but with the management of a small business. The executives at DTI have been very kind to me, and they play an active role in guiding my future. I have seen the hard work necessary in corporate management, and also the pleasure that success provides.
>
> As an afterthought, I will add that I think that my biggest achievement is not in just one facet of these three categories of my life: athletics, leadership, and scholarship. I am most proud and most pleased that I could achieve goals in all three aspects of life at the same time. This is my most valued accomplishment.

EXERCISES

1. Prepare some notes for class discussion on Andy's essay. How convincing is it? Will it help him get the job he wants?

2. Write an essay on your own "most valued accomplishments."

3. For yourself, make the scratch-paper inventory described above.

4. Make the complete inventory of your work experience, education, and activities suggested in this chapter.

5. Interview one of your instructors. Ask him or her: "What suggestions do you have for me in presenting my best self to an employer?" Write down the suggestions.

CHAPTER

20

The Application (Letter and Résumé)

What are we talking about? The term *résumé*, for instance, is not always used consistently, even in textbooks. So let's agree on these definitions:

1. A *résumé* is a summary of your relevant experience (relevant to the employer). The word has two accent marks: *résumé*. Without the marks the word is *resume* (re-SUME, meaning "to start up again").
2. A *cover letter* explains and supports the résumé, and vice versa.
3. The *application* consists of the letter, the résumé, and any pertinent extra material. One of our students, a senior in engineering, is assisting a professor in writing a computer manual. As extra material in his package, he will use a copy of the manual.

Note well the second definition, which explains the relationship between the résumé and its cover letter. One way to look at this relationship is to say that the résumé gives the facts while the letter explains the facts.

That is true enough, so far as it goes. But there is more. The two represent a package that sells you, and the elements of the package should be interwoven and strongly related. They support each other, but the way you create such support depends on the product (you), the material, and the type of reader (the employer). Analyze these carefully, and put your application together so that everything fits, without false emphases or unnecessary repetition.

To explain all this, now follows a typical package:

May 20, 1987

Lee Novak, Senior Partner
Novak, Preisler, and Bergeron
18 Koppel Street
Chicago, Illinois 60607

1   Dear Mr. Novak:

   I am answering your advertisement in the *Chicago Tribune* for a legal aide.
   I have trained specifically for this work since I started
5 college in 1983. First, I took all the courses Rendro Junior
   College offered in paralegal work. This meant that I had to
   attend an extra summer. Next, I majored in Administration
   of Justice at Southern Illinois University, specializing in the
   Legal Aide Program Curriculum. (I will graduate May 29.)
10 In the Spring of last year, I was an intern in the Rendro
   County District Attorney's office, where I performed the
   standard duties of a legal aide.
   You will note from my résumé that I have strong
   outside interests in music and sports. I would be glad to play
15 on your company's sports teams — if you have any. If you
   don't, I'd be glad to help organize them!
   I am not sure whether this would be of interest to you,
   but I have not missed a day of work since I started at
   Marwood Drugstore in 1980.
20 I am available for an interview at your convenience.

                                          Sincerely,

                                          Pamela Jarvis

RÉSUMÉ

Pamela Jarvis   May 20, 1987
1001 S. Mission Blvd.
Carbondale, Illinois 62901
555-322-1415

Job Objective: Legal aide in a private law firm

EDUCATION
    1985 to 1987 — BS in Administration of Justice,
                    Southern Illinois University,
                    Carbondale, Illinois
    1983 to 1985 — Two-year Arts degree, Rendro Junior
                    College, Rendro, Illinois

WORK EXPERIENCE
    Spring, 1986 — Intern, Rendro County District Attorney's
                    Office
                    Duties: Issuing subpoenas, taking
                            testimonies, performing various
                            clerical duties associated with the
                            District Attorney's office.
    1985 to 1986 — Part-time secretary, Department of
                    Administration of Justice, Southern
                    Illinois University
    1980 to 1982 — Part-time clerk, Marwood Drugstore.
                    Worked 12 hours a week.

ACTIVITIES
                — Member, Legal Aide Student Association,
                  1985 to 1986
                — Pitcher, girls' softball team, all-city
                  champions, 1982
                — President, Senior High Fashion Board,
                  Robeson's Department Store, 1982
                — Play guitar; started when I was eight
                  years old

PERSONAL DATA
    — Good health
    — Unmarried

WHEN AVAILABLE FOR WORK   The day after I graduate, May 29, 1987

REFERENCES
Professor Clarkson Smith, Department of Administration of Justice, Southern Illinois University, Carbondale, Illinois, 62901. (555-549-0409)
Ms. Clarice Harley, Rendro County District Attorney, Manla, Illinois, 62901. (555-549-7749)
Mr. John Hess, owner, Marwood Drug Store, 202 West 5th St., Urbana, Illinois, 62801. (555-367-5549)

Let us assume that you are Mr. Novak, the person to whom the letter is addressed. You are interested in hiring a legal aide, and you have twenty-eight applications on your desk. You begin by separating these into two piles labelled YES and NO. The applications put in the NO pile will not be considered again. You will read applications in the YES pile and recommend the top three as possible employees to another partner in the firm, who will check their references by phone. If the references of all three check out, you will interview each applicant.

Would you say that Pamela Jarvis, whose application we just inspected might be one of the top three in the "first cut"? (She was; can you guess why?) The line numbers in the margins of the résumé and letter help us refer to specific parts of the material.

DISCUSSION OF PAMELA JARVIS'S APPLICATION

Anyone who reads many applications learns one fact quickly: There is a surprising number of careless people in the world. Yet an application is one of the few instances in which the candidate for a job is not allowed any mistakes — at least, not any obvious ones that jump off the page at you.

A good friend of ours is a senior partner in an accounting firm. He reads the applications sent to his firm and makes the first cut. "I usually read them through fast," he told us. "When I find a misspelled word or faulty punctuation, I drop the application in the waste basket. We don't even answer those."

You may say that this is harsh. Perhaps it is. But it is typical, and you should know that it happens. Make your application mechanically perfect.

Here, possibly, is one reason Pamela Jarvis's application got her an interview. There are no mistakes in it. One mark in her favor.

But there had to be something else. In discussing her application, Novak supplied his reasons for wanting to interview her. Here is what he said:

> When I have to read many applications, I set aside an hour or two to make the first cut. In my *possibles* group, I put:
>
> 1. the really nice-looking applications — professionally printed, on fancy paper, for example
> 2. the ones that best fit the job we have
> 3. the ones that interest me the most or catch my attention in some way
> 4. a combination of the above
>
> Some of the nice-looking applications don't look so good when you read them carefully. The same can be true for the best job-fits and the most interesting ones.
>
> I do look hardest at the interesting applications, and I should say what I mean by *interesting*. Pamela Jarvis is a good example. I was struck by how

determined and consistent she seemed to be. She wanted solid training in her field badly enough to stay at her junior college an extra summer. I was also impressed by her internship; that sort of work is not easy for a woman in a rural southern Illinois county. She said at the end of her letter that she never missed a day of work. That is impressive. And in the context of her letter and résumé, I believe her.

Ms. Jarvis seems to have energy and stick-to-it-iveness. She has stayed with the guitar for a long time. She worked part-time all the way through her college career, and for some time in high school.

Everything in her application shows that she is not afraid of work, of applying herself.

But she doesn't sound like a grind, either. That remark in her letter about starting a sports team for us was a little thing, but I remembered it. It stood out.

In the Jarvis application, there is a personality — a definite one, but not a pushy one. Everything she has done shows that she can work with people. And lawyers, from the typical aide's point of view, are not the easiest people in the world to work with.

I guess what I'm saying is that Pamela Jarvis got an interview because she had the training we wanted (it fit the job); she appeared to be a strong, hardworking person; and, frankly, she made me curious. I just wanted to talk to somebody who pitches on a softball team and plays guitar.

Oh, by the way, one of the partners mentioned that I should be sure to talk to the woman who wanted to go to work "the day after I graduate."

That was all he remembered from her application.

One more point about the Jarvis application. There is nothing flashy about it. No tricks with language or visual effect; she made no statements about being a brilliant student or being super-active in the social whirl. Altogether, it is a pretty modest application built upon her careful analysis of her strong points as a person and a professional.

Did you notice that she said nothing about grades or honors? Novak didn't seem to be bothered by the omission, and he made no mention of it in his comments.

FORM OF THE APPLICATION

How does a person read an application? The answer tells us something about *form* as well as *content*.

Some people pick up the résumé first, some the letter. (Some people always read the résumé first. It's quicker, and if they see something they don't like they can put it in the NO pile right off.)

Next, whether particularly aware of it or not, a reader is likely to run his or her eye down the page, letting it be caught by an interesting detail, an unusual mass of information, or a single sentence that stands out, like the sentence in lines 17–19 in the Jarvis letter. But the reader's eye can't be caught if the appearance of the message is too massive. You should, therefore, make both your letter and résumé look light and airy: Use plenty of white space. (How many paragraphs are there in the Jarvis letter?) Separate the items so that your reader can tell one item from another. Notice that the dashes in the Jarvis résumé indicate where sentence units start. In addition, note her use of indentation, capital letters, and underlining.

Don't bury an interesting detail in the middle of the message. Look at lines 6 and 39 in the Jarvis résumé; and lines 17–19 in the letter. These are important and they are placed in positions of emphasis.

The typical résumé follows a form similar to the one Pamela Jarvis used:

RÉSUMÉ
- Name
- Job objective
- EDUCATION
- WORK EXPERIENCE
- ACTIVITIES
- PERSONAL DATA
- WHEN AVAILABLE FOR WORK
- REFERENCES
- Date

If you think your situation calls for a different form, try one. See, for example, Figures 20.1, 20.2, and 20.3 below.

The heading PERSONAL DATA is nowadays often omitted. Legally, an employer can't ask you for this information, and you don't have to supply it. You don't have to use a picture of yourself either, but if you think it is effective to use one, do so.

Adding a picture ordinarily means getting your résumé professionally printed, with the picture made a part of the résumé page, not clipped to it. Always staple letter and resume together; don't clip them. Paper clips were invented by the devil, who wanted to confound the human race with lost pages.

We should say something here about professionally prepared résumés. Generally, we don't approve of them; they are too often slick and phony-looking. In addition, we have never seen a professional job as good as one you can do for yourself, because *the professionals do not know you.* They usually work by formula, as if they were selling used cars.

If you want to hire a professional résumé-writer or a professional printer, demand that you design the messages and that you have final say in their content and appearance. After all, you are paying for the service. And check the proofs carefully. Some typesetters make errors.

WHAT NOT TO DO IN AN APPLICATION

- *Don't fib.* Tell the exact truth.
- *Don't try to make decisions for the employer.* Employers often complain about this sort of rhetoric in a letter: "I am the person you need for the job of _____."

    "Listen," said one executive. "I'll make my own decisions as to whether this is the 'sort of person I need for the job.'" Give the facts; let the reader decide.
- *Avoid widely used application models.* We asked a business writing class to use as a model the application package suggested in the placement office of the Commerce College in our university. It was a mistake. The resulting applications the students wrote all sounded alike. We couldn't tell one student from another.
- *Don't get nervous.* Relax. You'll do all right.

TYPICAL EMPLOYER COMPLAINTS

Here are typical complaints from employers about applications:

- Takes too long to say too little
- Hard to read; poorly reproduced; bad format
- Too much information that does not interest *me*
- Says the same thing too many times
- Contains spelling and punctuation errors
- Forgets that an application is a ticket to an interview, not an autobiography

Consider these complaints as you do the exercises below.

EXERCISES

1. Read the résumés in Figures 20.1, 20.2, and 20.3. Note that Résumé C was prepared by a person with some experience. Assuming that you as an employer had an opening in each of the three fields involved, which person would you hire first? Second?

2. Discuss the *strengths* and *weaknesses* of each résumé.

3. Would any of the three résumés stand alone, without a cover letter? Why?

4. Write a cover letter for the résumé that might need it most.

MARY ELAINE MAYS

1234 York Cove
Gropius, Indiana 46222

(555) 123-1234

IS AMBITIOUS
   Plans to take the CPA exam immediately after graduation
   Long range goal — partner in sizable firm

UNDERSTANDS ACCOUNTING WORK
   B.S. in Accounting, Memphis State University, May 1982.
   Overall grade point average 3.2

   Business My Specialty — overall Business Average 3.7
   Accounting, 24 hrs: 3.8   Business Statistics, 3 hrs: 4.0
   Business finance, 3 hrs: 4.0   Computer Science, 6 hrs: 3.6
   Economics, 9 hours: 3.6

COMMUNICATES WELL
   Salesperson, Goldsmith's Department Store, 1975 to present.
   Observed methods of controlling inventory, creation of
   primary source documents, effective utilization of data
   processing and computer. Supervised and trained new
   employees. Offered promotion and full-time work.

ASSUMES RESPONSIBILITY
   Beta Alpha Psi, National Professional Accounting Association.
   Membership Chairman.
   Married, manages a home and a child. Willing to travel.
   Paid all school fees.

IS PERSONALLY FIT
   5'6" tall; brown hair, blue eyes; missed two days of school/
   work in the last year.

Figure 20.1. Résumé A

QUALIFICATIONS OF JOHN D. COYL
FOR MANAGEMENT TRAINING
WITH XYC COMPANY

Qualified by Education

B. S. Memphis State University, May 1982. Major: Management with a concentration in Production Management. Grade point average in business: 2.8.

Qualified by Experience

Persuasive — A People Mover	Program Chairman, Society for the Advancement of Management Pledge Chairman, Delta Sigma Pi, Professional Fraternity Assistant Leader, Boy Scouts of America Dormitory Representative, Richardson Towers Campaign Manager, Student Government Campaign
Persistent	Ran for dormitory representative twice before being elected the third time. Competed for membership on University Golf Team, 4 years. Received an "F" grade on the first examination in Statistics, an "A" grade on the last examination, and a "B" in the course.
Imaginative	Earned an "A" on an Advertising presentation where I chose a product and designed a campaign.
Articulate	Gave election speeches for myself and others. Earned an "A" in Business Communication. Habitually earned good grades on term papers.
Dependable	Worked for Flagman, Arnold Construction Company, summers since high school without missing more than two days in eight years.

Figure 20.2. Résumé B

People Who Speak Well of Me

Ralph F. Smitherson	Don Carson, Vice	John H. Johnson,
Arnold Construction	President	Coach
(555) 123-1234	Student Personnel,	University Golf Team
	MSU	(555) 321-4321
	(555) 789-2134	

Contact Me

1234 Alpha Drive, Memphis, TN 38152
or phone (555) 123-4231

Figure 20.2. Résumé B (continued)

Sandra Jones

HOME ADDRESS
22 Cedric Drive
Urbana, Illinois 61801
217/367-3004

OFFICE ADDRESS
University High School
1212 West Springfield
Urbana, Illinois 61801
217/333-2870

JOB OBJECTIVE
Seeking a position as an instructor at a junior or community college, or at a small college or university in one or a combination of the following areas: speech communication, oral interpretation, theatre (acting, production, history, literature), English (rhetoric, literature).

EDUCATION
Master of Arts in Speech Communication, May, 1981, University of Illinois at Urbana-Champaign, specialization in Oral Interpretation
Bachelor of Arts in Speech Communication and English, May, 1977, Iowa State University, Ames, specialization in theatre and literature

EXPERIENCE RELATED TO JOB OBJECTIVE

Sept. 1981-present
University High School, University of Illinois at Urbana-Champaign
Teaching Assistant
Responsible for teaching freshman level course including units in literature, grammar, composition, and speech communication
Responsible for directing and producing two plays each school year

Sept. 1979-May 1981
Department of Speech Communication, University of Illinois at Urbana-Champaign
Teaching Assistant
Taught a course combining instruction in basic speaking and composition skills including public speaking, debate, group discussion, essay writing, research methods, and term paper writing
Production Manager
Oral interpretation productions presented at the University's Armory Free Theatre

June 1978-present
Celebration Company at the Station Theatre, Urbana
Actress, costumer, children's theatre director, and workshop leader
Created major roles in several productions; coordinated and built costumes for four major productions; directed three children's touring productions; conducted several workshops for children, teen-agers, and adults on a wide variety of theatre topics

June 1975-Aug. 1976
The Old Creamery Theatre Company, Garrison, Iowa
Actress, Assistant Costumer
Created several roles in major repertory and touring productions; assisted the costumer in building costumes for all productions

CREATIVE WORKS
Important acting roles:
Angel—*When You Comin' Back Red Rider* by Mark Medoff
Singer—*Marat Sade* by Peter Weiss
June—*Fifth of July* by Lanford Wilson
Betty—*Landscape of the Body* by John Guare
Lady Capulet—*Romeo and Juliet* by William Shakespeare
Mother Courage—*Mother Courage and Her Children* by Bertold Brecht

Directing experience:
Children's shows I adapted from children's literature for the Celebration Co.:
Rhymes, Creatures, A Who, A What, and All Kinds of Imaginary Features
Rhythm
Fun, Music, Rhythm, and a Washtub Bass (received a grant from the Illinois Arts Consortium for a Fall, 1980 tour)
Family with Karma Ibsen-Riley (a show conceived and written by a group of teen-agers participating in a workshop conducted for the Celebration Co.)
A Thurber Carnival by James Thurber, University High School
Yes, My Darling Daughter by Mark Reed, University High School
Director and narrator for The Rainbow Signing Company, a sign language theatre company in Urbana

HONORS
Regional Scholarship, International Thespian Society, 1972; Membership, Theta Alpha Phi, college theatre honorary, Iowa State University, 1975; Honor Scholarship for theatre, Iowa State University, 1976; Membership, I-Alums, theatre alumni honorary, Iowa State University, 1977; Dean's List, Iowa State University, last three years; Graduation with honors, Iowa State University, 1977

REFERENCES
Available upon request

Figure 20.3. Résumé C

PART 8

Oral Messages

CHAPTER 21

Picking a Form for Your Speech

You have three basic speech forms to choose from when you are invited to speak, although combinations of these three forms are also possible. The three basic speech forms are (1) impromptu, (2) extemporaneous, and (3) manuscript. Each one requires special skills and practice. In impromptu speaking you are expected to speak on the spur of the moment and think on your feet; in extemporaneous speaking you present material previously prepared from notes or an outline; and in manuscript speaking you deliver your speech from a written paper. Let us look at each form to see how each works in certain situations.

IMPROMPTU SPEAKING

An impromptu speech occurs on the spur of the moment or without advance preparation. You may be asked to comment on a report or plan, add information to someone else's analysis, or disagree or agree with an argument. You will seldom be asked to speak on something you know nothing about. It is therefore wise to be ready to speak whenever you are in a meeting, particularly when you are familiar with the subject matter under discussion. You can become a successful impromptu speaker by paying attention to these suggestions:

1. *Come prepared, so that you can feel confident.* Assume that you may be asked to speak. Bring files of information or notes that might help you in case you are asked to discuss the issues under consideration. Don't be ostentatious with your information — be as discreet as possible. But if you're prepared, you won't fall into panic, the worst enemy of the impromptu speaker.

2. *Listen and take notes.* Follow the speaker's line of reasoning and use of evidence. Respond to the speech by jotting down ideas. You might want to use two columns for your notes: *pro* and *con* or *I agree* and *I disagree*. (Do not be completely negative in your notes; otherwise, you may come off as being against everything the speaker says.)

3. *Take your time; organize your thoughts.* You need not rush into a speech if, without warning, you have been asked to comment. Your audience doesn't expect you to jump up immediately with a comment. In fact, your audience will respect you if you are cautious, careful, and reasonable. Take a few minutes, therefore, to put your notes together and develop a plan for your response. If you have taken good notes, they may form the basis for your speech. If you discover that your notes don't lead you the way that you want to go, you may find one of the following methods helpful:

    a. Discuss a point or issue that has been ignored.
    b. Agree or disagree with the plan by showing how it can or cannot be implemented.
    c. Show how the reasoning is sound or faulty — or partly sound and partly faulty.

EXTEMPORANEOUS SPEAKING

An extemporaneous speech is one delivered from notes or an outline. *Extemporaneous* originally meant "out of time." In speech-making, however, the term has come to mean a speech that has not been written out, but has been planned and practiced. You first plan carefully, following the methods described in Chapter 22. Then you practice the speech several times, so that it has a smooth delivery without sounding "canned" or memorized. (In an extemporaneous speech you memorize your basic ideas, not the speech itself.)

Most speech experts favor the extemporaneous speech because it is the best way to maintain a relationship with your audience. You are sensitive to your audience through eye contact. You are alert to their reactions. This technique is highly favored because a well-trained speaker can deliver a direct, sincere, stimulating speech that may sound "out of time" but is not.

Because extemporaneous speaking has these advantages, however, that does not mean it is an easy form to use. It requires meticulous planning and practice that takes time and patience. As you become an expert in your specialty, extemporaneous speaking will be much easier than it seems to you now.

MANUSCRIPT SPEAKING

There is considerable disagreement about whether to write out a speech. Some authorities say that a speech delivered from manuscript sounds artificial. In practice, however, speeches are being written and delivered from manuscript by the thousands. Consider the many written speeches delivered by politicians on television and on radio. In fact, many large corporations hire speechmakers whose primary responsibility is to write speeches for top management. Even leaders who do not have the services of speech writers continue to write out their speeches. Why are so many speeches written out?

First, leaders in government and business are busy people. A written speech can be more economical and efficient than one developed only from notes or an outline. Second, important people cannot afford to make mistakes. They need to say whatever is necessary in an orderly, developed fashion. It is easier to get sidetracked into irrelevancies when delivering a speech from notes than from a manuscript. Wordiness and imprecision may also be a problem for some speakers, and a written speech can be edited to remove these. A written speech, as you can see, has particular uses and advantages. If well done, it can also be as effective as one given extemporaneously.

If you choose the manuscript form of speech, you must remember that success depends upon the following:

1. Start with a clean manuscript, typed with large letters on one side of paper with lots of white space. Do not add last-minute notes that may cause you to lose your train of thought.

2. Do not use a speech manuscript more than once without re-evaluating your audience and the situation. Some speakers believe that a speech that works for one audience will be equally successful with another; this is not necessarily the case. We heard a talk in which the speaker, a professor of communication, read from a manuscript that he had used for several other audiences. Some of the evidence and points simply did not fit his new audience or the new situation. Instead of changing the speech to bring it up to date and for a different audience, he had tried to get too much mileage out of the old manuscript. The result was that he lost credibility.

3. Do not *read* the speech, *speak* it. Here are some techniques to use in delivering the speech:

    a. Present the speech in a conversational tone.
    b. Concentrate on the meaning as you talk. Such concentration will help you use inflections that are more like talking than reading.

c. Look ahead in your manuscript so that you can use eye contact with your audience. With practice, you can remember several lines in advance and deliver them extemporaneously.
   d. Take your time. Pause occasionally. Move away from the podium (or speaker's stand) to deliver a few lines without looking at the manuscript.

WHICH SPEECH FORM SHOULD YOU CHOOSE?

Each form of delivery is useful in its own way. None of them is necessarily better than others. You should pick the one that best fits the time allotted, the kind of information to be presented, and your confidence as a speaker.

Time Allotted for Speech

How much time can you take? The time allotted may influence the form of delivery you choose. If you have ten or fifteen minutes to make a speech, delivering it from notes or an outline will probably be the most practical method. Such a time limit will restrict the amount of material you can present; two or three main points will be the maximum, particularly if you support your points well. However, if your speech is much more than fifteen minutes long, you may wish to combine extemporaneous delivery with a written manuscript. Some of your points may be difficult to explain or full of detail. Having the speech written out will be an advantage.

If you have to speak for as long as an hour, you will have a great amount of material to present. For such a long speech it isn't likely that you will use extemporaneous delivery entirely. In this case a manuscript speech or a combination of extemporaneous and manuscript would be the best choice.

Density of Information

If your speech is full of statistics, facts, and arguments, then you should probably write it out. It is often very difficult to develop a reasoned argument, based on data, without having it in writing. Your points must be completely accurate. If you try to persuade someone to follow your line of reasoning and then take action based on that reasoning, your argument must be perfectly clear. So consider delivering this kind of speech from manuscript.

Let us consider three hypothetical situations to see which speech form would be most suitable.

   1. The management of your company has decided that a training session is needed to teach the employees of your division to write better memos and letters. A consultant visits your division for a day, reading memos and letters

in the files. Afterward, he meets with you and others in your organization, making several recommendations. You find that some of the recommendations are useful; others are simply impractical. Since you know the work of your division and your employees, you are able to respond to the consultant's proposal. This kind of speech comes under the heading of an impromptu speech. Your style needs to be casual; you may even be seated when you respond. You understand the situation, so you can handle the speech without having to practice or prepare an outline beforehand.

2. You have been invited to give a speech to the members of a service club in your home town. It is a luncheon meeting. Everyone has had a good meal, so the audience is relaxed and comfortable. Most of the members are friends. Even though the room is a small dining room, the twenty or twenty-five people are not crowded. The members want to be amused and entertained. If you can give them a few pieces of information, they would not reject them, but they do not wish to make any new decisions as a result of your speech. Delivering your speech extemporaneously from notes or an outline would be the appropriate way to handle this speech assignment.

You want your audience to know that you have thought about your topic and that you have come prepared to speak. Nothing insults an audience quite as much as thinking that the speech is purely impromptu. When someone has been invited to speak, the audience wants to know that some preparation has gone into the process. Your evidence of preparation is in the notes and outline that you bring with you. You may never refer to them, but the fact that you have them reassures the audience that you are serious about speaking.

3. You have been invited by your immediate supervisor to make a speech to the company's shareholders. The topic: Shareholder's dividends will be reduced next quarter. One hundred shareholders show up in a room that can seat 250 people. There are many empty chairs, and you must use a microphone to be heard. The room has bare floors and is ten degrees too cold. The audience is uncomfortable, some people wearing coats to keep warm. The audience is hostile because this is the second time in the year that the company has been unable to assign its customary dividend. You will probably want to write out this speech because you know you will be challenged, questioned, and perhaps disagreed with. You must have your facts straight, and you should not deviate from your speech until you have presented all the evidence. Your shareholders will trust your evidence more if you have it in written form than if you present it extemporaneously.

USE AN ORAL STYLE

Whether you choose to deliver your speech from a manuscript or from notes, you will want to use an oral style. This style is different from a written style in several ways.

1. Your vocabulary is simpler.
2. You use more colloquialisms, contractions, and rhetorical questions.
3. Your sentences are shorter.
4. You use more transitions to introduce the divisions of the topic.
5. You repeat key words and phrases.
6. You use direct dialogue with the audience.

Unless you are trained as an actor and are used to memorizing lines, don't try to memorize a speech. The time that it takes to memorize for a particular occasion is wasteful. Furthermore, a memorized speech, delivered by someone untrained in giving lines, sounds artificial. Your chance of forgetting part of a memorized speech is great, and omissions cause embarrassment for the audience and speaker alike.

The following speech, given by a speech writer for Illinois Bell Telephone Company, shows the qualities of the oral style. Read the speech, then answer the questions following it.

The Care and Feeding of the Executive Speaker
A FEW AGE-OLD PRINCIPLES OF EFFECTIVE ORATORY

By JOHN R. BONEE, *Corporate Communication Manager, Illinois Bell Delivered at the National Conference of the Public Relations Students Society of America, Chicago, Illinois, November 9, 1981*

1. Since I agreed to speak here today, I've had two letters and three phone calls from Nancy Theiss asking what type of audiovisual equipment I might need, another call reminding me that I hadn't made any requests, describing this meeting room and repeating the invitation to ask for I don't know what: slide projection, 16mm film, multi-media, whatever.

2. Well, I didn't want any audiovisual equipment and I am going to tell you why.

3. I'm here to talk about *speech* writing. And a speech is the *spoken* word.

4. You've heard the proverb, "One picture is worth a thousand words"? Well, if you believe that — then draw me the Gettysburg Address.

5. That says something about my attitude towards the spoken word, my work with the spoken word, and my love of the spoken. If the spoken word is eloquent, if it obeys the classical rules of acceptable rhetoric, it will be effective without visual aids.

6. Since my topic is the care and feeding of the executive speaker, I'm not going to treat you to a systematic treatise on speech writing. Instead I'm going to tell you how to care for the speaker for whom you write, or may be writing for someday in your career.

7. In the first part, I'm going to talk about the *theoretical* barriers to successful speech writing and to the successful management, if you will, of the speaker. Barriers that are rather intellectual than practical. In the second part I'll talk about some *practical* problems you meet in dealing with your client.

Picking a Form for Your Speech

8. What are the *theoretical* problems you will run into when you become a speech writer? There are at least four.

9. The first is a *prejudice in favor of logic over rhetoric*, of sweet reason over emotional appeal — a prejudice in favor of the facts, the data, the information over any other kind of argumentation. It's a *big* problem because so many speakers think all you have to do is give people the facts; tell them the statistics. Put up bar graphs and line graphs and pie charts, quote some research, cite Yankelovich, Skelly & White, call upon Roper & Gallup and Harris and ORC ... then you've got them. Your logic is impeccable, they will bow to it, you will convince them.

10. Okay, so you've convinced them, but have you *persuaded* them? Because conviction and persuasion are *not the same.* Conviction is intellectual, persuasion is in the order of action. If you have an emotionally loaded problem, you can convince people without persuading.

11. Think of a controversial social problem. Suppose you want to persuade people to accept — let us say — busing, as a solution to the problem of integrating our public schools. Sweet reason is not going to move parents to put their kids on that bus to ride ten miles to a school outside their neighborhood.

12. Sweet reason will not do it! Intellectually, you can make people accept integration as a reasonable goal, as a necessary goal, as the only right kind of goal to have in our society. But that doesn't put the kids on the bus, it doesn't stop the protests, it doesn't stop the angry speeches at the school board meeting. It just doesn't work.

13. Why? Because those people's *emotions* are involved. Strong emotions like fear and anger, resentment, even sometimes hatred. You've got to work with those emotions if you're going to write a persuasive speech and that's the only kind of speech worth writing. It's the only kind of speech worth giving.

14. You know, it's said that the human person is a rational animal. Okay, that's basically true. But don't count on people being *rational* animals all the time. Sometimes their animality takes over from their rationality. Not just sometimes — frequently. Not just frequently — more frequently than not.

15. There was a man who had everything going for him. He was rich, he was smart — high I.Q. — he was well educated. There was only one thing wrong with him. He thought he was dead.

16. So his family and friends prevailed upon him to visit a psychiatrist. The psychiatrist recognized that this man was intelligent, educated, successful in business. He thought, "Well, I'll *reason* him out of his illusion!"

17. So he asked him, "Listen, tell me, do dead men *eat*?" The patient said, "Well, as a matter of fact, maybe they *do.* In many cultures — in the Orient for example — they put food in the tombs so that the dead can come back and consume it. Apparently dead men do eat."

18. And then the psychiatrist asked him, "Well, do dead men *talk*?" And he said, "Well, maybe they do. You know, Houdini, for example, had a telephone put in his coffin so he could call back from the other world. And people apparently talk through mediums. Yeah, dead men do talk sometimes."

19   Next, the doctor asked, "Do dead men *walk*?" The man said, "Sometimes they do. There are documented cases, in England, for example, of haunted castles — the former occupant comes back and walks during the night, rattles chains. Yeah, dead men do walk."

20   In desperation, he finally asked, "Do dead men *bleed*?" And the patient said, "No, absolutely not. Dead men do not bleed."

21   The doctor said, "Roll up your sleeve." So he rolled up his sleeve and the doctor took a scalpel and made a small incision in the man's forearm. The blood began to roll down his arm and he put his finger on it and tasted it and he said, "What do you know . . . dead men do bleed!"

22   The point? You cannot *reason* people out of any proposition to which they have a strong emotional commitment.

EXERCISES

1. How does the speaker address his audience? How does he refer to himself? Discuss the effectiveness of this kind of dialogue.

2. Point out the use of colloquialisms and sentence fragments, which are not usually acceptable in formal writing. How do the colloquialisms and fragments add or detract from the oral style?

3. Speakers often repeat phrases, clauses, or single words, particularly those that are grammatically parallel. Find several examples in which the speaker repeats single words, phrases, or clauses. Why does he do this? Discuss the effectiveness of this device.

4. The oral style is effective when telling anecdotes and stories. Study the long story at the end of the example. Identify the devices Bonee uses to make the story sound like the dialogue of real people.

5. After Bonee tells the audience what he is going to talk about, he divides his speech into two parts. Why does he do this? What are the two parts? Discuss his method of keeping the audience "on track."

CHAPTER 22

Shaping a Speech for Your Audience

When you start to make a speech, you usually have certain preconceived notions about the way your audience will treat you. You expect people to wait until you have finished the speech before they get up out of their seats. You expect courteous treatment! You expect that they will not interrupt you, they will listen, and they will respond by eye contact and attentiveness. They may even take notes on what you say.

For extending you their courtesy, you repay them by treating your topic with originality. This does not mean that your audience wants a laugh a minute, but listeners do expect that you will present your material with a certain imagination and flair. "Put old information in new bottles" is a useful reminder for speech makers. Your particular way of approaching and dealing with the subject — with fresh insights and ingenuity — repays your audience for their courtesy to you. (See Chapter 23 for ways to vary your handling of information.)

You will probably not be invited to make a speech unless you have shown that you know something about the topic to be discussed. Your very presence in front of an audience is verification that you have experience and knowledge you are willing to share. The introductory remarks made about you before you speak also give the audience additional justification for accepting you as someone established in your field. So your audience expects you to live up to your reputation as someone who is accurate and honest in presenting information.

Since most audiences value honesty and trustworthiness, you owe them the courtesy of presenting facts accurately and qualifying your generalizations. Don't overstate your case by saying, "I know this to be true." Instead, say, "I believe this is true," or "Using my information, I conclude that...." Don't say, "Without doubt, my solution is the best one." Instead, say, "This is only one of the many solutions possible, but it is one that I favor." You can always expect to have at least one person in the audience who knows as much about the subject as you do — someone who can challenge your facts, if inaccurate, and your generalizations, if unqualified. Therefore be careful and cautious in your use of facts, figures, and generalizations. Don't get out on a limb and be forced to crawl back in front of an audience.

No two audiences are exactly alike. But the average audience is usually fairly predictable, particularly in its desire that as a speaker you treat its members with respect and courtesy. Never talk down to an audience or act as if you are the only one who knows about the subject. Nothing alienates an audience quite as much as a know-it-all. In addition, certain kinds of jokes and stories are unsuitable for many audiences. If you want to tell a story, be sure that it fits the subject matter and is not merely thrown in to get attention. Your listeners may reject your idea if you insult them with irrelevancies just for the sake of a laugh.

DEALING WITH INATTENTIVE OR HOSTILE AUDIENCES

Audiences have ways of showing whether they approve of you and what you are saying. Certain members of an audience may ignore you by thinking of something else — made obvious by their lack of eye contact. Others may refuse to laugh at your jokes. We have had hostile members of an audience interrupt to ask irrelevant questions or to argue against one of our facts. They may show by shrugs, slumping, or other body movements, how they feel about your speech. By contrast, they will often show approval by nodding in agreement, applauding, or laughing with you. As you become practiced at speechmaking, you will be able to identify these signs of approval or disapproval and respond to them.

If, for instance, you find that people are inattentive or becoming bored, liven up your delivery: move away from the podium to get closer to them. Speak faster and more briskly. Identify key persons in the audience and speak to them directly. Since nothing is more gratifying than having a responsive audience, make them respond. Don't allow their attention to wander. Command them by your actions and delivery to listen to you.

In this story, a trained speaker talks about handling a hostile audience:

> I was once invited to speak about a training program to workers in a large company. I learned, too late, that they were hostile to any proposals I

might make because they were under pressure from executives to develop a program they did not want. Consequently, when I came into the room to speak, they saw me as "a tool of the bosses." Immediately I became the enemy. Their minds had been made up; they had taken a position. Nothing I could say about the program would change their minds. As a result of their heckling, irrelevant questions, and criticisms of my proposals, I became defensive and antagonistic, making the situation worse.

In this encounter, I made three mistakes: First, I hadn't asked in advance the appropriate questions about the audience. I had gone into the situation "cold." Second, I was not alert to the clues the audience gave me. Third, I took the criticisms personally rather than as an expression of antagonism toward another proposal.

I should have solved these problems in the following ways: I should have realized that I had a problem when the irrelevant, heckling questions began. At that point, I should have shifted ground by asking the audience what they wanted to do about the training program. This action might have defused the situation. By allowing them to express their concerns to an outsider, I would have strengthened my role as an advisor. As it was, I made myself a victim.

If you find you have a hostile audience, pause for a moment. Assume that there is something you don't know about the situation. Try to find out what it is. Ask questions. Stay calm. Stay out of the argument as much as possible, but let the members of the group discuss the issues. Act as a moderator. After the audience has had its say, summarize and give a shortened version of what you intended to say in the first place.

If you are unwilling to take the necessary steps to fulfill the responsibilities to your audience (and also their expectations), refuse or avoid the speech assignment. If you don't know the kind of audience you will have or what your listeners may believe about the topic to be discussed, ask. Talk with those responsible for the meeting. Find out if any of the audience will be closed-minded or prejudiced against your topic. Get as much information as possible even if you are forced to get it at the last minute.

YOUR TOPIC

Most of the time, you will be invited to speak on a particular topic, either broad or limited. Here are examples of each:

A Broad Topic:	Public Action Committees
A Narrow Topic:	Your Company's Position and Rationale on Contributing to Public Action Committees

You yourself have certain limitations on the topics you can speak about. You may have a strong interest in Public Action Committees and know what you think your company should do about them. But you may not be privy to the kind of information that would allow you to talk on the narrowed topic suggested above. Therefore, your knowledge is by nature fairly restricted — restricted by your position in the company, your access to information, and your willingness to find out something about a topic you do not know from first-hand experience. We are all limited in the kind of topics that we are able to speak about. Look at your knowledge about PACs in a diagram form:

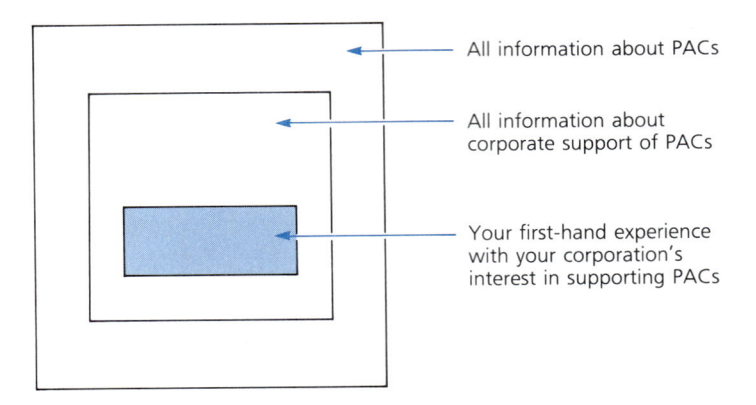

- All information about PACs
- All information about corporate support of PACs
- Your first-hand experience with your corporation's interest in supporting PACs

If you think of knowledge in this way, you will find it reassuring to understand that you can't know about everything. But you do know a lot, and when you are invited to speak about a topic, the process described in the following section will help you get your thoughts together.

FIND A POINT

Settle upon a point to your speech by following a three-step process: (1) Think about the topic and take notes; (2) classify your main ideas; and (3) outline or diagram your speech, using *hooks* (see the discussion of hooks in Chapter 1).

Think and Take Notes

Don't wait until the last minute to develop a speech. Begin to think about the topic as early as possible. Sit down on several occasions to think about what you know. Dig out any files that may help you. Using your knowledge, observations, and reactions, make notes on four-by-six-inch cards. Put a single idea on each card, using a title heading in the right-hand corner. If you were a ghost writer of speeches, like Carolyn Lomax-Cooke, you might make up cards like these:

> **Research**
>
> The ghost writer cannot write a speech without knowing a lot about the subject. Do the research.

> **Talk to the speaker**
>
> The ghost writer must know the speaker and find out what the speaker wants to say.

> **Speaker's style**
>
> Even though the ghost writes the speech, using the *speaker's* style is mandatory.

After jotting down everything that you know about the topic, you may find that you need additional information — facts, statistics, opinions, anecdotes. Go to the library and your company files to do research (see Chapter 25 for research methods). Take notes like the previous ones, but give the appropriate source if the ideas or materials are not yours.

Throughout the process, remember to continue taking notes. Additional ideas will come to you as you remind yourself about the topic and as you learn more about it. Increase your supply of notes until you feel quite certain that you have more information than you can possibly use. It is better to have too much material than too little.

Classify Your Notes to Find Main or Recurring Idea

After you have collected all your note-cards based on your thinking and research, you will find that certain key ideas reappear. Rearrange your cards in piles, classifying them according to those key ideas or broad subject headings. Suppose, for example, you are a regional supervisor of national parks. You are concerned about the number of automobiles and recreational vehicles that enter your parks in a year's time, so you consider suggesting changes in the way the National Park Service manages transportation. After doing some thinking and research, you find that your notes fall into four broad categories:

1. Growing number of cars and recreational vehicles in the parks
2. New roads and new camping sites
3. Serious traffic problems
4. Possible solutions

Diagram or Outline Your Point and Find Hooks

Your final step in developing your speech is to make a visual picture of your speech and to identify its hooks, those single words or phrases you plan to hang your ideas on. (See Chapter 1.)

Some speakers like to use an outline form to provide pictures of their speeches. The four ideas presented above about the park system can form the four main parts of an outline. See Appendix D for further information.

I. The number of cars and recreational vehicles using the National Parks is increasing.
II. The National Park Service creates some of the problem by building new roads and camp sites.
III. The popular national parks are encountering serious traffic problems.
IV. One solution would be to place limitations on traffic and camping in the most popular national parks.

Using these four ideas, you can draw a diagram — using hooks:

```
┌─────────────────────────────┐
│ THE PROBLEM                 │
│ I. Traffic and camping      │
│ II. Roads and campsites     │
│ III. Traffic problems       │
└─────────────────────────────┘
              ↓
┌─────────────────────────────┐
│ CALL FOR SOLUTION           │
│ IV. Limited traffic and camping │
└─────────────────────────────┘
```

(See Chapter 5 for other kinds of diagrams.)

By categorizing your evidence, developing an outline or diagram, and using your hooks, you have found your thesis or main point. You can summarize in one sentence what you plan to talk about:

> *Because of increased traffic and camping in the most popular national parks, the Park Service should consider limiting traffic and camping in those parks.*

You may think that three or four main ideas are not enough for a speech. Be aware, however, that most audiences cannot assimilate more than these in a ten- or twelve-minute speech. If you can fully develop that many ideas, you will be doing very well indeed.

USE SIGNPOSTS AND ORGANIZATIONAL SIGNALS

After you have identified your organizational pattern, you will notice that your speech falls naturally into blocks. These blocks are necessary for good speechmaking because an audience must be able to follow you and know exactly where you are taking them. Your audience will know where you are in the speech by the signposts and organizational signals you provide at the joints of the blocks. Certain words and phrases called *transitions* work particularly well for specific patterns of organization. Here are sample transitions for three important patterns:

CAUSE-EFFECT PATTERN:	*Because of this . . . ; The first effect* (second, etc.) *. . . ; I say this because . . . ; In effect . . .*
ACTION PATTERN:	*The first* (second, third) *problem we face . . . ; It is necessary to . . . ; I propose that we . . . ; One possible solution . . .*
COMPARISON-CONTRAST PATTERN:	*In contrast . . . ; Comparing X with Y . . . ; It is instructive to compare . . . ; On the other hand . . . ; That's only one side of the coin . . . ; Similarly . . .*

Use Enumeration and Graded Order

You will find enumeration useful to you, particularly if you are dealing with reasons or lists. Enumeration is just what the term implies — numbering your points from first to third (or fourth — more than that is usually unwieldy). You can, for example, use enumeration for questions:

First,	is the conservation of prime land going to force us into an anti-growth policy?
Second,	if we follow a conservation plan, which one should we use?
Third,	who has the authority to initiate a land-use policy?

Or the speaker could use the questions above and grade them according to importance, perhaps from the least important to the most important question. For speeches employing graded order, you would probably want to get the less important ideas out of the way quickly so that you can discuss fully the more important ones.

Use Restatement and Repetition

Don't be afraid to repeat the important points of your speech. Repetition and restatement are valuable tools to help keep the audience on track: Tell the audience what you plan to say; say it; and then tell the audience what you have said. See Figure 22.1 on pages 342, 343.

EXERCISES

1. Discuss the following excerpt from a speech to the Town Hall of California. Identify the pattern of organization that the speaker has promised to use. Identify also any signposts and transitions he has used. Discuss their effectiveness.

> It is an honor to be a guest of the Town Hall of California, and it's a real pleasure to trade the heat of a Texas summer for Southern California's breezes, if only for a day. I'm here today to talk about American industry and to point my finger at what I consider to be a fundamental challenge to its health and vitality.
>
> The driving force behind a successful business, of any kind, in any country, is the entrepreneurial spirit. It is my thesis that the stagnation affecting American industry today stems from a steady and serious erosion of that spirit in America's major corporations. We must regain that spirit if we are to restore vitality to the nation's economy. I want to talk about how it has been lost ... and then offer some possible solutions.
>
> I know that many who have preceded me in this forum have pointed out problems facing American industry. They have pointed to a host of real and imagined ills that affect and restrict our business environment — from trade imbalances and government regulations to labor costs and the price of imported oil. While we've pointed fingers at external causes of our problems, we've been less inclined to point a finger at ourselves — at American industry and American management.
>
> Despite all I've heard from Washington, it is my belief that no amount of corrective legislation is going to solve the problem for us. It will be up to American industry to create that economic vitality.
>
> Two Harvard Business School professors, William Hayes and Robert Abernathy, have told us exactly that. In their landmark article in *The Harvard*

Business Review, they argue that government regulations, labor costs, monetary policy, and so on, do not alone explain America's decline in productivity. They underscore the fact that other countries have these problems to an even greater extent than do we.

Europe's dependence on imported oil dwarfs ours, their labor costs are higher, and their government regulations are more restrictive, and yet both Germany and France have higher rates of productivity growth than do we. Even Hayes and Abernathy stop short of identifying the real villain. They argue that our primary problem is a shortage of technology on the factory floor.

In my opinion, all of these problems are really manifestations of a far more basic problem: the steady erosion of the entrepreneurial spirit in America's major industries.

Now, let me explain what I mean by the entrepreneurial spirit. It has two fundamental qualities. First, the ability to anticipate change, and second, the willingness to respond to it.

—W. H. Bricker

2. Make a list of from two to four topics on which you are knowledgeable. Explain what kind of audience would be interested in each of those topics, particularly if you were the speaker. Discuss other information you would need to know about the audience before making the speech.

    a. Choose one of the topics. Follow the three steps discussed in this chapter on finding a point for your speech: notetaking, classifying, and outlining.

    b. On your outline, indicate places where particular signposts or transitional phrases and words would be useful.

    c. Practice the speech from your outline and present it to the class.

INTRODUCTION

Tell the audience what you *plan* to say.

Or:
- Today, I will discuss three problems...
- In order to give perspective, I will discuss three problems...
- I have recently become concerned about three problems...

BODY

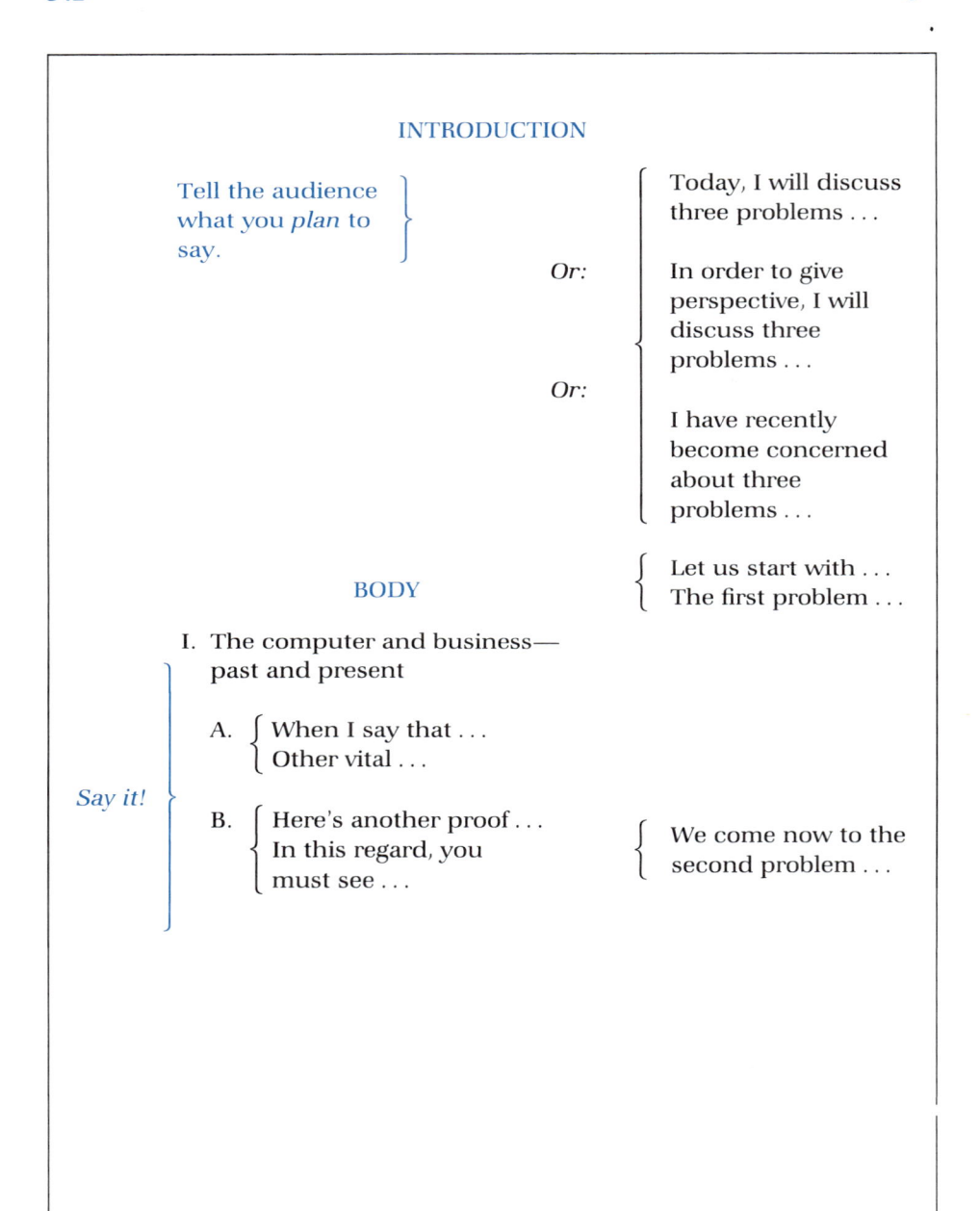

Let us start with...
The first problem...

Say it!

I. The computer and business—past and present

  A. When I say that...
     Other vital...

  B. Here's another proof...
     In this regard, you must see...

We come now to the second problem...

Figure 22.1. Outline of speech

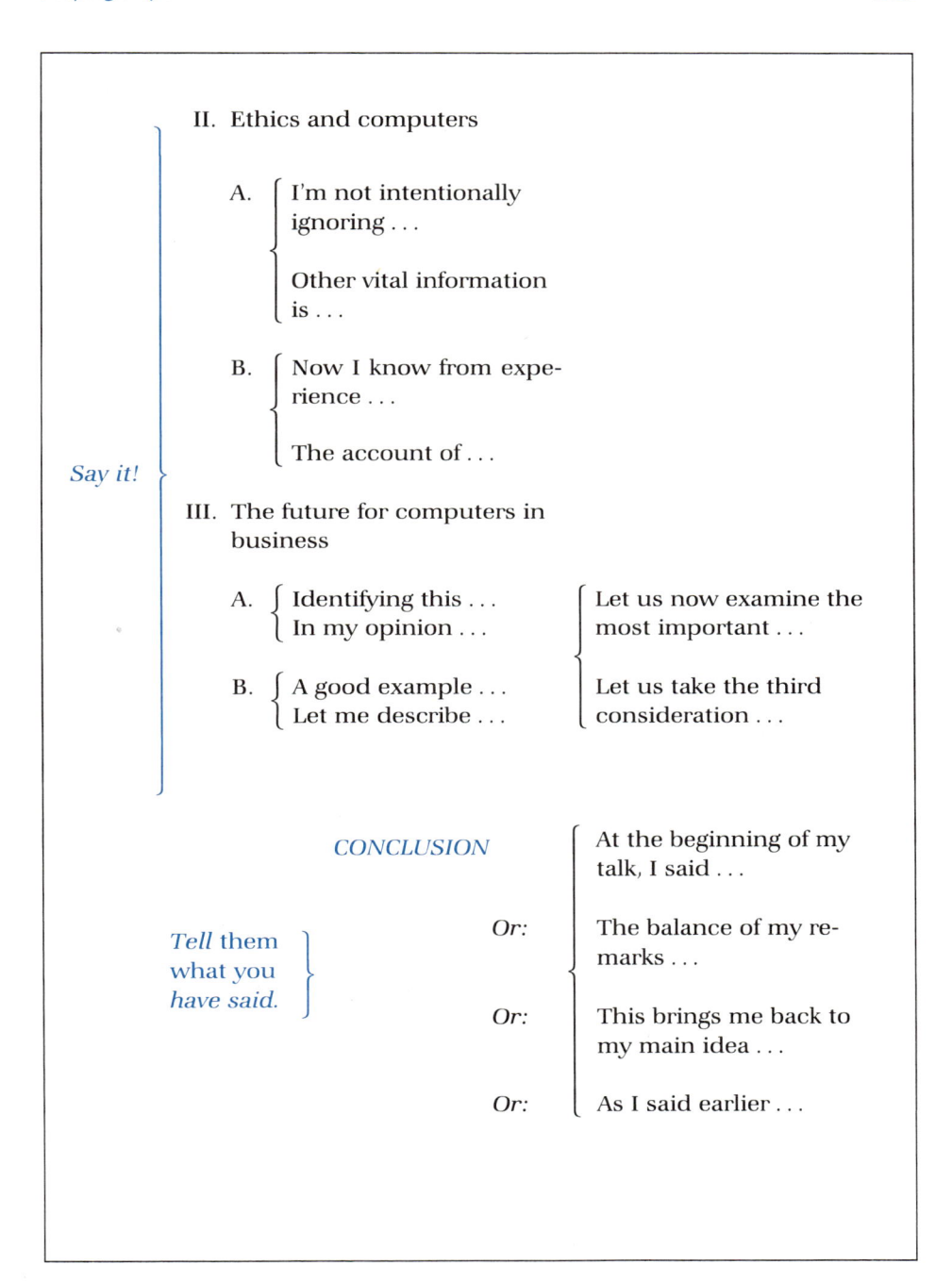

Shaping a Speech for Your Audience   343

Say it!
- II. Ethics and computers
  - A. I'm not intentionally ignoring...

    Other vital information is...
  - B. Now I know from experience...

    The account of...
- III. The future for computers in business
  - A. Identifying this...
    In my opinion...

    Let us now examine the most important...
  - B. A good example...
    Let me describe...

    Let us take the third consideration...

Tell them what you have said.

CONCLUSION

At the beginning of my talk, I said...

Or: The balance of my remarks...

Or: This brings me back to my main idea...

Or: As I said earlier...

CHAPTER 23

Convincing Your Audience

When you give a speech, you want to convince your audience. An audience will usually not be convinced by the bare bones of a speech. Your listeners expect you to support all your main ideas with details and evidence, giving credibility to your material. Here are four methods for using supporting evidence:

1. Convince with statistical information
2. Convince with examples or illustrations
3. Convince with comparisons (analogies) and contrasts
4. Convince with definitions

Convince with Statistics

In your supply of notecards for your speech, you may have numbers and figures — statistical information. Audiences cannot easily absorb a lot of dense information, and then synthesize it. You should therefore handle statistics so that they have meaning for your audience.

1. Be accurate, but not over-detailed. Round off your figures so that you don't have to reel off six- and seven-digit numbers. In addition, translate statistics into a form that audiences can understand. Percentages, for instance, are often easier to visualize than raw figures. Don't tell your audience that 25,557,000 families earn two paychecks. Instead, say sixty percent of American families do.

2. Avoid using statistics without interpreting them. Provide a generalization or summary statement that explains what they mean.

3. Use comparisons and contrasts to show the importance of the statistics. In other words, relate them to something else, such as statistics of the past or projections for the future.

Below is an excerpt from a speech that uses statistics to prove the need for new housing in the United States. Note how the speaker uses all three suggestions.

Earlier this year, Market Opinion Research Corporation conducted surveys on the subject of home ownership for the National Forest Products Association. That research shows that nearly 90 percent of Americans continue to place a very high value on home ownership. When asked about the goals and aspirations they have for themselves and their children, respondents ranked home ownership near the top of the list. While having a job was the most important, home ownership shared second place with quality health care. Further, they defined home ownership as owning a single-family home on its own lot with a lawn.	One main idea
	Definition
These findings shouldn't surprise us. They're simply the elements of the American dream that have existed for years. The dream hasn't died, or even changed much.	
Now add to that underlying American concept a number of demographic pressures that are building.	The problem introduced: demographic pressures
— The U.S. population is growing — from 227 million in 1980 to 287 million forecast for the year 2000.	Evidence #1 — statistics (number rounded off)
— The post-World War II baby boom generation is forming families and will continue to do so throughout the 1980s. More than 1½ million Americans will reach home-buying age each year in the 1980s — twice the rate of the 1970s.	Evidence #2 — comparison used
— People are living longer in the U.S. — nearly four years longer on average than just 20 years ago.	Evidence #3 — comparison
— More senior citizens want to remain in their own housing units. In 1970, 16 percent of those 65 and older lived in institutions or with someone else. By 1978, only 10 percent did so.	Evidence #4 — percentages used — comparisons

— More single heads of households want their own housing units. People stay single longer. People divorce more often. As a result, the number of people living alone has jumped from more than seven million in 1960 to nearly 18 million in 1980.

Evidence #5 — statistics and comparisons

Clearly, there's a strong and growing need for housing in this country. Let's examine for a moment how that demand's been exercised and by whom.

— John B. Fery

Generalization — interpretation of statistics. The argument stated: There is a need for housing.

Convince with Examples or Illustrations

Examples and illustrations form the largest class of supporting evidence. They do just what the terms imply: exemplify and illustrate your point. An example or illustration can be one of the following:

1. A relevant quotation or aphorism.
2. A testimony, usually a statement of opinion by an expert on a specific topic. (You may paraphrase or quote directly.)
3. A story or anecdote, real or hypothetical.

Quotations. Famous writers and thinkers often say things more clearly or creatively than we can. If you choose to use a quotation, be sure to identify the author. Audiences are suspicious of introductions like "A famous author once said...." or "A great man is known to have said...." They may believe you made it up.

Be sure that your quotation is relevant to the generalization you expect to make. Avoid quotations just for the sake of showing that you are well-read or knowledgeable. Use them because they are relevant and help to convince an audience.

Notice how a quotation from Pasteur has been integrated into a speech about management:

> The French scientist Louis Pasteur said: "Let me tell you the secret that led me to my goal. My strength lies solely in my tenacity." In the current business climate, you must persevere to survive. I know that stimulating a sales force today is a demanding task. You must be able to inspire yourself as well as others, to encourage those under you to carry on when they get weary. It's a tall order — because they're buffeted by a negative environment all day.
>
> — George R. Burns

Testimony. You can sometimes convince an audience to accept your point if you can assure your listeners that *others* — usually experts — support

Convincing Your Audience

your view. To gain credibility, the experts you choose must have certain qualifications.

1. The testimony should come from an expert who is experienced on the subject being discussed. In discussing the danger of a nuclear explosion, a nuclear physicist would be more believable than a movie star.
2. The expert should be reliable and unbiased. If the expert in nuclear explosions has a vested interest in a nuclear power plant, the audience might not respect his testimony as being fair and unbiased.
3. The expert's experience must be recent. If the nuclear physicist retired in 1975, his experience may be outdated.

If possible, give the expert's credentials before introducing his testimony. At the very least, give a title or place of employment.

In the following example, notice how Henry Ford II leads his audience through his argument by using selected quotations and testimony. When he finishes giving his supporting evidence, his audience is prepared to accept his conclusion or summary statement: The time has come for members of the Western Alliance to develop a collective approach to economic matters.

Perhaps in a curious way, we are indebted to the pipeline controversy for bringing the economic security interests of the West into sharper focus than ever before. And I am not alone in thinking so.	Problem stated
Just recently, Mr. Francis Pym [Britain's Foreign Secretary] spoke to Ford Motor Company's European Advisory Council. It was his feeling that although the pipeline dispute has been an unsettling one, it has had at least two beneficial consequences:	Expert (identified earlier)
First, it has forced the Atlantic Alliance to think more deeply about East-West trade and to address questions which we have been reluctant to tackle as energetically as perhaps we should have done.	Testimony #1 (paraphrased)
And secondly, said Mr. Pym, the dispute has reminded all of us that consultation and discussion are at the very heart of the Alliance. It is when we fail to consult properly and act together, when we take one another for granted, that we find ourselves at odds.	Testimony #2 (paraphrased)
Permit me to quote him exactly, because I share his sentiment: "If the pipeline dispute," he said, "forces us to make a fresh and more thorough appraisal of East-West trade, and how it should be integrated into an overall framework for	Testimony #2 (quoted directly)

East-West relations, it will have served a useful purpose."

My grandfather had another way of saying the same thing. "Don't find fault," the original Henry Ford jotted in his diary one day. "Find a remedy."

I believe we are doing just that.

It is in this spirit that I return to a comment made earlier in my remarks — that the time has come for members of the Western Alliance — including Japan — to develop a collective approach to economic matters that parallels what we most notably have done about defense matters.

Quotation (aphorism) and source identified

Summary statement and generalization (comparison with "defense")

Stories and Anecdotes. Choose stories and anecdotes that are appropriate for the audience, because its members must be able to identify with the characters or the situation. The story should be based on reality, even if it is hypothetical. One way for you to make a story realistic is by using lively and vivid language. Clear and precise examples will also help make the story come alive for an audience.

Here is part of a speech entitled "A Walk on the Wild Side," given to the New York Rotary Club by the president of the Trailways Bus Lines, J. Kevin Murphy. Murphy's point in his speech is that the Port Authority of New York City taxes bus tickets but provides no service for bus passengers. Notice how Murphy uses a hypothetical story in describing his idea of the typical bus passenger. Since the audience lives in New York City, its members know that the conditions Murphy describes are realistic.

Imagine, for a moment, that you have just arrived at the Port Authority Terminal in New York after a long bus trip. Perhaps you have come to see your new grandchild, perhaps to visit a son or daughter at college. Or, perhaps you simply want to see New York for the first time....

For you, the passenger in the bus terminal, the initial excitement of arriving in New York has probably worn off, replaced by a sense of anxiety as you make your way through a gauntlet of litter, fanatics, menacing-looking derelicts and truly ominous pimps poised to prey on the young girls who arrive daily on buses with no place to go. If concern with your own safety has not precluded thoughts of much else, you might reflect on what audacity allows the Port Authority of New York to charge bus passengers an incredible 17.5 percent

Hypothetical example

Description of "typical bus passenger"

Vivid language in description

of your ticket price. This is what the Port Authority charges for the questionable privilege of taking an unintended and undesired "walk on the wild side" through the Port Authority Terminal.

Point: reference to title, "A Walk on the Wild Side"

As you approach the exit and struggle to push through the heavy doors with your luggage, you might experience a fleeting sense of relief to be out of the building. Unfortunately, the area outside is worse — a human jungle of massage parlors, peep-shows, muggers, hookers, pimps and drug pushers. Yet, incredibly, the Port Authority has never sought to establish a buffer zone around the Terminal with the millions that are available for that purpose.

Vivid language and description

Point

Convince with Comparisons and Contrasts

Audiences want to understand the relationship between ideas. As we pointed out earlier, if you use a statistic, it is more meaningful if you can compare or contrast two figures. The same rule applies to other kinds of supporting evidence. If, for example, you discuss environmental concerns (littering, perhaps), you might want to take into account that twenty years ago non-returnable bottles were not widely used by soft-drink manufacturers. If you want to prove the need for a bottle bill in your community, a comparison of the limited use of non-returnable bottles two decades ago with their use today could help your argument.

Even quotations can be compared. Notice how Robert E. Allen's speech to Hampton Institute uses comparison to make a point.

In the course of my research for this talk, I consulted some of the standard sources of inspirational sayings and epigrams — more for my own inspiration than yours. What I found wasn't helpful.

Introduction: his motive

For example, Benjamin Franklin had a lot of his usual priggish advice about success — you know, "Early to bed," . . . "A penny saved," . . . "A stitch in time," . . . all that sort of stuff. I think he must have been a pain to be around for very long.

Another quote was by someone I've never heard of. It said, "If at first you don't succeed, you're running about average."

W. C. Fields had something to say about success, too. He said, "If at first you don't succeed, try, try again. Then quit. There's no use being a damn fool about it."

Three quotations used for humor, but each cast aside as unacceptable

But Henry Ford had the best thought. He said, "Before everything else, *getting ready* is the secret of success."

Let me repeat that thought. "Before everything else, *getting ready* is the secret of success."

And that goes right to the heart of what I want to say to you tonight. It's what you do right here and right now at Hampton Institute that's going to prepare you for opportunities in the corporate world, or anywhere else you want to go. And the better you do it, the better your chances are going to be.

Best quotation

Application of quotation to the point

An analogy is an extended comparison. Speakers often use analogies to clarify or explain something that may be unfamiliar, new, or strange. Let's assume that you are an executive discussing a new method of dealing with the gasoline tankers in your company. Before explaining your proposal, you might want to explain how tankers are loaded. Since you are trying to explain something relatively unknown to your audience, you might want to use the known (filling pop bottles) to explain the process:

A tank truck usually holds between 4,000 and 6,000 gallons of gasoline. Depending on the tanker and the oil company, there are three to six individual compartments which hold 600 to 900 gallons of gasoline apiece. The tank that contains the compartments is elliptically shaped to distribute the pressure equally and to allow a more complete flow of air when the gasoline is delivered.

Until recently the only way to load a tanker was to climb up on top, where the openings to the compartments are located. You can easily picture this by visualizing six pop bottles lined up in a single file on a table. A man wants to fill up bottle three, so he takes the cap off. He then inserts a small hose into the neck of the bottle and turns on a faucet which is connected to the hose.

A gasoline tanker is loaded in a similar way, but on a much larger scale. A man climbs on top of the tanker and opens a particular compartment by removing the cap. He then takes a hose with a four-foot metal pipe extension, about three and a half inches in diameter, and inserts the pipe down into the "bottle" (the compartment hole), which measures four inches in diameter. A pump is then turned on, allowing the gasoline to flow into the compartment.

Convince with Definitions

The more mixed your audience, the more you will be required to define your terms, particularly if your topic is complicated. If you are giving a speech to an audience of people working in your specialty, however, you might have to define only a few terms.

A variety of defining methods is available to you. You will find four methods most useful: definition by classification, definition by illustration or example, negative definition, and definition by operation.

Definition by Classification. In defining by classification, you put the term to be defined in its class (of things, people, activities, or ideas). Then you explain how the term differs from other terms in the same class.

Term		Class	Differences
Accountant	[is a]	trained person	who inspects or adjusts accounts. — *New World Dictionary*
"Engineering	[is]	the art and science	by which properties of matter and the sources of power in nature are made useful to man in structures, machines, and manufactured products."

— Robert Buckley

Definition by Illustration or Example. You can sometimes employ, implicitly or explicitly, illustration or example to aid in your definition. You can define a thing by giving an example of it: "*White collar crimes* range from fraud, embezzlement, conspiracy, waste and corruption, to false expense accounts, theft of materials and other various illegal acts" (Hershell Britton).

Definition by Negation. This method of definition entails explaining what something is *not*: A bucket is not a scoop. A debit is not a credit.

"Let me clarify what I mean by the word *support* . . . I do not mean *blind agreement* when I speak of women [in business] supporting each other" (Marilyn Loder).

Definition by Operation. You can define by operation when you state what something does or how it works: "A *word processor* is a computer that is used for providing multiple copies of the same letter."

"By *networking* I mean an expanding web of relationships with other women [in business] for the purpose of building support, solving common problems, and enhancing individual growth" (Marilyn Loder).

"*Inflation* is too much money chasing too few goods" (Robert H. Edmonds).

Knowing how to define doesn't mean that you just insert definitions anywhere in your speech. The same basic rule applies to definitions that applies to the other forms of supporting evidence: Integrate your definitions into your speech so that it flows smoothly and the audience understands your purpose in defining:

1. Define your term right after you use it the first time.
2. Make your definition clear by relating the term to things your audience knows about. Take plenty of time to define if the definition is crucial to understanding your point.
3. Stick to the definition you choose. Don't shift definitions or terms halfway through the speech.

Definitions not only provide clarification, they are also useful rhetorical devices: to emphasize a point, introduce a speech, or achieve humor. Some speakers like to give several definitions of the same term and then build the speech around the best definition.

Definitions in Introductions. Speakers often use definitions more informally than writers do, particularly epigrams and aphorisms that are definitional. You will find this kind of defining in many introductions. For example:

> I have spent most of my non-professional time in the last month studying about dyslexia. "Difficulty with words," it means literally, but it is widely interpreted as reading disability.
> My motivation, quite frankly, has been *guilt,* a general guilt that I was ignorant of an affliction which may affect as many as twenty-five million Americans, which would make dyslexia about the most widespread single malady in our society.
> — Melvin L. Vulgamore

EXERCISES

1. Make a list of words that you might need to define if you were going to talk to a mixed audience on the subject of your specialty. Define two or three words, using two or three different methods of defining.

2. Choose a speech topic you are interested in. Develop some statistical information on the topic. (Follow the suggestions in this chapter on using statistics.)

3. Develop an analogy for one of the following topics (or one of your own):
   a. Joining a company is like taking on citizenship (or being born into a family).
   b. Being president of a company is like being a football coach.

4. Discuss the use of example in the following excerpt.

Conventional engines can be modified to run — and run well — on any number of other fuels. I'm talking about propane, compressed natural gas, ethanol and methanol.

Propane is a petroleum-based fuel that has good short and medium term potential because the supply in some locations is abundant, and it's cheaper than gasoline. In the long run, these advantages are likely to fade. In the meantime, propane is finding growing use as an automotive fuel in Japan, Canada and several European countries. Ford is now building propane-powered heavy trucks in North America, and next year we'll introduce a factory-propane option, initially in Canada, for Granada and Cougar sedans.

Compressed natural gas is another excellent automotive fuel, already in limited use in Italy and New Zealand. It's cheap, clean and efficient, but energy density is low and vehicle range is limited. For special short-range urban applications, it may be better than electric propulsion.

Ethanol and methanol can be used in today's cars when mixed in small proportions with gasoline. They also give excellent results in their pure form with minor vehicle changes. Ethanol is distilled from farm products and wastes; methanol is derived from wood, coal or natural gas.

Brazil is converting a major part of its vehicle fleet to ethanol, and Ford of Brazil has built 34,000 cars so far that use pure ethanol. In the United States, Canada, Norway and other countries where coal or natural gas is abundant, methanol is a better choice. It gives equally good performance and efficiency, and it is a lot cheaper. A test fleet of 40 modified Ford Escort cars is now running on pure methanol in California. And we are ready to put more methanol-powered test fleets in the field to speed up on-the-road experience and evaluation.

The point is that we can convert engines to run on any of these alternative fuels right now. There are no major technical problems. Conversion costs are reasonable. Vehicle performance is at least as good as with gasoline. Operating costs — except with ethanol — are lower. And emission control is a lot easier.

The only thing stopping us is the presently limited availability of the other fuels and the absence of distribution systems. On the other hand, the energy companies can't move very far, very fast until we start selling vehicles designed for alternative fuels. — Donald E. Petersen

5. Discuss the following definitions and their possible use in a speech:

   a. "Social work is a healing profession; it deals with the walking wounded of society, the victims of hardship and neglect." — Vernon E. Jordan, Jr., in a speech to the Council on Social Work Education.

   b. "California is the motion picture and television studios where the nation's dreams are interpreted and turned into entertainment." — Russell S. Reynolds, in a speech entitled "Are California Business Leaders Different?" to Town Hall of California, Los Angeles.

   c. "Trial by Television" is the relatively standard technique in which television production teams become the accuser, judge, and jury of people and institutions with no real opportunity for the accused to get a fair hearing in the court of public opinion. Too frequently, the people in charge of those programs select story segments with their minds already made up, and proceed to choose the facts and quotes which make their case for them.

The "accused," of course, is almost always offered the opportunity to be interviewed for the program — but all the interview technique does is put the producer — that is, the accuser — in full control of deciding what the accused can say in his own defense. Since the producer — that is, the accuser — edits the interview before it goes on the air, he has the exclusive right to decide what portions of the accused's defense the public will be allowed to hear, and in what manner the defense will be presented. There is no way the accuser's conclusions or facts can be challenged. There's nothing very fair about that. — Ronald E. Rhody

d. You may ask: What makes a leader? What is a leader? That is a good question, since we know all too little about leadership. As I have said, "It is one of the most observed but least understood phenomena." Harry Truman had an adequate definition of leadership. He said, "Leadership was making men do what they didn't want to do, but making them like it." — Frank Forker

e. When I speak of "the West" I do not of course speak of that area on a flat map of our globe which by convention appears on its upper left-hand quarter. The term is — and again by convention — a kind of shorthand symbol for something located not geographically but politically, not in a particular region — though historically its institutional expression originated there — but in a particular vision. This is the vision, simply stated, that men might so order their affairs, that they have it within their capacity to create such political and social institutions, that they can live together as free citizens, without the oppression of the many by the few, or the few by the many, without undue or arbitrary constraints upon their lives and minds, and without the expropriation of what belongs to them, by their rulers, by the social collective, or by bandits wielding guns. In short, it is a vision, this vision I have for the sake of speed and convenience called "the West," of private rights, civil peace, and individual civic responsibility. This is the true meaning of liberty. It is also the *true* meaning of equality — that all men are equally entitled to keep what they have honestly earned, and to enjoy the fruits of civil peace, and that all are equally responsible for maintaining the civic order that protects them. And it is the true meaning of brotherhood, of fraternity.
— Midge Decter

6. Discuss the use of statistics in the following.

Consider today there are nearly 5,000 cable TV systems linking 19 million homes — 7 times more than there are commercial television stations. The demand for satellite circuits is insatiable — by 1986, will soar by some 85 percent — 24 new communications satellites are to be launched in the U.S., and at least 8 are on the drawing boards in Europe.

By 1990, cable TV will penetrate 55 million homes. We have some 79 million homes presently hooked into television.

By the middle of next year, fifty percent of all the commercial TV stations will have their own earth stations enabling them to pick off the satellite any program, thus freeing them from the dependency on the networks — by 1990, they will all have this capability.

By 1990, in my opinion, at least one quarter of the FORTUNE 500 companies will have their own television networks, broadcasting to conclaves of plants and employees over these low-watt, low range, low-cost mini-stations whatever they think necessary to communicate — quarterly profits, current developments, new product information, etc.
— John F. Budd, Jr.

7. Discuss the use of quotation in the following. What relation does the quotation have to do with the hypothetical example, for instance?

Many years ago a great philosopher asked:
"If men use their liberty in such a way as to *surrender* their liberty, are they thereafter any the less slaves?" What does that mean?

Have you tried to do *anything* lately without having to give your Social Security number? Buy a $50 savings bond at a bank as a gift to a high school graduate — and you have to give your SS number.

Pretty soon you will need to present your Social Security number to buy a bar of soap at a supermarket.

And, to help pay for the bureaucracy that imposes all these regulations on us, you will have to pay fifty times more for that bar of soap than you did in 1960, a bare twenty-two years ago. — Robert J. Buckley

CHAPTER 24

Managing the Dramatic Elements of Speaking

When you get up to talk, your body can be your worst enemy or your best friend, depending upon your attitude toward the speech. One authority on speech-making says: "I have made speeches when my mouth was so dry I could barely talk. During one speech, my heart beat wildly, and I imagined that I shook all over. Later, I discussed the speech with friends who were members of the audience. They were surprised to hear that I was nervous because it 'didn't show.'" Most nervousness you experience will probably not be apparent to your audience. People don't expect you to be nervous.

One of the best cures for excessive nervousness is to say to yourself: "I know a good deal about this topic, I have practiced the speech, and I *want* to tell the audience what I know."

It is true that a thorough knowledge of the subject and a desire to tell what you know are very important elements in maintaining confidence. But perhaps the most important preventive for nervousness is practice. One way you can practice is to discuss your topic with friends and acquaintances. You will be pleased to learn that you can become quite proficient in expressing yourself in this fashion.

Rehearse your speech

Begin by going through your speech once, using your notes or outline. (This advice is aimed primarily at extemporaneous delivery. If you give a

Managing the Dramatic Elements of Speaking 357

speech from manuscript, you will rehearse, but follow a different process, as discussed in Chapter 21). In this first run-through you will probably hesitate frequently, looking for the correct word. You may sound terribly stilted. Don't worry. You are at that stage of practice in which you are searching for words to express your ideas.

Rehearse the speech a second, third, and even fourth time. Notice that with every practice, your presentation becomes smoother. If possible, practice the speech in the room where you will speak. Pay attention to transitions (see Chapter 22). If your speech continues to sound stilted, don't worry. Once you are before an audience, you will be more natural because you will have someone to talk to. Do not rehearse so often that you memorize the speech. Memorizing can really create a stilted delivery.

Continue to talk about your speech topic to friends. This will improve your spontaneity before an audience, and it will help to keep you from getting nervous.

Manage Your Body for Effect

Gestures. You can use your body to emphasize your major ideas: tilt your head, raise a shoulder, point a finger, use a hand gesture. If you are truly interested in your subject, many of these movements will be natural. Practicing gestures for particular places in a speech seems to be a silly thing for grown men and women to do, especially since natural movements are much more convincing and effective. If you choose to practice movements, however, make them decisive. When you move forward or to the side, don't shuffle. Take a step. Walk. Don't rock. Move toward, not away from, your audience. Direct your gestures forward.

When you walk to the place where you will be speaking, take your time to arrange your materials. Compose yourself. Establish eye contact with your audience. Be sure that everyone is ready to listen to you. Be a little bit dramatic by using time to your advantage. At the end of your talk, wait until after you have concluded to begin collecting your material. Pause. Then collect your notes, and walk to your place on the podium or to your seat.

Clothes. A speaker should not attract attention to himself or herself or get between the audience and the ideas being communicated. If an audience goes away more impressed by what you wore that day than by what you said, you have failed. It isn't necessary here to go into detail about the kind of clothing that is appropriate for public occasions in business. Much has been written on the subject. We cannot, however, emphasize one point enough: Wear comfortable clothes that are appropriate for the occasion. We all have clothes that just don't "feel right"; they don't fit our bodies or our personalities. When you make a speech, wear clothes that you can forget about when you are before the audience.

Manage Your Voice

When you speak in public, it is necessary for you to be stronger and more resolute than you might be in small groups or in one-to-one meetings. One way to show your strength and resolution is to be confident and to act confident. Even more important, use a strong, resonant voice. To be convincing, you can't be afraid of the sound of your own voice. Unless you use a microphone, which calls for different techniques (to be discussed later in this chapter), speak loudly. The people in the last row must be able to hear you.

Speaking is like singing. You use the same muscles and the same vocal machinery. If you sustain your tones in the same way you do when singing, you will develop a resonant voice, one that will carry to the last row. Your vowels will be heard even when they are between difficult consonants — *B*s, *T*s, and *P*s. Words like *bad, mad, fad, patter;* phrases like *let me alone, the car is in the mud,* and *the cat is in the cab* are hard to understand. Learn to enunciate precisely.

Vary your speech patterns. Don't hit every word with the same force so that you have a monotone. Emphasize certain key words so that the audience can understand relationships. If you don't have a natural feeling for the stresses in English, go through your speech and mark those words that deserve some emphasis:

> Aŕson is a blíght.
> Whó hére would endorse aŕson?
> Aŕson is nót considered a májor críme.

Find places to pause:

> Hálf of aŕson today is "aŕson for prófit" — [*pause*] — not´ for reveńge.
> — Robert L. Geltzer

Manage Your Notes (or Manuscript)

Use your notes or manuscript unobtrusively. This does not mean that you hide them from your audience. By using good eye contact, you can take much of the attention away from your use of notes. In fact, by your smooth delivery you should be able to make your audience feel that you could make the speech just as well without notes.

Speechmakers manage notes in a variety of ways. One popular way is to write the outline and supporting material on four- by six-inch cards. This is especially practical if you have no speaker's stand. You can hold your cards at chest level, maintain eye contact, and glance at your notes occasionally.

Your cards can be arranged so that your supporting material will be in appropriate order.

Other speakers prefer to write an outline on a single piece of typing paper. (Supporting evidence can be included under the main headings.) This method works fine if you can be sure you will have a speaker's stand. You can put your paper(s) down on the stand and refer to them when necessary and still keep eye contact. But, if you get caught without a speaker's stand, you must either hold the papers in your hands or place them on a table where you have to bend over to see them. In either case, the larger pieces of paper cause problems without a speaker's stand.

Handling Questions

Ordinarily, you will not have to answer questions unless you have been warned to expect them. In many meetings a question period is scheduled, particularly if the topic under discussion is important to all the members of the audience.

It is not a good idea to entertain questions in the middle of a speech — it breaks the continuity. You must be a very clever and adaptable thinker to stop in the middle of a speech to answer questions. Furthermore, some of the answers may be in that part of the speech you haven't presented yet.

In order to field questions economically, efficiently, and logically, you should plan for them, keep your composure, and follow a particular process.

Plan Ahead. Try to predict the kind of questions you will be asked. Ask yourself if particular subjects in your speech may create controversy. If so, plan how to deal with them. In addition, anticipate irrelevant questions that might get you sidetracked. Ask yourself: What are the worst possible questions anyone could ask me? Then develop answers to those questions, or methods of dealing with them.

Keep Your Composure. Sometimes it is difficult to counter questions on the spur of the moment. Prepare as well as possible, and then keep cool. If you get questions that you can't answer, say so. Don't overstate your case or exaggerate. Admitting that you don't know something will help your credibility, not hurt it. Don't overreact under pressure and become defensive. If the questions get too hot for comfort, take a drink of water, compose yourself and move to another point, suggesting that the issue under discussion is not appropriate at this time.

How to Handle a Question

1. Keep the question-asker from giving a speech. After a minute or so, if the speaker hasn't come to the point, ask him or her to state the question.

2. Listen carefully to the question. Ask for a restatement if the question is unclear.

3. Repeat the question, then answer as briefly and concisely as possible.

4. If the question contains more than one sub-question, answer each of these separately; or choose the one that suits your topic best and answer it.

5. Include all the members of the audience when you answer the question. Don't look at the questioner all the time. Some techniques to use for including the entire audience: "That's a question we should all be aware of...." "I'm glad you asked that question..." "I neglected to deal with that particular issue because...." Make the questioner feel that he or she is actually contributing to the session, but include the audience in the interchange.

Managing the Environment

Well before you give the speech, visit the room in which you are scheduled to appear. Check the facilities: microphone (if necessary); audiovisual equipment; speaker's stand; and drinking water. No matter how much experience you have, your mouth may get dry during a speech. So if your speech is longer than ten minutes, be sure to have water available.

Check the temperature and lighting. If the lighting is dim, see that the light on the speaker's stand is adequate. Some convention centers have music piped in; check whether the sound system has been cut off in the meeting room. If the room and facilities are unsatisfactory, talk to the person in charge. All these problems can easily be solved if you notify the right people early enough.

EXERCISES

1. Read the following excerpt from a speech to the Charlotte, North Carolina, Rotary Club.

> Mr. Davidson has asked me to talk about the world food situation — or the problem of world hunger.
>
> As for the *dimension* of the problem, you've heard all the figures and seen the pictures on TV, so let me just mention two items: it is estimated that from one-fifth to one-fourth of the world's population is undernourished (not malnourished — many of us are malnourished from overeating or eating the wrong types of food); and in the poorer countries of the world one-third of the children die before reaching five years old from malnutrition or diseases associated with malnutrition.
>
> As for the *cause* of the problem, the cause is poverty, hunger simply

being a symptom of the disease, poverty, which is caused by low production, increasing population, and maldistribution of income.

As for the *solution* to the problem, there are three points I'd like to make: First, it is a problem that can be solved if we have the will to do it. The annual gross planetary product per capita is now running at about $2500 — certainly sufficient for every man, woman, and child on this planet to have a decent standard of living. But the one-fourth of us living in the high-income Northern countries receive four-fifths of the world income, while the three-fourths of humankind living in the low-income Southern countries must exist on one-fifth of the income. And it is estimated that there are 750 million people in what Robert McNamara terms absolute poverty — that is, living on less than $100 per year, their basic needs for food, shelter, education, and health unmet. In India, for example, Indian economists estimate that nearly half of the population — say 300 million — have monthly consumption of less than 65 rupees in rural areas and 75 rupees in urban areas; that's about eight or nine dollars per month — divide by 30 and you'll see what it is in pennies per day.

Second, it is a problem that must be solved if we are to avoid chaos, if we are to have peace. The Brandt Commission Report points out that war is usually thought of in terms of military conflict, but that an equal danger might be chaos — as a result of mass hunger, economic disaster, environmental catastrophes, and terrorism. And that's what the Hunger and Global Security Bill now before Congress is about: hunger being a threat to both military and economic security. The root of the military conflict in El Salvador is hunger (poverty), and look at the international ramifications such a problem as this can have! And the economic health of our economy depends increasingly on there being stability in the poor Southern economies. They are important markets for our products and sources of essential new materials.

Third (first, it's a problem that can be solved; second, it must be solved), let's look at how the problem might be solved. Four things need to be done: (1) increase the supply of food, (2) stabilize the market supply of food, (3) slow the increasing demand for food, and (4) reduce poverty, especially removing the 750 million from absolute poverty. Let's deal with each of these in a little detail.

— Charles E. Ratliff, Jr.

    a. Mark the words that you believe deserve stress or accent. Then read the speech aloud, using those stresses. How did it sound? Were your stresses natural? In reading the speech, did you change your mind about where the stresses should go?

    b. Where do you think gestures would be appropriate? What kind?

2. Review a speech you have read or heard (check *Vital Speeches* or look for reprints in the library; use one of your own speeches, if you wish.) Make a list of questions that an audience might ask the speaker. Then decide how you would answer the questions if you had made the speech.

USING VISUAL AIDS

We once attended the opening session of a business writers' convention. The purpose of the opening session was social: to welcome the members who had come long distances, and to introduce visiting dignitaries from the host company. After the opening remarks, a consultant in business communications gave the keynote address. Those of us attending expected a speech that would set the tone for the convention. We also expected to be entertained — but most of all, we wanted to learn something new that would make our teaching and writing better.

However, the visiting consultant did not fulfill our expectations. He played games with the audience, using flip charts as the main focus of the speech. His presentation consisted of jokes and riddles based on cartoons on his flip charts. The audience played a particular role in the speech because they were expected to respond to the riddles and jokes by answering his questions.

Most of the audience sat there stonefaced, while some of the younger, more energetic members played the games. No one knew exactly what the point of the speech was supposed to be. The visiting dignitaries were obviously bemused, and they must have left wondering if playing games with flip charts is what business communications is all about.

The consultant had forgotten three important rules about the use of the visual aids:

1. The aids should merely support the point of the speech, not be its primary focus.
2. The aids should be appropriate for the audience.
3. The aids should not be used as a gimmick. They should be treated as seriously as other sources of information.

It is tempting to pep up a speech with charts, graphs, and pictures, particularly if you feel unsure of your ability to get your point across. However, visual aids are inappropriate for some speeches. Indeed, they may detract, particularly if the speech is short and you have a limited number of examples to support your main point. Therefore use visual aids only if you cannot make your point without them. Here are some guidelines for their use:

1. Use visuals when you want to summarize facts, statistics, and other mathematical information. (Example: a company's profit-and-loss statement, perhaps in graph form)
2. Use visuals when you want to show how something works. (Example: how to assemble a food processor)
3. Use visuals when you want to describe an organizational structure. (Example: Showing the relationship between the executive, legislative, and judicial branches of government)

If you believe that a visual is necessary to support your point, then choose the one that works best, considering the audience, size of room, advance preparation necessary, and kind of information you want to present. The four most popular visual aids are handouts, charts, chalkboards, and overhead projectors. Each one of these aids has certain advantages and disadvantages. Particular care in preparation is necessary to avoid the pitfalls in using them.

Handouts

A handout is what the term implies: material that you give to each member of the audience.

Advantages of Handouts
1. The handout can be prepared in advance.
2. Members of the audience can write on it so that they have information for future reference. (This is important for training purposes.)
3. The handout provides an efficient means of communicating such "dense" information as graphs, tables, statistics, and other facts that may be too detailed for a chart, chalkboard, or overhead projector.
4. The handout shows that you have a professional attitude toward the information.

Disadvantages of Handouts
1. Information provided on handouts may become public. If you don't want your information shared with others, do not use a handout.
2. Rattling of paper handouts can be distracting to members of an audience.
3. Handouts take accurate, careful planning. Do not use them if you are not absolutely sure of your material — its quality and its sources.

Preparing Handouts
1. When you type the handout, double-space and use wide margins.
2. Proofread the manuscript, making sure that all statements are correct.
3. Don't skimp on quantity. Have plenty of copies for everyone.
4. If you take ideas from other people, give sources.
5. Distribute the handout to each member of the audience before you begin speaking. (You might get someone to help you if you need to be on the podium.)
6. Color-code the handouts so that you can refer to separate ones by color, making it easy for you and the audience to identify the correct one.

There are pitfalls in using a handout. For example you may be tempted to read it to the audience. You won't make this mistake if you think of yourself as a guide who must lead the audience through the handout, commenting and elaborating on the important points. A second pitfall is to allow the handout to become a distraction. If several members of the audience continue to read it after you have introduced a new point, stop. Pause. Get eye contact with most of the audience and proceed, repeating the point. Then lead them with you through your next points. The handout is an aid to your speech, not the speech itself.

Charts

A chart is a large poster containing information that supports your speech. The chart is usually displayed on an easel. Flip charts are posters, or pieces of paper, tied at the top so that they can be turned over to expose the charts in consecutive order. Flip charts are useful if you wish to show a series of informative items.

Advantages of Charts
1. Charts can be prepared in advance.
2. They are an efficient way to picture important information.
3. Charts are appropriate for small audiences.
4. Charts are inexpensive.

Disadvantages of Charts
1. Charts cannot be made at the last minute. If your material changes, therefore, you have to omit your chart.
2. Charts are bulky and difficult to carry.

Preparing Charts
1. Do not use more than six printed lines on a single chart.
2. Limit each line to from four to six words.
3. Use dark, clearly printed letters with lots of white space.
4. Have only one point or one idea per chart.
5. Check Chapter 3 to see how to use graphics.

Think of the chart as a mute straight man in a comedy routine. It feeds lines to you (the comedian) and displays information, but it is ready to upstage you at any moment. Don't let it take over. If you aren't careful, you will talk to the chart rather than to your audience. Be sure to maintain eye contact with your audience.

Don't allow your audience to pay more attention to the chart than they do to you. This may happen if the chart is too small for the room and the audience. People may crane their necks to peer at the chart and ignore you. Your straight man will become the center of attention.

Chalkboards (and white boards)

A chalkboard is a colored surface for writing with chalk. A chalkboard can be mounted permanently on the wall, or it can be movable, mounted on a pedestal. A white board requires liquid chalk or a washable felt marker. A white board can double as a projection screen.

Advantages of Chalkboards
1. You can design your information and display it in advance.
2. You can revise your information as you proceed in your speech.
3. Chalkboards are useful for small audiences.
4. They are useful for instructional purposes.
5. They are available in most convention centers, meeting rooms, and classrooms.

Disadvantages of Chalkboards
1. It is difficult to write without showing your back to the audience.
2. You must pay close attention to penmanship in order to write legibly — something that is difficult to do when you are talking.
3. The board may not be in the best position for the audience to see your information.
4. If you put your information on the board beforehand but you don't want the audience to see it until you are ready, covering the board is difficult.
5. Chalk dust is messy.

Preparing Chalkboards
1. Plan in advance the kind of information you want to put on the board. Identify key words so that you don't have to write all the time.
2. Bring your own chalk (or felt markers) and eraser.

Do not assume that because you have seen your teachers writing on chalkboards that it is easy to do while making a speech. You were not trained to write on a vertical surface a few inches from your nose. Because you are so close to your writing surface, you cannot focus on what you have just written. Consequently, you may misspell words and your writing may be illegible. Using a chalkboard while giving a speech takes more practice and skill than you might expect.

Practice writing on the board while speaking. To avoid standing with your back to the audience, limit your board work to the most necessary information. In addition, be prepared to do a lot of erasing because most boards hold less information than you think. Be ready to stand back and look at what you have written. It is very easy to make mistakes on a chalkboard.

Overhead Projectors

The overhead projector throws a picture on a screen by lighting a translucent page called a transparency. Since it is one of the easiest aids to use and control, the overhead projector is popular with speakers.

Advantages of the Overhead Projector
1. The machine is simple to operate.
2. Transparencies are cheap and easy to make.
3. You can cover up material that you don't want your audience to see until you are ready for it to be seen.
4. Most of the time, you can face your audience and maintain eye contact.
5. Compared to the chalkboard, the overhead projector is clean.
6. The room can be kept lighted, so that you are visible.
7. You can shut off the machine when it is not in use.
8. The overhead projector is excellent for instructional purposes.

Disadvantages of the Overhead Projector
1. In order to cool the high-intensity bulb, the fans of some overhead projectors run all the time. The noise of the fan can be distracting.
2. The bright light from the bulb shining in your face can be distracting.

Preparing Transparencies and Using the Overhead Projector
1. Use no more than six lines on each transparency, limiting each line to from four to six words.
2. Use clear lettering, not typing, unless you have a special key, called an orator, on your typewriter.
3. Arrange your transparencies in the order you plan to use, and label them accordingly. If you are speaking from notes or a manuscript, have the same material on the speaker's stand so that you don't have to look back at the screen or look at the bright light of the projector.
4. Before your presentation, place the machine where you get the best image.
5. Check fan, light bulb, and cord ahead of time. Bring an extra bulb and your own extension cord.
6. Have an alternate plan for use if the machine breaks down. Better still, bring your own machine.

In reply to a questionnaire asking about the use of visual aid machines, a friend of ours wrote: "The only visual aid machine that comes into my classroom is me." It takes only one machine to go bad during a presentation to make you vow never to use another one.

However, the overhead projector is such a useful aid that most speakers are willing to risk the problems that might occur. If you take proper precautions and check the parts of the machine, it will probably behave for you and add a great deal to your presentation.

Also check your room for "machine fit." Where, for example, are the electrical outlets? And since outlets are not always conveniently placed for machines, you need to watch where the cord stretches. If the cord lies in your speech path — that area in which you walk from the podium to the machine — you need to move it. This may seem to be a trivial matter, but when you stand in front of a crowd, changing your transparencies, trying to remember your next point and maintaining eye contact with your audience, you don't want anything to distract from your concentration. This is no time to stumble over a cord!

General Suggestions for Using Visual Aids
1. Rehearse with your visuals so that you are comfortable using them.
2. Talk louder when you speak — visual aids can be distracting for the audience. When you use visual aids, the audience must concentrate on more than one object.
3. Check the meeting room and your visual aid before the audience arrives. Don't take important time away from your speech to hand out papers, or to check the machine or charts.

USING A MICROPHONE

Think of the microphone in the same way you think of visual aids: a machine that can enhance your speech if used properly. Whether you use a microphone depends upon certain conditions. For instance, it is sometimes difficult to evaluate the acoustics just on room size alone. We have given speeches in a bare room seating 150 people, and needed no mike. Other times, in a speech to fifty people, in a carpeted room with upholstered chairs and drapes muting the voice, we needed one. Therefore take the furnishings into account if you have a choice of whether to use a mike.

Some convention centers, hotels, or businesses hire a technician to handle the problems of a sound system. Generally, however, you will be on your own to manage whatever equipment is in the room at the moment. If you have a choice of mike — fixed or lavalier — the kind of speech will dictate your choice. If, for instance, you want to move around, using visuals, a mike mounted on the podium can be a real hindrance. In that case, you probably won't use a mike unless a lavalier (one that will attach to your lapel) is available.

Check out the Mike

Finding an opportunity to test the microphone may be difficult. Nevertheless, try to check it out before your audience arrives. Place the stand of the microphone on the podium so that it suits your height. Your chin should be approximately six inches from the mike itself, which should be aimed at your collarbone. Saying a few words into the mike will give you an idea of how well it amplifies.

Let the Mike Alone

Once you have positioned the microphone correctly for your height, let it alone. Don't test or tap it in front of the audience. And don't blow into it. The microphone will pick up all sounds, so don't touch the mike stand or beat on the podium. Move away from the mike a moment if you need to clear your throat or cough. In other words, don't let your body work against the sound system; use it to your advantage.

EXERCISES

1. Mrs. Tibauld is making a speech to an audience of fifty people, using an overhead projector. In the middle of the speech, the fan in the projector suddenly makes a terrible racket, drowning out the speech. What should she do? (What should she have done?)

2. What would you recommend to a speaker who wants to use visual aids for the following speaking situations?

- **a.** An interior decorator giving a speech on the best way to arrange furniture in a typical living room.
- **b.** A heating specialist describing a duct system to his employees.
- **c.** A horticulturist providing a plan to a group of park supervisors on the best way to create ever-blooming gardens.
- **d.** An electrician explaining the methods for wiring the houses in a new subdivision.
- **e.** A supermarket manager trying to sell his or her plan for rearranging the store.
- **f.** A cost analyst proposing a new accounting system.
- **g.** A computer specialist selling a word processor to an office manager and ten employees.

3. Following are the outlines for two different speeches. What kind of visual aids would you choose for each speech?

   I. Beverage containers are a large part of Silver City's waste problem.
      A. They make up ten percent of all garbage in our landfill.
      B. They equal six percent of total municipal waste (by weight), both household and commercial.
   II. Since many of the containers are nonbiodegradable, they are filling up our landfills faster than anticipated.
      A. The present landfill was expected to last until 1990.
      B. At the present rate of use, the landfill will be full in 1985.

III. A mandatory deposit on beverage containers could save the city money in seeking out a new landfill.
   A. A new landfill agreement would cost the city thousands of dollars.
   B. A beverage deposit law would reduce the amount of solid waste by as much as twenty-five percent.
   C. The present landfill could last until 1988.

I. A growing number of vehicles causes serious problems in Sleepy Tree State Park.
   A. Ninety-two percent of all visitors to the park come in their own cars.
   B. Trailer camping has increased more than 100 percent in the last decade.
II. A new road would change the traffic pattern in the park.
   A. A main road into the park should start at Highway 19, ending at the spring in the northwest corner of the park.
   B. Five camping areas should branch off at half-mile intervals from the main road.
   C. One large picnic area should be built before the spring at the end of the road in the northwest corner of the park.

PART 9

The Library

CHAPTER

25

Using the Library

Here is a fact that may surprise you. After you leave college and become a professional person, you may use the library and do more research than you ever did as a student. In fact, libraries are so important to many businesses that they maintain their own collections and hire full-time librarians to organize books and magazines that are useful for the companies. You would expect, for instance, to find *Chemical and Engineering News* and *Chemical Abstracts* in the Dow Chemical Company library. In the Apple Computer, Incorporated, library, you would probably find *Computerworld*, *Byte*, and *Datamation*.

Not only will you find in a company library books and magazines geared toward the company's specialty, but you will also find the usual reference tools: encyclopedias, almanacs, statistical abstracts, and indexes. For in order to write reports business people and technicians need to check facts and use sources. Therefore, improving your skills in using a library may help you in your career, particularly in writing reports, verifying facts, and discovering new ideas.

In this chapter we will examine five efficient steps for finding information on a given subject. While you are following these steps you should keep bibliographic cards and take notes. Check a composition handbook for note-taking procedures.

Cathy Friedman, Commerce Librarian, Arizona State, Tempe, and Caroline Tibbetts, Reference Librarian, University of Delaware, Newark, acted as consultants for this chapter.

FIVE STEPS IN A SUBJECT SEARCH

A successful subject search depends more on organization and persistence than on brilliance. It is fairly easy to get information from libraries if you know how and where to look. Many technical advances have occurred in libraries, advances that improve your chances of finding what you need. The use of the computer, for instance, has improved book distribution. In the fairly recent past, if your library didn't have the book you needed, you would be out of luck. Recently, with the computerization of libraries in particular regions, getting books through interlibrary loan has become much easier.

Even though it is easier to get books, adequate preparation for a search is still necessary. We recommend the following steps.

1. Write a narrative description of your search, explaining its purpose. You should answer the questions: "What do I hope to learn? Why am I searching this subject?"
2. Search reference works for general information on your topic.
3. Search the card catalog (or computer catalog) for books available in your library. Search for bibliographies or abstracts that can lead you to books you might find in other libraries in your region, ones you could get on interlibrary loan.
4. Search the periodical indexes.
5. Optional: Search computer databases.

Step 1: Write a narrative description of your proposed search

Because of new technology, terms are very important in library research. We advise you therefore to write a narrative describing your topic and telling yourself (and any librarian who may help you) just what it is you want to know. You should also tell yourself why you want the information, using all the terms relevant to the subject. You will be surprised how the terms you use in your narrative may help you in your research.

Let's assume that you are a business administration major interested in learning about quality control in the Japanese management system. You think about your proposed research and write the following:

> I have heard a lot about the Japanese management of factories. Everything I read in the popular magazines and see on television suggests that the factory managers encourage input from the workers. I have also heard that decisions in Japanese industries are often made by consensus of the workers. As a result, factory workers believe that they have a stake in the product they manufacture. Consequently, Japanese quality control is reportedly better than it is in the United States. I know that excellence of

product combined with low prices has made Japan a formidable competitor, particularly in the automobile industry. Since my specialty is business administration with an emphasis on factory management, I need to know more about the Japanese system. I also need to know if what I have heard and read is accurate.

I may have to answer a question related to this subject if I am interviewed for a job; therefore I must be better informed than I presently am.

This is what I want to know: Is the Japanese managerial system one that could be adopted by American factories in order to improve quality control?

In your narrative, you have used a variety of terms. You will find some of these terms more important than others when you begin your search because they may be the ones chosen to index books and articles. In addition, certain combinations of these terms may be useful. Make a list of the terms (or combinations) you have used. Think also of synonyms that might be relevant.

- management/managerial
- factory/factories
- decision-making
- product
- quality control
- auto industry
- computer industry
- competitor
- Japan/Japanese
- United States
- manufacture
- industry/industrial

Since libraries and reference works depend upon a limited number of terms to index books and periodicals, you should probably check the *Sears List of Subject Headings* or *The Library of Congress Subject Headings* to see which of your terms, if any, are used in the library where you are doing your research. You will use many of these terms when you look for your subject in encyclopedias, the card catalog, and periodical indexes.

You will also find it useful to keep a copy of your subject terms with you any time you use the library. It is sometimes easy to forget important terms when you are scrabbling through many references and other card catalogs, trying to find information.

Step 2: Search Reference Works for General Information

The purpose of looking at reference works before using other resources in the library is to get an overview of your subject. Sometimes a general encyclopedia, such as the *Encyclopedia Americana*, can provide both information and bibliographies. Depending upon your own specialty, however, you may want to use encyclopedias that are geared toward your major. If, for instance, you are a finance major, you would probably find the *Encyclopedia of Banking and Finance* useful. Whatever encyclopedia you choose for your overview, you will follow the same procedure.

The most efficient way to use a multivolume encyclopedia is to turn first to the index, which is in a separate volume. There you may find the main entry for your subject. If you can't find it, you will need to look for related subjects. After checking the index entries for subjects that look promising, go to the volumes where the articles appear. Also check the bibliographies that follow most articles of any importance. These bibliographies will lead you to general reference books or texts on your subject. Sometimes they will also lead you to important periodical articles.

In your search of general encyclopedias, you will probably find only a little information on your topic. Therefore, you might find a more specialized encyclopedia like *McGraw-Hill Encyclopedia of Science and Technology* a better place to look. There you will find that *Japanese management* is not listed, but you will find the subject heading *Manufacturing engineering*. Even though there is nothing listed under that heading for *Japan*, you will find *quality control*. Figure 25.1 is a page from the index of that encyclopedia showing the information you need.

When using an encyclopedia, watch for *See* or *See also* references. They will often lead you to other articles that have important information related to your subject. Once you have read about your topic in a general or specialized encyclopedia, then seek out the items listed in the bibliography. Check any reference books (or periodical articles) listed to see if they give general information that might be useful. Be sure to examine the indexes, tables of contents, and bibliographies of these sources for ideas that might help you in your search for additional information.

To find out if these books and periodicals are available in your library, use the card catalog.

Step 3: Search the Card Catalog (or Computer Catalog)

The card catalog is an alphabetized collection of index cards that carry information on every book your library contains. For each book, you will find three types of cards: (1) author or main entry card, (2) title card, and (3) subject card. For periodicals, you will only find title and subject cards. If your book or periodical is listed, go to the shelf and look at it. If not, remember that most books can be borrowed from other libraries through interlibrary loan.

When you use the card catalog for a preliminary investigation of your subject, check the subject cards first. Start with a general classification, perhaps *Japan* and *Japanese*. Then start narrowing to more specific terms like *Manufacturing*, as you did when you used the encyclopedia.

You may find your material classified under some of the following subheadings:

> Manual welding **1** 670
> Manufactured gem **6** 119-120
> Manufacturing engineering **8** 116-119*
>   academic roots **8** 119
>   assembly methods **1** 766-767*
>   book manufacture **2** 378-380*
>   cost control **7** 90-91
>   functions **8** 116-117, 118-119
>   industrial engineering **8** 119
>   industrial robots **7** 105-114*
>   inspection and testing **7** 211-212*
>   mass production **8** 232-234*
>   material handling **8** 118
>   mechanical engineering **8** 119
>   plant engineering **8** 118
>   process engineering **8** 117-118
>   production methods **10** 844-846*
>   production planning **10** 846-847*
>   quality control **11** 156-159*
>   standards and methods **8** 118
>   tool engineering **8** 118
> Manuk **4** 504

Figure 25.1. From the *McGraw-Hill Encyclopedia of Science and Technology*

- Japanese Management
- Japanese Export Management
- Japanese Economy
- Japanese Manufacturing Techniques
- Japan — Commerce
- Japan — Industries
- Japan's Managerial System
- Industrial Management — Japan

Figure 25.2 shows the kind of subject card you may find under the classification of *Industrial Management — Japan*.

Once you have found a book under this subject heading, look at it to see if it is useful. If the subject is right for your research, look at the *main entry author card*. You will find this by looking under the author's name. On the bottom of this card you will find subject headings associated with the book you found. A sample card is in Figure 25.3.

These subject headings will be useful to you in the same way the *See* and *See also* references are when using the encyclopedia indexes. If you haven't checked the *Sears List of Subject Headings* or the *Library of Congress Subject Headings*, now is the time to do that. You should be using all the subject entries available to you.

If your library has an online computer catalog, your search procedure is similar to the one you used with the card catalog. You must enter into the computer the appropriate subject headings found in the *Sears List of Subject Headings* or the *Library of Congress Subject Headings*. The computer will respond either by asking you to narrow your search or by listing books found under the heading you entered. The more you focus your search through the

Subject		INDUSTRIAL MANAGEMENT—JAPAN.

Call Number	658 G356m	Gibney, Frank, 1924-
		   Miracle by design: the real reasons behind Japan's economic success/Frank Gibney.—New York, N.Y.: Times Books, c1982.
		   xv, 239 p.; 24 cm.

Note: This book has a bibliography		Includes bibliographical references and index. ISBN 0-8129-1024-9
	IU	830504 GCLCA UIUKdc 82-50043

Figure 25.2. Subject card from card catalog

Call Number	658	
Author	G356m	
Author		Gibney, Frank, 1924-
		Miracle by design: the real reasons behind Japan's economic success/Frank Gibney.—New York, N.Y.: Times Books, c1982.
		xv, 239 p.; 24 cm.
		Includes bibliographical references and index.
		ISBN 0-8129-1024-9
Related subject headings		1. Industrial management—Japan. 2. Industrial management—United States. 3. National characteristics, Japanese. 4. Japan—Industries. 5. Businessmen—Japan. I. Title
	IU	830504 GCLCA UIUKdc 82-50043

Figure 25.3. Main entry card from card catalog

use of narrower subject headings, the greater your chances are of finding materials closely related to your subject: for example, use *Management—Japan* rather than just *Management* or just *Japan*. By making your subject headings narrow, you reduce the number of unimportant or inappropriate titles listed by the computer.

Another way to find out what books on your subject your library contains is to check the shelf list, a listing of all the books in call-number order. After getting the call number of one book that deals with your subject, you can check the shelf list for books with similar numbers. If you are not allowed to go into the library's stacks, the shelf list can be a valuable way of finding other material on your subject.

Now is the time to see if the important books on your subject are actually in the stacks. If they are, check them out; if not, ask to have them saved, or order them through interlibrary loan. If your library has open stacks, browse through all the books shelved together on your subject. Check their tables of contents, indexes, and bibliographies. You may find pertinent or interesting material that will help you in your search.

When subject-searching the card catalog, it is a good idea to look at the subheadings identifying different types of sources. After the basic subject heading, there are sometimes phrases telling you what kind of information is included. An example of this is the subject heading *Industrial Management—Japan—Bibliographies.* This card tells you that the book listed is a bibliography. Some other subheadings that will be useful to you are *Periodicals, Indexes,* and *Congresses.* If you find these kinds of entries, look at them. They will not give you additional information, but they will lead you to sources of additional information.

Step 4: Search Periodical Indexes

Many periodical indexes are available for researchers; however, you will probably find the *Business Periodical Index* the most useful in your field. It lists recent articles published in more than 250 business periodicals. Published twice a month, combined every three months into a larger volume, it is then published yearly in one bound volume.

Most periodical indexes contain roughly the same format. To use an index efficiently, you need to be aware of the information presented in the front of each issue: (1) suggestions for using the index; (2) abbreviations of the periodicals indexed; (3) a list of the periodicals indexed; and (4) the key to other abbreviations. This information will tell you how to read such references and abbreviations as *Bull at Sci*, *jt*, *Ja*, *il*, and *por*, and will also give you other important help in using the index.

To look up your subject in a periodical index, again start with a specific term. If you can't find it, move to a broader subject. Periodical indexes use cross references in the same way encyclopedia indexes and card catalogs do.

After you have identified the items in the *Business Periodical Index* that may contain information on your subject, check the card catalog to see if your library has the magazines cited there in bound form. Current magazines, as well as older bound issues, may be listed in a Kardex file. Many librarians now have magazines on microfilm, in which case the microfilm number appears over the call number on the catalog card.

When you look up *Japan* in the *Business Periodical Index*, you will not find a subheading for *Management*; however, at the *beginning* of the entry for *Japan*, you will find a long list of *See also* references. *Management* is one. Figure 25.4 shows a portion of a page from Volume 24 of the *Business Periodical Index*. When you turn to *Management* in the *Business Periodical Index*, you will find fifteen references under *Management: Japan*, as shown in Figure 25.5.

Figure 25.6 explains the meaning of the symbols and abbreviations in an index.

Step 5 (Optional): Search computer databases

Many libraries now offer an online bibliographic search of periodicals indexed in a variety of databases. A database is the online equivalent of an index or abstract publication. Since the printing industry has moved almost entirely to computer-printed type, the printing tapes of indexes and abstracts can be transferred to computers to form another source of information for

JAPAN—See also—*Continued*
  Corporations, American
  Corporations, British
  Corporations, Swedish
  Credit cards
  Crime and criminals
  Drug industry
  Electronic industries
  Electric power plants
  Electric utilities
  Employment
  Engineers
  European Economic Community
  Fertilizer industry
  Fiber industry
  Finance companies
  Fish industry
  Fisheries
  Food service
  Forest products industry
  Heating and cooling industry
  High technology industries
  Holding companies
  Industrial relations
  Industrial research
  Insurance
  Insurance, Life
  Insurance companies
  Insurance laws and regulations
  Investments, American
  Investments, Foreign
  Labor
  Labor laws and legislation
  Loans, Bank
  Loans, Foreign
  Machine tool industry
  Management
  Marketing
  Metal working industries
  Monetary policy
  Money
  Motor bus industry
  Motor truck industry
  Motorcycle industry
  Museums
  Newspapers

Figure 25.4. From the *Business Periodical Index*, listing references for Japan

MANAGEMENT—*Continued*

Ivory Coast

In the Ivory Coast (Cote d'Ivoire): a mix of management methods. J. D. Harbron. map Bus Q 46:16-18 Summ '81

Japan

American myths vs. the real reasons for Japan's success. Mgt R 70:55-6 Je '81

Can America copy Japanese methods—or should we simply borrow some useful ideas? Mgt R 71:4-5 Mr '82

Explaining the Japanese miracle. O. B. Henriksen. Int Mgt 37:23 Ja '82

How the Japanese manage in the US [panel discussion] il Fortune 103:97-8+ Je 15 '81

How to go one better than Japan. R. Collard. Mgt Today p27+ Ja '82

Inscrutable world-beaters. B. Hammond. Director 34:28 N '81

Integrated management system: lessons from the Japanese experience. N. Hatvany and V. Pucik. bibl(p478-80) Acad Mgt R 6:469-80 Jl '81

Is Japan doing a better job managing inventory? R. E. Harvey. Iron Age 224:38-41 Je 1 '81

Japan and the excellent organization. J. S. Balloun. Managerial Plan 30:10-15 My/Je '82

Japan gives the B-schools an A—for contacts. Bus W p 132+ O 19 '81

Japan—where operations really are strategic. S. C. Wheelwright. Harvard Bus R 59:67-74 Jl/Ag '81

Japanese agenda for management development. H. Lim. Train & Devel J 36:62-7 Mr '82

Japanese and the American first-line supervisor. L. A. Bryan, Jr. Train & Devel J 36:62-8 Ja '82

Japanese approach to risk treatment. Y. Morimiya. tab Risk Mgt 28:46-9 N '81

Japanese are better managers, AMSA says. Iron Age 225:11+ F 19 '82

Japanese fix. R. Collison. Can Bus 54:36-43+ N '81

Japanese management: a skill profile. H. Lim. Train & Devel J 35:18-21 O '81

Japanese management in the United States. Res Mgt 25:3-4 Ja '82

Japanese management practices and productivity. N. Hatvany and V. Puick. il Org Dyn 9:4-21 Spr '81

Japanese perspective on management. Duns Bus M 119:52 Ap '82

Figure 25.5. From the *Business Periodical Index*, references for *Management — Japan*

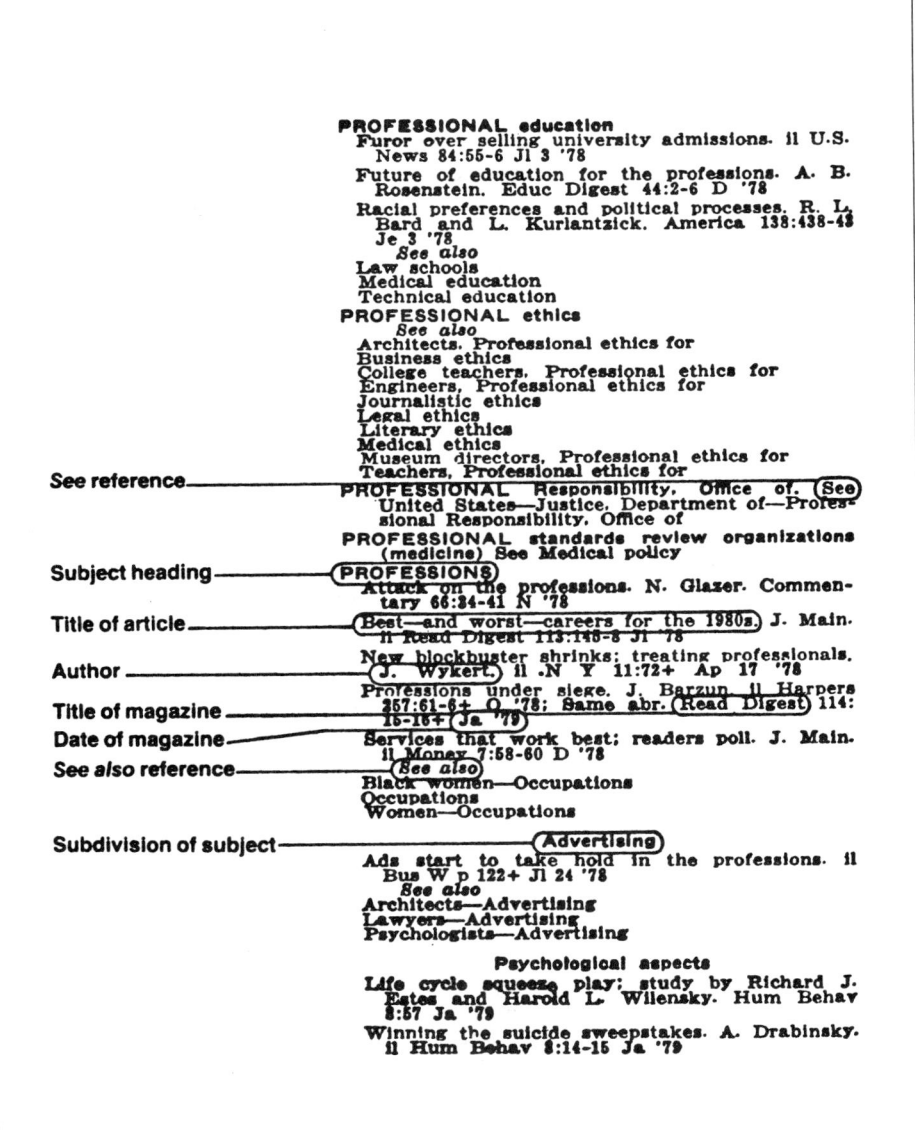

PROFESSIONAL education
  Furor over selling university admissions. il U.S. News 84:55-6 Jl 3 '78
  Future of education for the professions. A. B. Rosenstein. Educ Digest 44:2-6 D '78
  Racial preferences and political processes. R. L. Bard and L. Kurlantzick. America 138:438-43 Je 3 '78
    See also
  Law schools
  Medical education
  Technical education
PROFESSIONAL ethics
    See also
  Architects, Professional ethics for
  Business ethics
  College teachers, Professional ethics for
  Engineers, Professional ethics for
  Journalistic ethics
  Legal ethics
  Literary ethics
  Medical ethics
  Museum directors, Professional ethics for
  Teachers, Professional ethics for

See reference — PROFESSIONAL Responsibility, Office of. *See* United States—Justice, Department of—Professional Responsibility, Office of
  PROFESSIONAL standards review organizations (medicine) See Medical policy

Subject heading — PROFESSIONS
  Attack on the professions. N. Glazer. Commentary 66:34-41 N '78

Title of article — Best—and worst—careers for the 1980s. J. Main. il Read Digest 113:145-8 Jl '78

Author — New blockbuster shrinks; treating professionals. J. Wykert. il .N Y 11:72+ Ap 17 '78
  Professions under siege. J. Barzun. il Harpers

Title of magazine — 257:61-6+ O '78; Same abr. Read Digest 114: 15-16+ Ja '79

Date of magazine — Services that work best; readers poll. J. Main. il Money 7:58-60 D '78

See also reference — See also
  Black women—Occupations
  Occupations
  Women—Occupations

Subdivision of subject — Advertising
  Ads start to take hold in the professions. il Bus W p 122+ Jl 24 '78
    See also
  Architects—Advertising
  Lawyers—Advertising
  Psychologists—Advertising

      Psychological aspects
  Life cycle squeeze play; study by Richard J. Estes and Harold L. Wilensky. Hum Behav 8:57 Ja '79
  Winning the suicide sweepstakes. A. Drabinsky. il Hum Behav 8:14-15 Ja '79

Figure 25.6. Explanation of symbols and abbreviations in an index

researchers. Computer businesses, called vendors, rent the tapes of indexes to libraries.

At this point, individuals seldom do computer searches alone because it is complicated and expensive. Consequently, only librarians and researchers trained in online computer searching do them.

A computer search is complicated. Companies in the database industry are inconsistent in the way they index or manage their materials. Each database has its own vocabulary and its own indexing terms, symbols, and instructions. Librarians who are authorized to do online searches have an extensive library of manuals to help them use each database. For instance, after looking at the list of databases listed later in this chapter, suppose you decide to search *ABI/Inform* for your subject of *Japanese Management*. That would be the wrong choice. Your librarian, who knows the contents of each database, would probably advise you to use *PAIS International* because it indexes internationally-published business publications.

A librarian will also know if the kind of information you seek is available in a databank. The narrative description you prepared earlier will be a good resource when you discuss your research with the professional staff of the library. In addition, your manual search of reference works, the card catalog, and periodical indexes, which should be completed before requesting a computer search, will be invaluable to you and the librarian.

A computer search is expensive. One mistake in using the computer can cost a good deal of money. The library pays *PAIS* an hourly fee to rent its database. In addition, it pays the business, or vendor, who rents the tapes to the library. One librarian estimated that it cost her library fifty cents a minute to do a bibliographic search. You must pay for that service. Therefore, using the wrong subject term can be expensive. You cannot assume, for example, that *PAIS* would necessarily use the same index terms that your library's card catalog uses. Your librarian will have this kind of information when he or she does the computer search.

Since a computer search is expensive, it is very important to plan well before seeing the librarian. If your librarian believes that a database is available that covers your subject adequately, and you are willing to pay for the service, by all means take advantage of an online search.

Caution: A database is not like the card catalog. It has no relationship to your library's holdings. It is comparable to the *Business Periodical Index:* Your library may or may not carry the periodicals indexed in the database.

SELECTED REFERENCES

Dictionaries: Specialized

Ammer, Christine. *Dictionary of Business and Economics.* Rev. and expanded ed. New York: Free Press, 1984.

Auld, Douglas A. L., et. al. *The American Dictionary of Economics.* New York: Facts on File, 1983.

Brownstone, David M., and Irene M. Franck. *The VNR Investor's Dictionary.* New York: Van Nostrand-Reinhold, 1981.

Cooper, W. W., and Yuji Ljiri. *Kohler's Dictionary for Accountants.* 6th ed. Englewood Cliffs, NJ: Prentice-Hall, 1983.

Greenwald, Douglas. *The McGraw-Hill Dictionary of Modern Economics: A Handbook of Terms and Organizations.* 3rd ed. New York: McGraw-Hill, 1983.

Moffat, David. *Economics Dictionary.* 2nd ed. New York: Elsevier, 1983.

Pearce, David W., ed. *The Dictionary of Modern Economics.* Rev. ed. Cambridge, MA: MIT Press, 1983.

Rosenberg, Jerry M. *Dictionary of Banking and Finance.* New York: Wiley, 1982.

Rosenberg, Jerry M. *Dictionary of Business and Management.* New York: Wiley, 1983.

Encyclopedias: Specialized

Greenwald, Douglas, ed. *Encyclopedia of Economics.* New York: McGraw-Hill, 1982.

Munn, Glenn G. *Encyclopedia of Banking and Finance.* 8th ed. Rev. and expanded by G. L. Garcia. Boston: Banker's, 1983.

The McGraw-Hill Encyclopedia of Science and Technology. 5th ed. New York: McGraw-Hill, 1982

Directories

America's Corporate Families; the Billion Dollar Directory. New York: Dun and Bradstreet, Annual.

    This directory lists by industry, company name, and geographic location the largest public companies in the United States. To be listed, the companies must have annual sales of more than $50,000,000 and must do business from more than ten locations, so only the very largest of companies are included.

Kruzas, Anthony T., and Robert C. Thomas, eds. *Business Organizations and Agencies Directory.* Detroit: Gale Research, 1980.

Directory of Corporate Affiliations (Who Owns Whom). Wilmette, IL: National Register, 1985.

This directory provides two indexes: one by the parent company and the other by the name of the subsidiary.

Ward's Directory of 55,000 Largest U.S. Corporations: The All Purpose Marketing and Financial Directory. By the Editors of News Front Business Trends. Petaluma, CA: Baldwin H. Ward, 1981.

This directory ranks (by sales) the largest public companies in the United States. The rankings are given by industry, and additional financial information about the companies is included. There are alphabetical and geographical indexes.

Million Dollar Directory. New York: Dun and Bradstreet, 1959 to present.

This directory is divided into three volumes. Each of the volumes covers different sales amounts, with volume one listing the largest companies. Each volume is divided by geographical location, by industry, and by company name. There is a master index at the front of each.

Principal International Businesses. New York: Dun and Bradstreet, 1974 to present.

This one-volume directory lists major companies around the world. Basic information is given for each. This is a good source for addresses of foreign companies. The volume is divided by country, by industry, and alphabetically by company name.

Reference Book of Corporate Management. 4th ed. New York: Dun and Bradstreet, 1985.

This four-volume set provides short biographical notes on America's corporate management.

Standard and Poor's Register of Corporations, Directors and Executives. New York: Standard and Poor's, 1928 to present.

This directory is divided into three parts. The first part is an alphabetical list of companies, with basic information about each. The second volume lists alphabetically directors and executives of the companies with brief biographical sketches. The third volume is a geographic and industry index, a list of companies, a list of newly included executives, and an obituary section.

Thomas Register of American Manufacturers and Thomas Register Catalog File. New York: Thomas, 1905 to present.

This is a very thorough list of American manufacturing firms. The volumes are arranged by product and alphabetically by company name. There is also a list of product classifications and a list of leading trade names. The last three volumes are company catalogs.

Investment Sources

Standard and Poor's Corporation Records. New York: Standard and Poor's, 1940 to present.

This source provides very brief and concise information on corporations including corporation history (such as subsidiaries and the number of employees), stock data (such as number of stock holders), and price range of stock.

Value Line Investment Survey, New York: Value Line, weekly, 1936 to present.
This weekly looseleaf service attempts to predict stocks within the context of the industry overall. It provides investors with information concerning stock prices, timeliness of stock, and rank for safety.

Yearbooks, Almanacs, and Handbooks

Brusaw, Charles T. *The Business Writer's Handbook.* 2nd ed. New York: St. Martin's, 1982.

Levine, Sumner N., ed. *Dow Jones — Irwin Business and Investment Almanac.* Homewood, IL: Dow Jones Irwin, 1985.

Statistical Abstract of the United States. U.S. Bureau of the Census. Washington, D.C.: GPO, annual 1878 to present.

World Almanac and Book of Facts. New York: Newspaper Enterprise Association, annual 1886 to present.

Statistical Indexes and Business Ratio Sources

American Statistics Index. Washington: CIS, annual 1973 to present.

Statistical Reference Index. Washington: CIS, annual 1980 to present.

Index to International Statistics. Bethesda, MD: CIS, 1983 to present.

Troy, Leo, ed. *Almanac of Business and Industrial Financial Ratios.* Englewood Cliffs, NJ: Prentice-Hall, 1985.

Industry Norms and Key Business Ratios: Library Edition. New York: Dun and Bradstreet, 1984.

Standard and Poor's Industry Surveys. New York: Standard and Poor's, annual 1973.

United States Industrial Outlook. Department of Commerce. Washington, D.C.: GPO, annual 1975 to present.

Business Bibliographies

Daniells, Lorna. *Business Information Sources.* Rev. ed. Berkeley: University of California, 1985.
This is an excellent source. This bibliography is an annotated list of the most important business books, periodicals, and reference sources. The table of contents is a subject guide to finding materials on topics of interest in all aspects of business.

Wasserman, Paul, ed. *Encyclopedia of Business Information Sources.* 5th ed. Detroit: Gale Research, 1983.
This source is a detailed list arranged by broad subject category. It lists periodicals, general works, online databases, handbooks, indexes, bibli-

ographies, directories, and more, in all aspects of business and finance and for all types of industries.

Indexes

Business Index. Menlo Park, CA: Information Access, 1979 to present. (Microfilm format)

This alphabetized subject/author index covers more than 460 business periodicals and selected articles from pertinent legal and general-interest periodicals. It also indexes *The Wall Street Journal*, *Barron's*, and part of the *New York Times*.

Business Periodical Index. New York: H. W. Wilson, 1958 to present.

This is a basic index to more than 250 English-language magazines in different aspects of business. It is indexed alphabetically by subject and contains at the end a list of book reviews found in the indexed periodicals.

F & S Index. Cleveland, OH: Predicasts, 1960 to present (*F & S Index Europe* and *F & S Index International* also available).

This is a very good index to more than 750 financial publications, newspapers, trade magazines, and special reports covering economic, company, product, and industry information. The *Index* is divided into two sections: the first indexes articles by standard industrial classifications and the second alphabetizes by company name. The European and international editions are also indexed alphabetically by country name.

Index to U.S. Government Periodicals. Chicago: Infordata International, 1970 to present.

This index provides access to all United States government periodicals, including *Business America* and *Business Conditions Digest*.

Monthly Catalog of United States Government Publications. Washington, D.C.: GPO, 1895 to present.

This is a comprehensive listing of all United States government publications. The documents are indexed by subject, title, author, series/report number, stock number, and key word in context. The index is a good source for information on such general subjects as banking, finance, economics, and a variety of industries.

New York Times Index. New York: New York Times, 1913 to present.

This index is arranged alphabetically by subject and includes very useful cross-references. It is included here because of the *New York Times's* excellent business and political coverage. Indexing is based on the final city edition. (**Note:** Several other major city newspapers are also indexed; for example, indexes are available for The *Chicago Tribune* and the *Chicago SunTimes*.)

Public Affairs Information Service Bulletin. (PAIS). New York: Public Affairs Information Service, 1915 to present.

This is a very useful, selective subject index to more than 1,400 English-language periodicals, books, pamphlets, government publications, and reports of public and private agencies in economics, business, the social sciences, public administration, and so forth. One thing to remember about this index is that it selectively covers periodicals, indexing only those articles pertinent to its subject coverage.

Reader's Guide to Periodical Literature. New York: H. W. Wilson, 1900 to present.

This is a good basic index with author/subject access to approximately 190 general-interest periodicals.

The Wall Street Journal Index. New York: Dow Jones, 1958 to present.

This index to the most famous business newspaper in the world is divided into two sections. The first section is indexed alphabetically by company name. The second section, called "General News," is an alphabetical subject index. Indexing is based on the final Eastern edition.

Databases

ABI/Inform. Louisville, KY: Data Courier, 1971 to present.

This is one of the most widely used online management databases. *ABI/Inform* allows access to citations and abstracts from more than 475 English-language journals. Subjects covered include banking, finance, economics, law, marketing and management.

English-language journals. Subjects covered include banking, finance, economics, law, marketing and management.

Management Contents. Skokie, IL: Management Contents. 1975 to present.

This database provides access to citations and abstracts from more than 325 journals, both United States and foreign, but all in English, covering all aspects of management and related fields. It also includes some proceedings and transactions.

National Newspaper Index. Menlo Park, CA: Information Access, 1979 to present.

This database, also available as a microfilm index, gives complete coverage of *The Christian Science Monitor*, The *New York Times*, and the *Wall Street Journal*. Updating of the database is frequent, and indexing is very good.

PAIS International New York: PAIS. 1976 to present for English; 1972 to present for foreign language.

This database provides online access to the *PAIS Indexes*. Coverage is the same (see Indexes above)

Predicasts Indexes. Cleveland, OH: Predicasts, 1972 to present.

This database provides online access to the numerous Predicasts publications, including the main F & S indexes and the forecasting services.

EXERCISES

1. Choose a topic in business or a related subject that you would like to know more about — if not now, then in the future. Write a narrative, describing your interest in the subject. Answer the questions: "What do I know about the subject?" "What do I want to learn about the subject?" Use a variety of terms to discuss the subject. List the terms that you might use in searching the subject.

2. Look up the terms that you listed in Exercise 1. Use *Sears List of Subject Headings* or the *Library of Congress Subject Headings*, depending upon the indexing system your library uses. Which terms were included? cross-referenced? Did you find synonyms for the terms you listed? Which terms did you finally settle on?

3. Using the terms you finally settled on, look up your subject in an encyclopedia. Discuss the process you followed to find information on your subject.

4. Look for your subject in the card catalog. Notice how the terms found in *Sears* or *Library of Congress* match those in the card catalog.

5. Look up your subject in a periodical index. How much did you depend upon *See* or *See also* references? List the periodicals that were most useful for your subject.

6. Select a book covering your subject that your library doesn't have. Put in an order for interlibrary loan.

PART 10

Office Machines

CHAPTER 26

The Least You Should Know About Office Machines

What is the least you should know about office machines? The answer probably depends on several things:

1. What kind of work will you be doing?
2. Will your employer be using the high technology available today?
3. Will you be expected to dictate your letters, memos, and so on, to a secretary or to a machine?
4. Will you have a secretary at all? If you won't, what kind of support staff will be available to you? Will it be the people in a word-processing center, a central dictation system, or a typist who is expected to type and transcribe for several people?

Obviously, if you are a college student still anticipating your first major entrance into the real world of business, neither you nor we can answer those questions. We can pretty well assure you, however, that you won't have your own private secretary at the entry level in most businesses. Why? First, because nationwide the secretarial pool is diminishing by approximately ten percent per year. Second, those executives lucky enough to have a private secretary are usually at or near the top management level. If you are among the nontraditional students who will be using this text, the answers to the questions will depend on the type of work you do as well as your position in your company.

In either case, let's assume that you won't or don't have that Woman or

Man Friday and examine some of the office equipment that you should be familiar with. You don't need to become an expert; rather, you should become knowledgeable. With this knowledge you will be able to better judge the competence of a subordinate responsible for secretarial tasks, and you'll know whether what you ask others to do for you is reasonable and responsible. Finally, you will be able to perform certain tasks yourself when necessary, rather than waiting for a secretary to have time to do them. This knowledge, then, will serve you in many ways during your career in business.

REPRODUCTION EQUIPMENT: TYPES AND USES

Copiers

Most reproduction needs in today's business office will be met by one of the copiers currently on the market. Such copiers can be as sophisticated or as simple, as inexpensive or as costly, as your business justifies. There are plain-paper copiers, coated-paper copiers, and treated-paper copiers; copiers that collate, copiers that enlarge and reduce, and on and on. Some use a thermal process; some use the electrostatic process; others use any one of a dozen processes. All you need to know is how to use the one in your office. Most copiers are very simple: Put your original in, set an indicator at the number of copies you want, and push a button.

Now we can hear someone asking: "Why should *I* know how to run a copier? My secretary will do it for me." Maybe — if a secretary, yours or anybody else's, is available, and if they aren't working on a rush project you don't want to interrupt.

But what if you are working overtime on a Saturday morning on materials due in the manager's office Monday morning at eight o'clock — in triplicate? More than likely, secretaries won't be working on Saturday morning. You'll have to make the copies yourself. So familiarize yourself with the equipment in the office, just in case. It will be your face that's saved.

Or suppose you have to present a project to the Board of Directors at an early-morning meeting. You decide that your oral presentation would be more impressive if you used visuals to demonstrate some of the more important points. How would you make them? Most copiers can produce transparencies for an overhead projector. But you should acquaint yourself with your copier's idiosyncrasies. One brand of copier, for example, will not reproduce ball-point pen ink; another brand will. Each requires a different transparency sheet from which to prepare a visual. If, for instance, you tried to use the transparency sheet used on a treated-paper copier to prepare a transparency at a plain-paper copier, you would succeed only in melting the transparency sheet around the copier's fuser rollers. All of the office machines in your office will lighten your workload, but only if you know their capabilities and limitations.

There is a lot of difference in the speed and quality of reproduction as well as operational reliability among brands of copiers. These differences cannot always be accounted for in financial terms. As with any major business purchase in business, those in charge of purchasing will need to research the possible choices and determine the company's needs and preferences as to ease of operation, available technical assistance and service, capabilities of the equipment, and so on. A "Guide to Copiers," which provides practical assistance in assessing a company's needs and in selecting appropriate equipment to fit these needs, is available from Administrative Management Society, 2360 Maryland Road, Willow Grove, PA 19090.

Most companies will have a policy about the maximum number of copies to be made at a photocopier. Some will say no more than from seven to twenty; others, no more than 100. So you may also have a spirit-duplicating (commonly called a "ditto") or a "mimeograph" machine on which to reproduce large numbers of copies. You may also be expected to prepare your own master: type it, draw a graph, whatever. Suppose your machine is called a ditto or fluid-duplicating machine; how would you prepare your copy?

Ditto Machines

By means of a chemical reaction, the ditto machine transfers the ink from the back of a spirit-duplicating master onto paper as it passes over the sheets fed in by the machine. (The master usually consists of three pieces: a top sheet on which you type, a tissue insert that you remove before typing, and a carbon sheet, from which carbon is transferred to the back of the typing sheet as you type.) The copies are usually purple because the ink on the back sheet of the master is purple; however, ditto masters can be purchased in several different colors. These other colors are not as durable; therefore, you will not get as many copies from, say, a black or red master.

You can also prepare ditto masters with some copiers, using a special thermal master. Photocopies of the pages you wish to duplicate are run through the copier with the special master. These are not as sharp or as durable as the masters prepared on a typewriter. A direct write-on or type-on master, for example, will usually produce 100 or more copies, depending on the quality of your supplies. The thermal master will usually produce only forty readable copies.

Mimeograph Machines

The mimeograph machine usually produces black copy similar to typing. The master for use on this machine also consists of three layers: the backing sheet, a silk screen coated with a waxy substance, and a clear plastic film that prevents the wax from filling up your typewriter keys. This master is usually typed with the typewriter ribbon in the *off* or *stencil* position. As you type, the typewriter keys punch holes (in the shape of your keys) through the coating on the silk screen. When you put the master on the mimeograph machine, the holes allow the ink in the drum to seep out, so the ink is transferred onto the paper that your machine is feeding. The more common mimeograph stencil is capable of producing hundreds, even thousands, of copies, depending on the quality of your supplies. With the advent of word-processors and computers, however, newer stencils are being offered to accommodate the lighter touch of these new machines. These stencils are much less durable, and reproducing more than 200 copies from them is difficult, if not impossible.

The most commonly used ink is black, although there are mimeograph machines that boast of making multiple-color copies. Those, however, require that you change an "ink gun" or "drum" and make two or three passes over the paper. You'll seldom encounter them.

Another machine that you may work with is an electronic stencil maker, which burns the image into the waxed surface of a special master. The advantage of such a machine is that it will copy anything (chart, illustration, graph, handwriting). You prepare the original, adding any visual effects you think will help your presentation; then you photocopy the original and use the photocopy to prepare your stencil.

You may also be required to operate the machines used to reproduce your copies. The vast majority of them are simple enough to use. Put the master on the correct way, load the paper table, set the counter, push the *on* button, and push the *paper feed* lever. Some machines count for you; others do not. You will want to find an amiable soul to show you how to run these machines; a secretary in the front office, or a colleague. In any case, these lessons usually take only a few minutes because these types of reproduction machines are simple to operate.

Offset Printers

Some of you may be employed in a large corporation with its own in-house printing department. Most of these departments use offset presses to prepare the forms, letterheads, reports, brochures, annual reports, promotional and advertising materials, and so on, that are sent out under the corporation's name. The offset can be as simple or as complicated as your business requires, but it is not as easy to operate as a copier or the ditto or mimeograph machines. Most companies therefore have an in-house printing manager to supervise the work of that department. If this is the case, find out how such a department works. What kind of lead time does its manager require? How elaborate is the printing setup? What kind of authorization do you need to use the department's services? What does its jargon mean?

Printers' jargon can be confusing. Printers talk in terms of "ens," "ems," "points" of type, and leading. They measure by "picas" and "escapement" instead of inches and lines. An experienced printer can look at your typescript and estimate how much room it is going to take in, say, ten-point type (height of the letters) on twelve-point leading (including the space between lines of type). An association's production department manager once told us that before her association's publications were brought in-house, she was totally ignorant of picas, ens, and ems. Still, she produced the association's first in-house issue with only two hours instruction on an ESC (electronic selectric composer). She had successfully struggled her way through the job by combing through other association magazines looking for suitable formats, layouts, and type sizes. You can do the same thing when you are learning to deal with a large corporation's printing department.

Learn how to estimate type. There are many good books available that will give you the basics and help you learn how to interpret the printers' jargon. *Graphics Master*, by Dean Phillip Lem (Dean Lem Associates, P.O. Box 46086, Los Angeles, CA 90046); Walter B. Graham's *Complete Guide to Pasteup* (Philadelphia, PA: North American Publishing Company, 19177); and *Cameraready*, prepared by the Cameraready Corporation (Box 5812, Pasadena, CA, 1973), proved invaluable in this employer's search for competence as a production manager.

You won't need to typeset, pasteup, or design your work. But you should be knowledgeable enough about what the typesetters, the graphics department, and the designers in the in-house printing plant do, so that you won't be asking them to do the impossible — and so that you will be appreciative of the talents they bring to your work.

WORD-PROCESSING EQUIPMENT

New terms have crept into our language these past few years, among them *word processing*. Although we have been "processing" words since the time of the caveman who painted his images on stone, until recently we simply "typed a report," "wrote a letter," "prepared an abstract," or "dictated a memo" — without considering that we were processing words. Still, you should become familiar with the new terminology that has been introduced into the language with the advent of the high-technology era. A word processor can be a machine or a person (the one who operates the machine — sometimes called a "document copier"). You may even become a "word originator" or "document originator" in time (the person who dictates or in some fashion feeds the information to the word processor — the person or machine). We authors are both word originators and word processors, because we processed this chapter through a computer with a program called WordStar. But we're getting ahead of ourselves.

Typewriters

Realizing how fast technology is growing, we discussed this project with a representative of an office equipment firm and asked him, "What should we tell our readers about office machines?" Surprisingly, he replied, "Tell them *first* to learn how to type." That's sound advice, but some of you may think it an unnecessary skill. Still, consider this. When you become an executive with a firm, there will be times when you must know something about the equipment used to produce your letters and reports. The members of your support staff will usually work a thirty-five-hour week. You may find yourself some evening or weekend needing to correct a typo in a report that has to be in the mail that day or evening. If you can at least go to the typewriter, load the paper, perhaps change the ribbon, and use the typewriter's correcting feature, your problem is no longer a problem.

And there are other advantages too. Some of you will find yourself at a desk with a word processor or computer terminal at your elbow. Although you don't need the skills of an expert typist to use one of these, you will need to know the basics of the typewriter keyboard.

But what kind of typewriters are you likely to encounter? To count them is impossible. There are manual typewriters (slowly becoming an endangered species), electric typewriters, electric correcting typewriters, electronic, memory, electric selectric, intelligent, mag-card, disk, and many other models of typewriters on the market today. By the time this book is published, there will no doubt be many others.

Most of you know what an electric typewriter is. But what's the difference between an electric and an electronic typewriter? Most electronic typewriters have some capacity for storage — that is, retaining in memory frequently used words and phrases, paragraphs, even pages. A typical example of the kind of firm that would have use for an electronic typewriter is a law or insurance firm. Many of the documents such a firm prepares use the same phrasing over and over again. So the firm prepares on its electronic equipment segments that can be called up any time they are needed. Having such segments on hand is not only faster and therefore more efficient for the person preparing the documents, it also reduces proofing time.

A memory typewriter, for example, retains (in the machine, on tape) as many as 100 pages of material. The mag-card typewriter has unlimited retention, since the material is recorded on magnetic cards. These mag-cards are stored outside the machine and retained for future use. The mag-card typewriter uses the same principle as the tape recorder many of you own. The disk typewriter also has unlimited retention, recording on magnetic disks instead of cards.

All the new typewriters on the market today offer the advantages of more than one type style (accomplished by changing type elements or daisy wheels) and spacing options (elite, pica, proportional, and sometimes condensed) at the simple flick of a switch.

Today companies are developing voice-activated typewriters. Many of you will encounter them in your future offices — probably sooner than you expect. The primary drawback of development has been, of course, the difficulty of programming the machine to recognize the various dialects we encounter in a country as diverse as ours. How, for example, will a machine interpret the Bostonian's remark that he is "going to paak his cah" or the Southerner who is talking about how much he should pay his "hard ha-und." However, technology will, no doubt, conquer these problems. It is easy to see why there is such excitement and interest in the growing field of office automation.

Automated Office Systems

Automated office systems usually fall under one of two categories: (1) word processors with data processing capabilities, and (2) dedicated word processors. The categories are easily defined from their names. A word processor with data processing capabilities is capable of manipulating both words and data. The dedicated word processor is capable of manipulating only words. You could not, for example, set up files in a dedicated word processor and have the data in those files manipulated for reports, financial information, and so on. Nor could it be used for record keeping.

These systems are much more complex than any of the typewriters discussed earlier, but they are also more flexible and faster than typewriters. Most of them have some kind of printer attached to them. So while the secretary types the second page of a document the system can print the proofed first page. These systems are great timesavers, and in a firm that has a lot of paperwork they are fast becoming a necessity. (Some secretaries now insist on them as a prerequisite to accepting a position.)

Let's look at the speed and versatility of a few of the automated office systems to get an idea of their time-saving qualities. Most good typists can type between sixty and eighty words per minute, but an IBM mag-card composer prints 9½ cps (characters-per-second); the IBM mag-card typewriter 15½ cps; and the IBM Office System 6/450 prints 95 cps. The mag-card composer and mag-card typewriters are dedicated word processors. The office system is a word processor with limited data-processing capabilities. (A word about the differences between a mag-card composer and the mag-card typewriter: the composer uses type *fonts;* the typewriter uses typewriter *elements.* You'll read more about their differences in the section on typesetting equipment.)

All three of the automated office systems described in the previous paragraph offer great flexibility in composing; for example, you can take a paragraph from one page and insert it elsewhere, on the same or another page.

But it takes more manipulating — re-recording, and so on — to do that at either the mag-card composer or the mag-card typewriter (with external storage media) than it does at the office system (which has internal storage). With the system, for example, you have only to code a "block-and-save" and then a "get." With the punch of two or three buttons your sentence, paragraph, or page is moved, magically, from one point to another.

Here are just a few examples of the benefits of an automated office system, whether it is called a dedicated word processor, a word processor with data-processing capabilities, or a computer.

Suppose you are working with a large insurance firm that needs to notify its Midwest policyholders about a rate increase for automobile insurance because of the high accident rate in the metropolitan areas. By doing the following at your automated office system, your task is quickly and efficiently accomplished. (The terms used to identify these operations are IBM terms. They can be compared to the terms used by other systems, terms like "open a document," "edit a document," "mail merge," "print a file," "global search," "search and replace," and so on.)

Text Task. With the automated office system you would first prepare the letter announcing the rate increase. After it has been prepared, proofed, revised, and stored, you would then decide to whom the letter should go.

MergeFile/Text Task. Then you open your data file and "qualify" (identify) those people who are to receive the letter: policyholders in certain zip-code areas, for example. With a few instructions, generally requiring only a minute or two, the machine would print out personalized letters and addressed envelopes to those within the zip-code areas selected, no matter how many thousands of names are in the complete file. All of this can be done by the system, while you and other workers go on to other projects.

Search and Count. Perhaps you need to know how many policyholders in your file have $50,000 or less of personal liability insurance because you think this is inadequate protection. The system can tell you not only how many policyholders you have who fit this description (so you can order the quantity of brochures or letters you need), but it can tell you also who and where they are and how much of this kind of insurance they currently carry, all in a matter of minutes.

Output File. In our offices we edit and publish two magazines four times a year. Before automation, one record of the articles published was kept by our office manager and another was kept by our editor. The editor used his to keep track of when an article was published and who wrote it. The office manager kept one for the indexes published once a year. The editor's was a hand-written record — very sound logically but time-consuming and subject to human error.

The office manager's record consisted of four color-coded cards, one for each category of index (author/title, title/author, keyword, and book review). On three of these were recorded the name of the author(s), title of the article, volume, number, pages, and name of the journal in which the article was published. The fourth card was used to record information about the book reviews in the journals. Using a mag-card typewriter, it wasn't too difficult to prepare these four cards for each article. But when it was time to publish the index, the information had to be retyped — four times — at the mag-card composer. So the office manager's record, too, was time-consuming (and no less subject to human error).

Now the information is typed into the system once. The office manager can put out that file in any format desired: hard copy (paper) for the editor's working manuscript file, onto mag cards to be fed into the mag-card composer for the four categories of indexes published, in alphabetical or numerical order by author or title — and the keyboard is never touched a second time.

Figures 26.1 illustrates some of the many materials now being handled by some automated office systems with data management capabilities.

The advantages of the automated office are endless and exciting. In spite of the debate that still rages between warring factions, the evidence is in that

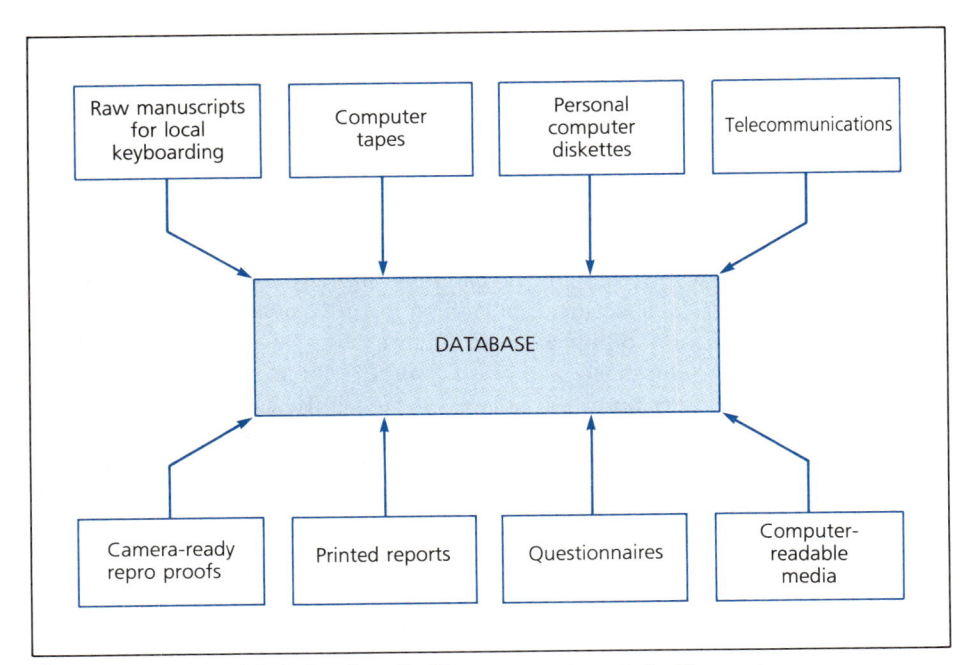

Figure 26.1. Materials being handled by some automated office systems

what we were once calling the office of 1990 has become the office of today. According to Larry Lynett, a noted management consultant, "The major thrust of office automation is actually directed toward management and professional/technical staffs. This is the level that has the most potential for realizing billions of dollars in savings through increased productivity." So more and more, the executive is going to have to cope with the spectrum of an automated office system on his or her desk, whether it is a word processor or a computer terminal.

Be consoled. There is nothing mysterious about using these systems. A logical mind and willing spirit will prevail. In the fourth chapter of his recent book, *Writing With a Word Processor* (Harper & Row, 1983), William Zinsser lists four blocks to learning to use such equipment:

1. Fear of loss (manuscript, the report, data, and so on).
2. Snobbery of liberal-arts types who don't understand science or technology and don't want to.
3. Conversely, the arrogance of those whose bent is for science and technology who think they don't have to bother to learn how to write clear English.
4. The typing block.

Zinsser's book is a delight to read, and we certainly call it required reading for anyone contemplating using a word processor. He described a "flurry of mishaps" in his first month not unlike those experienced by the majority of novice users when the automated office system is first introduced into their operations.

Typesetting Equipment

Today, companies are increasingly installing equipment that permits in-house typesetting. In addition to the so-called composers now on the market, many vendors are marketing devices that can work with a company's existing word-processing equipment. The possibilities are expanding so rapidly that we cannot attempt to describe them all to you. Be aware of the difference between your common typewriter or office system and typesetting equipment. They operate similarly, a few commands being the only variance. A typewriter and the more common office system use the same amount of space for each character (with the exception of proportional-spacing typewriters). Typesetting equipment uses "units" to measure characters: for example, the letter m uses nine units; an a five units; while an i requires only three. Lines are measured in picas rather than inches. (Six picas equal an inch.)

In-house typesetting becomes even more popular in times of recession because it is more economical than sending printing out to a firm specializing in that type of work. One production manager estimates, for example, that by using "strike-on" equipment she can typeset, proof, and prepare a cameraready page for from $4 to $7.50 (depending on factors like the complexity of the material, size of type and page, and including hidden overhead charges). Those same pages cost from $8 to $15 from a freelance typesetter and from $12 to $20 from a commercial printer; that's from two to three times what it costs to set it in-house.

In addition to the strike-on equipment described above, rapidly appearing in the marketplace today are small, relatively inexpensive systems that combine with computers to produce the typesetting needs of small business offices.

What if your company doesn't have any typesetting equipment but does have a word-processing system? With the use of microcomputers, another alternative to in-house typesetting is being offered by several companies. In many localities, those desiring typesetting services just call a local phone number and transmit (via modem and telephone line) formatted files that are converted to finished typesetting on the same or next day. To use such a service, users need a computer and an editing or word-processing program that can produce sequential files and store them on tape or disk. They also need a modem (telephone hookup) and transmission software that can communicate as a terminal and transmit previously stored files over the phone.

The potential behind typesetting output from a company's data storage is discussed further in "Late News on WP/Typesetting Interfaces," a special report from the National Association of Printers and Lithographers (NAPL), 780 Palisade Avenue, Teaneck, NJ 07666. The report points out trends that are combining to make word processor/typesetter interfaces desirable and accessible.

Shown in Figure 26.2 is one manufacturer's answer to an in-house publishing system that is to word processing what word processing was to the manual typewriter. It consists of forty-two distinct components, both hardware and software, from different manufacturers running under one operating system. The system integrates the cutting edge of word and graphic publishing into a single, easy-to-use system.

Computers

The subject of computers is difficult to more than highlight for you because the computer market is changing so rapidly that even the best sales representative has a hard time keeping abreast. When computers were first introduced, they were very large, delicate, and extremely expensive machines. These were called mainframe computers and were housed in their own rooms and needed whole departments for maintenance and service. Although the mainframe computers are still very much in use throughout the country, they are being challenged by today's microcomputers. (There are three classifications of computers: mainframe, mini, and micro.) The one that is enjoying a

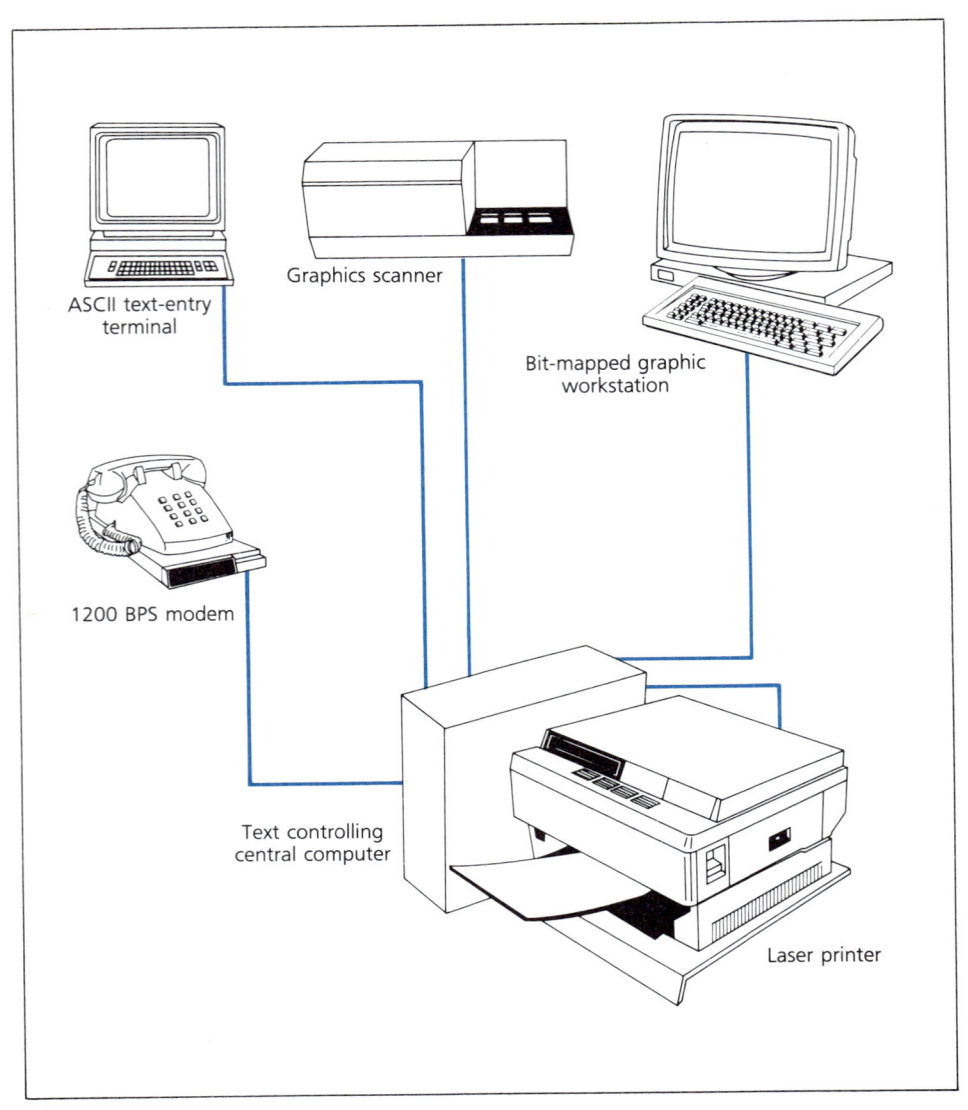

Figure 26.2. In-house publishing system integrating word-processing, typesetting, and printing

boom today is the microcomputer. This is also described as a personal or a small business computer, depending on which manufacturer you're dealing with.

A microcomputer sits right on your desk. It is small, relatively low-priced, and easy to use — once the user comprehends that a computer is simple-minded. In addition, some of these new computers contain as much computing power as the huge, isolated mainframe of years ago. The world of microcomputers is expanding rapidly to include most businesses and almost every profession. Computers give a real advantage to those people whose jobs are planning, decision-making, or organizing the vital records for a business. Today, a businessperson who is not planning to use some form of computing is in danger of falling behind the competition.

The Administrative Management Society reports that "until a few years ago small business [micro] computers were used strictly for data processing, and word processing was handled by a separate system. . . . Today, small business computers can handle both functions."

In addition to performing word-processing functions, a computer can handle most of the complex filing and correspondence, as well as the accounting, recordkeeping, bookkeeping, and list-sorting tasks that confront us at home and in the office.

Microcomputers offer the advantage of low prices, starting often at less than $500. Thousands of software packages are now available for them. However, prices go up depending upon the amount of memory needed, the number of software packages required, the amount of disk storage that is added, and the type of screen and accessories purchased. What starts out as under $1,000 may add up ultimately to a $5,000 or $6,000 package by the time the system is fully equipped.

With a computer you will also want a printer, and these also come in various price ranges. The least expensive ones (dot-matrix printers) sell for as little as $450. Letter-quality printers can sell for as much as $5,000. Laser and ink-jet printers are selling for as little as $850 and as much as $110,000. Not only do these printers vary greatly in price, they also vary considerably in quality of print, speed, and versatility.

Large businesses will usually hire a consultant to help them decide what type of system they need to fulfill their requirements. The consultant is paid to research the company's operations and then recommend the software needed (the programs that make the computer work) and the hardware (the equipment) required to support the software programs chosen. Small businesses will need to do a lot of research and shopping before making any decision as to (1) the software needed, (2) the classification (probably micro or mini), and (3) the brand of computer to purchase. While there are about thirty brands of copiers, twenty brands of typewriters, and sixty brands of dictation equipment on the market today, there are thousands of software packages to choose from and probably 250 or 300 brands of hardware out there in the marketplace. From an economic standpoint, the company's first purchase should be one that will serve the company well both now and over the long haul. If you are asked to help decide on what to buy, do your homework well. Ask yourself these questions:

1. What does the company want to do with a computer? Maintain customer lists? Perform payroll, bookkeeping, inventory, record-keeping functions? Do word processing?
2. Will the computer need to work with other computers? in branch offices? on-site?
3. How much storage capacity should it have?
4. Will it need communications capabilities?
5. Can the computer be upgraded as the company's needs grow?
6. Should it have multi-tasking, multi-user capabilities?
7. Will the brands of computers under consideration support the software packages you have chosen?
8. What technical assistance will potential users be given?

Many microcomputers are today offered complete with four or five software programs. Others require that you purchase software in addition to the terminal. Although the so-called bundled packages offer a substantial savings for the potential buyer, the savings will disappear if upon examination you find that the software packages are unsuitable for your operations. That is why a reliable dealer or consultant will recommend that you first choose your software and then find the hardware to support it!

The computer can be a valuable management tool, but it must be handled skillfully for the best results. The success of any computer system lies first in the establishment of proper controls for the purchase of such systems and, second, in the technical assistance potential users will be given. The second requirement may be easier said than done.

The user's manuals that come with computers are the worst we've ever read. Most of them assume prior knowledge of computers and lead the reader through their maze of instructions with unintelligible jargon. Further, getting employees to accept training on any new high-tech device may be more difficult than you expect.

Lura K. Romei, editor of *Modern Office Technology*, says: "There's a real 'optimism/pessimism gap' regarding the relentless march of technology into the workplace." On the one hand there are those who foresee the modern equivalent of sweatshops, where workers will become mere extensions of the machinery. On the other, there are those like Paul Strassman, a vice president of Xerox, who claims that the boost in productivity provided by technology will create more jobs and make those jobs more enjoyable.

So even when a conversion to computers has been based on technological facts and established needs, employees may not accept the change because they fear that it will affect their social relationships or status or security. Alvin Toffler, author and futurist, maintains that many technology-related problems can be avoided if we make "a massive investment — whether government, private, or a combination — in training, retraining, and reculturing."

The Least You Should Know About Office Machines

Fast replacing the personal (or small-business) computer, which normally supports only one operator at a time, is the mini system, designed to support many users. These are generally described as multi-user systems. They can be "local area network" (LAN) systems, which allow employees to use equipment to send and receive internal messages within the same office building or within a radius of from five to ten miles. There are also multi-user, multi-tasking systems that also support many users but in addition allow those users to share the same software. A system of this kind is shown in Figure 26.3.

It was predictable that the competition among computer and software designers would result in the proliferation of "terminals that don't work to-

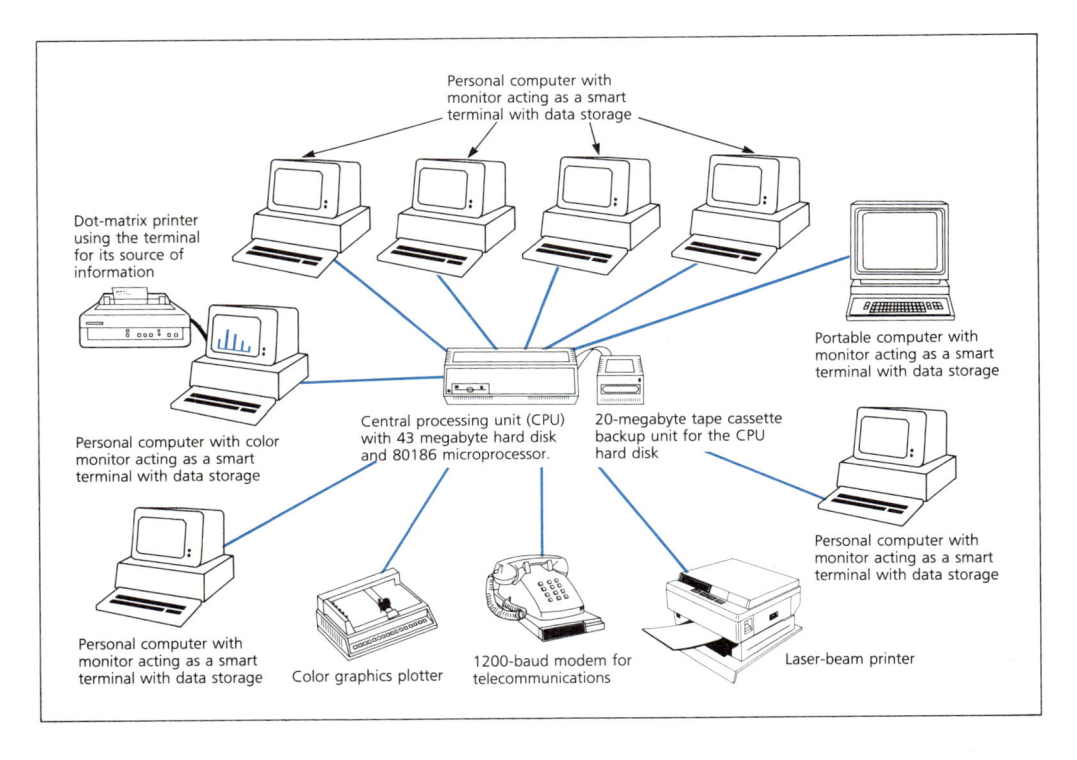

Figure 26.3. Multi-user, multi-tasking system

gether, equipment that's incompatible, hordes of suppliers each peddling a unique and distinctive system, a profusion of protocols, and a battle for the desk," according to the editor of *Modern Office Technology*. At maturity, the computer industry will offer universality: networks that can communicate with any type of personal computer, and different networks that will be able to communicate with ease. Some manufacturers have already seen the writing on the wall and are offering such compatibility now. Others are still in the battle for control of the field by guaranteeing a market through incompatibility and exclusivity. Until it becomes clear that universality is to everyone's benefit, the admonition to "shop wisely" should not go unheeded by those with purchasing power.

Dictation Equipment

A national survey conducted by the Administrative Management Society found that eighty percent of 360 companies had at least one type of dictation system in use, and many had more than one type available for their employees. In *Office Automation and Word Processing Fundamentals* (NY: Harper and Row, 1983), Shirley A. Waterhouse states that: "Improved features and a greater emphasis on machine dictation training will result in an increase in the use of machine dictation . . . a 75 percent increase in the use of machine dictation is expected over the next several years."

Three types of dictation equipment are commonly used: portable units, desktop machines, and central dictating systems that use a telephone dial-up or direct-wire handset to a central recorder. Dictation equipment is, in our opinion, an essential part of any office. It is a real booster of productivity.

Many secretaries take shorthand, but using shorthand means that two persons' time is being taken up for dictation: the dictator's and the transcriber's. In 1984 the cost of a business letter dictated face-to-face rose to nine or ten dollars, according to the Dartnell Corporation, a Chicago-based company specializing in training, communication, and personnel relations materials for business. The same letter transcribed by the use of dictation equipment represents a twenty-five percent savings over the face-to-face dictation and transcription method. The wise manager will therefore learn to use dictating equipment. The secretary can go about other tasks while the manager is dictating — a great timesaver for both.

Earlier we mentioned central dictation systems. Figure 26.4 explains some ways they can aid you in your dictation.

Many instructors of business communication are now realizing the need for their students to have dictation skills. If your instructor hasn't yet familiarized you with dictation equipment, ask about the possibility of a field trip to one of the offices in your community, or perhaps even on your own campus, where this (and sometimes most of the other equipment we've talked about)

The Least You Should Know About Office Machines 409

CENTRAL DICTATION SYSTEMS ALLOW YOU TO:

Start-stop-pause.	Dialing (or touching) a designated digit after gaining access to the system enables you to begin dictating, stop for a moment, start again.
Give special instructions.	These might be to insert something; ask for special formats, such as indenting, listing, or extra spacing; correct or delete something already dictated — whatever you want to tell the secretary.
Review the last few words.	You can rewind the tape or backspace the disk a little to hear what you just said. You'll get the last ten or twelve words. Sometimes you need that in order to decide what to say next. This feature is helpful in case of brief interruptions.
End a document.	With disk equipment each new document should begin on a new disk. Dialing a designated number ejects the disk you have been using and feeds in a new one. With tape equipment you can put a "privacy lock" on whatever you have finished, then no one else can play back your dictation. (Neither can you.) Dial again to continue dictating.
Rewind.	With tape equipment you can rewind to the very beginning of your dictation. With most disk equipment, you will have to call the attendant (sometimes called the "key operator") if you want an extensive review.
Listen.	You can do this with tape equipment after rewinding or fast forwarding.
Fast forward.	With tape equipment, use this command to get back to where you want to be.
Stop.	With this you can stop or pause longer than you can by using the start-stop-pause option.

Figure 26.4. The advantages of central dictation systems

is being used. If possible, your instructor might make some of this equipment available so that you could turn in one or more of your assignments on cassette.

Some instructors of business communication have reported success with an assignment that requires their students to dictate an assignment into a cassette tape recorder. The instructor then evaluates the assignment by returning a cassette of his or her comments to the student. The students thus get the opportunity to dictate and transcribe from this one assignment.

If you are attending a college that has a skills department — once called the Business Education Department — perhaps your dictated assignment could be transcribed in that department and returned to you with a critique from the transcriber. At the very least, you can sit down with a tape recorder and practice both dictating and transcribing what you have dictated. You'll be surprised by what you learn. In Appendix D, "Nice to Know," we've touched upon some of the methods you can employ to help you become a good dictator.

MISCELLANEOUS MACHINES

Of course there are other machines in the modern office than those touched on in this chapter. There are postage meters, calculators, collators, paper shredders, overhead projectors, and so on. A casual cruise through the most recent issues of *Modern Office Technology* finds described in their "Horizons" section such new technology as:

1. An automated records management system that can retrieve images from microfilm, microfiche, paper, aperture cards, and optical disk systems — and then send the electronic image of the document to the appropriate requesting station.
2. A copy editing machine that when connected to a plain paper copier, can delete text, trim unwanted copy, box, reverse, center, or transfer a given section of a document without making any changes to the original. All of the changes are done electronically in the copier.
3. An educated scanner that can convert typewritten pages, printed matter, drawings, photographs, and other visual matter into electronic files either in graphic form or as ASCII (American Standard Code for Information Interchange) data.
4. A compact self-contained microprocessor system that cuts lines of type from 24 to 192 points in size (¼ inch to 2 inches) from adhesive-backed colored vinyl, allowing sign making and lettering to be easy and convenient.
5. An overhead projector in a box 4¼ inches high, 13 inches wide, and 16½ inches deep. The folded projector weighs fifteen pounds and fits under the seat of an airplane.

6. A so-called intelligent document-filing machine that is as easy to use as an office copier. Image files can store up to ninety-eight documents, and, unlike ordinary fiche, can update original files.
7. An integrated voice/data workstation that combines the capabilities of advanced telecommunications and powerful desktop computers. The processor can run at either 7.14 megahertz or 4.77 megahertz; the lower speed allows the workstation to run IBM-PC compatible software.
8. A solid-state digital voice storage device designed to make the telephone receptionist's job easier by allowing the recording and playback of the company salutation. Once the salutation is recorded, it can be repeatedly played back so there is no verbal stumbling. Once the greeting is played, the operator takes over.
9. A copyboard that takes your ideas off the board and puts them on paper. It makes crisp multiple copies of notes, diagrams, equations — anything you write on the board — in seconds.

Our final advice, then, is: In your first weeks on the job acquaint yourself with all the departments with which you will deal. Show an interest in what the employees in those departments do, how they benefit the company, and how they may some day be of assistance to you. No matter how far down the corporate ladder a person's job may be, his or her contributions to the overall health of an organization cannot be minimized. Nothing is quite so appreciated by colleagues and fellow workers than your interest in and appreciation for the work they do.

EXERCISES

1. In this chapter you will find several terms that are special to high technology and are probably new to you. Using a dictionary or a user's manual for the machines described in this chapter, define ten of them. Then assume that you and a friend have decided after graduation to go into partnership in a small business (you decide what type of business). The two of you have been wondering just what amount of capital you will need to have in order to ensure success while you are building the business. Part of that capital will be spent for equipment. In a short, informal report that uses the ten terms you have chosen to define, describe to your partner what you consider to be the minimum amount of equipment you will need to get started in your business.

2. In 150 words or fewer, describe to your instructor what you envision your first job after graduation will be. What will your duties be? Which office equipment do you visualize yourself using?

3. Now assume that you are the purchasing agent for a small but growing company that up till now has had only electric typewriters for the secretaries in the front office to use. The business has been growing steadily, and with that growth the secretaries' tasks have multiplied, making the typewriters inefficient. The owner of the company has asked you to investigate other possibilities: electronic typewriters, a word-processing system, even computerization. After a thorough review of this chapter (and perhaps after a visit to a local office equipment store) make your recommendations to the owner in a memo report.

4. Assume the role of the in-house printing manager of your company. See if you can find copies of *Graphics Master, Complete Guide to Pasteup,* and *Cameraready* (see page 397 for bibliographic information) in your college library. (If the library doesn't have them, perhaps the printing services department of your college or the public library do.) Using the information in one of those references, describe to your subordinate one of the following:
- **a.** How to estimate type.
- **b.** How to enhance a publication page with a border that has four rounded corners.
- **c.** How to determine the percentage of reduction or enlargement of original copy.
- **d.** How to crop a photo or plate.

5. You are the executive development officer of your company. You know that there are at least two economic reasons for an executive to use dictating equipment. Yet in your company there are employees who have resisted all your efforts to get them to use the central dictation system. Write a persuasive memo to all employees (you cannot single out the resistant ones) describing the system and its benefits to both the company and to the employees, offering to train those who have little or no knowledge or experience with such equipment.

6. Your company has a small computer system with an inexpensive dot-matrix printer. You think this is adequate for in-house documents; however, you would like to see the external documents leave the company in letter quality. Visit a local computer and word processor retail store and choose three models to evaluate: these can be dot-matrix, daisy-wheel, laser, or ink-jet. There are several possibilities. However, your choices must consider compatibility. Choose three from your assumed knowledge of the system the company now uses. Then describe, in ranked order, to your superior in the company the models you would recommend for purchase. What are their differences? Explain them. (Perhaps you can design a table that will point out some of the more important features of each printer you choose to evaluate.)

The following questions (or descriptions) can be answered in only a paragraph or two. Your instructor will tell you what format your answers should take and who your audience should be.

7. Describe two inexpensive ways of reproducing a report or memo that must be distributed to more than twenty people.

8. Describe the differences between data processing and word processing. If you are not yet familiar with these terms, do some investigation on your own — this chapter has not gone deeply into the question.

9. What are the primary differences between electric and electronic typewriters?

10. What is an overhead projector? What are its uses? in the classroom? in your future job or profession?

11. What is the definition of a word processor?

12. Why should an executive be knowledgeable about office equipment?

13. What does *unlimited memory* mean? Which office machines offer unlimited memory?

14. William Zinsser described four blocks to learning word processing. What are they? Do you think he is right?

15. What are the primary differences between typescript and typeset print?

16. Why is in-house typesetting preferred in times of recession?

17. Why do employees resist change? How would you react if your instructor told you tomorrow that an assignment had to be prepared at a computer terminal or on word-processing equipment? Would you be intimidated? resentful? curious? excited about learning something new? Now assume that you are being interviewed for a position with a firm you would really like to work for. The recruiter says to you: "Oh, by the way. Our employees use small desktop computer terminals to maintain their sales records, customer files, and so on. Are you familiar with computers?" You are not. Answer the recruiter's question.

APPENDIX A

Extra Problems

Problem A.1

THE CASE OF THE CONSCIENTIOUS NURSE

Joe Adams had been Hospital Administrator about a month. It was a good hospital and Joe was settling in to his job with relish. All was going well until the head of the dietetics department spotted him Monday morning.

"Joe, you must do something about these nurses making up special trays for patients. They are coming into the kitchen area constantly and it's disrupting! Can you have the Director of Nurses put out an order that the nurses are to stay out of the kitchen area?"

Joe questioned the head nurse about the matter and was told that the dietetic department had recently refused to change some patients' diets. The head of the dietetic staff had instituted a policy that no lunch menus would be changed after 11:00 A.M. Physicians often visit patients between 11:00 and noon, and because of the dietetic department's new policy, and because new diets are sometimes requested by the physicians during that interval, the only alternative was for the nurses to attend to the matter personally.

What should Joe do?

Issue a memo outlining the course of action to be taken by the appropriate managerial personnel.

Problem A.2

ORDERS AND ACKNOWLEDGEMENTS, NO. 2

You are the sales manager of the American Historical and Commemorative Society, a publisher of books. What you produce and sell is of interest to private individuals as well as to school, public, and private libraries. These are expensive, well-printed, and authentic books on a variety of subjects — all of which relate to the history of the United States.

One of the recent publications from the Society is a set of three books on the American Revolution that, because of the recent Bicentennial emphasis, was quite popular. One of the books in the set emphasized the political, one the military, and one the economic aspects of our country's growth. All three contained a number of color pictures, as well as black and white pictures and drawings. The cost of the boxed set was $29.95, including postage.

Because of the quality of these books, they were sold out within eight months and a contract was made for reprinting. Inflation and other factors were at work, however; and the new price will have to be $35.95 plus postage. Shipping date will be no later than ninety days from the date of your letter.

Prepare a letter that can be individually typed on word processing equipment to explain the situation to those who have written to order the set at the old price. Offer the individuals the opportunity to confirm the order at the new price and tell them when the new shipping date will be. (If the order is not reconfirmed, there will be no shipment.) This may be a disappointment to some because of the increase in price, the delay in delivery, or both, so be tactful. Emphasize the quality of the product in order to retain customer goodwill.

Problem A.3

COLLECTIONS NOS. 3 & 4

Evaluate the following collection letter for organization, language, tone, and personal emphasis. Then write an effective solution to the placement office's problem.

Dear Graduate:

We wrote you soon after graduation, more than two weeks ago, requesting that you complete and return a form like the attached one. So far we have not received this information.

We would appreciate your completing and returning the attached form by return mail. This information is very helpful to the placement office in planning, participating in salary surveys, getting employers to visit the campus for the next class of graduates, for department information, and to help those who are employed after graduation.

It is expensive to have to write some graduates more than once and we are spending your money (taxpayer's). We would appreciate your cooperation.

Cordially yours,

Problem A.4

INQUIRIES, REPLIES, AND REQUESTS, NO. 5

Joseph Ragland received his monthly statement from the medical clinic where his daughter was examined. He noticed that the clinic had overcharged him $5 for a test that had not been performed, and he notified the clinic in writing about the overcharge. In a few days, he received this reply:

Dear Mr. Ragland:

We received your note with your recent October statement. We regret that you feel it is your prerogative to set the fee for our services.

We think this is an unusual procedure; however, we will adjust your account for the remaining $5 balance rather than incur the additional expense of keeping your account.

Yours very truly,

Jason Hobbs, Administrator

1. Evaluate the effectiveness of this letter for the following characteristics: (1) tone, (2) reader impact, (3) goodwill, (4) word choice, (5) mechanics, and (6) organization.

2. Rewrite the letter in a more effective and acceptable manner.

Problem A.5

PHOENIX POOLS, INC.

Phoenix Pools, Inc. officials decide to try writing sales letters in addition to using newspaper advertising. For the sales letter trial, they plan to obtain names of those families (within the company's sales radius) securing building permits, a list of names that currently has been running over 2,000 a month. The mailing will consist of a processed sales letter, a two-page, four-color descriptive brochure, and a postage-paid reply card.

Here are some features:

- wide choice of pool designs
- color harmonies for pool and equipment

- automatic filter and backwash
- automatic pool cleaner
- automatic pool heater; solar heater also available
- automatic chlorinator; recharge three times a year
- pool deck and coping in choice of color
- five-year guarantee on equipment
- lifetime structural guarantee
- financing plans available; up to seven years to pay
- prices start at $2,050
- buy now and have ready for use in 30 days
- plan landscaping with the pool
- wide selection of pool accessories (diving board, slide, flexible or rigid cover, vacuum)
- pool service contracts available at $15 a month

With these features you will fill in the details and analysis needed to persuade your prospects. Even though your letter will go to a list of good prospects, tailor your letter to talk to one reader. Be careful how you handle reference to children because you have no way of knowing which prospect has children. A careless reference may work against you.

Remember, to convince your reader, you must give details and picture the reader in action and in terms of some benefit to him or her. Don't just give physical descriptions. Determine what one feature is most likely to induce the reader to buy and build your letter around this theme. Further, even though you've enclosed a folder, don't just hand it to the prospect; you need to point out the important aspects and interpret it.

The purpose of your letter is to get your prospect to return the card naming a time a representative may discuss the prospect's needs and quote him a price. Write the letter.

Problem A.6

TEXCOM COMPANY

You are employed as office manager of the Texcom Company, which has approximately 100 office workers. It has been called to your attention that numerous office employees are using office supplies (stationery, envelopes, stamps, and so on) for their personal use. In addition, employees are using the WATS telephone line to make personal telephone calls. Write a memorandum to all office workers explaining the problems and the consequences if these practices continue. Caution: Think through very carefully the results you wish to achieve and wish to avoid with your memo.

Problem A.7

IN SEARCH OF THE SUCCESSFUL

You are a researcher for the Life Insurance Agency Management Association. Mr. Rigby Hawthorne is Director of Ordinary Agencies for the Western Home Office of the Megalaharlitan Life Insurance Company of America. A month ago he came to your organization with a problem, and you were assigned to the case.

Mr. Hawthorne's company is plagued with the same problem that faces other life insurance companies: high turnover of agents. Their retention rate has been averaging about eleven percent for those agents remaining with the company for more than three years.

He wished, therefore, that you would do a study on the importance of certain factors to the eventual success or failure of life insurance agents. Typically, the industry has recognized three major influences upon the productivity of such agents: selection, training, and supervision. The former is that upon which he expects you to concentrate.

The other two influences will be held constant in the following ways. All agents in your sample will have been exposed to the same precontract orientation (that is, training program). Then the retention rates of the supervisors of your sample agents will be studied. Those agents supervised by managers with either extremely high or low retention rates will be eliminated from your study.

Other restrictions placed upon your sample will be as follows: All agents will be male Caucasians who have had no previous experience selling life insurance. All of them also will have been contracted under the same financing arrangements.

You and Mr. Hawthorne jointly decided upon the following criteria for judging whether an agent was to be considered a success or a failure. A success remained with the company and either reached his sales quota for the first two years or was promoted to a supervisory position. A failure either left the industry or failed to reach his preassigned quota during both of his first two years with the company. Agents who had joined another insurance company and those who had reached their quota only one of their first two years were excluded from the sample.

Considering these restrictions, you were able to gather data on 932 agents hired by Mr. Hawthorne's home office from January 1970 to December 1971. According to the above criteria, 168 have proven successful, while 764 have failed. Judgment and availability of information determined the factors upon which data is presented in the following tables. All of this information pertains to the agents at the time of their application.

	Number Hired	Number Successful
AGE		
Under 25	373	47
25-29	280	38
30-35	93	36
36-39	46	17
40-45	75	15
over 45	65	15
MARITAL STATUS		
Single	186	23
Married	522	109
Divorced (or separated)	168	25
Widowed	56	11
LIVING QUARTERS		
Rent Furnished Rooms	93	17
Rent Apartment	205	34
Rent House	186	28
Own Home (mortgaged)	298	55
Own Home (clear)	103	29
Other	47	5
EDUCATION		
Less than HS Grad	0	0
HS Grad	65	10
Some College	280	45
College Grad	447	96
Graduate Training	140	17
LIFE INSURANCE OWNED		
$ 0-10,000	392	59
10,001-20,000	149	27
20,001-30,000	140	22
30,001-40,000	130	27
40,001 & over	121	33
ASSETS (excluding life insurance) LESS AMOUNT OWED		
$ 9- 5,000	261	47
5,001-10,000	112	18
10,001-15,000	177	30
15,001-20,000	186	32
20,001 & over	196	41
INDEBTEDNESS		
$ 0- 1,000	252	45
1,001- 5,000	261	55
5,001-10,000	233	40
10,001 & over	186	28

	Number Hired	Number Successful
MONTHLY INCOME FROM LAST JOB		
under 500	140	27
500-599	186	33
600-699	280	46
700-799	121	21
800 & over	205	41
EMPLOYMENT STATUS		
Student	177	28
Self-Employed	56	11
Unemployed	364	51
Full-time (employed)	270	58
Other and part-time job	65	10
NUMBER OF FULL-TIME JOBS HELD IN THE TEN YEARS PRIOR TO BEING HIRED BY MEGALAHARLITAN		
0	261	39
1	140	25
2	308	69
3	130	22
4 or more	93	13

Write a report to Mr. Hawthorne on the results of your study.

Problem A.8

SALES NO. 2

Your job is with the advertising department of a foreign car importing firm. Beginning three months ago, your firm began offering on a test-market basis a small car that is made in Germany and has an electric power mechanism. The car is extremely quiet, comfortable, and economical. It can be recharged at night with an extension cord plugged into any wall outlet. It takes about the same amount of electricity as two 110-watt bulbs to recharge the car and will run approximately eighty miles without recharging. It is ideal for in-town driving. Your research indicated that the average family drives about thirty-eight miles a day.

Your company discovered while test marketing the product that what seemed to clinch a sale was an actual test drive by the prospective buyer. As a result of your finding, you plan to promote the test-drive idea by offering prospective buyers a gift if they will visit the nearest dealer and try the car.

Extra Problems 421

Create a name for the car, decide on the type of gift that would be effective, and compose a sales letter that you feel would be effective in getting the desired action.

Problem A.9

INQUIRIES, REPLIES, AND REQUESTS, NO. 3

The William Penn Salt Company, located in Devil's Haven, Pennsylvania, has established an underground storage facility that can be used by business, government, education, and other groups for storage and safekeeing of documents. This area has controlled temperature and humidity and is located some 500 feet underground, which is safe from almost all factors (including nuclear attacks) that can damage or destroy documents.

The facility has been in operation for almost six years and has had a rather good history of success. It is located just eighteen miles from Philadelphia; and with its highly systematized locater system, the operators can locate and send most documents to a firm in Philadelphia in less than forty-eight hours — including the delivery time. The storage charge is minimal; the document search and delivery charge is competitive and equitable.

Obviously, because certain documents must be retained for as long as seven years, and others "forever," the need for document storage space is great. Furthermore, rent in Philadelphia is high; and such document storage is a nonproductive business operation. Inexpensive storage, therefore, is a much desired commodity.

As a student at Salt Creek State University, write to the Document Storage Facility of the William Penn Salt Company and ask whether your class in Administrative Management may visit the facility and have a guided tour. Inquire about the appropriate date and time, parking, lunch, handouts, and similar items. (Your university is only a forty-five-minute drive from the company; but because no buses are available, all transportation will be by private car.)

Problem A.10

SECURING A NEW WASTE-BALER

The Works Superintendent of the National Box Company has asked you to write a report to the Treasurer of the company requesting permission to purchase a new waste-baler.

Relevant Facts

1. The present waste-baler has been in operation for seventeen years.
2. Its present value is only $850. In two years, it will have fully depreciated.

3. Spare parts are no longer obtainable. When the machine breaks down, as it frequently does, National Box employees must manufacture their own parts. These don't always work satisfactorily, a fact that produces more breakdowns and generally unsatisfactory performance.
4. Because of poor performance, bales average only 728 pounds apiece and sometimes run as low as 350 pounds.
5. The low bale weight has in turn led to an increase in the labor costs for handling the bales and loading them onto freight cars. Two men are involved in this. Each receives $5.55 per hour. Each bale receives five minutes' worth of handling. Another five minutes per bale is involved in loading.
6. Repair costs have run $5,000 for the last two years.

Alternative Solutions

1. Continue with the present waste-baling machine despite its costly and inefficient operation.
2. Upgrade the present machine. This is not feasible because more recently designed parts cannot be integrated with the older design of this machine.
3. Purchase a new machine. Such a machine would produce bales averaging 1,100 pounds apiece. Over the year, this would mean that only 4,837 bales (in comparison to the present 7,302) would have to be handled and loaded onto the freight cars. A new waste-baler would cost $39,729.

Problem A.11

MERIT AND THE MANAGER

Under the guidance of Owen Langley, the personnel department of American Electronics had been transformed from a third-rate department into one that commanded respect and admiration from company executives and janitors alike. An often-heard remark among the men in the plant was "If you have a problem about the job, go see Langley; he'll give you a fair shake." In a recent attempt to relieve himself of part of the ever-increasing burden of making personal decisions, Owen had hired Ben Reed, a young man who had just received a degree in psychology.

Ben's first assignment was drafting an answer to the following letter from Samuel Wash, a technician:

> Dear Sir:
>
> I have been with American Electronics for only a short while, but am beginning to question the merit system as you seem to interpret it. In my division the supervisor makes all decisions concerning job advancement, and it is obvious that an advancement can be made only by his "good graces."
>
> Seemingly deliberately, information is withheld pertaining to job openings and the requirements of these jobs. At present there is no way for the

ordinary man to even know what jobs are available, let alone know the job requirements or how to go about getting the job. At times I wonder if the color of my skin has any bearing on the withholding of this information.

My question then, is this: Why don't we have a program that will give fair consideration to everyone for promotional opportunities?

Sincerely,
Samuel Wash

Following is the letter drafted by Ben as an answer to Samuel Wash.

Dear Mr. Wash:

   I have reviewed your note regarding advancement opportunities.

   Our Personnel Data System, which is used by our placement counselors to assist them in proper placement, does not at the present time include a skills inventory. It is planned, however, to make the skills inventory a part of the system, but it will be some time before this is completed.

   In the meantime, our Personnel Department relies on data made available to them through the employee appraisal program. From these records, managers' recommendations for promotions, the performance appraisal status, and other statistical information is constantly used in checking out applicants for jobs. In addition, information in this system is also available with regard to employee's requests for transfers or reassignment.

   We do rely largely on the manager's judgment to evaluate the performance of his people and their potential for advancement. There are means, however, by which an employee can express his personal interest for other types of work where he feels his background and experience might better be utilized. This can be done directly through the manager or through the completion of a Request for Transfer form. Either of these channels will be made known to Personnel and the employee will be given consideration as openings arise.

   I would encourage you to review this subject with your manager; however, if you prefer, you may contact Mr. Langley, our Personnel Director, for further discussion of the matter.

Langley okayed the letter (with some reservations) and it was mailed to Sam Wash. Within three days the following hand-written reply was received, with the letter attached:

Dear Mr. Langley:

What kind of double talk is this? I tried to tell you that my manager was biased and unfair, and you put the burden on me to shape him up. I've had just about all of this kind of "talking out of both sides of your mouth" that I can take. Just forget that I mentioned the problem.

Sincerely,
Sam Wash

Assuming the role of Owen Langley, draft a letter to Mr. Wash that will address his problems and assure him that he is not a victim of doubletalk.

Problem A.12

PARKING LOT QUESTIONNAIRE

The Brunswick Plant of Cummings, Incorporated, manufacturers of radio and television tubes, was built three years ago in an old section of the city. Many of the buildings surrounding the Cummings plant are vacant and available for sale. At present neither Cummings nor other companies in the vicinity provide parking facilities for their employees, with the result that employees who drive to work from other sections of Brunswick or from neighboring towns must find parking spaces in the narrow streets or in a relatively small public garage three blocks from the Cummings plant. The Brunswick Plant of Cummings, Incorporated, has 1,200 employees and operates on a day shift only.

As Manager of Building Operations, you have recommended that Cummings purchase space convenient to the plant, raze the old buildings thereon, and use the land for a free parking lot for Cummings employees. Your recommendation has been accepted.

Before you shop around for lots in the vicinity, you will have to determine the size of lot needed. You must thus find out the number of autos, motorcycles, and scooters that would have to be accommodated in the proposed parking space. You must also take into account the fact that some employees may form car pools. In case only limited space is available, or the number of driving commuters exceeds your expectations, what employees, if any should be given preference? If adequate space is available, should any employees have reserved spaces?

Construct a questionnaire to be sent to all employees in the plant to determine how many vehicles would have to be accommodated. Your questionnaire should contain clear directions as well as sample questions and answers.

Problem A.13

APPLE THEATRE DELAYED TICKETS

On March 3, Mrs. John Jones of Philadelphia sent a check to the Apple Theatre on Broadway in New York City for four tickets to the August 3 performance. She wanted to see the current show "I Don't, I Don't" on her vacation.

The manager of the Apple Theatre did not know whether the play would still be running August 3 and, therefore, held Mrs. Jones's check to "wait and see." In both April and May, Mrs. Jones telephoned long distance to inquire about the tickets and was told both times that they were still at the printing shop. Finally in June the Apple Theatre returned Mrs. Jones's check to her with a terse note stating that the show was closing at the end of the week.

Mrs. Jones felt annoyed at the apparent disregard of the manager of the theatre for the customer's need for communication, and said that she would not patronize the Apple Theatre in the future. She also told many of her friends and relatives of her disappointment.

Obviously, the theatre has lost goodwill with Mrs. Jones and probably many other playgoers who were treated in a similar manner. The management of the theatre should have contacted Mrs. Jones shortly after receiving her March check, thereby preventing the ill feelings.

What the Apple Theatre needs is an appropriate form letter to send to future customers when tickets cannot be mailed within a two-week period. Think of the various situations that could arise preventing the ticket distribution within a reasonable time, and write a form letter that will cover these situations.

Problem A.14

INTRODUCING BINDELL'S TRAVEL SERVICE

You have just been hired as the manager of Bindell's Travel Service at its new branch location in the Raintree Shopping Center. On your desk is a memo from the vice-president of Bindell's suggesting that you send a letter of introduction to all managers of stores in the shopping center. But what should you say in the letter? You will want them to know your name, of course, and the names of your company president and vice-president, your administrative assistant, and your three travel consultants.

Since you have been a travel consultant yourself for six years and since your agency has been serving the region for fifteen years, you feel that you can offer the other managers and their employees the help they need in planning transportation for business meetings or personal trips, whether regional, United States, or international. You cannot offer these businesses any discounts, but you can offer them special commercial accounts with twice-monthly billing. Besides, your business experience and your convenient location should convince them to handle their travel arrangements through your company. Write the letter.

Problem A.15

REQUESTS TO TENANTS AND LANDLORD

You are the manager of 20 Riverview Apartments (4231-4259 Riverview Drive, Spring Lake, IA 52522), for Miss Joan Harper (331 Trailer Court, North Miami, FL 11221).

The apartment tenants make a lot of work for you by setting sacks of garbage next to the overflowing garbage cans so that wind and dogs scatter the refuse that you must pick up to keep the grounds looking neat. The tenants also cut across the lawn from the parking lot, killing the grass and tracking mud down the apartment hallways.

You have argued, yelled, and begged them to smash their garbage so it will fit into the cans provided, to use the sidewalk, and to wipe their muddy feet on the entrance rug. The answers are sneers and snarls. "Why should I smash tin cans and milk cartons? If you're too cheap to provide enough cans, you deserve to pick up the stuff that blows around because it won't fit." "I'll cut across the lawn if I want to! I'm not going to detour clear around just to use that stupid sidewalk. Who cares about your lawn, anyhow?" "I *do* wipe my muddy feet on the entrance carpet — and get muddier! Why can't you provide a carpet that's more than two feet square, anyhow? You expect us to do your own work for you, and you don't care about making life easier for us! I can't even keep my own apartment clean, the hall's so muddy sometimes."

Write a letter to Miss Harper persuading her to provide more garbage cans, build a more direct sidewalk, and buy bigger entrance carpets. Then write a letter to all tenants persuading them that there is value in living in a clean, attractive apartment building.

Problem A.16

RESPONSE TO ADJUSTMENT LETTER REQUEST

You are the Vice-President of Field Operations for a national income tax preparation company, Tax Associates, Inc., 20 Northwest Plaza, (your town). Yesterday you received the following letter from a customer, Mr. J. C. Green, 151 Glacier Lane, Milford, TX 73516.

> In February I phoned the local office of Tax Associates, Inc., and asked about charges for computing my income taxes and completing the return. The receptionist inquired as to what forms would be necessary and then told me the charges would be $23.
>
> When I picked up my return one week later, I was told (by a different person) that the charges would be $41. When I questioned the $18 difference, I was told that I had been given the wrong information and that Tax Associates, Inc., employees were not allowed to quote rates over the phone. Was it my responsibility to know about this rule or was it the receptionist's responsibility?
>
> Since the fee quoted over the phone was an estimate, I did not expect the charges to be *exactly* that figure; but I surely didn't expect the fees to double. The only additional form needed that I did not mention to the receptionist was an "education expense form," which I was told would cost an additional $5. That would bring the total to $28.

I believe that you will agree that the mistake in the case was the fault of the Tax Associates, Inc., employee for quoting a rate rather than in my asking for that quote. I believe, too, that as a reputable firm, you will agree that the difference in the charges ($41) and the quote ($28 including $5 adjustment for education expense form) should be refunded to me — a total of $13.

Please restore my faith in your company by promptly making the requested refund.

a. Write to Mr. Green granting the $13 requested refund. Say whatever you can to develop and maintain goodwill with Mr. Green.

b. You feel that the $13 refund may not be enough to restore Mr. Green's faith in your company. Write to him offering what you feel is a better alternative. Say whatever you can to maintain goodwill.

Problem A.17

OPEN-UP PROGRAM

Assume that for the last two years you have worked in the Communications Unit of the Bank of Columbus Personnel Department. This bank employes 3,500 people in the service of six Western states.

For the last year, your unit has been responsible for operating the company's new Open-Up Program. This program was designed to stimulate the flow of open upward communication in the company.

Through the Open-Up Program, employees can mail questions or grievances to a program coordinator at the central office with the assurance that their identities will be kept strictly confidential. The coordinator seeks the necessary information or answers from the appropriate official and then responds to the person who made the request.

During the year that the program has been in operation, the coordinator has received 6,400 requests from employees. These letters have dealt with compensation, benefits, job opportunities, working conditions, supervisory policies and practices, and many other diverse subjects. The numbers of requests received each month are presented below in Table 1.

The president of your company recently decided that the program must be evaluated. You were commissioned to survey employees about the program. Specifically, the president wanted to know the extent to which the program has been used, the types of employees who were not using it, and the thinking of employees who have used the program.

TABLE 1

Monthly Requests

Jan.	Feb.	March	April	May	June	July	Aug.	Sept.	Oct.	Nov.	Dec.
492	553	577	628	600	566	533	509	496	498	484	464

In keeping with his expressed desires, you collected the information in the following tables. Your job now is to analyze that information and present it and your analyses and conclusions in a complete, coherent, objective report.

TABLE 2	
Have you ever used the "Open-Up" Program?	
No	220
Once	604
More than once	1102

TABLE 3	
Classifications of Employees Who Have Not Used the Program	
AGE	
under 25	84/421
25-40	36/719
41-55	55/563
over 55	45/223
SEX	
Male	90/1189
Female	130/737
RANK	
Nonmanagerial	121/1344
Managerial	99/582

The following tables contain responses of the 1706 people who had used the program.

TABLE 4			
How satisfied were you that your question(s) was (were) answered completely?			
	Completely satisfied	Partially satisfied	Completely dissatisfied
Used program once	300	223	81
Used it more than once	787	293	22

TABLE 5			
Do you believe that your question(s) was (were) handled confidentially?			
	Yes	Not sure	No
Used program once	139	328	137
Used it more than once	784	279	39

TABLE 6	
Do you intend to use the "Open-Up" Program again?	
Yes	1414
No	159
Undecided	133

Problem A.18

ROLL'S HOIST

Louis Roll is a second-shift supervisor in the assembly department of the PIX Company, a manufacturer of electronic office equipment. He has been with the company for twenty-six years and is looking forward to retirement in four years. You are his immediate superior.

This morning Joe Knapper, a first-line foreman under Roll, came to you with a distressing piece of information. Knapper had seen Roll leave the plant with one of the company's PIX-440 mini-calculators and had heard him tell a friend that his son in college would make good use of it.

You've known Knapper for some time now. You know that he is a trustworthy individual who has rather strong ethical convictions, so you see no reason for doubting his word or suspecting his motives. Furthermore, he seemed very disturbed as he related the incident to you. You feel that he probably would have preferred to ignore the whole scene. But he didn't, and now you are faced with a problem.

The general problem is not new. The company has always experienced some employee pilferage, but lately the estimated loss from such theft has climbed. Top management recently expressed some concern about it and asked department heads for ideas as to how this problem might be handled. Although you don't condone such theft, you personally feel that employees are rationalizing a justification for it from the rather meager wage increases they've been getting over the last two years. You also suspect that such theft is becoming more widespread; that is, that the same thieves aren't stealing more, but more people are getting into the act.

Despite the nature of the general problem, you have a specific one to deal with now. Roll's record is unblemished. In his long tenure with the company, he has been an efficient, effective, and (as far as you know) faithful employee.

What would you do? After you've made a decision, how would you communicate it?

Problem A.19

REILLY AND GREER, INCORPORATED

Reilly and Greer, Incorporated, sells and services swimming pools. The company's ten salesmen check in at the office at nine o'clock each morning. They call on customers and canvass prospective ones from about 10:00 until 3:30, at which time they return to the office to write up the deals they have completed and to enter new names and pertinent information in their prospective-customer file. Nine stenographers are employed to help the salesmen do the paper work connected with the completion of the deals.

After a salesman has tentatively completed a deal, the customer's credit must be checked before the final contract can be signed. In his hurry to write out the contracts upon his return to the office in the late afternoon, a salesman sometimes gives the stenographer incorrect or insufficient information to make a credit check, or he may give her the name of another customer. After she has worked on the credit check, she finds her time has been wasted and she has to start all over. (The next day when Mr. Reilly or Mr. Greer finds out the cause of the delay in making the credit check and in closing the deal, he is sharp with the salesman, who, in turn is sharp with the stenographer.)

Five o'clock comes and goes; the salesmen have written up the deals in longhand, recorded the names of prospective customers in the proper file, and gone home; and the stenographers are busily completing credit checks and typing contracts in order to have the material ready for the salesmen to pick up at nine o'clock the next morning. Seldom do the stenographers complete their work before 6:30; more often they do not leave the office until 7:30 or 8:00.

Because of the dissension, the long hours of overtime, and the rush of work after a day of waiting, there has been a 100 percent turnover of the nine stenographers during the past ten months.

Mr. Greer has asked you, as Office Manager, to find ways of reducing this high turnover of office help.

Before you write your memorandum report to Mr. Greer giving the details of the problem and your recommendations for alleviating the present undesirable situation and thus, one hopes, reducing the high turnover, consider the pros and cons of the following questions:

- Would it be practical to open the office late, perhaps at noon?
- Could only one or two stenographers check in at nine o'clock?
- Could the salesmen notify the stenographers during the day of deals completed so that they could get started on the credit checks?
- Could the salesmen use portable tape or disc recorders to record the information about deals at the time they are with the customers, so that the stenographers could get to work on the contracts as soon as the salesmen return to the office at 3:30? (Mr. Greer has indicated his willingness to buy five portable tape recorders.)
- Should extra part-time stenographers be hired for the busy hours?
- Could the contracts be delayed twenty-four hours so that the stenographers could work on them during the day while the salesmen are out of the office?

Write the report to Mr. Greer.

APPENDIX B

Message Format and Mechanics

For many years there have been only three or four standard letter formats: block, semi-block, simplified, and sometimes one that was once called conventional or modified block. You will probably be sending out letters in one of these formats. We doubt that any of your readers are going to look at your letter and say: Ah ha! XYZ Company uses the simplified letter form. Your reader doesn't really care. What is important is that your letter look attractive, be easy to read, and be understandable.

If your company insists on a particular style, by all means use it. Be conventional if you like. But don't be afraid to throw in a few surprises if they will help your reader better understand your message.

In our offices we use the Administrative Management Society simplified letter form, because it is efficient and easy on the typist. But we don't hesitate to modify it if the situation calls for it. We don't follow it blindly. If we need an indented paragraph, we use it. If we want to put some parts of our message in list form for clarity's sake, we put them in list form — and not always at the left margin, as the style recommends.

Figure B.1 shows several ways of varying letter style without committing any sins against letter form: leader dots at the end of the third line and at the beginning of the first paragraph; an indented paragraph for emphasis; and three uppercase lines at the beginning of the letter. None of these are specified in any letter form that we know of, but all of them provide emphasis, arouse interest, and improve readability.

IF YOU HAVE A
PROFESSIONAL INTEREST IN
THE COMMUNICATIONS OF BUSINESS ...

...you are invited to join the Association for Business Communication.

Membership offers you the opportunity to keep up with the important developments in research, teaching, and training, plus information about teaching and writing positions. Our members are university professors, junior college teachers, training directors, business executives, consultants, and all others seriously interested in business communication — written, oral, and graphic.

We publish quarterly *The Journal of Business Communication* containing major papers, research reports, and book reviews. We encourage you to submit your own papers for consideration.

> Our second quarterly publication is *The Bulletin,* which includes descriptions of courses (both senior and junior college) and company training programs; bibliographies; materials to use in classes and training sessions; and other useful material.

Special publications, sold separately, include *The Teaching of Business Communication* (an anthology of forty articles covering all aspects of classroom teaching of business communication), *Business Communication Casebooks* (problems and cases for assignment to classes), *Guidelines for Research in Business Communication,* and bibliographies on written communication in business, technical writing, and published research in business communication.

The seven spring regional meetings and the annual national convention enable you to meet and talk with leaders in the field.

To take advantage of these opportunities, just fill out and return the enclosed application along with your check for $35. Your membership will begin immediately and will continue for a full year. And we'll send you the current issue of the *Journal* and the *Bulletin.*

I'll be looking for your application.

[Signature Block]

Figure B.1. Varying your letter style to increase visual appeal. *This form letter is used by The Association for Business Communication to recruit new members. It is* block format, but the three all-caps lines at the beginning, the ellipses, and the indented paragraph are not standard parts of the block style. They do, however, tend to add variety, emphasis, and interest that a pure blocked format does not have.

Of course, there are a few things you should keep foremost in your mind when you start to decide on format. They are all commonsense: (1) Keep your paragraphs and sentences short and simple. (2) Allow white space. (3) Keep lines to six inches in length where possible (that's about as far as your eyes can scan without effort). All these things have been discussed in other chapters of this book. And they're all valid suggestions. They will all help your reader.

LETTER STYLES

Standard business correspondence styles are illustrated in some of the other figures that follow. Figure B.2 illustrates most of the standard business letter formats. Figure B.3 is a letter that has been typed in semi-block style with mixed punctuation (a colon after the salutation and a comma after the complimentary close).

However, should you choose not to indent paragraphs or punctuate after the salutation and complimentary close, you will create the block form with open punctuation. This style is shown in Figure B.4.

Further, you can type the letter with no paragraph indentions but still use punctuation after the salutation and complimentary close, to create still another style that is called block with mixed punctuation. The differences are so minor that they are not illustrated. But we would like to show you an example of the pure simplified letter form recommended so highly by the Administrative Management Society. It is shown in Figure B.5 with no deviation from their recommendations: date at the left; full address at the left; subject line instead of salutation; no indention; typewritten signature at the far left.

A suggestion: Although Figures B.3, B.4, and B.5 illustrate examples of some of the more common letter styles you'll be using, don't be afraid to experiment with them. None are cast in stone. All can be improved.

Use bullets, indented paragraphs, lists, and one-line paragraphs if you need them — if they will help your reader understand your message. But don't get carried away; use them sparingly, and only when needed. Don't let your surprises cloud the message.

Most important, don't give in to the paper-shortage scare. The institution that sent out the message in Figure B.6 must have feared that paper products were soon going to disappear from the face of the earth. The designers of this message must have recently discovered that if half-inch margins were used on all four sides, if the message were typed from border to border and then reduced photographically, they probably could save money on printing. We don't have any idea how much money was saved, but we do know no one read the message. No one could. Everyone got lost in the first paragraph. And

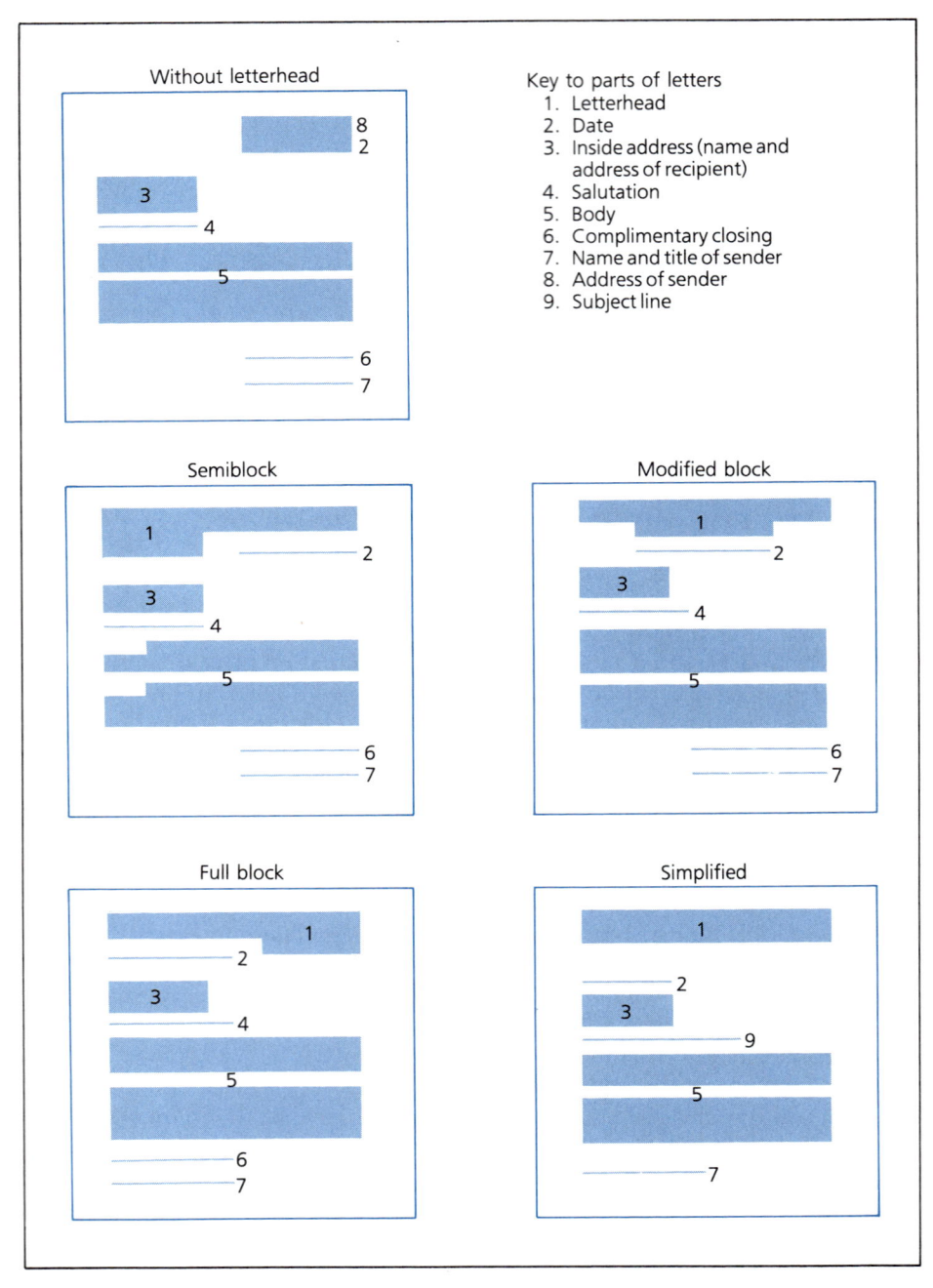

Figure B.2. Business letter formats. *This figure illustrates five different letter formats. The parts of the letter are keyed to the numbered list in the upper right-hand corner of the chart.*

August 24, 1986

Mr. David V. Smith
704 West Washington Road
West Lafayette, IN 46383

Dear Mr. Smith:

    We have no current information about jobs and careers in business and technical communication. Our career leaflet is out of print and being rewritten. We do not know when it will be available for distribution. We do not maintain lists of job openings, nor do we have a placement service.

    Probably the best ways to find the jobs are to read the help-wanted ads in local and national newspapers, and to inquire directly of companies.

    For information about careers in various aspects of communication, these publications should be helpful:

Your Career as a Writer, Mary Lewis Hanson, Arco Publishing Company, Inc., 219 Park Avenue South, New York, NY 10003.

Business Communication as a Career, International Association of Business Communicators, 870 Market Street, Suite 928, San Francisco, CA 94102.

Opportunities in Technical Writing Today, Jay R. Gould and Wayne Losano, Vocational Guidance Manuals, Inc., 620 S. Fifth St., Louisville, KY 40202.

Your Future in Technical and Science Writing, Emerson Clarke and Vernon Root, Arco Publishing Company, Inc., 219 Park Avenue S., New York, NY 10003.

                Good luck,

                [Signature Block]

Figure B.3. Semi-block with mixed punctuation. *Characteristics of this style are the indented beginning lines of each paragraph; the date and signature block at the right; the colon after Mr. Smith's name; and the comma after the complimentary close. This style is probably the most conventional in use today.*

August 26, 1987

Ms. Chris Steele
608 South Wright Street
Urbana, IL 61801

Dear Ms. Steele

Perhaps the best way to respond to your letter is to suggest the current approaches used in training undergraduates and graduates in business communication. Let me divide my comments into two categories:

Undergraduate work in business communication

The enclosed pages list those schools that offer a specific degree in business communication.

You will see that the phrase "business communication" is on a continuum — that is, at Baylor's Hankamer School of Business it applies to secretarial preparation, while at others it may emphasize behavioral activity.

Most often, however, students major in another department of a university or college — English, communication, psychology, speech — and then take business communication courses within a business school.

Graduate work in business communication

The enclosed document also makes comments on both the M.B.A. and Ph.D. degrees in business communication. You will find mention of those schools that profess to offer graduate training leading to an advanced degree.

I impose one caution; each school has a varying concept, from an emphasis on writing to one that is really organizational behavior. You will have to decide yourself on which direction you would like to follow.

Figure B.4(a). Block style with open punctuation. *As you can see, there is very little difference between this and Figure B.3. Block style is created when the first lines of paragraphs are not indented and "open punctuation" means only that you do not use punctuation after the salutation or complimentary close. Note the illustration of the second-page heading and the enclosure notation at the bottom of the page.*

Chris Steele   2   August 16, 1987

I have just learned that one school (The University of Texas at Austin) recently approved a joint M.B.A.-M.A. in Communication degree program. The program is sponsored by the Graduate School of Business and the College of Communication.

In summary, the most often followed path leading to an emphasis in business communication is to pursue a degree in a nonbusiness school or department, then add business courses, including business communication, as a minor to that degree.

Best wishes; I hope we have been of some help.

Cordially

[Signature Block]

Encl.

Figure B.4(b). Block style with open punctuation and second-page heading

August 22, 1986

Professor Gretchen Murphy
English Department
Illinois State University
Normal, IL 61761

YOUR NOMINATION FOR A SEAT ON THE BOARD OF DIRECTORS

The Nominating Committee nominated you for a seat on the Board of Directors, and your name will appear on the ballot we mail out on the first of the year.

So that members will know who they are voting for, we need to include with the ballot brief biographies of the nominees ... and that brings me to the point of this letter:

Please send me your professional history condensed to a few words.

To give you an idea of what is wanted, I'm enclosing an example from a previous mailing. Please, no more than 150 words, and send it soon?

[Signature Block]

Figure B.5. Simplified letter style. *First introduced by the Administrative Management Society, this style was a long time gaining favor from business. It is, however, extremely efficient. As you note, all lines are at the left; there is no salutation — it uses a "subject line" instead; and there is no complimentary close. Traditionally-trained executives are reluctant to use it because of the absence of the last two elements.*

Message Format and Mechanics

> ## A PROUD PAST — A PROMISING FUTURE
>
> In 1870, just three years after it opened, the University offered its first course in veterinary medicine and surgery. As the profession developed over the succeeding century into a highly sophisticated and specialized science, the University strived to expand its facilities to meet rapidly changing demands for modern veterinary medical education, research on human and animal health problems and service to the public. Today the University's College of Veterinary Medicine is one of only 18 in the nation. It is the only veterinary medical school in the state, and one of two colleges on the campus that awards a professional degree.
>
> Despite the fact that veterinary medicine has been taught at this campus for more than a century, the college itself is the youngest on campus. It grew out of the Department of Veterinary Science which was established in 1899 under the College of Agriculture, and later changed to the Division of Animal Pathology and Hygiene. Throughout the early decades of the twentieth century the division provided numerous services to veterinarians and livestock owners throughout the state. The diagnostic laboratory operated jointly with the State Department of Agriculture became one of the busiest in the nation, examining as many as 126,000 specimens a year between 1926 and 1946. Extension and disease eradication programs initiated by University personnel helped control such diseases as brucellosis and mastitis in cattle, fowl pox and pullorum disease in poultry, swine erysipelas, and parasites in horses. During most of this time all teaching, research and diagnostic work was carried out within the confines of a building constructed in 1904 as a beef barn. In recent years the structure has served as the Small Animal Clinic.
>
> In 1944 the Board of Trustees authorized "immediate establishment of a College of Veterinary Medicine at the University," and the following year the General Assembly allocated funds for construction of a basic science laboratory. Postwar shortages of building materials forced a delay in construction, however, and when the college accepted its first class in 1948, it was headquartered in a remodeled sorority house on X Avenue. The proposed Veterinary Medicine Building, along with a diagnostic and research annex, was finally completed in 1952. The following year funds were appropriated for a badly-needed Large Animal Clinic which was completed in 1955, leaving the former beef barn as the Small Animal Clinic.
>
> As classes continued to grow, facilities became more crowded and inadequate, and the inevitable next step was taken. Official planning of the new Small Animal Clinic began in 1962, and the area bounded by A Avenue, B Drive, and C Road was selected the following year as the relocation site for the College. Blueprints were completed and bids let in 1964, but every bid exceeded the budget by more than $1 million. The General Assembly increased its allocation, and bids were again solicited in January of 1968. This time an acceptable offer was received. The contract was awarded and groundbreaking ceremonies took place in March on the last day of the University's Centennial year. Construction began the following month, and, after many frustrating delays, is now nearly complete. Occupancy of the buildings, however, will be postponed until June to minimize disruption of classes.
>
> The new Small Animal Clinic and Obstetrical-Surgical Laboratory comprise Phase I of a three-phase building program planned to provide for much-needed expansion of veterinary medical teaching, research and public service in the state. Phase II is a Large Animal Clinic which will be joined to the Small Animal Clinic by a 250-seat teaching auditorium. This structure will provide more than

Figure B.6. Illegible brochure page. *The content of this page from a brochure is not important. What is important is its lack of readability and negative visual impact due to a lack of visual relief and small type size. It illustrates what not to do if you want readers to read your message. (To add insult to injury, the original brochure was printed in rust-colored ink on tan paper!)*

that's a pity, because it's an important message. The designers of this message broke every commonsense rule of readability: they used seven and a half-inch line lengths, no white space, and reduction of type to about half its original size.

In Figure B.7, the originators began by using many of the devices you read about in Chapter 3. They indented, underlined, listed, and left ample space between points A and B. But then they nullified their efforts by forgetting about ample margins and by reducing the whole thing to an unreadable type size. They didn't "listen to the look."

If you have used some of the suggestions outlined above and are still unsatisfied with the look of your letter, experiment with some unconventional ideas. Figures B.8, B.9, and B.10 illustrate three letter forms suggested a number of years ago by the late Henry Hoke, publisher of *The Reporter of Direct Mail Advertising* ("a monthly magazine of ideas and information for busy executives who use letters and printed promotion"). They are still as fresh today as they were when first introduced in Hoke's magazine; however, we can't assign them a name. They defy categorization. Yet they are useful, attractive, and economical. Make use of them when and if you can.

The following outline pretty well sums up the subject of letter format. We would like to give credit for it to someone, but it came to us unsigned.

MAKE THE LOOK OF YOUR LETTER COMMAND RESPECT
1. Learn the art of letter layout.
   a. Symmetry, proportion, and balance create advantageous first impression.
2. Put your letter in a picture frame.
   a. Put date near letterhead.
   b. Proportion your letter to the blank space remaining below the printed letterhead.
   c. Leave a slightly larger margin at bottom.
3. Use the picture-frame layout for all kinds, sizes, and shapes of letterheads.
   a. Plain paper — proportion letter to shape of sheet.
   b. Letterhead — adapt proportion to letterhead and sheet.
   c. Advantages gained from picture-frame layout:
      attractive to the eye
      high in attention value
      strong in visual contrast
      well-shaped
      well-centered
      interesting to look at
      easy to read
4. Don't skimp on white space — use a second sheet to avoid crowding the first.
   a. Crowding ruins the letter layout.

FACULTY INSTRUCTIONS FOR COMPLETING SPECIAL GRADE FORMS

A. Reasons for Creating Special Grade Form.

The original Grade Rosters will be scanned and then edited to detect error conditions. If no error is found, the student's grade will be recorded on his/her record. When an error on the roster is found, a Special Grade Form will be produced for each student who has a grade error. Special Grade Forms will also be generated automatically when the following course transactions occur after the production of the original Grade Rosters: a) course add, b) section change, c) credit change, d) add honors credit, e) drop honors credit. All the items shown on the Grade Rosters will be shown on the Special Grade Forms. However, the Special Grade Form will be used to assign only one student's grade.

The following error conditions will generate Special Grade Forms:

1. MISSING GRADE ON ROSTER. Rosters are "read" by a machine which recognizes only dark pencil marks. This error means that the instructor: a) did not mark a student's grade; or b) marked student's grade but the mark was too light for the scanner to record; or c) marked the student's grade in ink and the scanner could not read it.

2. UNMATCHED GRADES. The student's grade marked on a roster is different than the grade already assigned to the student's record. EXCEPTION: If a 'W' grade (withdrawn) was previously recorded for the student, a Special Grade Form will not be created and the 'W' grade will remain on the student's record. No error condition will be noted.

3. INVALID 'D' OR 'U' GRADE FOR THE COURSE. The 'S' or 'U' grade assigned to the student is not a valid grade because the course is not approved for use of 'S' or 'U' grades.

4. INVALID 'DF' GRADE FOR THE COURSE. The 'DF' grade assigned to the student is not a valid grade because 'DF' is not authorized for this course.

5. INVALID GRADE FOR MEDICAL SCIENCE COURSES. Only grades of 'O', 'S', 'U', 'DF', and 'EX' are valid for Medical Science 300, 301, 302, and 323 courses.

6. UNAUTHORIZED 'EX' GRADE. An undergraduate student was assigned an 'EX' which has not been approved by the Dean of the student's college.

7. MULTIPLE GRADES MARKED. The student was assigned more than one grade on the original grade roster and the Office of Admissions and Records cannot determine which grade is to be recorded for the student.

8. GRADE INVALID FOR 'DF', 'S' or 'U' COURSE. Only grades of 'DF', 'S', and 'U' are valid for 499 courses. All grades are valid for students taking other courses for zero credit.

9. GRADE INVALID FOR 'S' OR 'U' COURSE. Only 'S' and 'U' grades are valid for 499 courses. All grades are valid for students taking other courses for zero credit.

Figure B.7. Illegible instruction sheet. *The type on this instruction sheet was reduced to fit on one page. It looks like about six-point type (a size often used in newspaper classified ads to reduce cost). To use it for an informative message such as this defeats the purpose of sending the message.*

The Reporter of Direct Mail Advertising
A Monthly Digest of Direct Mail Ideas and Information
17 East 42nd Street • New York, NY 10017

February 15, 1987

Mr. Daniel Stowe
The Stowe, Beech Company
100 Fifth Avenue
Newark, NJ 07603

Sometimes, Mr. Stowe,

>it is necessary to write a short letter. One of thanks or acknowledgement.
>
>This form can be used for such a letter. It provides a change of pace. But, no matter how short the letter, it should be courteous and neatly typed.
>
>Courtesy and honesty of expression are appreciated by all.
>
>Sincerely
>
>Joan A. Overfield

JAO/ls

Figure B.8. Unconventional letter form. *This letter and those in Figures B.9 and B.10 originally appeared in the magazine,* The Reporter of Direct Mail Advertising. *Henry Hoke was publisher at that time. The magazine is now under the direction of his son, Pete, and it is called* The Reporter of Direct Mail/Marketing.

Message Format and Mechanics

The Reporter of Direct Mail Advertising
17 East 42nd Street ● New York, NY 10017

March 10, 1986	Your Answer
Mr. Henry Thompson Thompson & Company Warren, PA 16365	
Here, Mr. Thompson, is an out of the ordinary method of carrying on general correspondence.	
The message is typed left side of line, in triplicate.	
Original and one copy are sent to person addressed. Extra copy kept in company files.	
Recipient answers the letter on right side of line of the copy and keeps original.	
As soon as answer is received it is filed and the copy is torn up.	
Saves space, time, and effort. From all reports, it's working out very satisfactorily.	
Good luck always	
James Albert O'Neill	

Figure B.9. Message and reply on one page

The Reporter of Direct Mail Advertising
17 East 42nd Street • New York, NY 10017

March 10, 1987

Mr. Walter A. Roberts
602 Arcade
Johnsonville, NY 12094

This is a form, Mr. Roberts,
> that emphasizes the hanging paragraph. It can be used for short letters.

There is sufficient white space throughout the letter to encourage
> easy reading. And it is wise to keep letters just as short as possible.

Most letters could be shortened and still tell a complete story.
> Remember, it takes a really good letter writer to dictate a short statement of facts and still give complete information.

> Louise W. Steele
> Business Manager

P.S.
Little P.S. paragraphs are eye
catchers. Handwritten ones
are O.K. too.

Figure B.10. Unconventional letter form

Message Format and Mechanics

    b. Second sheet — should match first page in quality, weight, and size, but can have a smaller, similar letterhead.
5. Be sure people put you in the right pigeonhole — you may be judged by that first impression.
    a. Impressions determined by:
        quality of paper
        design of paper
        design of letterhead
        general neatness and accuracy of typing
        layout and placement of letter on the sheet
6. Use single spacing for most letters:
    business practice prefers it
    twice as much on the paper
    exception: the short letter can be double-spaced

What about the future? It is very likely that letter styles will be altered drastically with the use of computer-based word processors. Although most of them used in business will be hooked up to a letter-quality printer, some of them won't be. The style of type produced by a dot-matrix printer (figure B.11) and the capabilities of the software package itself may, in time, alter our thinking about conventional letter styles. Still, you can get variety and surprise with most of them. Experimentation will enable you to find a letter style that is both suitable and attractive.

MEMORANDUM STYLE

There's nothing mysterious about the style you would use when you are sending a memorandum. It's about as standard as you can get. The illustration in Figure B.12 has been marked so that you can tell how many spaces there are between the elements of the memo. (You will note that a memo is usually initialed rather than signed with your full name.) Of course, many of you will work for companies that have printed memo forms. These carry the same elements: author, destination, date, subject, copies to, references, and enclosures. If your company has these printed forms, you may be expected to use them.

OTHER STANDARDS OF BUSINESS CORRESPONDENCE

Following are some standards to follow now and on the job. But remember: these are standards, not rules. They are made to be broken if breaking them will enhance the look or readability of your letter or report.

Some of the questions students most often ask about letters are:

**ILLUSTRATION OF
ONE DOT-MATRIX PRINTER'S
RANGE OF TYPE STYLE POSSIBILITIES!**

This is an example of pica type (10 cpi).

This is an example of Elite type (12 cpi).

This is an example of compressed type (17 cpi).

This is an example of correspondence quality (in 10 cpi).

This is an example of expanded type (5 cpi).

This is an example of the underline mode.

This is an example of the 6-line-per-inch feed.
This is an example of the 6-line-per-inch feed.
This is an example of the 6-line-per-inch feed.
This is an example of the 6-line-per-inch feed.
This is an example of the 6-line-per-inch feed.
This is an example of the 6-line-per-inch feed.

This is an example of the 8-line-per-inch feed.
This is an example of the 8-line-per-inch feed.
This is an example of the 8-line-per-inch feed.
This is an example of the 8-line-per-inch feed.
This is an example of the 8-line-per-inch feed.
This is an example of the 8-line-per-inch feed.
This is an example of the 8-line-per-inch feed.

This is an example of the enhanced-print mode.

This is an example of the emphasized print mode.

This is an example of the super-script print mode.

This is an example of the sub-script print mode.

Figure B.11. Styles of type produced by dot-matrix printer

Message Format and Mechanics

August 22, 19-- [CR]
[CR]
[CR]
[CR]
Memo to: Alpha Beta Chi Advisers [CR]
[CR]
From: Bob Gieselman [CR]   *BG*
[CR]
Subject: Services to Local Student Chapters of _____ [CR]
[CR]
[CR]
It's good to see four chapters of Alpha Beta Chi going, and we at national headquarters want to do everything we can to encourage them. I'm sure we are all happy that student interest in business communication is increasing. A chapter of Alpha Beta Chi can be of real service to your students as well as to [association name]. [CR]
[CR]
Student chapters do require some special arrangements here in our office. It's difficult to keep an accurate mailing list of student members because of the turnover, and because they are not at school in the summer when our summer publications are delivered. [CR]
[CR]
Also, some student members find it difficult to pay both local chapter dues and national dues. The association's new student rate, as a result of our recent increase in dues, is $20. Therefore it is a good idea to allow students to join the local chapter without becoming national members and paying national dues. That entitles them to all the local benefits but not to national publications. Presumably they can read the publications in the library, or perhaps copies could be put on display at the local meetings. We can send you a few extra copies for display if you ask for them. [CR]
[CR]
Since student chapters are a new development for the association, we're still working out our procedures for managing the relations between our office and the chapters and with student members. Any ideas you have for creating a good relationship would be appreciated. We'll do everything we can to help you and your students.

    NOTES: [CR] = carriage return
           Note: A memo is usually initialed, not signed with a full name.

Figure B.12. Typing style of a memorandum

- "How do I set up a business letter?"
- "How many carriage returns do you use after the complimentary close?"
- "Where does the date line go?"
- "What heading do I use on the second page of a letter?"

The letter styles shown on the previous pages will give you some of this information, but let's "take a talk" down the page of a letter:

1. *Date line.* No matter where your date line is typed, it is always typed conventionally: all on one line.

[Four carriage returns follow your date line]

2. *Inside address.* Your inside address will consist of name, street address, or post office box number; city, state, zip code; and (sometimes) country.

The Postal Service has recently had something to say about addressing a letter. If your addressee has both a street address and a post office box number, the post office box should go on the line immediately preceding the city, state, and zip code. If you use only a street address, it, too, must immediately precede the city, state, and zip line. In other words, you could not reverse the order of the third and fourth lines of the examples below.

The inside address is almost always set up in the flush-left position on your page. Each element of your inside address should occupy its own line. If your reader has a title and it is short, it can go on the line with the name (as shown below). However, if your reader's title is long, such as "Assistant Vice-President of Marketing," you will probably want to put it on a line by itself, immediately following the name.

Amanda C. Clark, Editor	or	Amanda C. Clark
Good-Time Publishing Company		Assistant to the College Editor
Good-Time Plaza		Good-Time Publishing Company
P.O. Box 2680		Good-Time Plaza
Good-Time, U.S.A. 55555-0001		P.O. Box 2680
		Good-Time, U.S.A. 55555-0001

[Two carriage returns normally follow the inside address however . . .]

3. *Salutation or subject line?* Spacing depends on the style of letter form you choose. Take your pick. As we've stressed all through this part of the text, unless your company requires you to use a certain style, there are no requirements. Do what you are comfortable doing. You may choose to use a salutation:

Dear Mrs. Steele:

Use two carriage returns after the salutation.

If you use a subject line instead of a salutation:

> SUBJECT: PRINTING BID FOR <u>COMMUNICATION CONSULTING AND TRAINING IN BUSINESS, INDUSTRY, AND GOVERNMENT</u>

Use three carriage returns following the subject line.

4. *Your message: Single- or double-spaced?* Most business letters will be typed single-spaced, unless they are extremely short. Then you may choose to double-space a short letter so it will look better on the page (have good "visual impact"). (Your inside address will always remain single-spaced, even if you choose to double-space your letter.) When you double-space a letter, indent your paragraphs.

If you are following convention and single-spacing your letter, you will still return the carriage twice between paragraphs.

Enumerated material should be indented from five to eight spaces from the left margin. Two spaces follow the *1.* and *2.* (or A. and B.) and on down your list. You may hang indent items with two or more lines. This is hang indentation:

> A. Now is the time for all good persons to come to the aid of their party. Now is the time for all good persons to come to the aid of their party.

Or you may wrap them back to the left margin. This is wrapping back:

> B. This is a sample paragraph only. This is a sample paragraph only. This is a sample paragraph only. This is a sample paragraph only. This is a sample paragraph only.

No matter which you choose, to hang indent or wrap, you should single-space the material within each item and double-space between items.

Since spacing seems to be an aspect of typing that few students have had occasion to learn, here are a few additional conventions for you:

One space

- after a comma
- after a semicolon
- after a period following an abbreviation or an initial
- after an exclamation mark used in the body of a sentence
- before and after an *x* meaning *by*; for example, 4 x 6 card

Two spaces

- after a colon
- after every sentence

- after a period following a figure or letter at the beginning of a list of items

No spacing

- before or after a dash (two hyphens on the typewriter)
- before or after a hyphen
- between quotation marks and the material enclosed
- between any word and the punctuation following it
- between the initials that make up a single abbreviation: F.O.B., C.O.D., for example
- before or after an apostrophe, unless it begins or ends a word.

5. *Complimentary close.* If you use the complimentary close:

Cordially, Sincerely, Yours very truly, Best wishes,

Use four carriage returns following the complimentary close.

6. *Signature block.* Your name should be typed exactly as you sign it. If you sign your letters *J. R. Ewing*, then your name should be typed *J. R. Ewing*. If on the other hand, you sign your name *Jack Robert Ewing*, then have *Jack Robert Ewing* typed. If you have a title and it doesn't appear on the letterhead, it should be typed directly below your name. J. R.'s signature block, then would look like this:

J. R. Ewing
J. R. Ewing
Sole Owner, Ewing Enterprises

or

J. R. Ewing
J. R. Ewing, Sole Owner
Ewing Enterprises

But not:

J. R. Ewing
Jack Robert Ewing
EWING ENTERPRISES

or

Jack Robert Ewing
J. R. Ewing
EWING ENTERPRISES

A woman's signature block is usually typed as a man's is. However, if you have a preference as to *Ms.*, *Miss*, or *Mrs.*, you should so indicate it by setting up your signature block in this way:

Jean Ewing
(Ms.) Jean Ewing
District Manager

Note: If a woman states her preference in this way, honor her wishes. Don't use *Mrs.* or *Miss* just to satisfy your own biases.

Some companies will also require that you use the company name in the signature block. In that case the signature block will be set up this way:

EWING ENTERPRISES   or   EWING ENTERPRISES

J. R. Ewing   *Jean Ewing*

J. R. Ewing, Sole Owner   (Ms.) Jean Ewing
                                     District Manager

7. *Subsequent page headings.* These are normally placed approximately seven to ten lines below the top of your second sheet and spaced across the full width of your typing line. Your subsequent page headings should consist of three elements of information: name, page number, and date.

Amanda C. Clark   2   August 26, 1986

8. *The envelope.* Customarily, if the address block contains only three lines, double-spacing is recommended. If the address block contains more than three lines of information, then you should single-space the address.

NOW FOR THE ODDS & ENDS

Many older women executives started their careers as secretaries. When they were trained, certain amenities were part of a secretary's education. They were taught, for example, the feminine and masculine spellings of certain names. Teachers stressed correct grammar and spelling, drilled them on homonyms, homophones, and synonyms. This kind of training seems to be available now only from professional secretarial schools. Many colleges and universities have abandoned their skills departments, considering them too mundane for a prestige institution. Some high schools and junior colleges have succumbed to the "right to your own language" argument, abandoning the rigorous training in English usage that would make the student a competent secretary. Therefore, although many of the younger secretaries entering the workforce today are trained adequately in skills — typing, word processing, computer usage, and so on — they lack the ability to spell, to use language correctly, or to recognize ungrammatical constructions. Woe to the executive who gives machine dictation to a word-processing operator who has never learned to spell.

This lack of training has resulted in a proliferation of training seminars being offered by hundreds of companies across the country.

Some of the matters addressed here may seem trivial to you. They are not.

There is, for example, nothing quite so frustrating to a man whose name is Francis than to be addressed as *Ms.* or *Mrs.* The woman whose name is Frances has a similar problem. (This particular name you can remember as *FrancIs* for *hIm,* and *FrancEs* for *hEr.*) And few things will be quite so embarrassing to discover, after you've mailed a letter to an important client, than realizing that the person who typed your letter misunderstood your dictation (or didn't know better) and used the word *principle* instead of *principal*. ("The principle has been reinvested at 11.15 percent.") More about this below in the section on knowing what you are signing.

Be Sure You Know Whom You're Addressing

There are a number of names that could be either masculine or feminine: for example, *Chris, Sandy, Marion* (although this is traditionally spelled *"MariOn"* for a man, *"MariAn"* for a woman), *Bernie, Ashley*. If you do not know or cannot find out the sex of the person you're writing, IMPROVISE.

There is no rule that states that you must use *Mr., Mrs., Ms.* (or any other salutation). You can begin your letter with "Dear Chris Steele" or "Here, Chris Steele, is the...." or omit the salutation altogether. Below are just a few of the names that might prove puzzling to you:

Masculine	Nickname	Feminine
Adolph		Adolphe
Adrian		Adrienne
Alexander	Alex, Sandy	Alexandra, Alexandria
Alfred	Fred, Freddy	Alfreda
Benedict	Benny	Benedicta
Burl (Ives)		Berle
Charles	Char, Charlie	Charlene
Christopher	Chris	Christine
Denis		Denise
Edwin or Edward	Eddy	Edwina
Elbert	Bert	Elberta
Francis	Fran	Frances
Frederick	Freddy	Frederica
Gabriel	Gabe, Gabby	Gabrielle
James	Jamie	Jamie
Jesse	Jessie	Jessica
Joseph	Jo	Josephine
Juan		Juana
Louis	Lou	Louise
Lynn	Lynn	Lynda
Nicholas	Nicky	Nicole
Porcius		Portia
Simon		Simone
Vivian, Vivien		Vivian, Vivien, Vivienne

You can see that the possibilities for serious misjudgment as to whether a name is feminine or masculine are endless. Lists of masculine and feminine names appear in most dictionaries, although you can't put much faith in them today. If you look at the list above, you'll see that there are certain patterns. Some have been feminized by the simple substitution or addition of an *e* or an *a;* others by *enne;* still others by the substitution of *ria* for *er.* The addition of an *a* to *Elbert* should immediately alert us that we are addressing a woman. Yet a woman on our campus is named Michael — spelled *Michael,* not *Michelle.* And many of you have seen the vivacious blond nurse on "Trapper John" whose name is *Christopher* Lorrin.

So, if you are in doubt, leave the salutation out. Improvise.

More About the Conventional Salutation and Complimentary Close

When you are addressing a stranger, how do you know that he or she is *dear?* And why should you (in your closing) have to attest *sincerely* to your *truthfulness?*

Let neither tradition nor fads override your common sense in any situation. Be thoughtful and consider your audience. Few will take offense at a missing salutation or complimentary close. On the contrary, Francis will appreciate the fact that you were considerate enough to be concerned about his sex. And Chris Steele will appreciate your not addressing her as *Mr.*

One comment before we go on. Several persons we know begin their letters this way:

"It's been a long time, John,

since I've written to you...."

or:

"I wish I could help, Mr. Rodgers,

but we do not have the information you asked for."

This style seems much more friendly than a "Dear John:" letter. (It's certainly better than *Dear Gentlepersons*:!) However, your company may have ideas of its own, and you may be asked to accept them. Nonetheless, if you have a chance to experiment, experiment. Your readers will respond to personal treatment.

Be Sure You Know WHAT You Are Signing

If you read your letters before you sign them, it is unlikely that you will let this sentence slip by: "The cite of our next meeting will be the New Orleans Hilton." (This homophone sticks in one author's mind most vividly because a student once told her that she had been asked in junior high school to "write an essay on what you did this summer." Since she had spent a day in Appomattox where General Lee surrendered to General Grant thereby ending the Civil War, she wrote: "We spent one day visiting the sites of the Civil War." Later, she remembered, she went home angry and in tears because her teacher had given her a "B" and corrected her paper to read: "We spent a day visiting the 'sights' of the Civil War.")

Many executives seem to harbor the notion that it is insulting to check up on their secretary's transcription by reading their letters before signing them. Not true. A competent secretary welcomes such attention to detail. It's as embarrassing to the secretary as it is to the executive to have a letter leave the office with a misspelled or misused word. So always heed the lawyer's advice: Read the small print, even the letters typed by someone you trust. You are responsible for the contents of the letter you sign.

Be Sure to Consider Your Reader

There are many principles of business communication that you will learn to follow to enable you to consider your reader. But have you ever considered that format and mechanics can also help you make a favorable impression on your reader? Skillfully used, they can.

During your career, you will probably have to answer many inquiries that on the surface have only nuisance value. In our offices, for example, we daily get such inquiries as: "Tell me all about business communication." (As if we could!) "Where can I get a job in business and technical writing?" (We don't run a Placement Service.) "How many students in the country take business communication courses in any one given year?" This was our most recent:

Feb. 7, 1985

Dear Sir,

I am doing a Career Report for School. My report is on being a Humorist. Could you please sent [sic, but corrected to "send" by someone with a red pencil — his teacher, perhaps] me all the free information you can send me on a Humorist?

Thank-you for your prompt reply.

Sincerely,
TROY COPELAND
100 Market St.
Blueville, IN

Here is the reply:

February 13, 1985

Mr. Troy Copeland
100 Market Street
Blueville, IN

Dear Mr. Copeland:

I'm sorry to say that we're not very much in the humor business here at our association. However, if you are looking for good humorists, I would suggest

Message Format and Mechanics

> that you go to your local library and draw out the works of James Thurber, Robert Benchley, Ring Lardner, S. J. Perelman, and Ogden Nash. You should also consider some of the classic masters such as Mark Twain and your own Indiana writer George Ade. I'm sure the works of some of these great American humorists will be available in your local library.
>
> Lots of luck to you on your project.
>
> Sincerely,
>
> [Signature Block]

It may seem unnecessary for the staff to take time out from their busy days to answer such questions. But another quality you should acquire if you are going to be a good communicator is to care about your reader.

Another example, Figure B.13, is a letter written by a very successful freelance advertising copywriter answering an inquiry from a high school student about advertising and advertising copywriters. You can't pinpoint the letter style he used. There is nothing standard about the way the letter is set up on the page or in the way he emphasizes what he is telling his reader. But his reader must have felt very special about his taking the time to give her as much caring advice as he did. Notice how he takes her from one point to another with ellipses, indentions, enumeration, and so on. This letter proves that mechanics and format don't have to be formal and rigid. They can be useful tools of expression, too.

The conventions of letter style, mechanics, and the odds and ends that we have passed on to you are to business letter writing as gestures and body language are to speaking. They can set the stage for your presentation.

Many times during your career you are going to be puzzled about some aspect of letter style or mechanics. There is much more you should know. (Our offices are besieged by "What do I do if ... ?" questions from those who think we know everything.) But this is a book about writing and speaking, and we are under serious constraints as to how much we can tell you. (Most secretarial handbooks, where you can find other answers, are between 600 and 800 pages in length.) So, when you go into the business world, find out if the person who is going to be helping you has a good secretarial handbook. If not, you would be wise to buy one for your own reference. Of course, you won't use it daily. Maybe not once a month. But only one face-saving referral will repay you for your investment.

If we have succeeded only in making you conscious of to whom you are writing, what you are signing, how you can consider your audience, and why you should use format and mechanics to enhance your business correspondence, we will consider ourselves rewarded. And you should be well on your way to becoming a successful business correspondent.

November 10, 1986

Cheryl Ann Krueger
35 South Hill Street
Cleona, PA 17042

I thought...

Cheryl Krueger, that I had answered your letter a long time ago.

However... I can't find a carbon copy of that letter. So here we go.

You ask about advertising copy and copywriters. First to encourage you: If you learn to write direct mail advertising packages (letters and enclosures), there are many opportunities out there for you... *if* you are truly competent. So... let's take a look at what it takes for you to become a competent copywriter:

    1. You should have an intense interest in learning the various types of writing, including copy for advertising. This means all types of writing used out there in the business world. Learn copywriting for broadcast, print, public relations, direct mail, and so on. But also learn the essay and the short story and the editorial and news report.

    Each of the types of writing for advertising differs from the other. Learn those differences. Direct mail copy, for example, is written on the basis of one writer to one reader. Broadcast and print are based on addressing a group of people.

    Knowing these differences is vital to success in writing advertising copy.

    2. While in school, you should take as many writing courses as is possible. In high school, you must have courses in journalism and creative writing. Take them. The reason: to get the expressive mechanism that is your writing talent up to its best performance level.

    3. All the time... read the best of writing you can find. Reading is the key to learning to write. This reading should include everything from the classics to the paperback books. The reason for reading heavily is that you want to see how other people handle words. Since each of us sees the world differently, the way we handle words comes out of each of us in a different style.

Figure B.13(a). Answering an inquiry, first page

Cheryl Ann Krueger   2   November 10, 1986

    And what you want to learn is how to handle a variety of writing styles — from the objective use of words you see in company annual reports to the more or less "romanticized" use of language in the ads coming from the cosmetic industries.
    The reason: to give you a highly broad point of view on how words can be applied to various purposes in selling, in persuasion, in reporting, and so forth. The more you know about the many uses to which words can be put, the greater will be your ability to use words.
    4. Read some of the advertising books that tell how to write copy. Your school librarian can help you here. Usually, if one library doesn't have a given book, it can be borrowed from another library.
    5. Try to get some experience in writing advertising copy for the school paper, the school yearbook . . . or any local merchant who is willing to let you try doing his advertising.
    6. In college, take a major in advertising or else a major in English with a minor in advertising. The reason I add English is this:

> Maybe, just maybe, your talent is too good for advertising and should be devoted to the more literary pursuits. You will learn this difference as you get a little older. In any event, going this way gives you a skill that is readily salable in the marketplace — to help support yourself — and the possible skills to devote yourself to writing articles, fiction, novels maybe. This way you have all bases covered and your talent well developed.

    7. Advertising copywriting, especially in direct mail, can give you a good income. I know one woman who writes at home, types the copy at home. It comes out at a printer downtown, all set for printing. She makes about $100,000 a year.
    For a bit more information I suggest you write to the Direct Mail/Marketing Association, 6 East 43 Street, New York, NY 10017. Ask for information on copywriting and for a copy of their "Careers Booklet." They're very good about such requests.

Figure B.13(b). Answering an inquiry, second page

Cheryl Ann Krueger   3   November 10, 1986

    To sum it up: Learn to write as well as you can. Aim it at advertising. But, please, don't discard the possibility of becoming a writer of books, articles, and so on, too. Maybe you'll take a turn into that direction as you add years along the way.
    Good luck, Cheryl Krueger, and may your talent with words give you great pleasure and satisfaction.

Take care...

[Signature Block]

Figure B.13(c). Answering an inquiry, third page

APPENDIX C

A Short Handbook of Grammar and Punctuation

INTRODUCTION

Be Sensible About Grammar

Grammar is very important.
Grammar is not important at all.

Which statement is true? Neither, probably. The truth lies somewhere in between. Our reason is that issues in grammar are not always as simple as they seem. For example, two of us wrote a letter to the *Wall Street Journal*. In the letter we used the expression *none are*, as in "None of these people are going to remember certain grammatical points."

Readers of the *Journal* were shocked. How could two specialists in English make this mistake in grammar — a singular subject with a plural verb? Terrible! Yet if you look at the major books on grammar and usage, you will find that none of them condemn the usage. (We just did it again: none . . . condemn.)

In fact, *none are* has been standard usage for hundreds of years. You don't need to be an expert in grammar to know this. You don't even need to consult one of the grammar and usage books listed in Chapter 6. Most standard desk dictionaries give a "usage note" on *none*, allowing it to be used with a plural verb. (No writer should be without a desk dictionary; it is as useful for points on grammar as it is for spelling, defining, and so on.)

The best way to avoid errors in grammar is *to write clearly and simply* — that is, you should follow the suggestions in Chapter 6. Using *who does what* and chunking your sentences will clean out most errors automatically. Long, involved sentences are breeding grounds for grammatical disease.

But how do you know whether something is an error in grammar or usage? Is it wrong to split an infinitive, for instance (as in "to badly write")? To change number, as in "Each employee should receive their W-2 form on Wednesday"? In the course of a working day, several questions like these may arise. When they do, check this *Handbook* and, if necessary, your dictionary.

N   MISUSE OF NOUNS

N₁   Use the Right Form of Plural Noun

Ordinarily, nouns form their plurals by adding *s* or *es:* auto/autos, bus/busses, chair/chairs, tomato/tomatoes, ache/aches, tax/taxes.

If you are doubtful about a plural form, check your dictionary.

N₂   Use a Possessive with an -ING Noun (Gerund)

Gerunds are verbal nouns like the italicized words below:

Taxing those properties is a good idea.
She does not believe in *renting; buying* is best for her.

When you have a noun or pronoun before the gerund, use a possessive form:

JOHN'S *taxing* those properties was a good idea.
I didn't agree with HER *renting* an apartment.

Wrong:	Is there any reason for *them* avoiding Japanese products?
Right:	Is there any reason for *their* avoiding Japanese products?
Wrong:	*Me* asking for that report was my own idea.
Right:	*My* asking for that report was my own idea.
Wrong:	That was the reason for *Germany* dominating the market then.
Right:	That was the reason for *Germany's* dominating the market then.

PN MISUSE OF PRONOUNS

PN₁ Check Pronouns for Agreement

This agreement is faulty: "They ordered *everyone* to pick up *their* tools and go." Since *everyone* is singular, the pronoun *their* does not agree with it.

    Wrong: I told *each plumber* coming to the site to bring *their* own helper.
    Right: I told *each plumber* coming to the site to bring *his or her* own helper.
    Right: I told *all the plumbers* coming to the site to bring *their* own helpers. (Instead of making the pronoun agree with the expression appearing earlier in the sentence, start the sentence with a more logical word. *Each plumber* refers to *all the plumbers*.)

    Wrong: If you ask a *supervisor* to give you a big raise, give *them* several reasons you deserve it.
    Right: If you ask a supervisor to give you a big raise, *give him or her* . . .
    Right: If you ask your *supervisors* for a big raise, give *them* . . .

You can often avoid errors in pronoun agreement by deciding early in the discussion whether you want to be in the singular or the plural. Should you refer to supervisors in general, or one of them as an individual? After you decide, be consistent when you choose pronouns.

For a comment on the "generic pronoun," see "Sex and the Language," in Appendix D.

PN₂ Avoid Shift in Pronouns

Before choosing pronoun forms, plan ahead. Try to be consistent.

    Wrong: If *one's* car breaks down, the dealer provides a loan car for *you*.
    Right: (1) If *one's* car breaks down, the dealer provides a loan car for *him* or *her*.
                (2) If *your* car breaks down, the dealer provides a loan car for *you*.
                (3) If cars break down, the dealer provides loan cars.
                (4) For any car that breaks down, the dealer provides a loan car.

As you can see, there can be several ways to avoid a shift in pronouns.

PN₃ Use Right Form of Pronoun

To find most errors in pronoun form, set the construction off by itself.

Wrong:	The salary structure was specially designed for *we* part-timers.
Set off the pronoun:	The salary structure was specially designed for *we*. (*We* should be *us*.)
Right:	The salary structure was specially designed for *us* part-timers.
Wrong:	Would you call Jill and *she* on the phone?
Set off the pronoun:	Would you call *she*? (*She* should be *her*.)
Right:	Would you call Jill and *her* on the phone?
Wrong:	Clinton and *me* will walk to the meeting with you.
Right:	Clinton and *I* will walk to the meeting with you.

Who vs. *whom*. Use *whom* when it is the object of a preposition: "*for* whom," "*to* whom," *with* whom." Use *who* with everything else.*

PN₄ Avoid Vague Pronoun References

Make pronoun references clear:

Wrong:	In discussing the accounting requirements, it made us feel that we had the wrong idea about the limitations of accounting. (What does *it* refer to?)
Right:	As we were discussing the accounting requirements, we began to realize that we had the wrong idea about the limitations of accounting.
Wrong:	The policy had several benefits listed on page 4 that clients had trouble understanding. This required me to get help from an insurance expert. (What does *this* refer to?)
Right:	Since the policy had several benefits listed on page 4 that clients had trouble understanding, an insurance expert helped me rewrite the section for clarity.
Wrong:	She left three bills and two new checks on Ms. Bartlett's desk last night. We discovered two of them missing the next morning. (Does *them* refer to bills or checks, or to one of each?)
Right:	She left.... We discovered the two checks missing the next morning.

---

*See "Whom's Doom," in T. M. Bernstein, *Dos, Don'ts & Maybes of English Usage* (New York: Times Books, 1977), pp. 238-244. Bernstein declares that *whom* is unnecessary except with prepositions.

A Short Handbook of Grammar and Punctuation 463

V MISUSE OF VERBS

V₁ Avoid Errors in Agreement

Verbs should ordinarily agree with their subjects:

Economists *are* able to predict the future.
The Englishman *was* an engineer.

If you are in doubt, let the meaning determine the agreement.

    Problem: A *number* of these parts *was* (?) *were* (?) rejected.
    Right: A *number* of these parts *were* rejected. (Clearly, *number* designates more than one part.)
    Right: (1) *Several* of these parts *were* rejected.
           (2) A *few* of these parts *were* rejected.
           (3) The inspectors rejected some of these parts.

Consider the typical problems in verb agreement in V_2–V_6 below.

V₂ Be Wary of Clumsy Joiners

In addition to, as well as, and *along with* can give problems with verbs.

    Problem: My module, together with three other modules in the assembly process, *was* (?) *were* (?) saved by the procedure.
    Right: My *module*, together with three other modules in the assembly process, *was* saved by the procedure. (A singular subject uses a singular verb.)
    Note this solution: My *module* and *three other modules* in the assembly process *were* saved by the procedure. (Where you can, use *and* instead of clumsy joiners.)

V₃ Use Verbs Properly with Group Nouns

    Problem: The research team *is* (?) *are* (?) surprised by *their* discovery.
    Right: The research *team is* surprised by *its* discovery. (Consider the team as a unit.)
    Right: The *members* of the research team *are* surprised by their discovery. (Use a plural subject.)
    Problem: A *dozen feet* of tape *is* (?) *are* (?) enough for this box.
    Right: A *dozen feet* of tape *is* enough for this box. (Consider a *dozen feet* as a unit.)
    Right: We need a dozen feet of tape for this box.

V₄ Use Verbs Properly with Pronouns

Problem: She is one of those women who *is* (?) *are* (?) up for promotion.
Right: She is one of those women who *are* up for promotion.

(Make the verb agree with the noun (*women*) that the pronoun (*who*) stands for.)

Right: She is the kind of woman who is up for promotion.

(Put the whole thing in the singular.)

V₅ Use Verbs Properly with "Subject-Is-Noun" Clauses

Problem: The main issue *is* (?) *are* (?) strong currencies.
Right: The main *issue is* strong currencies. (Make the verb agree with the subject.)
Right: The main *issue is* that *currencies are* too strong.

V₆ Use Verbs Properly with Expletive ("It-There") Statements

Problem: There *is* (?) *are* (?) dissatisfied executives in the department.
Right: There *are* dissatisfied *executives* in the department. (Make the verb agree with the subject, *executives*.)
Right: In the department, some executives are dissatisfied.

V₇ Avoid Errors in Tense ("*Time*")

Wrong: She said to me that she *is* ready. (Both events are in the past.)
Right: She said to me that she *was* ready.
Wrong: Economists then *believe* that the national debt *was* related to interest rates.
Right: Economists then *believed* that the national debt *was* related . . .
Right: Economists now *believe* that the national debt *is* related . . .

V₈ Use the Subjunctive Properly

The subjunctive is a verb form used mainly in contrary-to-fact statements and after wishes (or requests or demands). The verb form may be *were, be,* or the verb without the final *s*.

Contrary-to-fact statements:

If he *were* truthful about that he would not be so nervous. (*He is not truthful.*)
He would not do that if he *were* thinking. (*He is not thinking.*)
If this *be* militance, then I am not a militant. (*This is not militance.*)

After wishes, requests, or demands:

I wish this *were* Friday.
Let her *live*.
We demanded that they *be* heard.
I request that Jones *be* reprimanded.

V₉ Avoid the Split Infinitive

Do not "split" the *to* from its verb if awkwardness results:

Wrong:	*To* quickly go
Right:	*To go* quickly
Wrong:	I want you *to* properly *do* your work.
Right:	I want you *to do* your work properly.
Right:	I want you *to do* your work as well as you can.
	I want you *to do* good work.
	Please do good work.

M MISUSE OF MODIFIERS

Modifiers are sentence elements that limit, qualify, or describe the meaning of an expression.

M₁ Do Not Misplace Modifiers

Wrong:	She nearly tried to make all her board members happy.
Right:	She tried to make nearly all her board members happy.
Wrong:	She left for Portland on a plane two thousand miles away.
Right:	She left for Portland, two thousand miles away.
Right:	I got on a plane bound for Portland, which was two thousand miles away.
Wrong:	We destroyed the old well near the south corner of the Chicago plant, which was full of green, rotted wood. (The *plant* was full of rotted wood?)
Right:	The old well that we discovered in the south corner of the Chicago plant was full of green, rotted wood.

M₂   Avoid Dangling Modifiers

Most dangling modifiers occur at the opening of the sentence:

Having eaten her breakfast, the flight departed.

Make sure that your opener modifies the subject of its following main clause:

Having eaten her breakfast, she boarded the departing flight.

Wrong:	Turning on the word processor, the report was quickly finished.
Right:	Turning on the word processor, she quickly finished the report.
Wrong:	Angry at the contract, his feet inadvertently kicked over the wastebasket.
Right:	Angry at the contract, he inadvertently kicked over the wastebasket.
Right:	He was so angry at the contract that he kicked over the wastebasket.

S   FAULTY SENTENCE STRUCTURE

S₁   Use Coordination Properly

Do not put unequal ideas into equal main clauses; you may create faulty coordination:

Wrong:	They had no time, *and* they skipped their morning break.
Right:	*Because* they had no time, they skipped their morning break.
Wrong:	Georlene was a trainee, *and* she won the top award for performance.
Right:	*Even though* she was only a trainee, Georlene won the top award for performance.

S₂   Avoid Faulty Comparisons

A faulty comparison: "Smith's *solutions* were the same as *Lentz.*" The problem is that the writer is comparing the wrong things, *solutions* and *Lentz.*

Right:	Smith's solutions were the same as Lentz's.
Right:	Smith's solutions were the same as those described by Lentz.

S₃ Avoid Faulty Parallelism

Parallel elements should be written in the same grammatical form. Examples:

Selkirk and *Miller* wanted to use their own attorneys.
Consulting in and *teaching* business law are not activities for lazy people.
A few smaller companies decided to *stop* and *wait* in order to see what the bigger companies would do.

Put parallel *ideas* in parallel *form:*

> She *believes* in the company and *having* faith in it.
> She *believes* in the company and *has* faith in it.
> The credit report had too many *graphs, tables,* and *the statistics were faulty.*
> The credit report misused *graphs, tables,* and *statistics.*

P   SOME HINTS ON PUNCTUATION

P₁   When to Use a Comma

a. When you use coordinate adjectives:

new, practical computer

New and *practical* are *coordinate* because you can logically put *and* between them — "new *and* practical."

honest, capable person (honest *and* capable person)
cold, dark office (cold *and* dark office)
But: *last spring* semester (not last *and* spring semester)

b. When you write a parallel construction of three or more units:

inquiries, claims, and *credit*
We must not ignore the *Sales, Accounting, or Transport* Departments in our discussion.
We finished our work, we left early, and *we beat the heavy traffic out of the city.*

c. When you use a coordinating conjunction (*and, or, but, so, for*) to join two main clauses:

The committee approved your proposal, *and* they agreed to fund it.
Ms. Mason agreed with the statement, *but* she asked that it be checked with the Director of Publicity.
The photocopier needs adjustment, *so* be sure to call the repairman before you leave tonight.

d. When you add a sentence unit to a main clause — before, after, or inside the clause.

Because the auditor will be here tomorrow, we will not have our customary meeting at 2:30.
The company could not expect more credit, *even considering its greatly improved financial condition.*
That is what they intended, *to improve the flow of work in the Planning Section.*
Our design of the grommets, *which had been suggested by Bill Plant,* was turned down by the technical staff.
You typed her memo, *not mine!*

e. When you use *direct address:*

Mike, please complete the order.
Ms. Rosenthal, could you determine the costs of the project?

f. When you use places or dates:

San Antonio, Texas
February 23, 1987
On August 14, 1946, in Teaneck, South Carolina
The package arrived in Columbus, Ohio, on October 14, 1985.

g. When you need to prevent ambiguity:

By speaking of the dead, Reagan appealed to Polish patriotism.

If you write "By speaking of the dead Reagan . . .", your reader may be confused and have to reread the sentence.

The deductions allowed, the taxpayer is able to. . . .

"The deductions allowed the taxpayer . . ." may be confusing.

P₂   When to Use a Semicolon

a. When you join two main clauses with conjunctive adverbs like *however, moreover, therefore, thus, indeed.*

You should be commended; *indeed,* we will ask for a written commendation for you.
Natalie and David bought good stocks; *however,* they didn't get rich.
The company overpaid its income tax; *therefore,* the Internal Revenue Service will return a large amount of money.

b. When you join two main clauses without a coordinating conjunction or a conjunctive adverb:

A Short Handbook of Grammar and Punctuation   469

Secondary recovery is important; we are not finding new oil fields.
His style as a leader is careless; he doesn't seem to care whether his employees understand his ideas or not.

c. When you need to clarify a series complicated by internal punctuation:

Unclarified: At the dais were Prentice the president, Gilbert the vice president, and Tchou the comptroller.
Clarified: At the dais were Prentice, the president; Gilbert, the vice president; and Tchou, the comptroller.
Unclarified: The janitor tells us what kind of cleaner to use, the same as he uses, when to use it, the same time he does, where to place the furniture, the same place he wants it, and, most obnoxious of all, which kind of trash goes in which wastebackets.
Clarified: The janitor tells us what kind of cleaner to use, the same as he uses; when to use it, the same time he does; where to place the furniture, the same place he wants it; and, most obnoxious of all, which kind of trash goes in which wastebaskets.

P₃ When to Use a Colon

a. When you introduce a quotation:

At the end of the year, she sent this memo: "Please reorganize the Delta Section and re-assign extra personnel."

b. When you introduce a list:

Do consider these stocks: U.S. Steel, Bell Telephone, and Illinois Power.

Sometimes it is better to omit the colon:

Do consider U.S. Steel, etc.

c. When you punctuate a salutation:

Dear President Ryan:
Dear Mr. Slope:
Dear Ms. Perez:

P₄ When to Use a Dash

A dash indicates a break in thought, usually a fairly strong one:

He was made president twenty-five years later — the oldest person ever to have the job.
Are there — be careful with your answer — any extenuating circumstances in this unusual case?

P₅   When to Use Parentheses

Parentheses set off an expression or a single word from the rest of the statement:

> The company I am writing to (Smithson, Inc.) is very important to our success.
> There are too few women accountants in this firm (this was her claim).
> As it passed under the bridge, the mast (which had been weakened by the storm) suddenly snapped in two.

P₆   When to Use an Apostrophe

a. When you need a possessive form:

> *Myra's* arm
> *Ross's* administrative style
> the *book's* point (one book)
> the *books'* point (more than one book)

With personal pronouns you do not use the apostrophe: "his job," "it is hers."

b. When you form a contraction:

> *It's* wrong to think that.
> *She'll* understand your report.
> But I *can't* understand it.

c. When you form plurals using letters or numbers:

> Next semester, she is hoping for two *A's*, 3 *B's*, and no *C's*.
> I remember two *5's* in the missing serial number.
> Let us hope for peace in the *1980's*.

P₇   When to Use Quotation Marks

a. When you refer to titles of relatively short works like articles in *Business Week* ("Is There a New Boom in Auto Sales?"). Typically, report titles are put in quotation marks:

> Mr. Finerty wants to see the second Jackson report, "Tactical Efficiency of Short-Range Missiles."

In the business world, the rule of length is generally quite simple: Book-length titles are italicized (*Renewing American Industry* or *The Termination Handbook*). Any title of a work that is distinctly shorter, like an article or a chapter in a book, will be put in quotes:

A Short Handbook of Grammar and Punctuation 471

Before Tuesday, read "Why are Employees Discharged?" in *The Termination Handbook*.

b. When you quote the exact words of another person:

As Robert Coulson says, fighting usually brings "disciplinary action, often against both participants."

Another example:

In *How to Write and Publish a Scientific Paper*, Robert Day says: "I herewith ask all young scientists to renounce the false modesty of previous generations of scientists. Do not be afraid to name the agent of the action in a sentence, even when it is 'I' or 'we.' "

If you need to quote more than four lines, block the quotation like this:

> I herewith ask all young scientists to renounce the false modesty of previous generations of scientists. Do not be afraid to name the agent of the action in a sentence, even when it is "I" or "we." Once you get into the habit of saying "I found," you will also find that you have a tendency to write "*S. aureus* produced lactate" rather than "Lactate was produced by *S. aureus*." (Note that the "active" statement is in three words; the passive requires five.) — Robert Day

P₈ When to Use a Hyphen

a. When you need a syllable break at the end of a line:

sup-ply   illu-minate   dosim-eter

b. When you use a prefix before a syllable starting with *e* or *o*:

co-op   pre-empt   re-entry

c. When you make a compound word:

ex-premier   *all*-powerful   *pro*-Soviet

d. When you use a compound modifier:

out-of-work painter   *one-year* clause   *deep-well* drilling

If you are in doubt about hyphenation, particularly for prefixes and syllable breaks, check your dictionary.

P₉ When to Use Italics (Underlining)

a. When you emphasize a word or phrase:

It must be done by *Wednesday*.
Have the cleanup done by *Howitch*, not Klein.

b. When you refer to specific words or phrases:

The word *antidote* is not hyphenated.
Did the Chinese understand what we meant by *democratic capitalism?*

c. When you refer to the titles of magazines, books, stage productions, movies, or newspapers:

The Art of Technical Reporting (book)
The Right Stuff (book)
The Right Stuff (movie)
Newsweek (magazine)
St. Louis *Post Dispatch* (newspaper)

The relative length of works determines whether you use quotation marks or italics. An article on economics in *Fortune* is put in quotation marks; a textbook on economics is italicized.

EXERCISES

1. The following sentences contain examples of grammatical errors covered in the handbook. Correct them.
   a. My list of supplies were so long the company refused to pay for all of them.
   b. Be sure to really inspect the computer handbook before turning it on.
   c. It says in the handbook to not allow temperatures in the room to rise above eighty-two degrees.
   d. Mark and me understood that from the beginning.
   e. Inflated to an enormous size, Thomason checked the rubber floats in the system.
   f. Business jargon makes Ms. Arkham just as disgusted as those people who talk endlessly of nothing but ballet and Bach.
   g. Fewer people went to the movies in the 1970s; more and more they bought cable TV instead of watching their neighbors.
   h. By refusing to allow smoking in the lounge, there was a belief that the habit might be reduced.
   i. If you check with Personnel, they will tell you how to handle the problem.
   j. No one appreciates Smith working more than I do.

2. These sentences also contain examples of grammatical errors. Correct them.
   a. There have been many customers who have approved of this service, and I think it is a good one.

A Short Handbook of Grammar and Punctuation   473

 b. Sheila says my handwriting is easier to read than her secretary.
 c. Concentrating hard, the report was written quickly.
 d. Each person in Advertising should submit their own proposal.
 e. A legislature does not like to tax its citizens, and they will usually attempt to raise money some other way.
 f. I wish this was payday.
 g. This type organization is one of those that surprises you when you first encounter it.
 h. Neither the CEO nor the Board of Directors were responsible for the losses this year.
 i. To quietly and peacefully retire at seventy is all these workers are asking for.
 j. I wish you could have stopped them taking the fine print so seriously.

3. The following sentences contain punctuation errors covered in the handbook. Correct them.
 a. The instructor said Read the section called Business Practice in Jones book Economic History.
 b. The boss opinion is that the word hopefully should not be used in our ad copy.
 c. My job is not in danger neither is yours.
 d. The contract was well written clear and to the point but it was still missing one clause we had agreed upon.
 e. Jarelson flew her own plane a new Piper to the meeting in South Carolina.
 f. At the end of the year however ones job get easier.
 g. Before the Saturday morning session be sure to pick up the statements forms and all pertinent literature at the main desk.
 h. Its accounting system failing the company asked for suggestions from a consulting firm for improvements.
 i. The admissions office called and wants to know what to do with the student program requests for pre registration.
 j. Royalties from the song Oklahoma have over the years paid for the entire original production of the musical Oklahoma.

4. In the paragraphs below, we have numbered each space where the author originally placed a punctuation mark inside a sentence. After you have punctuated the sentences, explain or defend in a brief phrase each mark you used.

 Similar readaptive changes are taking place at the edge of the industry where the steel service centers are assuming larger responsibilities for distribution. The earliest steel service centers[1] or warehouses[2] stored standardized products for customers in transportation and industry as the big companies turned out steel instead of orders. Most of these warehouses were independently owned[3] although some major firms have acquired them in order to locate near customers or to absorb excess capacity. At first the warehouses[4] or service centers[5] merely stockpiled standard items such as bars[6] rounds[7] and structural shapes. In the past thirty years[8] however[9] the service centers have become increasingly active in finishing products and pursuing customers. Robert Welch[10] president of the Steel Service Center Institute[11] estimates that service centers now modify about 80% of the products they handle. Such modification includes cutting[12] welding[13] pressing[14] rolling[15] and stamping. In short[16] the service centers have become finishing mills for steel and other metals.

[17]I think that what has happened over the past ten years[18,19] says one service center executive[20,21] is that the metal service centers have gained more expertise[22] and we have been willing to make heavy capital commitments in terms of equipment.[23] In contrast to most steel companies[24] the service centers have been quick to detect and respond to customers[25] needs.[26] We are extremely aggressive investors in our ability to serve the customer[27,28] says another service center manager.[29] I think we're alive and well and eager to do anything that is necessary to serve the customer's needs.[30]

Such attitudes are borne out by the growth of the service center industry. Service centers now consume about 20% of all domestic steel shipments[31] up from less than 15% a decade ago[32] by the end of the 1980's[33] according to some projections[34] that figure may reach 30%. Service centers buy metal from foreign as well as domestic producers[35] and the most efficient of them turn over their inventory forty to fifty times a year. Like the mini[36] mills[37] the service centers profit from proximity to customers[38] but they also have set about their business with a competitive spirit that the major firms would do well to emulate. — Paul Lawrence and Davis Dyer

APPENDIX D

Nice to Know

Here is some handy information for you on five topics that might occasionally cause you difficulty: *writer's block, outline forms, sex terminology, legal issues*, and *dictation*.

AVOIDING WRITER'S BLOCK

Imagine that one morning you get in your car to go to work. You back out into the street and start to drive away, when suddenly you notice a huge pile of rocks blocking the entire street.

What do you do? If you are like many writers who encounter a block when they stare at an empty sheet of paper, you will just sit there in your car, race your engine, and mutter to yourself. If you are like a few unfortunate hotheads, you will drive your car right into the pile of rocks; this is known as The Approach Direct. It is hard on cars *and* writers, and tends to raise the blood pressure. If you pass by someone's office and hear angry noises and see a dozen crumpled pieces of paper on the floor, and there is somebody behind the desk with his head in his hands, you will know immediately that The Approach Direct has failed again.

As the title suggests, the solution to writer's block is to avoid it — even to outwit it, tame it, dissolve it, make it disappear. Your weapons are not direct attack, but guile and dissimulation.

You will know when you start to block. When it happens, here are some suggestions:

1. *Don't think about the writing you have to do.* Instead:
2. Take your pencil and start moving it on the sheet of paper in front of you. Any movements will do:

Or:

These warm-up exercises will help keep your muscles from tensing.
3. Write familiar words on the sheet:

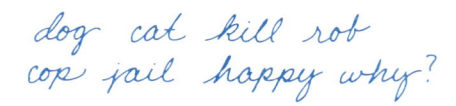

dog cat kill rob
cop jail happy why?

4. Alternate the words with the loosening-up exercises in No. 2.
5. Start writing little sentences about the things you can see in your office or room:

My walls are green. The color is ugly. Must ask Levinson a question. Can I get the place repainted?

6. Suddenly, before worry overtakes you, start writing the message that was originally blocked. Write one simple sentence after another. Is the message flowing well? Don't stop to think; just write.

If steps one through six work for you, you have avoided the block and can finish your message. If you block again, you may need other techniques.

Writers find that blocks often occur when the message "hooks" are not sharp (Chapter 1), or when they are unsure of their facts, or when they are unsure of what they want the reader to *believe* or *do* (see Overview).

If one of these is the case, then steps one through six won't be of much help because the source of the block lies in lack of preparation for writing. When this happens to you, there is really only one thing to do: go back and fill in on your areas of ignorance. Get the facts. And make sure you know what your reader should believe or do.

After you have done that, start again. Are you blocking now? If so, don't waste time getting angry with yourself. (It's not your fault; the devil did it.) Put pencil to paper, and just start to write the familiar words in your hook or main point:

project finance Evans finance Evans Evans Evans project finance

And write your reader's name over and over:

Marsh Marsh Marsh Marsh

Do both of these at once, loosening your muscles and keeping your brain warm and focussed on the subject of your message. Now start to write . . .

Mr. Marsh, I really wish you would change your mind about financing the Evans project. The Evans project is dear to my heart; it is also one that will help the company in our Fall campaign ⸺click⸺ *Mr. Marsh would you please reconsider the financing of the Evans project...*

Right at that *click* everything fell into place. You were relaxed; your mind was engaged on the problem; you knew where the message was going; your muscles were warmed up. The block just disappeared. You exercised it out of existence.

Some people never suffer from writer's block. Good for them. But for those of us who do, we are like baseball pitchers who need extra warm-up time before beginning to throw hard. If we don't warm up carefully, there goes the old arm, tied in knots and extremely painful. The main cure is to warm up carefully and not to worry.

Our example, as you have seen, is of a writer who uses pencil and paper. The same method works for those who dictate. For those who type or use a word processor, warm up by hitting keys at random and then typing cliches:

cnvmbj24343434 45trtfgf hjhjykopdhs ajcbghtuypio Now is the time for Now is the time Now is Now Now Now Now Now for the all good men to come to aid of their country men and women.

To be or not to be that is the question Who cares whether that is the question Hamlet was a dummy he should have run away from the castle with Ophelia and had a bunch of little great danes. etoain shrdlu.

Now you are warmed up and can start writing.

If you dictate your messages, you are lucky. You can just start talking about anything on your mind until you are warmed up. (Be sure to warn your secretary.)

The key to removing all blocks is action. Get your muscles, hands, and mind moving. When they are warm they will continue moving easily and with less effort on your part.

OUTLINE FORMS AND HOW THEY ARE USED

An outline is essentially a classification of ideas arranged according to levels of subordination. In other words, it arranges main ideas over subordinate ideas.

Express the main ideas using roman numerals:

Introduction
  I. First main idea
  II. Second main idea
  III. Third main idea
Conclusion

If you wish, you can start numbering with the Introduction and end with the Conclusion.

Subordinate ideas are expressed with letters and arabic numerals, in this fashion:

I. _____
  A. *(first-level subordination)*
  B. _____
II. _____
  A. _____
    1. *(second-level subordination)*
    2. _____
      a. *(third-level subordination)*
      b. _____
      c. _____
    3. _____
  B. _____
III. _____
  and so on.

Theoretically, you are not supposed to subordinate a part of your outline with only one point ("You can't have an A. without a B.; a 1. without a 2."). Actually, unless you are striving for geometric neatness in the appearance of the outline, you *can* have a single point. This happens, for instance, when you have only one example to support a particular idea. If your instructor objects to single subordinations on an outline, simply put the offending single point with the last item in the section to which it belongs.

We will consider three standard outline forms: sentence, topic, and mixed.

In sentence form, you write out the parts in full sentences. Here is a sentence outline of an early version of Chapter Four in this book:

   I. Should you write an outline?
      A. For some writers, an outline is necessary for good organization.
      B. For some other writers, an outline is useless or unnecessarily constricting.
      C. The term *outline* can mean different things.
         1. It can mean a few jottings on a piece of scratch paper.
         2. It can mean a detailed formal affair with many headings and subheadings.
      D. A formal outline is valuable if it helps *you*.
         1. Use it if the situation warrants.
         2. Use it if you are comfortable with it.
  II. Try the one-idea-to-a-card method.
      A. Put ideas on cards, one idea to each card.
      B. Classify the cards — that is, classify the ideas on them.
      C. Look for a logical pattern, one that "blocks out" your subject and your approach to it.
 III. Draw your organizational "blocks" (the graphic for your message) on a large sheet of paper.
      A. Any blocks you use should fit your purpose, subject, and audience.
         1. Try question-and-answer blocks.
         2. If you want your reader to *do* something, use *action* blocks.
            a. Need*
            b. Description of an action
            c. Why action is practical and beneficial
         3. There are two basic report forms.
            a. For scientific papers
            b. For engineering and business messages
      B. Create your blocks — your organizational pattern — for the situation.
  IV. Concluding remarks: re-emphasize point III. B. And:
      A. Consider the value also of "graded order."
      B. Note that some materials seem to demand a particular arrangement — for example, the materials of a process.

---

*At this level of our outline, you can save time and space by using fragments instead of complete sentences.

In the topic outline, you use fragments for all headings, both main and subordinate:

    I. The outline — when necessary?
       A. For some writers, improves organization
       B. For other writers, useless or constricting
       C. Meaning of outline
          1. A few jottings
          2. A detailed formal affair
       D. Helpfulness of outlines
          1. When situation warrants
          2. When comfortable with it
   II. The one-idea-to-a-card method
       A. Ideas on cards
       B. Cards classified
       C. Logical pattern: use "blocks"
   III. Blocking as organization—
      and so on.

In the mixed outline, you put your main points, as represented by roman numerals, in sentence form. Put everything else in topic or fragment form:

    I. Should you write an outline?
       A. For some writers, improves organization
       B. For other writers, useless or constricting
       C. Meaning of *outline*
          1. A few jottings
          2. A detailed formal affair
       D. Helpfulness of outlines
          1. When situation warrants
          2. When comfortable with it
   II. To help you organize your material before outlining, try the one-idea-to-a-card method.
       A. Ideas on cards
       B. Cards classified
       C. Logical pattern: a system of "blocks"
   III. Draw your organizational blocks (the graphic for your message) on a large sheet of paper.
      (and so on)

Each of these types of outline — the sentence, the topic, and the mixed — has advantages. Using the sentence outline, you have a strong control over everything you plan to say. In effect, with this kind of outline you have almost said it already. The topic outline is somewhat more flexible, and you can write it quicker. For some people, the mixed outline is the best because it combines the good qualities of the other two, without their weaknesses. Since it uses sentences for its main points, the writer has good control over the larger elements of the message. And the topic fragments in the other parts of the mixed outline are easy to manage and provide some flexibility in writing the first draft.

Your instructor may want you to write outlines in a certain way. Be sure to follow his or her wishes.

SEX TERMINOLOGY

SEX AND THE LANGUAGE
Charlene Tibbetts

When I started to write this brief comment, I thought it was going to be easy. After all, I know about the situation from the ground up. I have long experience in business and education, and I'm a professional writer with a feel for the language and its problems. Moreover, as a professional woman, with three grown daughters working as professionals, I have more than a little sympathy for the situation regarding sex and the language.

Alas, writing this comment has not been as easy as I thought. Let me give you the reasons.

To begin with, any comments that someone in my position (and yours) might make should be truthful — should accord with the facts. But some of the "facts" regarding sex and English usage are right now somewhat confusing.

Twenty years ago, they were not confusing. *He* and *his* were accepted (by most educated people) as generic pronouns. *Salesmen* sold things. *Mankind* referred to people on earth. A committee had a *chairman*. Women were either *Mrs.* X or *Miss* Y.

Ten years ago, we were told that all this was changing. And so it seemed to be changing. People used *chairperson, he or she, salespeople, humankind, Ms.*, and so on. At least some people did.

What we call English usage is a funny thing. Indeed Usage, as I keep reminding my students, is a sniffy, narrow-minded old bachelor with a set of prejudices as long as your arm. He will accept *am not*, but will drive from his door a much more vivid word, *ain't*. He will take *as* (as a conjunction) to his bony bosom, but throw a tantrum at *like*. He will insist on using *whom* in situations where nobody but a copy editor can remember how to use it. He will accept *salesperson*, but not *chairperson, fireperson,* or *mailperson*. If you say to Usage, "You don't make sense," he merely sneers: "I don't *have* to make sense."

I have made Usage a man, but of course she is also a woman — really, all of humankind that speak English. *Standard usage* refers to the way educated people use the language when they are being more or less proper and careful. Don't expect usage to be consistent, or expect the English language to be consistent. The language is made by human beings, and you know what *they* are.

Language changes, but not constantly or regularly. Generally, you don't notice changes in standard English because most of them come slowly or when you aren't looking. As I write, we are in the middle of some changes in a few parts of the language denoting or implying sex. And those changes are still going on, but not consistently — or in the same direction.

Competing Usages

English has more words than it can possibly use. I was looking up loose synonyms for the word *robber* the other day, and stopped after finding about forty of them. Words and phrases compete with each other, and the same person will employ competing terms without being conscious of doing so. On a recent long flight I heard a young woman refer to people doing her job as *flight representative*, *stewardess*, and *stew* — the latter being her own term for herself.

My daughter is a dispatcher for a fire department. She refers to the men she works with as firefighters. "What do the men call themselves?" I asked her. "Oh," she said, "they use *fireman* most of the time, but they use *firefighter* when the new contract comes up and they want more money." The other day, I saw both terms employed in a front-page story in the Chicago *Tribune*. *Fireman* is often used in headlines because it is shorter. Shortening frequently happens: When *salesman* became *sales representative*, some people immediately shortened it to *sales rep*, which later became simply *rep*. But all three terms are available for use.

The facts show that instead of offensive terms being replaced in standard English, most of them remain in the language as *competing terms:*
Ms., Mrs., Miss
Chair, chairman, chairwoman, chairperson
He, he or she (plus avoidances — see below)
Man, humanity, humankind, people, human beings
Salesperson, sales representative, salesman, saleswoman.

What Do We Do?

In public we are pretty much stuck with standard usage, whether we like it or not. (In private we can do what we please.) This means that whenever we find competing usages, we can usually employ any one of them without fear. Of course, much depends upon your audience; I would not use *salesmen* when writing for any group who might be unhappy with the term. *Chairperson* is often used in colleges and universities, but it is less used in the business world — and it is rare in the halls of power. I have never seen it used for a CEO (Chief Executive Officer). In fact, the *-person* compounds are not consistently used in business.

Sometimes it is hard to know what to use. Take *Ms.*, for example. For reasons that I don't understand, in the late 1970s some people began to turn against *Ms.* In 1979, the Roper Organization conducted a nationwide poll, reporting that only sixteen percent of American women preferred to be called *Ms.*, while seventy-seven percent preferred *Miss* or *Mrs.*

In May of 1982, Carol Hymowitz, a reporter for the *Wall Street Journal*, looked into the situation of *Ms.* and found it most unhappy. For example, she reported the president of a mailing-list company as saying: "Such a small number of women are choosing it [now] that we aren't using it on order forms in a lot of our mail campaigns."

Some of the women professionals Ms. Hymowitz interviewed said that they preferred using *Ms.*, but others weren't interested. Said one woman: "I really don't care what I'm called as long as I'm getting paid the same as the man sitting next to me who's doing the same job."

I approve of *Ms.*, and use it myself. But as the editor of *Webster's New World Dictionary* remarks, *Ms.* "hasn't replaced *Miss* or *Mrs.* and become the universally used title that we thought it would."

Before using *Ms,* nowadays, I try to find out what my audience thinks of the word.

Suggestions for a Rule on the Generic Pronoun (*he* and *his*)

The word *generic* refers to a class, group, or species. The English language is full of generics. Most of them we don't notice because they are so normal and idiomatic. As linguist Otto Jespersen pointed out, there are generic nouns, pronouns, adjectives, phrases, abstractions, judgments — even generic verbs and numbers, as in: "We *used to go* there every summer." And "The golf scores were all in the *70s.*" Such things are built into the language; they are a part of its brick and mortar.

The generic *he* is standard, and you can use it if you want to. If you don't want to, or if you think your audience would not like it, here are other choices:

1. Avoid *he* by using plurals.
2. Avoid *he* by using *you.*
3. Use *he* and *she* sparingly. And don't repeat the phrase in clause after clause.
4. Write "around" the problem — for example, instead of writing *The student sees his chance*, write *The student sees a chance.*
5. Use the pattern of *everybody . . . their.*

Don't use *he/she* or *s/he.* The slash mark (/) is not used in standard English to make such compounds.

It is of some interest that the major authorities you most often turn to (the dictionaries) still allow *he.* The latest *Webster's Collegiate* (1985) says that *he* is "used in a generic sense and when the sex of the person is unspecified."

But not one of the six solutions I just gave seems entirely satisfactory by itself. In many instances, I would prefer the pattern of *everybody . . . their* — although I don't have the courage to use it very often. *Everybody* can be clearly plural in meaning, just as *none* can be. Indeed, the authorities agree that *none* is more often than not a plural, so why can't we accept *everybody* (or *anybody*) as a plural in some sentences? (Check with your instructor before using *everybody* as a plural.)

You can use *you* in a larger number of cases, like this one. I like *you* because it loosens up a writer's style, making it more conversational and direct.

He or she is all right if used sparingly. Many readers don't like it because it is both redundant and awkward. In one chapter of this text, I first wrote:

> As the interviewer, you may have a great deal of influence over the person's future in the company, or the choice of job that he or she will take. Therefore you should empathize with him or her and recognize that he or she may be nervous or afraid. It is up to you to put him or her at ease.

That sort of thing just won't do — it's too clumsy.

In this book, we authors have experimented with replacing *he* and *his*, and have managed to remove most of them. The ones that remain seem more or less unavoidable. Incidentally, I would not mind if we passed a law making *she* a generic pronoun — we need one of some kind. A generic is necessary in the passage just quoted, considering the logic of the passage and its context.

LEGAL ISSUES

LEGAL ISSUES IN BUSINESS COMMUNICATIONS
Iris I. Varner, Illinois State University
Carson H. Varner, Attorney-at-Law

Most textbooks in business communication mention the importance of the law in communication, but they seldom discuss the issue in detail. The law is cited most often in connection with selling substitutes, and with writing personnel reports, application letters, résumés, interviews, collection letters, and sales letters. Usually the textbook authors simply state what is considered legal or illegal without further explanation.

Of course authors seldom have a legal background. They are trying to teach business communications, not the subtleties of legal issues. Thus we find that the "legal" rules given are usually sound and prudent but not necessarily a separation of "legal" from "illegal" practices. The purpose of this article is to discuss common legal issues in business communication, show their complexity, and give guiding principles rather than lists of *do's* and *don'ts*.

What is a Law?

Under our federal system, laws may be passed either by the individual state or by the central government in Washington, D.C. A Georgia law, for example, would have no effect in Illinois — although a Federal law would apply throughout the country and have precedence over conflicting state laws. The United States Constitution is the supreme law and takes precedence over conflicting statutes (a *statute* is a law passed by Congress or a state legislature). Once a statute or law is on the books there is still the problem of interpretation and meaning of the law.

For example, 21 U.S.C.A. §2000e-2 says, in part: "It shall be an unlawful employment practice ... to fail ... to hire ... any individual ... because of ... race, color, religion, sex, or national origin." (U.S.C.A. is the United States Code Annotated.) This is the Federal Civil Rights law, but who is to say what it really means? There are several sources of interpretation: a government agency, an executive order, a district attorney interpreting law. But the courts have the final say on the matter. Congress gives a government agency, under the executive branch, power to enforce the law. Thus, for example, the Equal Employment Opportunity Commission issues guidelines giving its interpretation of the Civil Rights law. The Internal Revenue Service also issues regulations which interpret the tax law passed by Congress. It is not unknown for the courts, who have the final say, to decide whether the agency has overstepped its authority. In saying what the law is, one should distinguish between statute and regulation.

Some laws are *federal*; other are *state*; and some are merely municipal ordinances. A newspaper, for example, once stated that there was a law that people must keep their alligators on leashes when taking them for a walk. Such a law, if it in fact exists, would probably be a municipal ordinance. In Normal, Illinois, it is against the law to discriminate against students, but a store right across the city limits could refuse to do business with students because there is no state or federal law forbidding discrimination against students.

Frequently people say that something is the law because of a court decision. Several warnings apply to this. First, don't fully trust newspaper accounts because journalists can be biased or (more frequently) simply ignorant of what the court decided. Each time a court makes a decision it is deciding a specific case based on a set of facts. As soon as the facts change, the decision can change (see below for the discussion of the requirement of a high school diploma for a job). Finally, a court decision is only precedent in the court's jurisdiction. A court decision from Texas is the law only in Texas.

In summary, when one hears about a law one should ask:
Is the source of the law ...

1. a constitution (state or Federal)?
2. a statute (Federal, state, local)?
3. a regulation (government agency's interpretation of a law)?
4. a court decision? — if so ...
    a. which court: Supreme court, other — Federal, state?
    b. what did the court really decide?

If you ask these questions, then you can better evaluate just exactly what the "law" is.

Here are a number of legal issues that typically come up in business communications classes:

Does the company name below the complimentary close provide more protection for the writer against legal involvement than if the name of the company is missing?

Assume you are the purchasing director of a company and you order office furniture for the company. When you act *for* the company, you act as the agent of the company and the company is the principal. The question arises whether the agent (call her Mary Jones) can be sued on the contract she made if the company for some reason breaches the contract. The general rule is that, as long as the agent made the contract for the company, she is not liable. The agent acts for the company if the agent identifies herself as the agent or if the other party should reasonably have known of the agency. The agent identifies herself by giving the title in the complimentary close; for example, "Mary Jones, Purchasing Director, Enterprises International, Inc."

One could be even more precise by adding to this: "As agent for . . ." but the title would normally be sufficient. Suppose she had signed only "Mary Jones"? For an order of $10,000 worth of office furniture on stationary with the company letterhead, the title would not be necessary to establish agency. On the other hand, suppose Mary Jones was ordered to buy a fur coat and used her title but did not say the coat was for company use. In this case Mary Jones might reasonably be held liable if the company refused to pay because the seller might reasonably have thought he was dealing with the credit of Mary Jones as Purchasing Director and not that of the company.

"I am acting only as agent for Enterprises International, Inc., and not in an individual capacity" should protect a person in all cases, but this phrase is awkward and strange.

To repeat, the name of the company below the complimentary close will not in itself prove agency, and omitting the name does not mean one can be held liable. Important are the facts of the particular situation.

Can a customer keep a substitute of an ordered product without having to pay for it on the basis of not having ordered it?

Based on 39 U.S.C.A. § 3009, the answer to this appears to be quite simple. The law clearly says, "Unordered merchandise . . . may be treated as a gift by the recipient. Who shall have the right to retain, use, discard, or dispose of it in any manner he sees fit without obligation whatsoever to the sender."

Suppose you come home and find an Apple II home computer — the kind you have always dreamed of — in a package addressed to you. Yet you did not order it. Apple calls you the next day and requests the return of the computer, saying they made a mistake. Ethical considerations aside, is the Apple legally yours? The text of the law appears to give it to you, but of course Apple won't give up without a fight in court. Apple will argue that the apparent meaning of the law is not the meaning that Congress intended when the law was passed. Congress intended to stop the unscrupulous practice of sending unordered merchandise to people and then trying to collect on it. Apple will argue that this being the purpose of the law, truly accidental mailing is not included. While there are no reported cases on this issue, our professional judgment as well as common sense indicates that Apple would win despite the clear language of the statute.

Let us turn to a typical business problem. A company receives an order for a $60 briefcase in brown, and the order says, "Please send this as soon as possible because it is for my wife's birthday, which is in two weeks." The company is out of stock on the item but does have a slightly more expensive model selling for $67. If the company sends the more expensive model, which was clearly not ordered, can the receiver keep the briefcase as a gift? The law is quite clear that this is unordered merchandise.

Again, the intent of the law has to be examined. The law was intended to stop the unscrupulous businessperson. It was not intended to hinder the businessperson's acting in good faith. If a company makes a frequent habit of sending out higher priced merchandise than that ordered, the court would probably decide against the business. Each case must be analyzed individually and one must balance good will against the letter of the law.

This piece of legislation is about a dozen years old. And at this point there is only one reported case (Kipperman v. Life Indemnity 544 F.2nd 377 (1977), giving an interpretation of the statute. The insurance company sent a term insurance offer to college students. The offer stated that if students sent in $9 they would have $2000 of term insurance for a stated period. Kipperman sued, claiming that the insurance under the code should be treated as a gift and that he should be entitled to the insurance without payment. Furthermore, all who had sent in the $9 should be given a refund. The case made it to one level below the Supreme Court of the United States. The court said the insurance company made an offer, not a gift, and furthermore this was not the sort of abuse the statute was designed to correct. Kipperman lost, but in our system litigants pay their own attorney fees, so the insurance company had to pay substantial lawyer's fees.

Can one threaten in a collection letter?

Threats in collection letters are governed by recent Federal legislation, which has not yet been interpreted by an extensive body of case law. Abundant evidence of debt collection abuses is cited as reason for passing the law. The law (15 U.S.C.A. § 1692) points out, "Business debt collection practices contribute to the number of personal bankruptcies, to marital instability, to the loss of jobs, and to invasions of individual privacy." This passage does not give rules of conduct, but it will aid in the interpretation of the other passage in the law because it clearly states the background of the law.

There are certain things you may not do in collecting a debt. You may not communicate by postcard (the postman and neighbors could read it), threaten violence, call repeatedly with intent to annoy, use obscene language to abuse, falsely say one is a lawyer, misrepresent the legal status of the debt, or falsely suggest that the debtor has committed a crime. The thrust of the law is to prevent unreasonable annoyance, lies, and holding the debtor up to public ridicule. But threats as such are not forbidden. The law does recognize that while some people are clearly unfortunate and are in debt without faults of their own, others are simply irresponsible. Their failure to pay their debts raises prices for the rest of us and poses a burden for society.

Debt collection is by necessity a tough business and one is not required to say "please" and "sir" in dealing with the debtor. Depending on whom one is dealing with, one could say, "You have to pay this debt *now!*" (the italics being for emphasis, not abuse). If one intends to follow through, one may say, "If you don't pay this in one week you will be summoned to court!" It is perfectly legal to sue someone for not paying a debt, and to sue someone naturally involves bringing him or her to court. There is clearly a threat here; it is tough talk, but not the abuse the federal law seeks to prevent.

One case shows how the law is applied. Involved is a sixty-year-old widow with high blood pressure and epilepsy. (From her lawyer's point of view she is an ideal plaintiff because she will appear to be the proverbial "little old lady" who is helpless, in ill health, and obviously abused by the collection agency. By contrast, under similar facts a twenty-seven-year-old in good health will come across as a deadbeat and collect nothing.) The widow owed $56 on a bill she had thought Medicare should pay. The defendant told her, "You owe it, you don't want to pay, so we're going to have to do something about it." She got a letter (with the return address clearly marked) saying that the collection agency would investigate in the neighborhood and with her employer. The company overstepped fair bounds and the woman could claim damages.

The teeth of any law are in the enforcement mechanism. The law says one may sue for actual damage, and up to $1,000 in additional damages, as the court may allow. The court will thus give an award it thinks fair. Also the law allows "the costs of action, together with a reasonable attorney's fee." Normally in our system, in contrast to those in England and Europe, each party pays its own lawyer.

Is it illegal to provide unsolicited information in a personnel report?

There is no statute on the books of the Federal Government or of any state which forbids the giving of unsolicited information in a personnel report recommendation. The issue of unsolicited information arises in our laws on libel and slander, which must be balanced against our rights of free speech and free press. Our courts have held consistently that free speech does not cover the spreading of vicious rumors, like accusing someone of being a criminal or having a loathsome disease, or accusing a woman of being unchaste (this bit of sexist common law remains with us). Speech that holds a person up to hatred, contempt, or ridicule, or causes him or her to be shunned or avoided, is generally considered slander and "illegal."

Normally, a person is not put in jail for making slanderous remarks, but the individual slandered may sue for damages.

A person accused of slander may raise certain defenses to the charge. The two defenses in such a case are truth and privilege. Truth is generally an acceptable defense to the charge of slander. Truth was not a defense as common law because the action in court was supposed to be an alternative to satisfaction. Truth, even today, may not be a defense if the speaker is acting out of malice to destroy the reputation of a person.

The second defense to the charge of slander is privilege. A person can assert in court that what was said was untrue but that because of privilege damage may not be recovered. For example, a member of Congress speaking in Congress has absolute privilege and may be maliciously slanderous without incurring liability.

The writer of a letter of recommendation or a personnel report has qualified but not absolute privilege. In a personnel report it is generally believed that the writer owes a moral duty to state what is known about a former employee. What is stated honestly and in good faith is privileged communication even if it is shown subsequently to be untrue. One does not have to prove that everything said in the letter is true beyond any doubt as long as the writer says what he or she honestly and in good faith believes to be true. It is not illegal to provide unsolicited information in a letter of recommendation, but in this case the standard for truth is higher.

Suppose you are writing a recommendation for an employee who has worked as a janitor and is applying for a job as a bank teller. The inquiry to which you are responding is: "How has the candidate been as an employee?" You know the janitor has been in jail, and it is generally believed that he was convicted twice for embezzlement. You write this in your recommendation. Suppose it turns out the janitor had been in jail for involuntary manslaughter, not embezzlement (the distinction might be critical for a bank job), and the janitor sued you for libel. Normally, the recommendation is privileged, but does this apply here? Here you were asked only to comment on the janitor's performance on the job and not about the background. Therefore the information is not privileged but subject to another standard.

Were you careless or negligent in stating what you knew? If so, you could be held liable for damages caused. On the other hand, let us assume the janitor had started the rumor, or everyone had believed it for years, and the janitor had made no attempt to correct the rumor. In this case the jury could find that you were not careless in your statement and therefore not liable. In summary, if you provide unsolicited information, you will be held to a higher standard of truth. If you speak or write maliciously, you may be held liable in any case. In response to an inquiry, you should basically have no fear of saying what you know or of adding information in good faith — because good faith is the standard normally applied.

Again, the precise facts of a case are essential in interpreting the court rulings. For example, in one case a person was held liable for speaking the truth beyond the scope of the inquiry. An examination of the facts revealed that he had sent a letter warning a supplier not to sell goods to a competitor because the competitor was a bad credit risk.

The court decided that the writer acted maliciously and was out for personal gain. The result of this case has to be seen with this background and should therefore not lead to the general fear of being sued for providing unsolicited information in good faith. To receive all the important facts in a personnel report it might be advisable to make in the inquiry a statement to the effect, "Is there anything else you know about this person that you would like to add?"

What questions can an employer legally ask in an interview?

The civil rights law has already been stated above. It says rather simply that one may not discriminate in hiring on the basis of race, color, religion, sex, or national origin. There are other sections which somewhat qualify this to allow, for example, Methodists to discriminate based on religious belief when hiring ministers, or to allow a designer to discriminate on the basis of sex when hiring models for a new line of fall furs.

There is nothing in the law that forbids the asking of any question in an interview *per se*. Discrimination is forbidden, not the asking of certain questions. If, however, an application asks about race, color, religion, and so on, a court (in trying a case) might want to know: *For what purpose are the questions asked, if not to discriminate?* Thus the asking of these questions might be used as evidence of discrimination. Most problems today deal with questions which do not appear to discriminate at first sight, but in fact do.

If a company asks about marital situation and children, the company might use the information to discriminate against women with small children. A question about height could be used to discriminate against Mexican Americans or Orientals. In fact there are few questions that could not somehow lead to discrimination by prospective employers. Being president of Alcoholics Anonymous reveals things which may be used to discriminate. Even questions about formal education and job experience could be seen to be discriminatory because white males tend to have more formal education than any other group.

Any question in an interview or on an application could somehow be seen as a way to discriminate. Even asking the name or address of a person could in some minds be seen as a discriminatory question.

What is the real law? Simply stated, it is illegal to discriminate on the basis of race, color, religion, sex, or national origin unless one has a valid reason. Furthermore, the party alleging discrimination has the burden of proving discrimination. All the facts and circumstances will be considered. Thus if a woman claims she was not promoted to a managerial position because she is a woman she might find discrimination easier to prove if the company has never had a woman manager. Discrimination would be much harder to prove if the company had many women managers and her evidence for sex discrimination was the fact that one day her supervisor had inquired into the health of her small children.

After reviewing numerous cases, it is our professional opinion that the courts are fair, equitable, and reasonable in applying the law. The Equal Employment Opportunities Commission, which holds its own hearings, tends to favor those who complain of discrimination.

Let us review a few actual cases and see how the courts apply the law. In one case, a man sued Safeway stores because he had been fired for refusing to wear a tie. He claimed he was the victim of discrimination because women in similar positions were not required to wear ties. The court said that conditions of employment were covered by the civil rights laws. Dress and grooming regulations were not intended to be covered by those laws.

In another case a company instituted the requirement of a high school diploma for supervisory positions. Blacks complained that this was discrimination. Although the rule was neutral on its face, it disproportionately affected blacks. The court found that the rule was implemented soon after the passage of the civil rights law, that blacks had in the past not been considered for supervising positions, and that whites had done well in the positions despite lack of the diploma. The new rule eliminated almost all blacks from promotion. In considering all the facts and surrounding circumstances, the court found that the requirement constituted discrimination. (This case does not suggest that schools and colleges can no longer ask about educational qualifications and discriminate against those who lack certain degrees.)

Suppose, hypothetically, that a company has a job opening for a traveling salesperson. The job requires the employee to be on the road thirty-five weeks a year, four weeks at a time. A company could under these circumstances refuse to hire persons with small children or single parents with children at home. But it would be illegal discrimination to ask women about their marital situation and their children and not apply the same rules to men. It would also be illegal to give the job to a man with small children and refuse to consider a woman in the same situation.

When a lawyer formulates a policy for a company, the lawyer is not interested in winning cases in the Supreme Court but in keeping the company out of court and out of trouble with the E.E.O.C. Thus policies and advice from legal departments tend to be cautious. Lawyers find it much easier to tell others that certain things are illegal rather than to explain exactly what the law says. The courts know they must separate the merely disgruntled or unqualified employee from the one discriminated against, and most courts do so by taking into account all of the evidence. Lawyers know that the cases will be easier if there are as few things to explain away as possible.

In a conversation with a personnel officer we were told, "All I want my people to think about is how well the person can do the job and not even to think about race, age, sex, and so forth." This is exactly the good faith standard that the law requires.

Summary

If you understand a few basic legal principles as well as how the law works, then you can bring this knowledge to a logical solution of legal problems as they arise in business communications.

If you have a serious legal problem you should, of course, consult a lawyer. But if you simply hear about a law or decision which seems funny, you should look it up. State and Federal statutes as well as decisions of the

Supreme Court are found in many libraries. The United States Code Annotated (U.S.C.A.) contains not only Federal statutes, but also notes on cases interpreting them.

Many public and university libraries carry the legal encyclopedia, *American Jurisprudence (Am. Jur.)*, which is a vast encyclopedia of the law. It is well indexed and fairly easy for the nonspecialist to read. These tools are not beyond the range of laymen who want to make their own judgments on what the law is.

HOW TO BECOME A GOOD DICTATOR

Although considered by some to be an "art," giving good dictation is an acquired skill — a skill to be learned much like ballroom dancing, baseball pitching, or card playing. Practice is the keyword; and no motto could be more appropriate than that of the Boy Scouts and Girl Scouts: Be Prepared!

Preparation

Before you start to dictate, be certain that you have all the necessary materials at hand. Have you had prior correspondence with this or another reader on the subject? Get it out of the file in case you need to make reference to earlier discussions. Is there a document which you will be referring to? Have it at hand so you won't have to fumble (and mumble) while you search your desk for it. Are you going to be enclosing some materials with the letter or memo? Gather them now so that they can go forward to the transcriber with the correspondence you are answering.

Plan what you are going to say before you try to say it. Read the letter you are answering carefully, underlining key words in the letter and jotting notes in the margin to guide you through your answer: can a request be granted? must you refuse the writer's request? why? can your refusal be justified? when is the order to be shipped? etc. These marginal notes will keep you on track and eliminate the tendency to wander around a subject because you're uncertain of your information.

If your message requires more than a short reply, make a key-word list or prepare an outline which identifies the purpose of the message and itemizes the main points you want to make. Such an outline needn't be extensive; one or two words — at most a phrase — will identify for you the information you need to give your reader:

Para. 1: Thanks for the order
Para. 2: Shipment will be made October 15
Para. 3: Quantity disc. of 20% earned; add'l discount 2/10

Para. 4: New "gidget" available 1st of year/price
Para. 5: Close

Tone

Establish the tone of the letter. If, for example, you are answering a letter of complaint, make certain that *you* remain objective. Even if you consider the complaint unjustified (*especially* if you think the complaint unjustified), counter-attacking your reader will be unproductive. If you can't write objectively, put the letter aside until you can. If possible, visualize your reader. Put yourself in his or her situation and choose your words accordingly.

Dictating the Material

With your preparation complete, you can now begin to dictate your material. Be sure to give your transcriptionist adequate instructions: identify yourself immediately; ask for priority handling if the message is urgent; if you want a rough draft first, ask for one; tell how many copies are needed and who gets them; identify the format you require (*memo, block format, simplified letter,* and so on). Try to visualize your message: how long will it be? or how short? Tell your transcriptionist that you expect this will be a rather short or a very long message, and so on. After identification and instructions are complete, you can then begin to dictate your message.

Remember to speak and enunciate clearly. Dictate the name and address of the recipient of the message; spell out all names unless you are going to give the transcriptionist a source document to use. And, unless you have absolute confidence in your transcriptionist, emphasize numbers for accuracy and spell out unusual words and homophones.

The pairs of words listed below are examples of words that sound similar and thus may confuse your typist.

- accept/except
- addition/edition
- advice/advise
- affect/effect
- allusion/illusion
- already/all ready
- altogether/all together
- always/ all ways
- assistance/assistants

- bases/basis
- brake/break

- capital/capitol/Capitol
- cite/sight/site
- complement/compliment
- confidently/confidentially
- council/counsel

- elicit/illicit
- eligible/illegible
- eminent/imminent
- extant/extent

- farther/further
- formally/formerly
- intense/intents
- personal/personnel
- principal/principle
- role/roll
- stationary/stationery

During dictation, indicate punctuation and format by saying: "period," "comma," "semi-colon," "colon," "paragraph," and so on. If you come to a part of your message that you want put in list form, say something like: "Louise (or Louis), this next should be in list form." The use of the transcriptionist's name immediately alerts her or him that what you are saying at that moment doesn't need to be typed; rather he or she is to listen for your instructions. When you have finished enumerating, tell your transcriptionist "end of list."

When you have finished your message tell your transcriptionist again how many carbon copies are needed; what special mailing notations are required; thank the transcriptionist; and say "end of dictation."

Checking the Completed Work

Remember our earlier admonition that *you* are responsible for the contents of your messages. So, read the entire message for accuracy of spelling, punctuation, grammar, *and* content. Sign the letter or initial the memo. And, then, if warranted, thank the transcriptionist for excellent work. (This latter suggestion is so often overlooked by the busy executive that you will have made a friend for a life and be assured that your dictation will receive extra care in the days to follow.)

Subject for number 2, page 98:
"Should the Drama Department start a new course in television soap operas?"

INDEX

Abbreviations, 450
ABCA Bulletin, The, 5
ABI/Inform, 384, 389–390
Abstractions, 137
  boneless, 108
Abstract nouns, 133–134
Abstracts, 251
Acknowledgments, 415
Action (s)
  blocking method for, 81, 82
  in message writing, 15, 16, 20
  request for, 283
  for sales, 157
  sentences of, 135
  vs talking and writing, 10
Action statements for readability, 121–122
Address, 440
  inside, 448, 449
Adjustment letter, 229–232
  exercise in writing, 425–426
  exercise in writing a response to, 426–427
Administrative Management Society, 405, 431, 438

Almanacs, list of, 387–388
American Jurisprudence, 492
Analogy in speeches, 350, 352
Analysis, 77
And/or as bizbuzz, 110–111
Anecdotes, 270
  in speeches, 348–349
Annual reports, 21–22
Aphorisms, 352
Apostrophe, 470
Appendixes, graphics in, 67
Application, job, 310, 314–317
Approval, credit, 192–193
Arguments in oral messages, 328
ASCII (American Standard Code for Information Interchange), 410
Attention getters, 157
Audience (s)
  hostile, 334–335
  oral messages and, 326, 327, 333, 344–349
  See also Readers
Authorship, 258
Automated office systems, 399–401, 402
Averages, 59

495

Background, and context, 9
Balance, 440
Bar charts, 61, 62
Barron, Clarence, 3
Bateman, David, 52
Bibliographies, and subject searches, 375, 376, 379
Bizbuzz, 108–111
  exercises about, 116–119
  glossary of standard usage and, 111–116
  See also Doubletalk; Jargon
Block, writer's, 475–478
Block method of organization, 76, 77–78, 84–85
  examples of, 79, 81–82, 83
Block style of letter writing, 436–437
Body
  of a report, 243
  of a speech, 342–343
Body language, in speaking, 357
Boldface headings, 13
Boldface type, 38, 41
Bonee, John R., 330–331
Boneless abstractions, 108
Brain, and data assimilation, 10
Brevity in reports, 242
Buffers in letter writing, 224
Bullets, 47, 433
Bureaucracy, and unsuccessful companies, 9
Business, reports and world of, 242–244
Business bibliographies, list of, 388
Business Communication Concepts, 52
Business Periodical Index, 380
Business Week, 5–6

Cameraready, 397, 412
Capital letters, 47, 50
Card catalogue of library, 376, 378–380
Cards
  for speeches, 358
  subject, 376
  three-by-five-inch, 76, 77–78
Central dictating systems, 408–409, 412
Chalkboards, 364–365
Character references, 195
Charts
  bar, 61, 62

  pie, 64
  as visual aids, 364
Chesterton, G. K., 13–14
Chronology, 77
Chunks, 10–11, 13
  as openers, 132–133
  sentence, 129–131, 138–140, 460
  visual effect and, 43, 44, 47
Civil Rights Law, 485, 490
Claims letters, 182–183
  examples of, 184–187
  exercises for writing, 188–190
Clarity. *See* Readability
Classification, definition by, 351
Cliches, 108, 146
Close, complimentary, 438, 450, 453, 486
Clothes, and speech making, 357–358
Collection letter, 201–203
  examples of, 204–207
  exercise in writing, 207–209, 415–416
  legal issues and, 487, 488
Colons, 469
Color, as visual effect, 41
Columns, 59
Commas, 467–468
Communication, successful
  action writing in, 15–16
  answering questions in, 5–7
  chunking for, 10–11, 12
  correct image and, 2
  exercises for, 16–27
  familiar words in, 13–14
  influencing readers in, 4–5
  reader's viewpoint and, 3–4
  simplicity for, 9–10
  situation and context and, 7–9
Comparisons
  faulty, 466
  in speeches, 349–350
Compatibility, computer, 408
Complete Guide to Pasteup, 397, 412
Complimentary close, 438, 450, 453
  and liability, 486
Computer catalogue, of library, 378–380
Computer databases, 380, 384
Computers, 403, 404, 406–407, 408
  manuals for, 405

Index

Conclusions
   in a report, 257
   of a speech, 343
Condolence, letter of, 151
Confessions of an Advertising Man, 129–130
Constitutions, 485
Context, and message form, 8–9
Contrasts, 349–350
Copiers, 394–395
Copyboard, 411
Copy editing machine, 410
Correspondence. *See* Letters; Messages
Court decisions, 485
Cover letter, for job application, 310, 314–317
Credit
   rating of, 302
   refusal of, 228–229
Credit letters, 191–194
   examples of, 194–197
   exercises for writing, 198–200
Cross references, 376, 378, 380, 385

Daisy wheels, 398
Dana Corporation, 9
Dangling modifiers, 137–138, 466
Darian, Steven, 6
Dashes, 50, 450, 469
Data assimilation and human brain, 10
Databases
   computer, 380, 384
   list of, 389–390
Date line, 448
Debtors, 201–203
Definitions, in speeches, 350–352, 353–354
Designing Technical Reports, 3
Deupree, Richard, 10
Diagramming of speeches, 338–339
Dictation, 492–494
   equipment for, 408–410
Dictionaries
   list of specialized, 385–386
   visual effects of, 52
Differentiation, and visual effects, 47, 50
DiGaetani, John, 135
Dirck, John, M. D., 106

Directories, list of, 386
Discrimination, in hiring practices, 490
Ditto machines, 395
Document-filing machine, 411
Dot-matrix printer, 405, 412, 445, 446
Double signpost, 92–93, 96–97
Double spacing, 449–450
Doubletalk, 422–424. *See also* Bizbuzz; Jargon
Dow Jones, 3
Dramatic elements in speaking, 356–357
   body language as, 357–358
   exercises in, 360–361, 368–369
   handling questions and, 359–360
   microphones as, 367–368
   and notes, 359–360
   visual aids as, 362–367
   voice as, 358–359
Dun and Bradstreet, 307
Dust jacket, 52
Dx + Rx: A Physician's Guide to Medical Writing, 106

Echoes, 93–95, 96–97
Economics, 96–97
Educational experiences, and job application, 306
Electronic stencil maker, 396
Emotional strengths, 304
Emotions
   money and, 304
   and oral messages, 331
Emphasis, points of, 51
Encyclopedia of Associations, 307
Encyclopedia of Banking and Finance, 375
Encyclopedia of Business Information Sources, 388
Encyclopedias, 375–376
   list of specialized, 386
English usage, 13–14, 106–108
   glossary of standard, 111–116
   training in, 451
   See also Bizbuzz
Enumeration, 339–340, 449
Envelopes, 451
Epigrams, 352
Equal Employment Opportunities Commission, 490, 491

Evaluation and recommendation, letters of, 210–212, 216
Evidence, weight of, 241
Examples in speeches, 346–349, 352–353
Experts, 346–348
Expletive statements, 464
Extemporaneous speaking, 326–327, 356–357
Eye contact
  and charts, 364
  for dramatic effect, 357
  and extemporaneous speaking, 326
  and handouts, 364
  and manuscript speech, 358
  and overhead projectors, 366, 367

Fadwords, 108–109
Familiarity in word usage, 13–14, 106–108
Farkas, David, 5
Federal laws, 485
Felt marker, 365
Feminine spellings of names, 451–453
Filing machine, document, 411
Flip chart, 364
Ford, Henry II, 347–348
Formal reports, 243
Format, message. *See* Message format
Free speech, 488–490
Friendliness, in letter writing. *See* Goodwill letters

Generic pronoun, 483–484
Gerunds, 460
Gestures in speaking, 357
Gieselman, Robert D., 96
Glossary of standard usage, 111–116
Goodwill letters, 145–147, 415, 424–425
  exercises for writing, 154–155
  samples of, 148–153
Gowers, Sir Ernest, 15
Graded order, 339–340
Grade-point average (GPA), 306
Graham, Walter B., 397
Grammar course, 306
Grammatical errors, 459–460
  exercises in correcting, 472–474
  faulty sentence structure as, 466–467

  incorrect punctuation as, 467–472
  misuse of modifiers as, 465–466
  misuse of nouns as, 460–461
  misuse of pronouns as, 461–462
  misuse of verbs as, 462–465
Graphics, 54, 55, 64, 66–68
  bar charts as, 61
  exercises about, 68–69
  line graphs as, 62, 63
  pie charts as, 64
  tables as, 59, 61
  when to use, 57
Graphics Master, 397, 412
Graphs, line, 62, 63
Group nouns, 463
Grow, Gerald, 118
Guide to Copiers, 395

Half-inch margins, 433
Handbooks
  list of, 387–388
  secretarial, 455
Handouts, 363–364
Hang indentation, 449
Harvard Business School, 135
Headings, 50, 91, 96–97
  boldface, 13
  page, 451
  in reports, 255
Hewlett Packard, 103
Hiring practices, legal aspects of, 490–491
Hobbies, 306
Hoke, Henry, 440, 442
Hoke, Peter, 442
Homophones, 493–494
Hooks
  message, 31–36
  for speeches, 338–339
Hostile audience, 334–335
Hyphen, 450, 471

Illegibility, examples of, 439, 441
Illustration(s)
  definition by, 351
  in speeches, 346–349
Image, writer's, 2
Impromptu speaking, 325–326
Indentation, 47, 433, 449
Indexes
  of computer databases, 384

Index

list of, 388–389
periodical, 380
and subject searches, 376
Influence of readers, 4–5
Information, request for, 170–171
Ink-jet printers, 405
Inquiries, orders and replies, 170–173, 415
exercises for answering, 179–181
exercises in writing, 416, 421
examples of answers to, 174–179, 456–458
In Search of Excellence: Lessons from America's Best-run Companies, 9, 103
Inside address, 448, 449
Interlibrary loan, 379
Interview, legal aspects of job, 490–491
Introduction
definitions in, 352
for predicting, 91–92, 96–97
of reports, 253
to speeches, 333, 342
Investment sources, list of, 387
Irrelevancies, 2
Italics, 471–472

Jargon, 14, 108–111, 121
chunking and, 131
printers', 396–397
See also Bizbuzz; Doubletalk
Job hunting
application for, 310, 314–317
campaign in, 303–309
and discrimination, 490

Key words, underlining, 1–2
Kipperman v. Life Indemnity, 487

Laser printers, 405
"Late News on WP/Typesetting Interfaces," 403
Lavier, 367
Laws of visual effect, 41–43
Layout, letter, 440
Leader dots, 431–432
Legal action, threat of, 201–203
Legal issues, 484–485, 491–492
examples of, 486–491
in letters of evaluation and recommendation, 211

Legal jargon, 14
Legal Writing: Sense and Nonsense, 14
Lem, Dean Phillip, 397
Letter(s)
of adjustment (*see* Adjustment letters)
claims (*see* Claims, letters for)
collection (*see* Collection letters)
of condolence, 151
credit (*see* Credit, letters for)
of evaluation and recommendation, 210–212, 216
exercise in writing, 425
job application cover, 310, 314–317
of transmittal, 247
See also Messages
Letterhead, 53, 440, 445
Letter-quality printers, 405, 445
Letters of recommendation. *See* Evaluation and recommendation
Letter styles, 433, 440, 445
samples of, 432, 434–439, 441–444
Liability. *See* Legal issues
Libel, 488–490
Library(ies), 373–376, 378–380, 384
exercises in using, 385
and job hunting, 307
selective bibliography for using, 385–390
Library of Congress, 385, 376–378
Library of Congress Subject Headings, The, 375, 378
Line graphs, 62, 63
Liquid chalk, 365
Lists, parallel, 47
Local area network (LAN) computer systems, 407
Logic, 331

McDonald, Daniel, 20
McGraw-Hill Encyclopedia of Science and Technology, 376
McPherson, Rene, 9
Machines, office. *See* Office machines
Mag-card typewriter, 398
Manuals, computer, 405
Manuscript speaking, 327–328
Margins, 433, 440
Masculine spellings of names, 451–453
Mathes, J. C., 3
Mellinkoff, David, 14

Memorandums, 7, 8
  style of, 445, 447
Memorization speech, 330
Memory typewriter, 398
Merge file/text task, 400
Message format, 431–433, 451–454
  of letters (see Letter styles)
  of memos, 445
  readers and, 454–458
  standards of (see Standards of business correspondence)
Messages
  to answer inquiries (see Inquiries)
  claims (see Claims, letters for)
  for collection (see Collection letters)
  about credit (see Credit, letters for)
  of evaluation and recommendation, 210–212
  form of, 7–9
  format of (see Message format)
  goodwill (see Goodwill letters)
  negative (see Negative messages)
  oral (see Oral messages)
  to order products and services, 171–173
  organization of (see Organizing techniques)
  outlining (see Outline)
  patterning in, 77
  persuasion in, 241
  planning (see Planning messages)
  and replies on one page, 443
  sales (see Sales messages)
  successful communication of (see Communication, successful
  writing (see Writing messages)
  See also Letters; Reports
Microcomputers, 404–405
Microfilm in libraries, 380
Microphone, 358, 367–368
Mimeographs, 395–396
Mini system, computer, 407
Mixed outline, 480
Modern Office Technology, 406, 408, 410
Modifiers
  dangling, 137–138, 466
  misuse of, 465–466
Money, and emotion, 304
Motivators for selling, 158
Ms., use of term, 482–483

Multi-user computer systems, 407
Municipal ordinances, 485
Murphy, Kevin, 348
Murphy's Law Perfected, 284

Names, masculine or feminine, 451–453
Negation, definition by, 351
Negative messages, 223–227
  exercises in writing, 232–237, 417, 429
  for refusing adjustments, 229–232
  for refusing credit, 228–229
  for refusing requests, 227–228
  sandwiching of, 212
Newspaper indexes, 389
News reports, 82, 83
New York law, for readability, 120
New York Times Index, 389
Nonspecialists, as readers, 105
Notes for speeches, 336–338, 358–360
Not-stand-alone chunks, 139
Nounophilia, 133–134
Nouns, 464
  abstract, 133–134
  group, 463
  misuse of, 460

Office Automation and Word Processing Fundamentals, 408
Office machines, 393–394, 410–413
  reproduction equipment as, 394–397
  word processing equipment as (see Word processing equipment)
Offset printers, 396–397
Ogilvy, David, 129–130
One-line paragraphs, 433
Opening chunks, 131–132
Operation, definition by, 351–352
Oral messages, 333–334
  comparisons and contrasts in, 349–350
  conclusions in, 343
  definitions in, 350–352
  diagramming of, 338–339
  dramatic elements in (see Dramatic elements in speaking)
  examples or illustrations in, 346–349

exercises for making, 340–343, 352–355
form of, 325–329
hostile audiences and, 334–335
point of, 336–338
signposts in, 339–340
statistics in, 328, 344–346, 354–355
style in, 329–332
topic of, 335–336
Order in messages, 77
Orders. *See* Inquiries, orders, and replies
Organizational signals in speeches, 339–340
Organizational structure, 362
Organizing technique(s), 75, 89
　blocking as (*see* Block method of organization)
　echoing as, 93–95
　introduction as, 91–92
　signposting as, 90–91, 92–93
　transitions as, 95–96
Outline(s), 75–76, 79
　forms of, 478–481
　modified (*see* Block method of organization)
　for proposals, 285–287, 297
　in speech making, 338–339, 359
　sentence, 479
　of a typical report, 243
Output file, 400–401, 402
Overhead projectors, 365–367, 368, 410

Page headings, 451
Paging of a report, 258
PAIS International, 384, 390
Paper feed lever, 396
Paperwork, 9–10
Paragraphs
　development, 89, 90
　indentations of, 43, 433
　linking of, 93
　sentence chunks as, 47
Parallel headings, 50
Parallelism, 127–128
　faulty, 467
Parallel lists, 47
Parallel structures, 127–128
Parentheses, 470
Passive construction, 121, 258
Pasteup, 397, 412

Pasteur, Louis, 346
Patterning, in messages, 77
Pedantic writing, 258
Percentages, 64
Periodical indexes, 380
Personal data, and job application, 316
Personality traits and job hunting, 304–305
Personal pronouns, 134–135
Personnel reports, and unsolicited information, 488–490
Persuasion, 241
　in oral messages, 331
Peters, Thomas J., 9, 103
Photographs, 57, 67
Picas, 402
Picture, and job application, 316
Picture-frame layout, 440
Pie charts, 64
Placement office and job hunting, 307
Plain English laws, 120
Plain Words: Their ABC, 16
Planning messages
　hooking for, 31–36
　visual effects for (*see* Graphics; Visual effects)
Pleasure, as motivator, 158
Plural nouns, 460
Point(s)
　of emphasis, 51
　of messages, 1–2
　of speeches, 336–339
Possessive noun form, 460
Prediction, 91–92, 96–97, 125–126
　parallelism and, 128
　strong signal words for, 128–129
Prefactory, of reports, 243
Printers, 399, 405
　dot-matrix, 405, 412, 445, 446
　offset, 396–397
Privilege, as legal defense, 489
Problem definition, in proposals, 284
Procrustean solution, 7
Procter and Gamble, 10
Products, answering orders for, 171, 172–173
Product sales. *See* Sales messages
Product substitution, and liability, 486–487
Progress reports, of employees, 211, 298–300

Projectors, overhead, 365–367, 368, 410
Pronouns, 464
  generic, 483–484
  misuse of, 461–462
  personal, 134–135
Proportion, 440
Proposals, 283–287
  examples of, 288–297
Prose
  and graphics, 61
  running, 47
Public Affairs Information Service Bulletin (PAIS), 389
Punctuation, 467–472, 473–474
  dictation and, 494

Questionnaires, 424
Questions
  readers', 5–7
  speech making and handling of, 359–360
Quotation in speeches, 346, 349–350, 355
Quotation marks, 470–471, 472

Readability techniques, 120–123, 124–125, 135–136
  checklist for, 138
  chunking as, 129–132
  exercises in, 123–124
  need for, 439, 440
  nounophilia and, 133–134
  parallel structures as, 127–128
  personal pronouns and, 134–135
  prediction as, 125–126
  revision as, 136–138
  sentence length and, 11, 13, 132–133
  strong signal words as, 128–129
Reader(s), 241
  effect of format and mechanics on, 454–456
  and graphics, 57
  influence of, 4–5
  nonspecialists as, 105
  pleasure as motivator of, 158
  retaining attention of (*see* Organization techniques)
  viewpoint of, 3–4
Reader's Guide to Periodical Literature, 389

Reading
  from left to right, 41–43
  revision and aloud, 136–137
  from top to bottom, 42–43
Recommendations
  letters of, 210–212
  in reports, 257, 488–490
Records management system, 410
Redundancies, 109–110
References
  character, 195
  cross, 376, 378, 380, 385
  for job hunting, 305
Reference works, 375–376
Refusal(s)
  of adjustments, 229–232
  of credit, 193–194, 228–229
  of requests, 227–228
Regulations, 485
Rehearsal, speech, 356–357
Repeated words, 93–95, 96–97
Repetition, 340
Replies. *See* Inquiries, orders and replies
Reporter of Direct Mail Advertising, The, 440, 442
Reporter of Direct Mail/Marketing, The, 442
Reports, 241–244
  annual, 21–22
  blocking, 82, 83
  case studies for writing, 272–281
  conclusions in, 257
  examples of, 244–256, 260–271
  headings in, 255
  to inform, 418–420, 421–422, 427–428
  paging of, 257
  personnel, 488–490
  progress, 211, 298–300
  proposals as (*see* Proposals)
  recommendation, 257, 448–450
  of results, 83
  student, 258–259
  style of writing in, 258
  topics for student, 271–272
Reproduction
  equipment for, 394–397
  of graphics, 67
Requests
  for action, 283
  refusal of (*see* Refusals)

Restatement, 340
Results, reporting, 83
Resumés, 310, 312, 314–317
Revision, techniques for, 136–138
Rhetoric, 352
　in speech making, 330, 331
Ribbons, changing of, 398
"Right to your own language," 451
Role, writer's, 2
Romei, Lura K., 406
Rowboat effect, 59
Rowland, David, 16
Running prose, 47

Sales messages, 156–158, 171–172
　examples of, 158–165
　exercises for making, 166–169, 416–417, 420–421
Salutation, 448–449, 453
Samuelson, Paul, 96
Scanner, educated, 410
Search and count, 400
Sears List of Subject Headings, 375, 385
Secretarial handbook, 455
See and *See also* references, 376, 378, 385
Self-assessment for job hunting, 304–305
Selling yourself, 297. *See also* Job hunting
Semi-block letter style, 433, 435
Semicolon, 468–469
Sentence(s)
　action, 135
　faulty structure in, 466–467
　length of, 11, 13, 132–133
　listing of elements of, 127–128
　motion of, 125–126
　topic, 90–91
Sentence chunks, 129–131, 138–140, 460
Sentence outline, 479
Services, sale of. *See* Sales messges
Sex preference, and signature, 450
Sex terminology, 481–484
Shelf list, library, 379
Signal words, strong, 128–129
Signals, speeches and organizational, 339–340
Signatures, 450–451, 453–454

Signposts, 90–91
　double, 92–93
　in speech making, 339–340
Simplicity
　of language, 13–14, 103, 105–106
　in message writing, 9–10
Simplified letter form, 431, 438
Single spacing, 445, 449–450
Situation, and message form, 7–9
Slander, 488–490
Social ability, vs grade point average, 306
Social relationships, and computers, 406
Software, computer, 406
Space
　double, 449, 450
　single, 449–450
　white, 47
Speech
　free, 488–490
　patterns of, 358
Speeches. *See* Oral messages
Spelling
　of homophones, 493–494
　of names, 451–453
Split infinitives, 465
Stand-alone chunks, 138–139
Standard and Poor's Corporation Reports, 307, 387
Standards of business
　correspondence, 445, 448–453, 454–455
　examples of, 446–447, 456–458
　salutation and close in, 453
Standard usage, glossary of, 111–116
State laws, 485
Statistics in oral messages, 328, 344–346, 354–355
　and visual aids, 362, 364
Statutes, 485
Stencils, 395–396
Stevenson, Dwight, 3
Stories in speeches, 348–349
Strassman, Paul, 406
Stresses in English language, 358, 361
Student reports
　sample of, 258–271
　topics for, 271–282
Style, oral vs writing, 329–330

Style of writing in a report, 258–259
Sub-hooks, 34–35
Subject cards, 376
Subject-is-noun, 464
Subject line, 8, 51, 438, 448–449
Subject search in libraries, 374–376, 378–380, 384
Subjunctive verb, 464–465
Supplements of a report, 243
Symmetry, 440

Table of contents, 36
   of a report, 249
Tables, 59, 61
Tense, verb, 464
Testimonials, 158
   in speeches, 346–348
Texas Instruments, 9
Text task, 400
Thomas Register of American Manufacturers, 307
Three-by-five-inch cards, 76, 77–78
Tibbetts, Arn, 306
Tibbetts, Charlene, 481–484
Time line, 299–300
Title pages, 245
Toffler, Alvin, 406
Topic outline, 480
Topic sentences as signposts, 90–91
Topics
   speech, 335–336
   for student reports, 271–282
Transitions, 95–97
   in speeches, 357
Transparencies, 366, 367
Truth, as legal defense, 488–489
Typesetting equipment, 402–403
Typewriters, 398–399
Typing, 397, 449

Underlining, 471–472
   of headings, 50
   of key words, 1–2
United States Code Annotated, The, 492
Universality, computer, 408

Vagueness, in word usage, 14
Value Line Investment Survey, 387
Verbs, misuse of, 463–465

Visual effects, 37
   charts as, 364
   chunking and, 43, 44, 47
   color as, 41
   of dictionaries, 52
   exercises about, 38–41, 43, 52–53
   graphics as (*see* Graphics)
   how to create good, 47, 50–51
   laws of, 41–43
   negative, 439–440
   in speech making, 362–367
   and variety, 432
Vital Speeches, 361
Vogue words, 108–109
Voice-activated typewriters, 399
Voice/data workstation, 411
Voice in speech making, 358–359
Voice storage device, 411

Wall Street Journal Index, The, 3, 116, 389, 459, 482–483
Waterhouse, Shirley, 408
Waterman, Robert H., 9, 103
Weight of evidence, 241
White space, 47, 59, 440
"Who does what" in message writing, 15–16, 121–122, 126, 460
   examples of, 21–22
"Who is what" in message writing, 122–123
Word-processing equipment, 397, 399–403
   computers as, 403, 405–407, 408
   and letter styles, 445
   typewriters as, 398–399
Words
   cutting unnecessary, 137
   repeated, 93–95, 96–97
   signal, 128–129
   underlining key, 1–2
   See also Bizbuzz; English usage
WordStar, 397
Work experience, 305
Wrapping back, 449
Writing messages, 103, 105–106
   action in, 15, 16, 20
   bizbuzz in, 108–111
   familiar words in, 106–108
   glossary for, 111–116
   imitation of speech in, 135–136

readability and (*see* Readability)
  writer's block in, 475–478
  writer's role in, 2
Writing style of a report, 258–259
Writing with a Word Processor, 402

Xerox, 406

Yearbooks, list of, 387–388,

Zinsser, William, 20, 402

Credits

CONTINUED FROM PAGE IV

Felker, et al. *Guidelines for Document Designers*. Reprinted by permission of Document Design Center.

Page 62, Figure 3.11: 1960/1970 Population from Felker, et al., *Guidelines for Document Designers*. Reprinted by permission of Document Design Center.

Page 63, Figure 3.12: Money Invested by Acme (in millions) from Felker, et al., *Guidelines for Document Designers*. Reprinted by permission of Document Design Center.

Page 63, Figure 3.13: Investment Expenditures of Three Companies (in millions) from Felker, et al., *Guidelines for Document Designers*. Reprinted by permission of Document Design Center.

Page 64, Figure 3.14: Line graphs from Felker, et al., Guidelines for Document Designers. Reprinted by permission of Document Design Center.

Page 70, Figure 3.17: Gains Chart and Graphic Representation of Gains Chart from John Stevenson's, "98% Negative Database Holds Power of Expansion Benefits" from *Direct Marketing*, March 1985. Reprinted by permission of Direct Marketing, 224 7th Street, Garden City, New York 11530.

Chapter 4

Pages 86–87: James Fleming. "My Favorite Assignment." From the *ABCA Bulletin* September 1978. Reprinted by permission of the author.

Chapter 5

Page 94: William H. Whyte. "The Language of Business" reprinted from *Fortune* (c) 1950 Time Inc. All rights reserved.

Pages 96–97: Excerpt from Paul Samuelson's *Economics*. 10th edition, pp. 237–238. Copyright 1976, 1973, 1970, 1967, 1961, 1958, 1955 by McGraw-Hill, Inc. Copyright, 1951, 1948 by McGraw-Hill. Copyright renewed 1976 by Paul A. Samuelson. Reprinted by permission of McGraw-Hill Publishers.

Chapter 6

Page 104: "Keep It Simple." Advertisement for United Technologies. Reprinted by permission of United Technologies.

Pages 118–119: Gerald Grow, "Ten Steps to Clearer Writing" from "How to Write 'Official' from *Simply States ... in Business*, April, 1982. Document Design Center. Copyright 1981 Gerald Grow. Reprinted by permission of the author.

Chapter 7

Page 134: Bruce Price. Excerpt from "An Inquiry into Modifier Noun Proliferation," from "Book World" (April 1970). Copyright (C) 1970 by *The Washington Post*. Reprinted by permission of *The Washington Post*.

Chapter 9

Pages 164–166: Terrance B. Ahern. Letter describing the Xerox Memorywriter. Reprinted by permission of Xerox and Terrance B. Ahern.

Chapter 16

Pages 272–277: "Word Processing Case study—An Opportunity for Improving Production of Messages and Documents" by Francis Weeks and Louise Steele. Reprinted by permission of the authors.

Pages 277–282: Bonnie Brothers York, "Candipop, Incorporated." From the *ABCA Bulletin*. Reprinted by permission Bonnie Brothers York.

Chapter 19

Pages 307–309: Andrew J. Wisniewski, "My Most Valued Accomplishments are My Non-Academic Activities." Reprinted by permission of Andrew J. Wisniewski.

Chapter 20

Pages 318–320: Nancy A. Dittman, "Job Winning Resumes" from the *American Business Communication Association Bulletin*. Reprinted by permission of Nancy A. Dittman.

Page 321: Sandra Jones resume. Reprinted by permission of author.

Chapter 21

Pages 330–332: John F. Bonee, "The Care and Feeding of the Executive Speaker," p. 199, *Vital Speeches*, January 15, 1982. Reprinted by permission.

Chapter 22

Pages 340–341: H. W. Bricker, "Opening Windows of Opportunity," *Vital Speeches*, p. 747, October 1, 1982. Reprinted by permission.

Chapter 23

Pages 345–346: John B. Fery, "The Future of Housing," *Vital Speeches*, p. 158, December 15, 1982. Reprinted by permission.

Page 346: George Burns, "Management by Inspiration," *Vital Speeches*, p. 5, October 15, 1982. Reprinted by permission.

Pages 347–348: Henry Ford, II, "The Search for a Better Idea," p. 144, *Vital Speeches*, December 15, 1982. Reprinted by permission.

Pages 348–349: J. Kevin Murphy, "A Walk on the Wild Side," p. 625, *Vital Speeches*, August 1, 1978. Reprinted by permission.

Pages 349–350: Robert E. Allen, "Effective Preparation for Career Opportunities Within the Corporate World," p. 110, *Vital Speeches*, December 1, 1982. Reprinted by permission.

Page 352: Melvin Vulgamore, "The Place of the Fourth Miracle," *Vital Speeches*, p. 662, September 15, 1982. Reprinted by permission.

Page 353: Donald E. Petersen, "The Future Task of the Worldwide Auto Industry: To Manage for the Long Term Benefit," p. 664, *Vital Speeches*, August 15, 1981. Reprinted by permission.

Pages 353–354: Ronald E. Rhody, "The Conventional Wisdom is Wrong," from p. 22, *Vital Speeches*, November 1, 1982. Reprinted by permission.

Page 354: Frank Forker, "The Call for Leadership to Young America: Be an Innovator", from p. 745, *Vital Speeches*, October 1, 1981. Reprinted by permission.

Page 354: Midge Decter, "Expanding World Freedom", from p. 724, *Vital Speeches*, September 15, 1981. Reprinted by permission.

Page 355: John F. Budd, Jr., "Are We 'Smart Enough' for Tomorrow?", from p. 730, *Vital Speeches*, September 15, 1982. Reprinted by permission.

Page 355: Robert J. Buckley, "Can We 'Engineer' Ourselves Out of the Crisis of Costs?", from p. 724, *Vital Speeches*, September 15, 1982. Reprinted by permission.

Chapter 24

Pages 360–361: Charles Ratliff, Jr. "Food: Peace or Chaos?", from p. 17, *Vital Speeches*, October 15, 1981. Reprinted by permission.

Chapter 25

Page 377: Page 394 from *McGraw-Hill Encyclopedia of Science and Technology.* Copyright (C) 1982, 1977, 1971, 1966, 1960 by McGraw-Hill, Inc. Reprinted by permission of McGraw-Hill Publishers.

Page 381: Business Periodicals Index. Volume 24 (August 1981–July 1982). Copyright (c) 1981, 1982 by The H.W. Wilson Company. Material reproduced by permission of the publisher.

Page 382: Business Periodicals Index. Volume 25, #5, January 1983. Copyright (c) 1983 by the H.W. Wilson Company. Material reproduced by permission of the publisher.

Chapter 26

Page 409: Francis W. Weeks, "Centralized Dictation System" from the *ABCA Bulletin.* Reprinted by permission of the author.

Appendix A

Pages 414–415, 422–424: Evan E. Rudolph, "The Case of the Conscientious Nurse" and "Merit and the Manager" from the ABCA's *Business Communication Casebook 1.* Reprinted by permission of the author.

Pages 415, 421: John E. Binnion, "Orders and Acknowledgements, No. 2" and "Inquiries, Replies and Requests, No. 3" from the ABCA's *Business Communication Casebook 2.* Reprinted by permission of the author.

Pages 415–416: G. Pepper Holland, "Collections, No. 3 & 4" from ABCA's *Business Communication Casebook 2.* Reprinted by permission of the author.

Pages 416, 420–421: Mary J. Nelson, "Inquiries, Replies and Requests, No. 5" and "Sales, No. 2" from the ABCA's *Business Communication Casebook 2.* Reprinted by permission of the author.

Pages 416–417: Charles B. Smith, "Phoenix Pools, Inc." from the ABCA's *Business Communication Casebook 2.* Reprinted by permission of the author.

Page 417: Donald E. English, "Texcom Company" from the ABCA's *Business Communication Casebook 2.* Reprinted by permission of the author.

Pages 418–420, 429, 427–428: Donald J. Leonard, "In Search of the Successful" from the ABCA's *Business Communication Casebook 2* and "Roll's Hoist" and "Open-Up Program" from the ABCA's *Business Communication Casebook 3.* Reprinted by permission of the author.

Pages 421–422: Robert S. Rudolph, "Securing a New Waste-Baler" from the ABCA's *Business Communication Casebook 2.* Reprinted by permission of the author.

Pages 424, 429–430: Ruth G. Batchelor, "Parking Lot Questionnaire" and "Reilly and Greer, Inc." from the ABCA's *Business Communication Casebook 1.* Reprinted by permission of the author.

Pages 424–425: Lois Bachman, "Apple Theatre Delayed Tickets" from the ABCA's *Business Communication Casebook 3.* Reprinted by permission of the author.

Page 425: William Donald Payne, "Introducing Bindell's Travel Service" from the ABCA's *Business Communication Casebook 3.* Reprinted by permission of the author.

Pages 425–426: Pat Pearson, "Requests to Tenants and Landlord" from the ABCA's *Business Communication Casebook 3.* Reprinted by permission of the author.

Pages 426–427: Stephen D. Lewis, "Response to Adjustment Letter Request" from the ABCA's *Business Communication Casebook 3.* Reprinted by permission of the author.

Appendix B

Pages 442, 443, 444: Letter forms (to Mr. Daniel Stowe, to Mr. Henry Thompson and to Mr. Walter A. Roberts) by Henry Hoke, Jr., in *Direct Marketing*, March 1985. Reprinted by permission of Direct Marketing, 224 7th Street, Garden City, New York 11530.

Page 447: Robert Gieselman, "Letter to Alpha Beta Chi Advisers". Reprinted by permission of Robert Gieselman.

Pages 456–458: John T. Maguire, "Letter to Cheryl Krueger". Reprinted by permission of John T. Maguire.

Pages 473–474: Excerpt from *Renewing American Industry* by Paul R. Lawrence and Davis Dyer. Reprinted by permission of The Free Press, A Division of Macmillan, Inc. Copyright © 1983 The Free Press.

Pages 484–492: Carson and Iris Varner. "Legal Issues in Business Communications" from the *ABCA Bulletin.* Reprinted by permission of the authors.